Egon Erwin Kisch,
The Raging Reporter

Caricature of Kisch as robot by
Umbehr from the 1926 edition of
Der rasende Reporter.
Courtesy Aufbau-Verlag

Egon Erwin Kisch, The Raging Reporter

A Bio-Anthology

Harold B. Segel

Purdue University Press
West Lafayette, Indiana

01   00   99   98   97   5   4   3   2   1

∞ The paper used in this book meets the minimum requirements of American National Standard for Information Sciences—Permanence of Paper for Printed Library Materials, ANSI Z39.48-1992.

Printed in the United States of America
Design by Anita Noble

Library of Congress Cataloging-in-Publication Data
Kisch, Egon Erwin, 1885–1948.
      Egon Erwin Kisch, the raging reporter : a bio-anthology / [compiled by] Harold B. Segel.
         p.   cm.
      Includes bibliographical references and index.
      ISBN 1-55753-100-5 (alk. paper)
      1. Kisch, Egon Erwin, 1885–1948. 2. Journalists—Czechoslovakia—Biography. 3. Journalists—Germany—Biography. I. Segel, Harold B., date. II. Title
PN5355.C95K43 1997
070'.92—dc21   97-10194
   [B]   CIP

In memory of

Dmitry Chizhevsky and Roman Jakobson,

two of my greatest teachers,

who were at home on this terrain as well

Once the catchword for everything under the sun was "nervous," then "fin de siècle," then "Übermensch"; after that "inhibitions" were big, and today the rage is "reportahsche," which is how the word should always be spelled. Dear Egon Erwin Kisch, just see what you've gone and done! At the very least you're a reporter, and a very good one at that; but why does everything now have to be called reportage?

> —Kurt Tucholsky, "Die Reportahsche" (1931)

Kisch is creating a new type of reportage; he is letting the wealth of today's reality speak.

> —Georg Lukács (1935)

Kisch is one of Europe's most interesting personalities—a superb reporter, raconteur, and linguist. His insatiable curiosity has led him into the remote corners of the earth.

> —*The New York Times Book Review* (February 3, 1935),
> Alfred E. Knopf ad for Kisch's *Changing Asia*

He had all the curiosity, the ingenuity and the inventiveness of his modern successors, as well as that unusual sixth sense that tells him he is on the trail of a good story just because of a hunch.

> —*New York Herald Tribune Books* (December 14, 1941)

Contents

Preface

Egon Erwin Kisch (1885–1948) led an extraordinary life, and he is credited with virtually defining reportage as a literary genre. His dazzling, adventure-filled career included combat in Serbia as a soldier in the Austro-Hungarian army in Word War I; leadership of an abortive left-wing coup d'état in Vienna in 1918; unauthorized entry from Tajikistan into Afghanistan in 1931 to hunt tiger; illegal travel through a turbulent China in 1932; arrest by the Nazis and incarceration in Spandau prison; leaping ashore from an ocean liner after being denied entry into Australia in 1934; and participation in the Spanish Civil War in 1937–38.

Kisch's pursuit of adventure, his restless, doggedly inquisitive spirit, his lifelong preoccupation with crime, and his scrupulous regard for decency and justice in human affairs make him an exceptionally interesting figure. His experiences the world over became the stuff of books that together represent an enormous journalistic achievement. The collected edition of his works that the Aufbau-Verlag of Berlin began publishing in 1960 now runs to twelve volumes; individual collections of his reportage have gone through many editions, with new ones continuing to appear. Kisch, in fact, has never been better represented in print than at the present.

Kisch has not been unknown in the English-speaking world, but the interest in him seems to have peaked in the 1930s and 1940s when his collections of reportage about Soviet Central Asia and China, *Changing Asia* and *Secret China*, were published in the United States and England. The books have never been reprinted. In light of the cause célèbre that Kisch became in Australia in 1934, the Australian interest in him is understandable. His account of his experiences trying to disembark in Melbourne to take part in an antiwar congress there appeared in Australian and English editions in 1937, the former edition reprinted in 1969. *Marktplatz der Sensationen,* Kisch's highly entertaining collection of autobiographical sketches, was published in New York as *Sensation Fair* in 1941 but has long been out of print. The only other English translation of a full-length book by Kisch is *Tales from Seven Ghettoes,* a small collection of sketches on Jewish themes. "Die Drei Kühe" (The Three Cows), a story with a Spanish Civil War setting, was also published separately in English translation in London in 1939.

The wave of new interest in Kisch in the German-speaking world in the 1980s and 1990s—reflected in new hardcover and paperback editions of his works, and in new critical and scholarly studies—underscores the appropriateness of a book about him in English. Although Kisch is indeed a fit subject for a full-length biography, it seemed to me at this juncture that the reader would be better served by a book with two objectives: the first, to provide an introductory narration of Kisch's extraordinary career and his contribution to reportage in the twentieth century; and the second, through a fairly broad collection of his own works in translation, to allow the reader to meet Kisch directly through his writings.

The introduction is thus a concise yet reasonably comprehensive account of Kisch's life and career. The selections in translation include representative sketches from nearly all of Kisch's collections, either translated by me for the first time or, if previously translated, newly translated by me. Although the English translations of Kisch's works from the 1930s and 1940s are by and large respectable, they are stylistically antiquated, lack any commentary or annotation, and in some cases contain errors and omissions. Hence my feeling that for the sake of stylistic consistency, my best course would be to translate anew everything I wanted to include in this book.

Although not obligatory, my interest in Kisch perhaps merits a few words. For several years now I have been studying literary and theatrical "small" (or short) forms—genres of literature and drama lacking the esteem of the major genres of high literature but widely cultivated from the turn of the century well into the 1920s and 1930s. Examining the social and artistic reasons behind the new interest in such small forms prompted my studies on the cabaret and on the feuilletonistic sketches produced in the environment of Vienna's coffeehouses. Kisch first attracted my attention because of the possibility of fruitful contacts between Kisch and Russian writers, but after reading a great deal of his reportage, I felt that a plausible case could be made for the reportage sketch as a literary small form, and that its rise to prominence especially between the First and Second World Wars could in part be related for the enthusiasm for the small form going back to the turn of the century.

The organization of this book needs no special elucidation. My introduction proper, which combines the biographical and critical, is preceded by a synoptic account of Kisch's career, the purpose of which is to provide a bridge to the longer and more detailed discussion that follows. The selections from Kisch's reportage follow chronological lines, with the sole exception of sketches from *Sensation Fair,* which because of their autobiographical nature seemed appropriately situated at the beginning. Because of its almost programmatic nature, the very short essay "A Dangerous Literary Genre" precedes the other pieces.

My translations are based for the most part on the Aufbau-Verlag collected edition of Kisch's works in individual volumes. I hereby express my deep gratitude to Aufbau-Verlag for their blanket permission to translate whichever of Kisch's works I chose. In a few instances, where I had ready access to original editions of a few of Kisch's collections, I preferred to use these for the translations, checking them for later changes with the Aufbau-Verlag edition.

Apart from certain words and idioms common to the Prague German of Kisch's time and some military and police terminology, his language poses no extraordinary problems to the translator. Kisch is usually casual in style, often colloquial, and the effort was made to preserve these qualities as much as possible. In a few selections, I have chosen to carry over into English Kisch's use of the present tense to describe events in the past. As a reporter who kept notes as he traveled and on some occasions appears to have written, or to have begun writing, his sketches either during the events themselves or shortly thereafter, his journalistic use of present narrative makes for a sense of immediacy, and even spontaneity, that I though worth preserving, where feasible, in translation.

My sincere thanks are due the following publishers, institutions, and individuals who made this book possible:

Aufbau-Verlag of Berlin and Weimar for their permission to translate from the various editions of Kisch's work published by them, and their willingness to be of help in other ways. I especially appreciate the efforts of Frauke Jung-Lindemann and Christian Karpus.

Verlag Kiepenheuer & Witsch of Cologne for their kind permission to reprint pictures from their two-volume anthology of Kisch's writings, *Nichts ist erregender als die Wahrheit.*

The Federal Bureau of Investigation for allowing me access to their file on Kisch, albeit in censored form.

Dr. Eva Wolfová, director of the Památník národního písemnictví in Prague, for making available to me photographic material from the Kisch archive.

Dana Klocurkova of the IREX office in Prague for her very kind help in expediting matters at the Památník národního písemnictví.

Hanns-Peter Frentz of Ullstein Bilderdienst (Berlin) for his great help with photographic material when I visited his office.

Anita Noble of Purdue University Press for her usual fine work with layout and design.

Once again it is a happy occasion for me to be able to express my deep gratitude to Dr. Margaret Hunt, my editor at Purdue University Press. Her very close attention to the text, her many helpful suggestions in the area of translation, and her usual efficiency—to which ease of communication and friendliness were never sacrificed—made publishing another book with Purdue as much a pleasure as the first truly was. For any errors of fact or lapses in translation that may yet be discovered in the book, I alone bear full responsibility.

The Raging Reporter Introduced

His friends and wife called him "Egonek," a combination of his first name and the Czech diminutive suffix "-ek"; the rest of the world came to know him as "the raging reporter." He was Egon Erwin Kisch, born in 1885 in Prague, when that city of Czech and German cultures was one of the adornments of the Austro-Hungarian Empire; he died in 1948, in his native city, then the capital of the independent Czechoslovakia that had been created out of the ruins of the Habsburg Empire following World War I. In a sense Kisch traded one empire for another, the Austro-Hungarian that was destined to crumble notwithstanding Kisch's efforts to hasten the process to the best of his ability; and the post–World War II Soviet empire of which Czechoslovakia was firmly a part and which had now become Kisch's only true homeland.

Kisch's early work as a reporter was intimately bound up with his native city; but by the time he returned to Prague in 1946, a year after the end of World War II, he had traveled the world over in a long and remarkable pursuit of experiences from which he crafted an extraordinary number of sketches collectively representing one of the great achievements of modern reportage. A workaday journalist in the conventional sense only when he covered the back streets of Prague as a local reporter for the German-language *Bohemia* in the early years of the century, Kisch's subsequent career was devoted wholly to the elevation of reportage to the level of literary art. So admirably did he

1

succeed in that goal that he is now acknowledged as the central figure in that development in the German-speaking world in the twentieth century.

Kisch's flirtation with the writing of poetry, fiction, and drama came at a fairly early age, but was rapidly overtaken by his commitment to reportage. Once set on that path, he never wavered or retreated. Unlike other writers who began as journalists and moved on to the more respected, and usually more lucrative, cultivation of fiction, Kisch determined by his own example to change attitudes toward reportorial writing, to transform reporting into reportage, a literary art form indebted to fact but shaped by the creative genius of the writer.

The determinants of Kisch's success were many. A restless, energetic, immensely curious individual with a flair for adventure, the world, literally, became his beat. His early Prague newspaper sketches, subsequently collected in three books, laid the cornerstone of his career. Admired for their vividness and color, their keen eye for detail, their offbeat characters and settings, they also evidenced a social consciousness barely concealed beneath the apparent objectivity and lightheartedness. Kisch's sense of fair play and justice, his sympathy for the socially overlooked and marginalized, carried over into his World War I war diary, often composed under fire, in which his concern above all is with the ordinary soldier. The published diary was a considerable success and confirmed Kisch's position as one of the leading reportorial writers of his day. When he uncovered and leaked the sordid truth behind the suicide in 1913 of Colonel Redl, a high-ranking officer in military intelligence, he was well on his way to celebrity. His later detailed account of the Redl treason, *Der Fall des Generalstabschefs Redl* (The Case of the Chief of the General Staff Redl, 1924), was one of his most acclaimed publications.

The sobriquet "the raging reporter" derives from the title of Kisch's first real collection of reportage after the early Prague newspaper sketches, his war diary, and the Redl exposé. The collection was first published in 1924 and has been republished many times since. Widely divergent in its topics, from a piece about a shelter for the homeless in London to impressions of the ravaged Albanian city of Scutari in the Balkan War of 1913, *Der rasende Reporter* could not have come at a better time, in the literary sense. The devastation of World War I understandably diminished the appeal of literary make-believe. How could the work of imagination vie with reality when reality was more powerful, more terrifying than anything the human mind could devise? Interest now arose in a literature of fact, of reality, a literature dealing with the concrete issues of the here and now. This enthusiasm for the "factographic" coincided with the "New Objectivity" ("Neue Sachlichkeit") of postwar Weimar Germany. Half a world away, in postrevolutionary Russia, similar forces were at work but for dissimilar reasons. The massive undertaking of rebuilding Russia greatly enhanced the appeal of nonfictional writing, and the campaign of the new regime to shape attitudes toward various aspects of reconstruction and the building of a new system placed great value on the talents of the journalist.

As the most dynamic centers of political and artistic culture in Europe at the time, Germany and Russia—whose appetite for news about the other was prodigious in the 1920s and 1930s—became the focus of keen attention throughout the world. When Kisch's *The Raging Reporter* appeared in 1924, it entered a cultural-political environment that was extraordinarily hospitable to a literature of fact. Reportage was hailed as the most timely of literary forms and, in the German-speaking world, Kisch was regarded as its contemporary master. How committed this master of reportage was to the elevation of the stature of journalism in general is manifest in one of his greatest labors of love, the compilation of a huge anthology called *Klassischer Journalismus* (Classical Journalism) and illustrating the varieties of the journalistic experience from ancient times to his own. The book was published in 1923, a year before *The Raging Reporter* and as a kind of grandiloquent preface to it.

The continuity of the past, reflected in *Classical Journalism,* formed the basis of Kisch's next collection of sketches, *Hetzjagd durch die Zeit* (Pursuit through Time), which, while carrying a copyright date of 1926 in the original edition, was actually published in 1925. Kisch's experience with crime and police detection acquired in his work as a local reporter in Prague piqued his interest in criminal cases of the past. But rather than pursue the already well researched, Kisch characteristically struck out into darker, more obscure corners. In 1931, he published a book of sketches about historical criminal cases in the Czech lands, which he called *Prager Pitaval* (Prague Pitaval), after a seventeenth- and eighteenth-century French writer who began the fashion of such writing. But after beginning *Prague Pitaval,* Kisch temporarily put it aside in order to come out sooner with *Pursuit through Time,* which Kisch assembled out of some of the historical sketches intended for *Prague Pitaval,* other sketches with a historical focus, and pieces previously written but not included in prior collections of reportage. Ever the man in a hurry, anxious to produce a new book before the print in the preceding had dried, Kisch similarly combined new and old reportage in subsequent collections. Moreover, he was not averse to returning to an old sketch and revising it for inclusion in a new collection.

By using the techniques of twentieth-century reportage with events in the past, above all criminal cases, and writing about them in a vivid, casual, and contemporary way, Kisch extended the frontiers of the genre, further enhancing its image. His reputation as a writer thus secure, Kisch embarked next on a series of far-flung travels that would give rise to several more well-received books of reportage and further validate the sobriquet of "raging reporter."

His trip to the new Soviet Union from December 1925 to May 1926 was predictable. Convinced before World War I had ended that the Austro-Hungarian Empire was doomed to collapse, Kisch threw his lot in with revolutionaries committed to building a new society on its ashes. Inspired by the events in Russia—and the revolutionary climate building in Central and Eastern Europe in the immediate aftermath of the war—Kisch headed a small revolutionary force known as the Red Guards, made up mostly of army veterans, and plotted to take over Vienna on the day it was to be declared a republic in November 1918. The plot failed miserably, but Kisch's sympathies remained overwhelmingly with the political left. By the time he embarked on his trip to Russia he had already joined the Communist Party.

Kisch's political outlook, which was shaped by his experiences as a local reporter in Prague and even more so during World War I, remained consistent without becoming doctrinaire. His awareness of social and economic injustice inclined him to the political left in the absence of any viable alternatives, from his point of view. The widespread economic instability after World War I, felt so profoundly in Germany and Austria, and spreading political turbulence placed him squarely on the left. When Hitler and the Nazis came to power in Germany in 1933, Kisch's identification with those forces opposed to fascism and totalitarianism was complete.

Sympathetic to the great changes then taking place in Russia, Kisch nevertheless resisted making reportage a mere handmaiden of politics and wrote a richly detailed, variegated, and objective account of what he observed in the Soviet Union. If the reader carries away from it a certain respect for Soviet efforts at reconstruction following the awesome devastation of war and revolution, Kisch's abiding interest in crime and punishment guarantees that the enormous weight of the problems remaining makes no less an impression. When it came out in 1927, *Zaren, Popen, Bolschewiken* (Tsars, Priests, and Bolsheviks) was recognized as an impressive collection of reportage. It was followed in fairly rapid succession by four more collections of travel sketches. In late 1926 and early 1927, Kisch was off to North Africa, producing in *Wagnisse in aller Welt* (Worldwide Exploits, 1927) a colorful book of his experiences among the Algerians, Tunisians, and Jews of North Africa. Although the focus of the book falls on the indigenous populations of the region, the colonial presence is felt throughout and in ways that leave little doubt that Kisch was no more hospitable to colonialism than he was to fascism.

With barely a pause after his North African journey, Kisch embarked on a nearly half-year trip to the United States in late 1928. The impact of the United States on the European consciousness between the two world wars easily rivaled that of the Soviet Union, and Kisch could not long have resisted the natural impulse to compare the colossus of capitalism and that of communism. But no overt comparison mars the readability of *Paradies Amerika* (Paradise America, 1929), his ironically titled book of reportage based on travel in the United States from New York to California and back. Kisch's reputation as a red-tainted reporter preceded him to America and caused him some anxious moments when he applied for a visa. But he was able to enter the country, to travel freely, and even at one point to work for his passage as an ordinary seaman on an American merchant ship sailing from New York to California. It is the entertaining account of this experience as well as his encounters in Hollywood (observing Charlie Chaplin at work on a picture, for example) that set the tone of *Paradise America* as much as those pieces clearly intended to show the darker underside of American life. While Kisch hardly shrinks from the unflattering in his book of Soviet reportage, he is equally candid in his depiction of American life, and yes, the abiding interest in criminals, police, and prison is well represented.

If Kisch was never a communist activist in the true political sense—his Red Guards adventure in Vienna in 1918 doubtless tempered his revolutionary zeal—he was always a willing speaker at international antifascist and anti-militarist conferences of one sort or another sponsored by the Soviet Union or its fellow travelers in the West. One such conference in Kharkov, Ukraine, in 1930 served as the springboard for Kisch's next two episodes of grand adventure travel. The first was through Soviet Central Asia in 1931, a journey that produced *Asien gründlich verändert* (Changing Asia, 1932), Kisch's first book of reportage to be translated into English. The trip through Central Asia extended his earlier enthusiasm for the exotica of Islamic lands and peoples. It also afforded the inquisitive, indomitable reporter the opportunity to examine the impact of a rapidly industrializing secular society on the ancient customs and traditions of the Muslim populations of Uzbekistan, Turkmenistan, and Tadjikistan, which had recently been incorporated into the Soviet Union and were in the process of being conscripted into the twentieth century.

For an adventurous spirit like Kisch, the temptation to head farther east from Central Asia was irresistible. So instead of returning to Europe, he went on to China, entering that country illegally. Caught between the turmoil of civil war and Japanese invasion, mired in corruption and foreign intrigue, China attracted journalists from all over the world in the 1920s and 1930s. With their own high stakes in the outcome of the political conflict there, the Russians also followed events closely, with a number of on-the-spot observers, journalistic and otherwise. *China geheim* (Secret China), published in Berlin the year after *Changing Asia* and also translated into English, is among Kisch's most engrossing collections of reportage. It was also the last book he was able to publish in Germany. Concentrating often on less obvious aspects of Chinese society, attentive to its cultural traditions, keenly observant—and critical—of the foreign role in its economic life, Kisch avoids the overtly political and yet succeeds admirably in conveying a sense of the turmoil in the country and the crosscurrents struggling to shape its future.

When Kisch finally returned to Europe and resumed residence in Berlin, the Nazi assumption of power abruptly ended his stay there. Imprisoned for a while the day after the burning of the Reichstag in 1933, which provided the Nazis a pretext for rounding up real or imagined enemies of the state, Kisch was released on the strength of his Czechoslovak citizenship. From the time he was escorted across the German-Czechoslovak border, Kisch wholeheartedly identified with the plight of German anti-Nazi exiles and became active in émigré cultural circles, mostly in Paris.

It was while he was in Paris in 1934 that Kisch was asked by the International Committee against War and Fascism to participate in an antiwar congress being held in Australia in October of that year. Kisch grabbed the opportunity to set sail for a faraway land he had never visited, and he was no less eager to promote the agenda of the antifascist movement. German diplomatic officials in Australia saw the matter differently and conspired to block his visit. The eventual ban on his disembarkation by the Australian authorities, his leap ashore at Melbourne—which resulted in a broken leg— and his subsequent arrest, imprisonment, release, and participation in political rallies throughout the country, constituted a real cause célèbre. Kisch's account of it makes up the greater part of *Landung in Australien* (Disembarking in Australia, 1937). Here the author, thinly veiled under the persona of "unser Mann" ("our man"), becomes the subject of his own reportage. The rest of the book comprises sketches on different aspects of Australian life and society.

After his return to France in April 1935, Kisch occupied himself primarily with the writing of *Disembarking in Australia* and with involvement in the cultural and political life of the German anti-Nazi emigration in Paris. Before the Australian episode he had completed and published two new books of reportage, *Eintritt verboten* (Entry Prohibited, 1935), a collection of sketches dealing mostly with industrial life in Belgium, Holland, and France, and essentially Marxist in inspiration, and *Geschichten aus sieben Ghettos* (Tales from Seven Ghettos, 1934), a medley of stories about Jewish life past and present. Although a nonobservant, culturally Germanized Jew, Kisch always sought out Jewish communities on his travels around the globe, viewing them primarily as sources of colorful literary material. Following the pattern of *Pursuit through Time, Prague Pitaval,* and *Kriminalistisches Reisebuch* (A Travel Book of Crime, 1927), which consists mostly of previously published crime-related sketches, Kisch combined past and present in his Jewish reportage by bringing together accounts of contemporary Jewish life in such disparate locations as London, Mexico, New York, Shanghai, and Tunis, and little-known historical criminal cases involving Jews.

When the Spanish Civil War erupted in 1936, Franco's rebellion against the socialistic republic became the rallying point of right and left alike throughout Europe and America. The formation of the Loyalist International Brigades and the participation of German and Italian units internationalized the conflict and lured any adventurer and reporter worth his salt to Spain at the time. André Malraux was there, and Arthur Koestler, and Ernest Hemingway, and such leading Soviet journalists as Ilya Ehrenburg and Mikhail Koltsov, and many others, including Kisch. Attaching himself to units of the International Brigades made up primarily of volunteers from Central and Eastern Europe, Kisch was in Spain in 1937 and 1938, saw some action, and wrote a few sketches, though no collection of reportage resulted from his experiences. Nevertheless, the longest of his Spanish Civil War sketches, "Die drei Kühe" (The Three Cows), about a couple of Austrian farmers who leave home to fight on the side of the Loyalists in Spain, became well known and was translated into several languages, including English.

Kisch returned to France in April 1938 and was married that same year to his longtime literary assistant, Gisela Lyner,[1] who under the name Gisela Kisch and in cooperation with Kisch's friend, the German writer Bodo Uhse, edited several new editions of his works after his death, including the collected edition that Aufbau-Verlag of Berlin began publishing in 1960. The rapidly deteriorating European situation, beginning with the German annexation of Austria, the capitulation of Czechoslovakia, and finally the German invasion of Poland in September 1939 convinced Kisch that as a well-known anti-fascist and anti-Nazi, a communist, a writer whose works were now banned in Germany, and as a Jew, the time had come to get out of Europe. As his place of exile, he finally chose Mexico, where he was admitted and where he and his wife remained from 1940 to 1946.

When he settled in Mexico City, Kisch joined a small but energetic community of fellow émigré writers from Germany and Austria. Kisch made the most of his time in Mexico and produced two of his best works there, *Marktplatz der Sensationen* (Sensation Fair, 1942) which eventually became his best-known book, and *Entdeckungen in Mexiko* (Discoveries in Mexico,

1945). Both books were published by the small anti-Nazi German-language publishing house established by Kisch and his fellow émigrés in 1942. A collection of sketches based on his youth and early career in journalism in Prague, Vienna, and Berlin, *Sensation Fair* is the closest Kisch ever came to writing an autobiography. The work was begun before the outbreak of World War II and Kisch's emigration to Mexico but was finished in Mexico City. Thousands of miles from his native Prague, in a different part of the world and in a very different culture, Kisch obviously took great pleasure in recalling the distant past and shaping his warm memories of it into some of his most delightful prose. *Discoveries in Mexico* is a different sort of work, reportage on the grand scale in the manner of Kisch's previous collections, with Mexico approached not as a place of refuge but as another exotic land to which Kisch the adventurer was irresistibly drawn and whose culture he came to know intimately.

With the war at an end, it was time for the Kisches to return to Europe. But where in Europe specifically? Paris in its time had been a place of exile like Mexico. The ties to Vienna and Berlin were strong, but Vienna had lost much of its appeal to Kisch, and Berlin lay in ruins. So the exile went home to Prague, where he was raised and for which his affection was as strong as ever.

Prague welcomed him with open arms. He was a native son and a world-famous writer; he was also politically correct. But Kisch was a product of another era. Gone were the vibrant German and German-speaking Jewish communities that had so enriched the cultural life of the city in Kisch's younger days. Never having written in Czech, less than perfectly fluent in the language, having used it so rarely in his life, Kisch might well have continued writing in German and been published in that language in Germany or Austria as well as in Czechoslovakia; but he was plainly an anachronism. Before death claimed him, he succeeded in writing a few more sketches, the most interesting of which is an impeccably researched reconstruction of the visits of Karl Marx to Karlsbad (Karlovy Vary, in Czech). But Kisch's health began declining within a year of his return to Prague, and his career was virtually at an end. He suffered a stroke in November 1947, followed in March 1948 by a second stroke, which killed him.

Kisch's funeral was a state event carefully orchestrated by the communist authorities of Czechoslovakia for maximum ideological effect. A member of the political left most of his career, Kisch, however, had never lived under a communist regime. His experiences in the Soviet Union were just those of a well-received visitor and observer. His only direct exposure, as a citizen, to a totalitarian regime was in Germany in 1933; the memory of his brief incarceration in Spandau and subsequent summary expulsion remained with him the rest of his life. When Kisch returned to Prague in 1946, Czechoslovakia was ruled by a coalition government and had not yet slipped into the firm grasp of the communists. It was also the only state in Eastern Europe at the time that was not yet regarded as a Soviet satellite. Kisch's ability to pursue his literary career more or less without outside interference and to maintain a network of foreign contacts was unimpeded. Apart from the problem, if indeed it was one, of his continued writing in German, his transition to postwar European life in Prague was reasonably smooth. He was lionized and provided living quarters and other perks. Kisch had by now become an icon and the Czechs were glad to have him. How long the romance would have continued after the communist coup in February 1948 is anyone's guess. Kisch prized independence and freedom, championed them his whole life, and abhorred totalitarianism. That the "raging reporter" would meekly have accepted the numbing curtailments of individual liberties that became everyday reality in Czechoslovakia is difficult to imagine. When death finally overtook him, Kisch was spared the necessity of having to confront the greatest challenge to his beliefs, the destruction of liberty in the land he called home.

The Career of Egon Erwin Kisch

Local Reporter: Pubs, Prostitutes, and Perpetrators

Kisch was born in Prague when the Czech and Slovak lands were part of the Habsburg Empire and was a typical product of the ethnic and cultural heterogeneity of the empire. Like the majority of Czech Jews, his first language was German and his cultural identification was wholly German. He was educated in German-language schools in Prague and entered the German Prague University to study literature and philosophy. But he broke off his studies after a semester in favor of volunteer military service for a year. If not exactly a natural rebel, Kisch nevertheless was uncomfortable with authority and developed a reputation for defying it while a schoolboy. Wearing an army uniform did not make much of a difference; of his 365 days of service, 147 were spent in the brig.[2]

His interest in journalism manifested itself early. In 1905, when he was barely twenty years old, he signed on with the *Prager Tagblatt* as an apprentice. But restlessness again got the best of him—as it would throughout his life—and he left after a short while to enroll in a private journalism school in Berlin. By the time he returned to Prague six months later, his choice of a career in journalism had been firmly resolved. In April 1906 he joined the staff of the *Bohemia*, Prague's second-largest German-language paper and the *Prager Tagblatt*'s leading competitor. He remained on the staff of the paper until 1913.

Although a cub reporter's first assignments may not make much of a difference in shaping the future course of his career, this was not so in the case of Kisch. When he joined the *Bohemia,* it was as a replacement for a *Lokalreporter*—a reporter who covered news of local interest—named Melzer. But the kind of news covered by Herr Melzer related mostly to crime, and specifically the crime of homicide. Kisch fit comfortably into his predecessor's shoes. In the seven years he was with the *Bohemia,* he earned a reputation as Prague's best local reporter with a definite penchant for criminal cases of every hue and stamp.

In writing about crime in general, and murder in particular, Kisch demonstrated attributes as a reporter that were to remain with him for most of his career. Since most of what he reported on was generated from the margins of society, from the back alleys and nocturnal haunts of the big city's social dregs, he developed an extraordinary sense of place, personally rummaging about every nook and cranny of a crime scene. It was in many of these same neighborhoods that he found a trove of material for the sketches of local color that he began writing alongside his crime stories. Almost no detail was insignificant to Kisch, and if there is any criticism to be made of his earlier reportage, it is that his passion for precision and minutiae seems at times to go too far.

Attracting Kisch to criminality was also an undeniable taste for the sensational, which shows up in much of his writing and which he forthrightly acknowledges in *Travel Book of Crime* (1931):

> A new broom, I swept all the streets thoroughly for the sake of catching some criminal case. There wasn't a single pickpocketing I didn't try to develop into a cause célèbre by interviewing the victim, sniffing out the scene of the crime, and conducting investigations on my own. Nights I crawled around police headquarters hoping to become a witness to some exciting scene or at least to be able to steal a look at some sensational record.[3]

Although there is undoubtedly an element here of sensationalism for its own sake, Kisch seems to have been more attracted to the sensational as a means of heightening the narrative appeal of factual writing. But in drawing attention to the sensational, even highlighting it, Kisch never invented anything. As a journalist, Kisch had a passionate respect for truth and would have considered it beneath his dignity as a reporter to embellish a story for the

**Sketch of Kisch as a young man before
World War I.
Courtesy Kiepenheuer & Witsch Verlag.**

mere sake of adding zest to it. Nevertheless, there are those who saw Kisch's fascination with crime as rooted in the desire to attract attention through sensationalism. This is evident, for example, in Max Brod's reminiscences of the old Prague German-speaking literary community:

> That his reportage had been written on the basis of thorough factual studies; that he possessed the talent to see much of what others did not see; that he responded, moreover, to an inner compulsion to express the warm compassion he felt for the most underprivileged—all of this (and much else that was praiseworthy) seems to me to be as beyond questioning as it is to his thousands of admirers. . . . But what a shame that in his many books what Kisch experienced, or pretended he experienced, in the criminal world, in the milieu of whores, and so on, is written with this reaction in mind: How the good citizens of Prague, the subscribers to the chauvinistic bourgeois German paper *Bohemia* (for which Kisch worked for years) will be astonished at my wickedness! This sidelong glance at the impression he produces is really an unartistic element in Kisch's work.[4]

In his pursuit and reporting of criminal cases as well as in his stories with local color, Kisch became a Prague *Lokalreporter* in the fullest sense of the term. There was no section of the city that he did not come to know well, but his predilection was for the out-of-the-way places, the narrow lanes and alleyways, the cheap pubs, wine cellars, cafés, and raunchy cabarets, where most of the characters and situations of his early sketches proliferated. His nose for detail combined with an uncanny ability to ferret out the quirky and the offbeat. But there was more to the young reporter's fascination with the underside of his native city than the mere pursuit of the unfamiliar. Besides the criminals, pimps, prostitutes, vagabonds, and flophouse tenants he met on his rambles, Kisch also discovered the "little people" of the city, from laundresses to petty shopkeepers. Although his leftist political views were yet to cohere, the writings of his *Bohemia* years reflect a growing awareness of want, neglect, and exploitation. Never one to distance himself from anything he wrote about, to remain aloof from his subject, to see it coldly as little more than the raw material of reportage, Kisch plunged into whatever milieu he entered, unafraid and able to take it on its own terms. If he was writing about the homeless, he made a point of living among them, as he did, for example, for his sketches "Eine Nacht im Asyl für Obdachlose" (A Night in a Homeless Shelter), in *Aus Prager Gassen und Nächten* (Out of Prague's Alleys and Nights), and "Unter den Obdachlosen von Whitechapel" (Among the Homeless of Whitechapel) in *The Raging Reporter.* He became as familiar a face in Prague's bordellos as the most compulsive client, and in such early collections as *Prager Kinder* (Prague Children) and *Die Abenteuer in Prag* (Adventures in Prague), he wrote about the whores and their pimps with the familiarity of a family member. In his "Magdalenenheim" sketches in *Prague Children* and *Sensation Fair,* about homes for "wayward girls," his hosts were shocked to discover that Kisch and the "Magdalenen" ("Magdalenes," a more socially acceptable term for prostitutes) were on a first-name basis.

The sketches Kisch wrote about Prague for the *Bohemia* appeared as a regular series in the feuilleton section of the paper's Sunday edition under the title "Prager Streifzüge" (Prague Rambles). They became tremendously popular and laid the foundation of Kisch's career. In response to their popularity, Kisch decided to collect a number of his "Prague Rambles" and publish them in book form. The collection appeared in 1912 as *Out of Prague's Alleys and Nights.* Although the mostly short sketches cover a broad spectrum of the small life of the big city, Kisch's abiding interest in criminality is much in evidence. The success of *Out of Prague's Alleys and Nights* prompted Kisch to publish two more collections of "Prague Rambles" in book form. *Prague Children* came out the following year, 1913. It includes a mini-cycle of some his best stories about seamier Prague life under the title "Szenen aus Spelunken" (Scenes from Dives). *Adventures in Prague,* the last of the "Prague Rambles" collections, appeared in 1920.

Between the appearance of *Prague Children* and *Adventures in Prague,* Kisch published his first novel, *Der Mädchenhirt* (The Pimp), in 1914; the subject was one he knew well as a Prague local reporter. Kisch himself referred to the novel as "Prague's first naturalistic novel," immediately establishing a train of associations with Zola, whom Kisch much admired as a novelist and social thinker and on whom he obviously patterned himself in *The Pimp.* Erich Reiss Verlag of Berlin, the publisher Kisch was to have the longest relationship with until his expulsion from Germany in 1933, issued the book. Kisch's only surviving novel, *The Pimp* was by far his most successful work of fiction, twice serving as the basis of a movie. The Austrian director Karl Grune, whose film *Die Strasse* (The Street, 1923) pioneered the melodramatic so-called "street" film genre about big-city degradation, prostitution, and crime, in fact began his career as a filmmaker with *The Pimp* in 1919.[5] A less successful version of the novel was made in Prague in 1929 by the German director of Fox Film's European operations, Hans Tintner; it starred the Austrian matinee idol Werner Fütterer. Before settling on a career in journalism, Kisch had also published a book of poems when he was nineteen years old, *Vom Blütenzweig der Jugend* (The Flowering Branch). The poetry was followed two years later by a collection of short stories, *Der freche Franz und andere Geschichten* (Fresh Franz and Other Stories). Although he enjoyed some success and recognition as a writer of fiction and, later, as a playwright, Kisch was not lured into believing that fiction and drama were his proper literary métier. Once fame as a writer of reportage came his way, he all but abandoned further efforts at imaginative literature, preferring instead to develop reportage into a true literary art and advocating it as more responsive to the needs of post–World War I society than fiction.

The Redl Affair

Although Kisch found many occasions in his career as a journalist to write about crime, the high point of his criminal reportage was related to the notorious espionage case involving Colonel Alfred Redl. The case became so well known that it served as the subject of four movies: the silent film *Oberst Redl,* with Robert Valberg in the lead role; the sound picture *Der Fall des Generalstabschefs Redl;* the film *Sabotage,* directed by the Austrian Franz Antel and with Oskar Werner and Ewald Balser in the lead roles; and finally the German-Hungarian movie (*Oberst Redl*) directed by István Szabó and starring the German actor Klaus Maria Brandauer as Alfred Redl. The English dramatist John Osborne also drew on the case for his play *A Patriot for Me,* which deals with espionage.

Since a translation of Kisch's longest account of the Redl case (*Der Fall des Generalstabschefs Redl*) is included in its entirety in this book, there is no need for any detailed account here. Kisch is generally credited with being the first journalist to break the news that Redl's death was in fact a hushed-up commanded suicide because of the colonel's activities as a spy. As in the case described in the sketch "Unforeseeable Consequences," Kisch's discovery of the truth of the affair came about entirely accidentally. Fearing that publication of the report of the true circumstances of Redl's suicide would be blocked in Prague, Kisch sent it to a Berlin paper, which carried it in the form of an unsigned denial of a rumor. In its morning edition the next day, 28 May 1913, the Prague *Bohemia* repeated the report, thereby assuring its broader dissemination:

> Vienna, 27 May (Private). The *Zeit* reports: Rumors are circulating throughout Vienna that Colonel Redl of the General Staff committed suicide because of his involvement in an *espionage affair.* The officers with whom he had been together shortly before his death confronted him with the *gravely incriminating material* that they had in their possession. Colonel Redl preferred to use the time granted him to avoid any further investigation by taking his own life. Those in official positions are saying little about the matter and providing no additional information as to the accuracy of these rumors.[6]

Since Kisch of necessity kept his name from the report, it was not immediately common knowledge that it was he who had lifted the veil of official secrecy surrounding Redl's suicide. When eventually Kisch was identified as the man behind the revelatory denial, and his full account of the Redl case was published in Berlin in 1924, he was hailed as the leading investigative reporter of the day. The appearance around this time of his first major collection of reportage with the provocative title *The Raging Reporter* confirmed his celebrity both as a reporter and as a writer of literary reportage in the best sense of the term.

Kisch in the Great War

A little over a year after the exposure of the Redl affair, Archduke Franz Ferdinand was assassinated in Sarajevo and Austria-Hungary declared war on Serbia. World War I was about to begin. Kisch was called up for active service on 31 July 1914 with the rank of infantry corporal. Whatever misgivings he may have had about going into combat, he did not follow the example of other Austrian writers (Hugo von Hofmannsthal and Franz Werfel, for example) who accepted press corps and military "archivist" assignments that kept them out of harm's way. Whatever dangers and uncertainties awaited him, Kisch was unwilling to settle for anything less than direct, firsthand experience of war. He got his fill of it. In early August, the 11th Infantry Regiment, in which he was serving, was sent into action on the Serbian front, which saw some of the most bitter fighting of the war. Kisch went through the entire southern campaign, including the disastrous Austrian retreat across the Drina River. He was wounded and moved up in rank from corporal to first lieutenant. That Kisch saw the war through the eyes of a born journalist with a taste for adventure is manifest in his writings about it. Although he contributed eyewitness accounts to the Prague and Berlin newspapers with which he was affiliated, his most detailed, personal, and trenchant observations about military life and combat were reserved for the diary he began compiling on 31 July 1914. Jotting notes and impressions, often while dodging bullets, Kisch was so concerned about his account eventually reaching the public that he passed his notebooks on to his mother in Prague by means of fellow soldiers returning there on leave. Excerpts from the work appeared in 1918 in the Vienna weekly *Der Friede* and in 1921 in the Prague daily *Prager Tagblatt*. The diary was first published in book form, unrevised, in 1922 under the title *Soldat im Prager Korps* (Soldier in the Prague Corps). Two more editions of the book were published that same year. Responding to the growing popularity of his wartime memoirs as well as favorable critical notice, Kisch expanded the book for a new edition published by the Erich Reiss Verlag of Berlin in 1929. This new edition, which has been reprinted several times, was given a different title—*Schreib das auf, Kisch!* (Write It Down, Kisch!)—referring to the good-natured ribbing Kisch got from his trench-mates because of his constant writing during the war, even under enemy fire. When the new edition of the diary appeared, Kurt Tucholsky, the outstanding Berlin satirist and critic, praised it as "The new edition of Kisch's old war diary, with a few masterful descriptions that belong in every textbook. . . . And the crossing of the Drina belongs in a literary museum."[7]

As the excerpts from *Write It Down, Kisch!* included in this book demonstrate, Kisch never flinched from describing the horrors of war. The tedium and lethargy that eventually overcame men exposed to long periods of frontline duty are also almost palpable. Kisch came to despise war for its cruelty and senselessness. When he received word that his youngest brother,

Wolfgang, had been wounded in action near Lublin, Poland, was captured by the Russians, and subsequently died in a Lublin hospital on 2 November 1914, his grief gave way to an intense hatred for war. What had once been approached as a great adventure (and, indeed, not by Kisch alone) had now become an unmitigated horror, aggravated all the more by his observations of the cynical, self-serving behavior of many officers.

The Great War ended for Kisch temporarily on 18 March 1915, when he was wounded in the head by shrapnel from a grenade in a village in Galicia (Austrian Poland) to which his regiment had been transferred following the disaster in Serbia. Since he preferred to recuperate in a hospital in Prague rather than in a war zone, he requested promotion to officer's rank, which made that possible. His request granted, he returned to Prague on 22 March 1915 and entered a Red Cross facility in the Karolinenthal Hospital. Officially declared unfit for active duty on 18 November 1915, Kisch spent the next four months in the military censor's office in the Hungarian town of Orszova. In March 1916, he was reexamined, judged fit for field service, and was returned to the front. Despite a ten-day detention brought on by an unauthorized report from the front while he was in the town of Gyula, in southern Hungary, Kisch was held in high esteem as a soldier and was decorated on more than one occasion. When a subsequent medical examination revealed that he was now suffering from a variety of neurotic symptoms from his grenade wound, Kisch was reassigned from the front to the press section of the War Office in Vienna. He began his work there on 1 May 1917. In March 1918 he was transferred to the editorial staff of the *Heimat,* a newspaper published for frontline troops whose editor-in-chief at the time was Robert Musil.

His experiences in World War I had a profound impact on Kisch's outlook. Anxious to share with readers the unvarnished reality of warfare as opposed to the sanitized, feel-good coverage of the big newspapers, the former local reporter from Prague also intended for his diary of the bitter Serbian campaign to serve as an antidote to the official pap spooned out by members of the War Office press corps. Although not in the style of what Kisch had previously written, a developing social consciousness links the Prague sketches and the war journal. Kisch's focus at the outset of his career was on the socially marginal, on the "little people" of his native city. This was the milieu in which he found the colorful characters and stories that caught his literary imagination and gratified his fondness for discovering the unusual in the ordinary. He had no cause or issue to champion at the time; there were no clear signs of a social activist or revolutionary in the making. This changed during the war. Kisch saw the wide gap between the enlisted men, who bore the brunt of the fighting and dying, and the pampered, arrogant officer class, whose frequent blundering cost many lives. War became the crucible of Kisch's social and political coming-of-age. Sharing the disaffection and disgruntlement of so many of his fellow soldiers returning from the then costliest war in human history to a society on the verge of collapse, Kisch threw his lot in with the enthusiasts of revolution. In so doing he was following the path of many in the tottering empires of World War I Europe. Restless and energetic by temperament, however, Kisch was not cut out to be a follower and instead cast himself in the role of a revolutionary commander intent on leading his Red Guards to political victory in Vienna in 1918. The failure of the revolution and the establishment of the interwar Austrian republic returned Kisch to his literary career. But like so many artists and thinkers in the immediate aftermath of World War I and the subsequent revolutionary fervor that swept the European continent, Kisch remained true to his views on social and political injustice and the need for radical reform.

Postwar Vienna:
The Red Guards and the Attempted Coup of November 1918

The success of the Bolshevik coup d'état in Russia in November 1917 and the imminent end of World War I nurtured the belief among revolutionaries that history was on their side and that the inevitable collapse of the Austro-Hungarian Empire would present them their golden opportunity to raise up a socialist republic on its ashes. A "workers' council" was formed in Vienna in the wake of the dramatic events unfolding in Russia, and when it was joined by disaffected military officers before the war's end, it was transformed into an illegal "workers' and soldiers' council." That Kisch was among those who joined the organization and who served it as a political activist among soldiers may not come as much of a surprise.

Reconstructing the evolving political thought of someone as mercurial as Kisch has its pitfalls. Notwithstanding his affiliation with a nationalistic German-language Prague paper such as *Bohemia,* Kisch demonstrated a maturing social consciousness in his "Prague Rambles" and drew no distinction between Czech, German, or Jew. Hardly a didactic writer, and with no agenda to advance at the time, Kisch gravitated toward the socially marginalized and disadvantaged. He commiserated with their plight—despite the objectivity of his reporting—and seemed progressively more aware of the injustice around him. The war only better defined and sharpened these perceptions, as is evidenced by his diary. Social consciousness bred political conviction, and before long Kisch had aligned himself with the anarchists and revolutionaries who hoped to replace the antiquated and discredited imperial system with a socialistic republican government.

It does Kisch an injustice, however, to seek to draw a simple trajectory of political engagement from a basically liberal but politically unfocused outlook to Communist Party affiliation. Kisch's evolving social and political attitudes favored the left. But his insatiable appetite for adventure, his quest for the exciting and sensational, would have set him on that path even, I believe, with a less developed political outlook. World War I buried the old imperial order in Europe and washed away the props of the liberal bourgeoisie. Without a viable middle, the gravitational pull was strongest to either end of the political spectrum. The left and the right were the self-declared architects of change, the revolutionaries of a new post-imperial order. Nationalistic, fascistic, and anti-Semitic political parties would obviously have repelled Kisch. Only the left remained, and with it a role in the drama of revolutionary upheaval and change.

The opportunity that the revolutionaries had been waiting for presented itself in the form of a general strike by more than 100,000 workers in Vienna that lasted from 14 to 20 January 1918.[8] A mutiny a month later by Austrian sailors in the Bay of Cattaro destabilized the situation all the more. Kisch seems to have taken no part in the January strike, despite the involvement in it of the Workers' and Soldiers' Council. Whatever his reaction to the events, he also wrote nothing specific about them, nor is there any documentary or even anecdotal evidence suggesting that he was any more than an interested observer. Through a network of spies and informers, the police had managed to keep fairly close tabs on the activities of illegal revolutionary groups, and several members of the Workers' and Soldiers' Council were arrested. When his superiors at the military press section became apprised of the fact that

Kisch too was under suspicion, they hastily arranged to reassign him as press officer to the big Austro-Hungarian naval base of Pula on the Adriatic.

While Kisch was sitting out the remainder of the war on the sunny Adriatic, economic conditions on the home front were deteriorating as rapidly as the military situation. Food and energy supplies had dwindled alarmingly, unrest began spreading, the great influenza epidemic of 1918 took a terrible toll, and monarchy and empire were teetering on the brink. When Emperor Franz Josef died in November 1916, he was succeeded by his grandnephew Karl. By the time Karl was persuaded by the pace of events to all but formerly abdicate, no one in his right mind still believed that it might yet be possible to halt the dissolution of the Austro-Hungarian Empire. The huge Slavic minorities—Poles, Czechs, Ukrainians, Serbs, Croats, and Slovenes—could no longer be reasoned with as to their future participation in some sort of postwar federation that would grant them self-governing status while preserving the outward semblance of empire. The political leadership of the German population meanwhile nourished its own ideas as to the future, envisioning a separate and sovereign German state to be known as "German-Austria."

Emperor Karl's withdrawal from the affairs of state in early November 1918 set the stage for the convocation of the Provisional National Assembly in the Parliament on the twelfth of the month. By the time the work of the assembly was finished, all that was left of the Austro-Hungarian Empire was a very small state to be known as the "democratic republic" of "German-Austria."

As these momentous events were unfolding, Kisch had sunk deeper into revolutionary scheming. Arrests and natural attrition had taken a heavy toll on the Workers' and Soldiers' Council. But the disarray in the military and uncertainty over the future created a fertile ground for the recruitment of disaffected soldiers for revolutionary causes. Kisch had kept up his friendship with other officers who had previously been affiliated with the council. These associations, now buttressed by contacts with a variety of veterans' groups, emboldened him to devise a plan to form a military revolutionary organization on the Soviet model, to be known as the Red Guards. Kisch set forth the platform of the Guards as succinctly as possible: "Its program was simple: to defend the revolution, to protect the republic from republicans who were riding out for audiences with the emperor in court automobiles."[9] The "republicans" referred to were leading Social Democratic politicians, such as Victor Adler, Karl Renner, and Karl Seitz, who were in fact holding meetings at the time with the emperor in Schönbrunn Castle concerning the transfer of power.

A mass antigovernment demonstration by workers and soldiers before the Provincial Parliament building in Vienna on 30 October 1918 provided the occasion for active recruitment by Kisch and his closest collaborators at the time—Stephan Haller, an army corporal and friend, and Leo Rothziegel, a former leader of the Workers' and Soldiers' Council.[10] The formal establishment of the Red Guards took place on 1 November 1918 at a mass gathering on the Ringstrasse in front of the Deutsch-Meister monument. Numbering about seven hundred (the organization was to grow to about two thousand at its peak), the Red Guards made their one and only attempt at a coup the day the new Austrian republic was to be proclaimed (12 November) from the steps of the Parliament building. But hardly had they displayed red flags during a speech by the president of the Parliament when they were caught off guard by the report that a machine gun had been set up on the roof of the Parliament and was about to fire on them. Some of the Red Guards then burst out of the huge crowd massed on the Ringstrasse and, firing their guns wildly, rushed the Parliament in a vain attempt to occupy it. However, they were easily repulsed by members of the legislature inside the building and finally driven off by the police. The aborted coup cost two lives, and nearly fifty people were injured.

If Kisch in his Red Guards days exemplifies the activist impulses of the man of letters, he was surely rivaled in flamboyance by his friend Franz Werfel, who came in from Prague to join him in the great revolutionary adventure then in the making. It was Werfel more than Kisch who climbed monuments to inflame the crowds to action. In his roman à clef about the Vienna of his time, *Barbara oder die Frömmigkeit* (Barbara or Piety; translated into English under the title *The Pure of Heart* in 1929), Werfel, who appears in the work under the name of Ferdinand, describes the events of 12 November 1918 in considerable detail and introduces Kisch in the guise of the character Ronald Weiss. Here, for example, is how Werfel recalls Kisch's sudden transformation into a revolutionary commander:

Kisch as commander of the Red Guard in
Vienna. To his left is Leo Rothziegel.
Courtesy Museum of National Literature,
Prague.

Weiss cleared a path for himself to the podium. At first a cool and distrustful mood prevailed in the hall. Ronald began timidly. His phrases didn't hit home. Accent and shading rang false in the ears of the crowd. But suddenly Weiss had the brilliant idea of tearing his gold medal for bravery from his chest and throwing it into the audience with a magnificent gesture. This was the first strong moment of the entire evening. People stormed . . . The name "Comrade Weiss" rang loudly through the hall. Three minutes were all it took, and a new leader had arisen. . . .[11]

Where had Weiss suddenly come by that thoroughly plucky tone with which he imposed his will on the crowd? He was demanding that elections for soldiers' councils be held tomorrow in every barracks and hospital in Vienna. It would then be the duty of the chosen representatives to see to it that no arbitrary and hasty action occurs. Yet, arms at the ready, everyone must be ready for the call to duty at a moment's notice. Until it came, every revolutionary soldier was obliged, by means of tireless educational work, to win over vacillating and recalcitrant comrades. The orator finished with the cry:

"Down with war! Long live the revolution!"

After this speech, "Comrade Weiss" was the most popular name in the entire hall. A staff of young soldiers had already formed and stuck close to him. He had become a power.

Werfel himself became a member of the Red Guards' military committee, and Rothziegel, the communist for all occasions, its Soviet-style political commissar. After its first stormy demonstration in front of the Parliament, during which a huge red banner was raised, the Guards, now armed with machine guns, sallied forth to take over an army barracks preceded by a band playing the Marseillaise. Werfel offers an evidently accurate eyewitness account of the initial enthusiasm of the Red Guards and then their dismay when fighting actually broke out and the Parliament did not fall to them, as they had expected:

Around midday the great workers' demonstration and march on Parliament had begun. It was something that Vienna, the imperial city, had never before experienced. . . . (497)

An awareness of their strength and what they had achieved, despite all their misfortune, made the crowds of people oblivious to any danger and put them in a good mood. Eddies of laughter rippled all along the broad slope of the festive stream. The Red Guards also exhibited a pleasant gaiety. Men had left the ranks and stood about in groups, laughing. Their rifles were carelessly slung over their shoulders. . . . (500)

What developed next happened so breathtakingly fast that an accurate analysis of the exact sequence of events cannot plausibly be disentangled and then reconstructed. Wimpel [Weiss's orderly] dashed forward, panting, as if he had run not ten steps but a long distance. In an instant Ferdinand and Weiss were surrounded by a cluster of gesticulating guardists. One voice rose above the others:

"Comrade Weiss! Machine guns aimed at us! Up there . . . An officers' putsch!". . . (503)

Weiss was the most changed of all. He, whose mouth was still full of the words with which he characterized the shadowy theatrics of such events, fell instant victim to the force of the drama, and plunged right into the midst of it. Ferdinand had never seen him like this. His eyes had narrowed from intoxication, the skin over his cheekbones flushed deep red. Weiss no longer knew that he was only the actor of this moment. Trembling from powerful longing for great experiences, he screamed, his voice cracking:

"Attention! Machine guns! Fall in!" . . . (503–4)

What had happened? Who fired? The assembled masses understood nothing. Even the troops of the Red Guards, who were peppering the coping of the Greek temple [the Parliament building], took the echo of their own shots for an enemy attack, and now began firing in all directions. The heavy Parliament doors did not give way beneath the savage pounding. (505)

Not long after the publication of Werfel's novel, a reporter asked Kisch if he was upset by the portrait Werfel had painted of him in it. Kisch declared that he was not in the least, since, after all, he had been partly responsible for Werfel's getting involved in the Red Guards and the November Revolution in the first place. Moreover, Kisch expressed his admiration for Werfel's astonishing memory, which had managed faithfully to recreate scenes and conversations that had taken place ten or more years before.[12]

As operetta-like as it appears to have been, the failed Red Guards coup has to be seen in the larger context of the communist fervor that swept across Eastern and Central Europe in the wake of the successful Bolshevik seizure of power in Russia in 1917. Béla Kun's short-lived communist regime in Hungary and the shorter-lived "Soviet Republic of Bavaria" were similar, and initially more successful, manifestations of the campaign to exploit the political instability that followed the dissolution of the Habsburg, Hohenzollern, and Romanov empires during and after World War I.

The "Golden Twenties" in Prague and Berlin

After his expulsion from Vienna following the Red Guards fiasco, Kisch spent nearly the next two years in Prague. He was now a citizen, after all, of the new Republic of Czechoslovakia, and Prague was emerging as a vibrant national capital after its long subordination to Vienna within the Austro-Hungarian Empire. Cultural life flourished, and Kisch threw himself into it with delight. The Prague community of German writers, consisting principally of Max Brod, Willy Haas, Franz Kafka, Rainer Maria Rilke, Franz Werfel, and Ernst Weiss, welcomed him into their circle, and before long he was a regular at such landmark coffeehouses as the Café Continental and the Café Central. Since the Conti was the preferred hangout of journalists affiliated with the German-language *Prager Tagblatt,* to which Kisch soon began contributing, he made it his favorite as well and staked out his own reserved table there. Late-night haunts such as the Café Montmartre and the Lucerna brought him back to his early days as a Prague local reporter.[13]

Kisch's return to Prague in 1920 also enabled him to resume old friendships with members of the Czech literary world, above all Jaroslav Hašek, the creator of the immortal *Good Soldier Schweik* (1920–23) and the outstanding dramatist František Langer. Despite their use of different languages, the three writers had common literary interests. Hašek and Langer were very much at home in the milieu of Kisch's early collections of Prague sketches, and Langer especially shared Kisch's appetite for the criminal and sensational. The two Czech writers also held similar liberal social views, and both had seen military service in Russia with the Czech Legion during World War I. Langer published several works about his wartime experiences, while Hašek did a complete turnabout after the Russian Revolution, deserted the

Czech Legion, joined the Red Army, and served for a time as a political commissar in Siberia. It would be hard to imagine that Hašek's and Langer's stories about Russia did not add fuel to the growing fire of Kisch's interest in that country and desire to travel there.

Another Czech writer who crossed Kisch's cultural horizon in Prague in the early 1920s was Emil Artur Longen. A member of the left-leaning Prague bohemian crowd whose uncrowned king was Hašek, Longen in 1920 opened a short-lived avant-garde cabaret-theater in Prague named Revoluční scéna (Revolutionary Stage). Kisch soon began collaborating with it, happy to have an excuse to resume his interest in the stage, which went back to the spring of 1914, when he was briefly employed as dramaturge by the troubled Deutsche Künstlertheater of Berlin. Two of his early works—the story "Himmelfahrt der Galgentoni" (The Ascension of Toni the Gallows Girl), about a Prague prostitute who, despite her profession, goes to heaven, and the novel *The Pimp* were dramatized in Czech and staged by Longen for the first time in October and November 1921, respectively. Kisch's amusing sketch "Die Reise um Europa in 365 Tagen" (Around Europe in 365 Days), about an actual, very protracted trip by tugboat from Prague to Bratislava via Germany, was dramatized by Hašek with Kisch's help and staged at the Revoluční scéna at the end of December 1921.

Kisch continued his theater work after he left Prague and settled in Berlin in the fall of 1921. Although deeply attached to Prague, with which he continued to maintain close ties, he was ready to move on in search of new experiences. Notwithstanding its postwar malaise and economic and political instability—or perhaps because of them—the German capital in the 1920s was a magnet for writers and artists throughout the German-speaking world. It was a time of exciting challenges and creativity, and Kisch had to be in the midst of it. Not one to let any grass grow under his feet, he was soon renewing old acquaintances and making new ones, reestablishing contacts with Berlin newspapers and publishing houses, striking his tent in the city's great literary cafés, above all the legendary Romanisches on the corner of Tauentzien and Budapester Strassen, hurling himself into a frenzy of writing.

The Weimar period became one of the most fruitful of Kisch's career.[14] Still entertaining thoughts of theatrical success on the heels of the well-received little productions in Prague, Kisch wrote two more stage works, *Die gestohlene*

Stadt (The Stolen City), a historical comedy based on an episode during the Seven Years' War, and *Die Hetzjagd* (The Pursuit), about the last day in the life of Colonel Alfred Redl. *The Stolen City* had its premiere in the New German Theater in Prague in June 1923 and was performed in Czech the following year by two small Prague theaters, the Apollo and Rokoko.[15] Between 1923 and 1925 the Rokoko also staged five more works based on Kisch's sketches, among them a dramatized version of the shorter account of the Colonel Redl treason and one dealing with the legendary flea circus owner, Ferda Mestek de Podskal.[16]

Although Kisch was glad to see his few original plays and dramatizations of his sketches performed in Prague, it was obvious that he was not going to take the Berlin stage by storm and that there was no real future for him in the theater. His dramatic works are of uneven quality, mostly fair to good comedies, and assume an importance in his overall creativity only insofar as the lessons he learned from playwriting about dialogue and dramatic structure were put to far more effective use in his reportage. Fortunately for his career, Kisch diverted little time from his journalistic writing to other literary pursuits. In 1922 he published two works, his play *The Stolen City* and the first edition of his war diary, *Soldier in the Prague Corps,* which he had finally completed in Prague and Berlin. The later edition of the work, *Write It Down, Kisch!* was published in 1929. The year after *The Stolen City* and *Soldier in the Prague Corps* appeared, Kisch's monumental anthology *Classical Journalism* was published in Berlin. It was followed the next year, 1924, by two of Kisch's most resonant works, his account of the Colonel Redl affair, *The Case of the Chief of the General Staff Redl,* and his first great collection of reportage, *The Raging Reporter,* an eclectic assemblage of previously published and new pieces which began his fame as the "raging reporter" and sent his literary stock higher than it ever had been.

If Kisch was "raging" by virtue of the astonishing variety of subjects he wrote about and his breathless racing from one locale to another, with hardly time out for military service and attempted revolution, he was also "raging" in the feverish tempo of his literary output: publication of a play and his war diary in 1922, his sweeping anthology of journalism in 1923, the account of the Redl treason in 1924, and *The Raging Reporter* the same year. And there was no slacking off after these achievements. A second collection of wide-ranging reportage with a largely historical orientation under the title *Hetzjagd durch die Zeit* (Pursuit through Time) was published by Erich Reiss Verlag the year after *The Raging Reporter* began showing up in bookstores. Two more collections—*Worldwide Exploits* and *Tsars, Priests, and Bolsheviks*—appeared in 1927, but by now Kisch had greatly expanded his horizons and had cast his net across the globe. The "raging reporter" had burst his European confines.

The Worldwide Traveler

Worldwide Exploits marked a new departure for Kisch. Whereas his previous books of reportage had a European focus, this one reflected a growing enthusiasm for far-flung travel, in this case North Africa. It seems likely that Kisch would have dashed off to that part of the world sooner or later. He may even have been thinking about it when a stranger approached him one day in a Berlin coffeehouse and offered him the job as an extra in a film being shot partly in Algeria. This is how Kisch explains the circumstances surrounding his first trip to North Africa in his amusing sketch "Memoiren eines Filmstatisten" (Memoirs of a Movie Extra), which is included in *Worldwide Exploits*.[17] Shortly after he reached Algiers, he also sent a report about the film to the Prague journal *Internationale Filmschau,* together with a photograph of himself and the other actors and actresses.[18] The film, it turns out, was something called *Die Frauengasse von Algier* (The Bordellos of Algiers), and it was being produced by the famous UFA cinema company of Berlin. Once his movie debut was over, Kisch was on his own to travel elsewhere in North Africa, and he headed to neighboring Morocco and Tunisia.

Strongly attracted by the exotic elements in North African society and culture, which he writes about with the same keen eye for detail and the offbeat as in his previous books, Kisch also gives evidence in this collection of a greater willingness to comment on political life. In the context of North Africa in Kisch's time, this meant the reality of French rule and the different colonial structures in Algeria, Morocco, and Tunisia. Although he avoids overt condemnation of French colonialism, Kisch makes it clear that natural resources and native labor serve primarily French interests and that resident French landowners and businessmen are exploitive, arrogant, and unafraid to use force to preserve their privileges. Kisch's sympathies lie almost wholly with the indigenous peoples, whose mores are the main focus of his reportage. This excludes, however, the native political authorities who exercise power only at the pleasure of the French and are portrayed as little more than puppet figures. Well aware of growing resistance to the French, Kisch also writes about the various North African political crises and military clashes before, during, and after World War I. *Worldwide Exploits* is a colorful and readable collection of North African sketches by a fascinated observer who is at the same time well versed in the history and politics of the region.

In the Land of the Tsars and Bolsheviks

Hardly had he returned from his travels in North Africa when the peripatetic "raging reporter" was off again on another lengthy trip, this time to the Soviet Union. But it was more than just his political views that impelled the former commander of the Vienna Red Guards to make the journey. This was no mere pilgrimage to the mecca of communism. The downfall of the Romanov dynasty and the coming to power in Russia of the Bolsheviks had electrified the world. To the Germans, whose fascination with things Russian goes back to the seventeenth century, Russia had never seemed more interesting. The success of the Bolshevik coup represented a model for German revolutionaries, just as it had inspired its Austrian admirers in the days of the short-lived Vienna Red Guards. The more successful but ultimately ephemeral attempts to create Soviet-style republics in Germany not long afterward left a legacy of admiration for Russia among German leftists, who took advantage of any and every opportunity to visit the Soviet Union. They were joined by many other Germans, not all of whom traveled east for inspirational purposes. The liberalism of the Weimar period created a climate of openness toward Soviet and Russian culture. This was particularly true of the literary community, which opened a real dialogue with its Russian counterpart and created an impressive body of travel literature. Kisch, therefore, was not the first German-language writer to travel extensively throughout the Soviet Union in the 1920s and publish a detailed account of his impressions and experiences. He was preceded by Arthur Holitscher, Leo Mathias, and Joseph Roth; Heinrich Vogler and Klara Zetkin were there around the same time he was; his *Tsars, Priests, and Bolsheviks* appeared a year after René Fülop-Miller's *Geist und Gesicht des Bolschewismus* (The Spirit and Face of Bolshevism) and Erich Mäder's

Zwischen Leningrad und Baku (Between Moscow and Baku); three other accounts of travel through the Soviet Union appeared the same year as Kisch's book—Otto Friedländer's *Hammer, Sichel, Mütze* (Hammer, Sickle, and Cap), Emil Julius Gumbel's *Vom Russland der Gegenwart* (Russia Today), and Max Tobler's *Moskauer Eindrücke* (Moscow Impressions); Walter Benjamin's *Moskauer Tagebuch* (Moscow Diary), which covers his travels in the Soviet Union not long after Kisch's, was published for the first time only in 1980.

Ideology was obviously one of the things that attracted Kisch to the new Soviet Union. Besides being the former commander of the Vienna Red Guards, Kisch had been a member of the Communist Party of Austria since its founding in November 1918, and on 18 November 1925 he had joined the German Communist Party.[19] Although party membership eased his travel in the Soviet Union and facilitated contacts that otherwise might have been difficult to make, Kisch did not travel to Russia as a worshipping, uncritical observer. He was, however, not as easily deterred by the negative aspects of the new Soviet society as were, for example, Benjamin and Erich Kästner, who also made the almost obligatory trek east in the 1920s. It would perhaps be too cynical to suggest that once having planned the trip to the Soviet Union Kisch made a point of equipping himself with a German Communist Party card along with such necessities as a passport and a visa. His ideological outlook had developed over a period of time, and his credentials as a well-known left-leaning journalist of high repute would have been enough to open doors for him without the imprimatur of the Communist Party.

Kisch's interest in Russia should be seen, however, in the broader context. The erstwhile revolutionary and now card-carrying communist would obviously have felt a strong attraction to the Soviet Union. But, as I have pointed out, curiosity about the new Russia, commingled with admiration and even a sense of excitement, ran high among German-speaking artists and intellectuals in the 1920s, and Kisch was in good company.[20]

The inspiration, moreover, of two exceptional foreign journalists, one American, the other Russian—both of whom, in an odd twist of fate, died of typhus in their early thirties—also shaped Kisch's plans. The first was John Reed, the young American reporter who eventually became one of the founders of the Communist Party of the United States. Reed was in Petrograd in 1917 in connection with his coverage of World War I in Eastern Europe[21] and in

Ten Days That Shook the World (1919) wrote an astonishing eyewitness account of the early days of the Russian Revolution. The distinguished American diplomat and historian George Kennan has described *Ten Days That Shook the World* in these words: "Despite his exuberant and uninhibited political bias, Reed's account of the events of that time rises above every other contemporary record for its literary power, its penetration, its command of detail. It will be remembered when all the others are forgotten."[22] Kisch was indeed familiar with Reed's work. Besides his introduction to the German edition of *Ten Days That Shook the World,* "John Reed, ein Reporter auf der Barrikade" (John Reed, a Reporter at the Barricades), Kisch also wrote a short appreciative sketch, "Our Own Correspondent John Reed" (title in English in the original; 1928). As his writings on Reed make clear, Kisch admired the young American reporter above all for his fearless objective reporting despite the enormous circumstantial pressure on him to slant his coverage to comply with the Allied plan to keep Russia in the war against Germany at all costs. While obviously sympathetic toward Reed's prorevolutionary outlook, Kisch would in any case have held the American in high esteem for his commitment to reporting the facts as he saw them. As Reed himself wrote candidly: "In the struggle my sympathies were not neutral. But in telling the story of those great days I have tried to see events with the eye of a conscientious reporter, interested in setting down the truth."[23]

The other foreign reporter whose coverage of the Russian Civil War made a lasting impression on Kisch was Larisa Reisner.[24] A young Russian woman of an aristocratic, cultured, and well-to-do background, Reisner fervently embraced the Bolshevik cause and went on to become one of the monumental heroines of the Civil War. A courageous combatant as well as journalist, Reisner won the respect and admiration of battle-hardened Red soldiers and seamen. Her compelling account of the bitter fighting in Kazan and Sviazhsk on the Volga, in which she took part aboard a Red flotilla, appears in *Front* (Front, 1924), undoubtedly some of the best reportage to come out of the Russian Civil War. For Kisch, Reed's *Ten Days That Shook the World* and Reisner's *Front* were the "only two journalistic war books" that still had critical importance in his own time and would "still have it in a hundred years."[25] Although different in style, Reed and Reisner both grasped, according to Kisch, that "current events should be dealt with journalistically only from the angle of eternity and that each individual fate and each episode should mirror the great destiny of humanity" (193). Kisch had also linked Reed and Reisner together in his introduction to the German edition of *Ten Days That Shook the World:*

> No one withheld this literary recognition from Reed's work, just as bourgeois criticism acknowledged, in amazement, that there was nothing in the journalistic literature of the world war even approximately comparable to Larisa Reisner's book *Front* (the events of which are the sequel to the "Ten Days"). To be sure, the only one who might have been amazed at this is the person whose judgments are made from the purely aesthetic point of view.
>
> No, it is no accident that Reed and Reisner succeeded in shaping books from bare facts and unadorned events that in power, excitement, and tension leave far behind the overwhelming bulk of novelistic literature and can be compared only to those novels whose contemporary historical significance sprang from the same sources: a pitiless rendering of the truth and an *uncompromising* social will.[26]

Although she was more spontaneous, poetic, and less disciplined a journalist than Reed, Reisner's appeal to Kisch would not have been limited just to her coverage of the Russian Civil War. As a young girl, Reisner lived in Berlin from 1903 to 1908. Not only did she learn German fluently, she maintained a lifelong interest in Germany and returned there in 1923—as a Comintern agent as well as journalist—to cover the uprising in Hamburg that year. Her major work of reportage dealing with that event is *Gamburg na barrikadakh* (Hamburg at the Barricades); a German translation was published in 1925. The work circulated widely despite an official and controversial ban on it.[27] A 1927 German collection of Reisner's reportage, under the title *Oktober* and including most of the sketches in her *V strane Gindenburga* (Hindenburg's Country, 1925; *Im Lande Hindenburgs: Eine Reise durch die deutsche Republik,* in German), the fruit of a return trip to Germany in 1925, did not include *Hamburg at the Barricades.*[28]

Kisch's collection of Russian sketches, *Tsars, Priests, and Bolsheviks,* followed the same basic pattern of his more recent books of reportage. The travel ranges far and wide, from Leningrad to Moscow and thence to the

Caspian Sea, Georgia, Armenia, and Azerbaijan. His antennae ever tuned to the dramatic, Kisch concludes the book with an account of his arrival in Warsaw the day after the coup d'état by Marshal Józef Piłsudski in May 1926. Although Moscow and Leningrad are given their due, there is a slight bias in the book in favor of the Caucasus and the Soviet Union's non-Russian peoples. It includes, for example, pieces on professions and religions in Tiflis, the capital of Georgia; theater life in Azerbaijan; a morning stroll through the streets of Yerevan, the capital of Armenia; a visit to an authentic Turkish bath; an audience with Katholikos, the head of the Armenian church; the oil fields in the Caspian Sea; a community of German peasants in Georgia; and a masked ball in Tiflis. Coming on the heels of his sojourn in North Africa, Kisch may have felt a certain affinity at this point with the non-European parts of the great communist empire. In this sense, *Tsars, Priests, and Bolsheviks* can be regarded as something of a warm-up for Kisch's extensive journey through Soviet Central Asia in 1931, a trip that yielded *Changing Asia.*

Despite its resemblances to Kisch's previous reportage—the seeming randomness of the experiences, the sharp eye for detail and color, the preoccupation with the everyday, the fascination with crime and punishment—his book about the Soviet Union marked in some ways a departure from earlier writing. Obviously anxious to be as journalistically conscientious as possible in his reporting from the Soviet Union, Kisch sometimes allows his characteristic fondness for detail to slip into a recitation of dry statistics. This shows up most where one would most expect it, in pieces devoted to industry and economics.

Coming to the Soviet Union as a former revolutionary and a member of the German Communist Party, Kisch seems to have approached his task as a writer of reportage with a greater seriousness of purpose than ever before. This is reflected in the style of *Tsars, Priests, and Bolsheviks.* The casual, often conversational narrative of previous collections of reportage—for which he had been faulted by orthodox communist critics—gives way now to rare *gravitas.* Sentences and paragraphs are longer and more ponderous. The reading, while interesting, is slower—inevitably, no doubt, in view of the amount of information Kisch sought to communicate. But his stance throughout is by no means that of an awestruck admirer of the Soviets who has nothing but good to relate. In sketches such as "Männer und Frauen im

Gefängnis" (Men and Women in Prison), "Moskaus Polizeichef antwortet dem Interviewer" (Moscow's Police Chief Answers the Interviewer), and "Erziehung durch den 'Geschlechtskranken'" (Venereal Disease as Education), he shows no reluctance to confront seamier sides of Soviet society, though he is careful to acknowledge progress where it is being made. He also deals frankly with the situation of the Christian church in the Soviet Union and the campaign to suppress it. Perhaps it was for its candor that *Tsars, Priests, and Bolsheviks* was never published in the Soviet Union.

While not the easiest of Kisch's reportage to read, *Tsars, Priests, and Bolsheviks* has much to recommend it. Kisch was never content to go where others went and kept a sharp eye out for the less obvious, the novel, and the ironic, even when writing about the seemingly banal. The book was a great success when it appeared—ten editions were published between 1927 and 1930—and it would be naive to attribute its success primarily to the interest in the Soviet Union in the German-speaking world at the time.

Although Kisch's itinerary and contacts in Russia are difficult to reconstruct with any great degree of precision, his reputation as well as his political sympathies preceded him and eased his way. In general, wherever he went he made friends easily and was anything but shy about seeking out fellow writers. Within the Russian literary community at the time, his most fruitful contact might well have been with Sergei Tretiakov, despite disappointingly sparse documentation. At a time of great international interest in the political events in China, Tretiakov's sojourn there in the mid-1920s and his writings on Chinese subjects—including the "factographic" play *Roar China!* and his "bio-interview" *Deng Shi-hua*—attracted much attention outside the Soviet Union. Tretiakov also had his admirers in the German-speaking world. An innovative, avant-garde, and cosmopolitan poet and dramatist, Tretiakov was a leading practitioner of reportage to whom, one imagines, Kisch would naturally have gravitated. Tretiakov spent time in Germany in the early 1930s and became a close friend (as well as translator) of Bertolt Brecht's. Although there is little to go on, a relationship was certainly possible between Kisch, Tretiakov, and Brecht in Berlin before Kisch was arrested in 1933. There is no hard evidence, however, that Kisch and Tretiakov developed any real relationship, whether in Russia in the mid-1920s or in Berlin the early 1930s. In an homage of sorts to his friends, Tretiakov wrote a series of literary portraits under the title *Lyudi odnogo kostra* (People of One Campfire, 1936), in which he mentioned that Kisch, Ludwig Renn, Ernst Toller, and Erich Weinert should have been included, but that he had to limit himself to those individuals whom he knew personally.[29]

Kisch's growing reputation as a writer, his communist affiliation, and contacts established during his first trip to the Soviet Union in 1925 and 1926 led to his being invited back in 1930, this time as a delegate to the congress of the International Association of Proletarian Revolutionary Writers held in Kharkov, Ukraine.[30] The congress was the first of such scope and magnitude. It drew representatives from twenty-three countries and lasted for three days. In his brief account of the affair, Kisch mentions that America was represented by Michael Gold, the author of *Jews without Money* (1930) and an ardent American champion of "proletarian" literature, who was accompanied by colleagues from *New Masses* (New York), and members of the John Reed Club of Chicago.[31] Whether Tretiakov had anything to do with the invitation to Kisch, or with his appointment the following year as visiting professor of journalism in the Artem Communist University in Kharkov, remains to be determined. As secretary of the new Writer's Union, Tretiakov was certainly in a position to arrange such invitations.

Tsars, Priests, and Bolsheviks, the fruit of Kisch's first trip to the Soviet Union, appeared in 1927. That same year, Kisch brought out *Travel Book of Crime,* a small collection of fourteen of his favorite crime sketches. It was followed in 1931 by *Prague Pitaval,* which contains forty pieces of reportage. This title sheds some light on Kisch's knowledge of the history of the genre with which he himself became so closely identified early in his career. François Gayot de Pitaval was a French journalist whose reputation was based on his crime reporting; in 1734 he published the first volume of his *Causes célèbres et intéressantes avec les jugements qui les ont décidés* (Famous and Interesting Cases Together with the Trials That Decided Them). The collection became a classic before the end of the eighteenth century.[32] Kisch was familiar with Pitaval's work, which he may have read in the original or in German, and saw Pitaval as a model for his own criminal reportage.

Kisch had another reason to think of Pitaval while in Berlin in the mid-1920s. As a contributor to the crime section of the *Berliner Montagspost,* he was asked to write a short article for the paper commemorating the two hundredth birthday of Pitaval. Around the same time, Kisch was also approached by Rudolf Leonhard of the Berlin publishing house Die Schmiede to contribute to a new "Pitaval series" on crime to be called "Aussenseiter der Gesellschaft" (Outsiders of Society). The series eventually comprised fourteen volumes; Kisch contributed the second volume in 1924 in the form of a synopsis of *The Case of Colonel Redl.* Tucholsky had high praise for it: "This is a bestseller of the first order."[33] Following on the success of its "Pitaval series," Die Schmiede planned another series of nonfiction of a more socially problem-oriented nature, in the spirit of "Neue Sachlichkeit." It was to be called "Berichte aus der Wirklichkeit" (Reports from the Real World). Kisch was again a logical contributor to the new series. Between 1925 and 1928 he had published more than fifty sketches on different criminal cases and was regarded favorably as a specialist in this area of journalism. The book that Kisch came up with for "Reports from the Real World," *Kriminalistisches Reisebuch*, appeared in 1927. Kisch often drew on previously published material for his books of reportage, but he used the occasion of a new collection to revise and generally expand earlier sketches for *Travel Book of Crime* and for *Prague Pitaval.* In the case of the former, Kisch validated the book's title by combining old sketches from his criminal reporting days in Prague with later sketches from his experiences in such places as Berlin, The Hague, Amsterdam, Algiers, and Moscow. Since crime and punishment long excited Kisch's enthusiasm and reportorial instincts, he found plenty of new material to write about on his travels through Europe, Russia, Central Asia, and North Africa. His own arrest and imprisonment in 1933 and his difficulties with Australian authorities a year later were to broaden his range with experiences of a far more personal nature.

Paradise America

After his visit to postrevolutionary Russia, the center of world communism, Kisch had an understandable urge to visit its polar opposite, the United States of America, the center of world capitalism. When he actually began the trip, and in what circumstances, are somewhat unclear. Michael Horowitz has Kisch boarding the English luxury liner *Olympic* in London on 30 October 1928, while Dieter Schlenstedt dates this a month later. Horowitz, like other commentators on Kisch, also subscribes to the notion that because he was thrice denied an entry visa by the American authorities, Kisch entered under false pretenses.[34] There is no evidence, however, supporting this claim. The first sketch in *Paradise America*, "Der Doktor Becker vor den Pforten des Paradieses" (Doctor Becker at the Gates of Paradise), introduces the figure of a "Doctor Becker," who effectively becomes Kisch's persona throughout the book. The sketch begins with the sentence: "Doctor Becker, as our man is called, is aboard the English passenger ship with mixed feelings." As Horowitz tells it, Kisch had false papers identifying him as Doctor Becker, a writer. When asked what kind of a writer he was, Kisch declared that he wrote stories and novels. As to his interest in politics, his answer was that he had none.

While acknowledging Kisch's difficulties in obtaining an American entry visa, Schlenstedt disputes the contention he entered the United States under a pseudonym. That Kisch might have had problems with American immigration authorities at the time would not be too surprising. His recent travels in Soviet Russia, with the appropriate stamps in his passport, would certainly have aroused some curiosity, and possibly also suspicion. American distaste for communism was well known, and the American intervention in the Russian civil war was still a recent memory. Kisch's enthusiasm for Reed and his opposition to the execution of Sacco and Vanzetti were further possible impediments to the easy acquisition of an American visa. Although Kisch's leadership of the Red Guards might conceivably have caused him greater problems with entry into the United States, it was doubtless unknown to the American authorities. But there is no evidence that Kisch traveled under any name but his own; the invention of the figure of "Doctor Becker" served primarily literary aims in *Paradise America*. Schlenstedt is quite right, I think, when he writes that "'Doctor Becker' might be punishable not as a false name, but as a proper literary method, with the imaginative element built into the reportage and this way achieving such a convincing effect. The figure goes about naively, is itself presented now and then as the bearer of a false consciousness that is to be corrected, and through attention to facts is corrected; the process by which the veil of illusions can be torn will be carried out on it. One of the attractions of Kisch's reports about America, of the grande reportage, as contemporaries called the form, is that it was not the [immigration] officials but rather we the readers who are provoked to observe the observer, to adopt a critical stance toward his ways and conclusions."[35]

In the several months that he was the United States—the longest time that he had yet visited a foreign country for purposes of reportage—Kisch saw a great deal, enough to provide ample material for the forty-one sketches that make up *Paradise America*. How varied his experiences were in the United States is evident from the subjects he wrote about: the presidential election of 6 November 1928, which brought Herbert Hoover to the White House; the New York jail known as the Tombs; Washington, D.C.; the piers of New York; Harlem; the Welfare Island prison in New York City; his service as an ordinary seaman sailing from New York City to California—the longest piece in the collection; gold digging in California; San Francisco and Oakland; the American gum industry; Philadelphia; a cemetery for the dogs of the wealthy in Hartsdale, New York; the stockyards and Board of Trade in Chicago; a Wall Street bank; the execution of David Shanks at the Cook County Jail; a New Year's Day parade in Philadelphia; Ford's Theatre in Washington; Sutter's Fort; the Ford factory in Detroit; American football; Sing-Sing; and hat-making in Danbury, Connecticut.

Excited as so many others by the birth of cinema and the emergence of Hollywood as the world capital of the new medium, Kisch made it the focus of his stay in California. His introduction to the movie world was arranged by the writer Upton Sinclair, who shared his social and political views. Always impressive in the research he conducted in advance of a new trip, Kisch came to the United States armed with a respectable knowledge of contemporary American society and culture, the American film industry included. This is evident, for example, in his "Erstes Gespräch mit Upton Sinclair" (First Conversation with Upton Sinclair). When Kisch reached California and looked up Sinclair, whom he had first met in New York, he lost little time in asking him to arrange a meeting with Charlie Chaplin. At the pinnacle of his career as an actor and director, Chaplin was a must visit for Kisch. Recognizing in him another kindred spirit, Kisch quotes Sinclair's description of Chaplin in his "First Conversation with Upton Sinclair" as "a wonderful person, even if, unfortunately, he never answers any letters. He is a socialist and hangs around with radicals, which is why he is viewed with dread in certain circles."[36] Kisch and Chaplin apparently hit it off together, and Chaplin even invited Kisch into his studio to observe work in progress on the film *City Lights*. The detailed

**Composite photograph of Kisch and Upton
Sinclair with Charlie Chaplin.
Courtesy Museum of National Literature,
Prague.**

description of Chaplin's working methods in "Arbeit mit Charlie Chaplin" (Working with Charlie Chaplin) in *Paradise America* surely is a valuable contribution to the literature on Chaplin the artist.

Kisch's enthusiasm for America was tempered by his awareness of social and economic inequities, which he draws attention to whenever relevant without belaboring the point, lapsing into the propagandistic, or losing his sense of humor. This was Tucholsky's assessment as well: "Kisch saw a great deal in America, and what he saw he relates well, in a fresh, lively way. One doesn't have the impression that he went to America with the idea in mind of finding everything bad." Nevertheless, Tucholsky reminds his reader, Kisch "is a trained Marxist and doesn't have any illusions."[37] Hollywood, in a way, was a microcosm of American society, at least from Kisch's point of view— alluring, brash, aggressive, exploitive, and cynical. Little wonder that he made friends so easily with Chaplin and with the author of *The Jungle, King Coal ,* and *Oil!* A few of the sketches in *Paradise America* deal with less glamorous aspects of the film capital. For example, Kisch writes about the hardball business practices common to the film industry and the garish architecture and sculpture of Los Angeles. But Kisch's casual style and humor soften the edges of any implied social criticism:

> The architectural logic isn't always understandable. Why, for example, does a restaurant have the shape of a stiff brown hat? Why is Hollywood's biggest movie house in the style of a Chinese theater? Why are Jewish religious services conducted in a church adorned with crosses and bearing the inscription "Unitarian Church"? Hold on a second! We almost made a fool of ourselves! This cross-adorned church really is a church and no synagogue, except that on Jewish holidays it covers up its saints, altars, and holy-water fonts and rents itself out to the pious of the film industry. Until a few years ago it was made available just for the Day of Atonement; but it proved to be more profitable for both parties to rent it out or rather lease it for all Jewish holidays. Great possibilities for imitative Europe: the head rabbi of Berlin preaches in the Kaiser Wilhem Memorial Church, and in the Old-New Synagogue the prince archbishop of Prague bestows his blessings on all the faithful. Naturally in return for good old American dollars.[38]

The fascination with "Americanism" and "American tempo" throughout Europe and Russia in the 1920s and early 1930s created a ready market for books on American life and culture. The entry of the United States into World War I and the appearance of large numbers of Americans in Europe during and after the war had a profound impact on the European consciousness and led to an intense interest in everything American. This was paralleled by the tremendous interest in Russia in the wake of the revolution in 1917. It was as if events had conspired to pull European awareness to the periphery. The hunger for knowledge about the vast countries of America and Russia and their very different societies inspired every conceivable type of publication and above all books of travel and reportage. Kisch's *Paradise America,* with its breadth of coverage, information, and revelation, its light, readable style, and its ironies, proved an extraordinary success. Besides its popularity in the German-speaking world, within two years of its publication the book had already been translated into Czech, Finnish, Polish, Russian, Serbo-Croatian, Spanish, Swedish, and other languages.

Soviet Asia and China

After his stint as a lecturer in Kharkov, Ukraine, Kisch decided to take advantage of his second stay in the Soviet Union to expand his knowledge of the non-Russian republics. Having visited Georgia, Armenia, and Azerbaijan on his first trip, he was now enthusiastic about the prospect of traveling farther east, to Soviet Central Asia, to such regions as Kazakhstan, Kyrgyzstan, Tajikistan, Turkmenistan, and Uzbekistan. In the summer of 1931, Kisch left by plane from Moscow to Tashkent and proceeded thence by train to Samarkand, Bokara, down along the Afghan border, and finally up to Stalinabad (formerly Dushanbe), the capital-in-the-making of Tajikistan. As the youngest Soviet republic—it had been admitted to the U.S.S.R. as an independent republic in July 1929—Tajikistan was the principal goal of Kisch's journey to Asia. Here, he believed, he would have the best chance to observe the modernization of a backward Central Asian region under Soviet rule.

When it was published in English in 1935 by Alfred A. Knopf, Kisch's account of his trip through Soviet Central Asia was given the title *Changing Asia.* Although the English title has a nice ring to it, it is not entirely accurate.

"Changing Asia" suggests a process of change taking place, in this case specifically the far-reaching changes brought to Central Asia under Soviet rule. The German title, *Asien gründlich verändert,* literally means "Asia fundamentally changed." For Kisch, the changes had already taken place and were so revolutionary in nature that they affected basic patterns of life and society. Semi-nomadic Islamic peoples had become settled, and the foundation of a modern industrial economy stood where not long before centuries-old tribal commerce was practiced. Wherever Kisch looked, he could not help being struck by the changes wrought on the land, cities, institutions, and even peoples. Having familiarized himself with the history of the region, he geared his reportage toward the contrasts between past and present, between vestiges of the past resistant to change, or begrudgingly yielding to change, and the relentless forces of change at work. He designated these contrasts with color in his sketch "Zweifarben-druck von Taschkent" (Two-Color Print of Tashkent), gray signifying the past, red (obviously) the present and future. Addressing the situation of women, who were often the most resistant to change, Kisch writes:

> Gray: Many women in the Hamsa Theater can be seeing wearing the *chadshvan,* a veil made of horses' hair.
>
> Red: They see other women on the stage belonging to their tribe, speaking their language, singing their songs, and wearing no protective shield before their faces. And the veiled women applaud their unveiled sisters.
>
> Gray: The better to appreciate this, it must be understood that there are still districts in Uzbekistan where women who dare show themselves without *chadshvan* are stoned to death. Sitting next to one of the veiled members of the audience is her daughter.
>
> Gray-red color transition: Like her mother she is covered from head to foot in the national costume, the *parandsha,* but she is not veiled.
>
> Red: And the girl next to her—a friend? her sister?—wears her hair short and has European attire. Many young Uzbek and Tajik women are already sporting the olive-green uniform of the Komsomols.[39]

Although favorably impressed with the modernization of Central Asia under the Soviets, Kisch's account of everything he sees and experiences is factual without lapsing into an exercise in pro-Soviet propaganda. The narrative is that of the enthusiastic, well-informed traveler with notebook in hand. Unlike *Tsars, Priests, and Bolsheviks,* the style of *Changing Asia* (to keep to the title of the published translation) is lighter, more casual, often more conversational. Of particular interest to Kisch, who was always respectful of the cultures of non-Europeans, was the extent to which the meaningful relics of the indigenous culture—above all those related to Islam—were being preserved and where necessary adapted to the new political-economic system.

In its ad for *Changing Asia* in the *New York Times Book Review* on 3 February 1935, Knopf sought to convey the basic appeal of Kisch's book: "[it is] the exciting record of a recent journey. It is a very unusual travel book, describing what is happening in the land of romance once ruled by Genghis Khan and Tamerlane—now in the throes of an amazing transformation. The ancient East is becoming a modern industrial region—but not without struggle, banditry, and comedy."[40] A. M. Nikolaieff's review of *Changing Asia* in the *New York Times Book Review* a week later took particular note of its style but also expressed a cavil: "The conversational form, to which the author often resorts, reproducing the words of his native informants, and his historical and 'editorial' digressions, are of added interest and enliven the narrative which, however, is not without bias."[41] The bias referred to has to do mostly with Kisch's claim in *Changing Asia*—which the reviewer Nikolaieff disputes— that the existence of "tens of thousands of dirty, ragged *bezprizorni* [juvenile waifs and strays]" was a legacy of tsarism. Nikolaieff acknowledged, however, that "doing away with this evil of the earlier years of the Bolshevist regime unquestionably should be considered an important attainment of the Soviets." While most reviews of *Changing Asia* were favorable, Marguerite Harrison, writing about it in the *New York Herald Tribune Books* on the same day the *New York Times* review appeared, credited its informational value but took issue with its "mass" of statistics:

> Egon Erwin Kisch, the author of "Changing Asia," is a thoroughly honest, sincere Marxist. In addition he is a well trained reporter of the German school with a veritable passion for data and statistics. . . .
>
> Kisch's picture of the economic and social forcing process by which the Bolsheviks are modernizing this section of Central Asia leaves

nothing to be desired in the way of completeness. It is in fact so complete that it is next to impossible to absorb the colossal mass of statistics bearing on every field of Soviet endeavor and the vast amount of information imparted to the reader.[42]

Ever the adventurer, Kisch could not pass up the opportunity to inject himself into potentially hazardous situations. On one occasion, he slipped across the border into Afghanistan to go on a tiger-hunting expedition, an episode he recounts in "Im afghanischen Dschungel" (In the Afghan Jungle), which is included in this book. In "Die Besiegung der Räuber" (Robbers Vanquished), Kisch describes in detail, and with due attention to the historical past, the events that transpired on 23 June 1931 in the village of Koktash. He had gone there in order to witness a holiday organized by the Red Sticks, a volunteer group of peasants founded to defend the village against raids by nearby bandits. Their foremost antagonist is the once popular tribal chief and now outlaw, Ibrahim Beg, an avowed foe of Bolshevism and the leader of the Bassmachi organization, whose uprising in 1921 had been harshly suppressed by the Soviets. While Kisch is in Koktash, Ibrahim Beg and his "chief of staff," Sahib Kommandir, sneak into the village late at night, armed to the teeth, but are apprehended before anyone is slain.

While in Soviet Central Asia, it would also have made sense to travel farther to China, which is what Kisch did, illegally, from March to July 1932. Again, Tretiakov's possible role in the formulation of these travel plans may be worth considering. Tretiakov had been a visiting lecturer on Russian literature at the National University of Northern China in Beijing for a year and a half in 1924–25 and while there collected material for his play *Roar China!* and the "bio-interview" *Deng Shi-hua,* a formally innovative work that used the raw oral narrative of one of his students to create the biography of a young non-communist Chinese. The purpose of the work was to capture the essence of China at such a turbulent juncture in its history and at the same time oppose what Tretiakov referred to as the "colonial-exotic" fiction about China by Western writers. During Deng Shi-hua's recitation, in broken Russian, Tretiakov acted, he recalls, as "interrogator, interviewer, confessor, conversational partner, and psychoanalyst,"[43] guiding the direction and shaping the order of his student's thought. Then drawing on his own knowledge and experiences,

Tretiakov fashioned his biography of Deng Shi-hua out of the oral auto-biography, hence the term "bio-interview."

China was a very different experience for Kisch from Soviet Central Asia, which he had traveled through just the year before. Instead of modernization, industrialization, and campaigns to overcome mass illiteracy and disease, he found a land of appalling corruption, retarded in its economic development by the self-serving policies of the great Western powers, rent by civil war, and brutalized at the time by Japanese invaders. Kisch's interest in crime and punishment found much to write about in China and is reflected in a number of sketches. Sensitive, as always, to the human condition, Kisch described the economic exploitation of children and the degradation of Russian women whose families fled Russia after the defeat of the White armies and who were trying to eke out a living as prostitutes. The colonial exploitation of China is a dominant theme in *Secret China* and is effectively but not dogmatically portrayed. Traditional aspects of Chinese culture and society form the subjects of two pieces on the Chinese theater and on the still more venerable institution of the Chinese eunuch. The contemporary political turbulence is addressed, as is the Japanese presence in the country.

The Burning of the Reichstag, the Coming to Power of the Nazis, and Exile

The burning of the Reichstag on 27 February 1933 ended Kisch's stay in Berlin, and Germany generally, after his return from the exhausting but exhilarating travels in Central Asia and China. That Kisch must already have been under Nazi surveillance seems obvious from his arrest and incarceration in Spandau prison the very next day after the Reichstag fire. His stay in Spandau, along with many others caught in the same dragnet, is described in chilling detail in the reportage "In den Kasematten von Spandau" (In the Dungeons of Spandau),[44] which is included in this collection. Because he held Czechoslovak citizenship at the time, and relations between Germany and Czechoslovakia had not yet reached the point of no return, Kisch was able to secure the intercession of the Czechoslovak authorities for his release. Since remaining any longer in Germany was now out of the question, he left Berlin for Prague the day of his release, 11 March. A civilian guard escorted him as far as the border. Although he threw himself into a whirlwind of anti-Nazi activity once in Prague, the growing German threat to Czechoslovakia and the desire of the authorities to avoid undue provocation made the continuance of such activity highly unlikely. Kisch thus remained in Prague for just a few months, moving on to Paris toward the end of May. In the French capital he became an active member of the growing community of German antifascist artists and intellectuals—Jews and Gentiles—who were in the process of making Paris a new center of German culture and the European hub of anti-Nazi resistance.[45] The presence of such writers as Alfred Döblin, Lion Feuchtwanger, Leonhard Frank, Thomas Mann (before he moved on to Switzerland), Heinrich Mann, Walter Mehring, René Schickele, Manès Sperber, Fritz von Unruh, Stefan Zweig, Benjamin, Koestler, Graf, and Tucholsky—to mention only some of the best known—and the possibility of publication by émigré journals and book publishing houses went a long way toward easing any doubts Kisch may have had concerning his ability to continue functioning as a German writer. As with many of the émigrés, money was a constant problem, but Kisch managed to get by and rarely made much of an issue of it.

The small world of the German exiles in Paris was anything but idyllic. The fervor of active anti-Nazi opposition was offset by factionalism (mostly along pro- or anti-Soviet lines) and the usual abrasions of close contact. After about four months in Paris, Kisch was ready for a change, ready for more travel and the new experiences that fueled his reportage. In October and November 1933 he traveled widely about Spain, a harbinger of his return to that country as a journalist reporting on the Civil War in 1937 and 1938. January and February 1934 found him on a tour of Belgium and the Netherlands accompanied by his Dutch translator, the journalist Nico Rost.[46]

When he returned to France, Kisch took up residence not in Paris, as might have been expected, but in Versailles. While he obviously wanted to stay in touch with the rest of the German exile literary community in Paris, it was equally obvious that Kisch also preferred to keep a certain distance from it. Once settled in Versailles, he threw himself into a study of the French Revolution (about which he subsequently wrote two novels, later lost during the German occupation of France) and prepared two new collections of reportage based mostly on his recent travels. The first collection, *Entry Prohibited,* the title indicating the uninvited (and unwelcome) investigative nature of the reportage, contains Kisch's observations on working conditions in the silk industry in Lyons, diamond cutting shops in Belgium and Holland, and silver mines in Spain; one sketch deals with an insane asylum in Belgium. The collection was published in July 1934 by the Paris exile publishing house Edition du Carrefour, which also brought out a French edition of the work. Subsequent German editions were published in 1934 by Universum-Bücherei, a Berlin publishing house that moved to Prague and Zurich in the wake of the Nazi takeover in Germany, and in 1935 by the Verlagsgenossenschaft ausländischer Arbeiter (Publishing Cooperative of Foreign Workers) in Moscow.

Kisch's second collection of reportage from 1934, *Tales from Seven Ghettos,* deals exclusively with Jewish subjects and is especially interesting for his resurrection of old criminal cases involving Jews. The collection was published by the Amsterdam exile publishing house of Albert de Lange. An English translation appeared in London in 1948. In a review of the original German edition in *Books Abroad,* the reviewer noted: "This temperamental volume of grotesqueries from various Jewish quarters in Europe and elsewhere has documentary value and atmosphere, color, and above all, odor."[47]

Kisch's last major literary effort before his notorious trip to Australia in 1934 was yet another collection of reportage—*Abenteuer in fünf Kontinenten* (Adventures on Five Continents)—comprised of previously published reportage as well as material collected on his recent trips to Spain, Belgium, and Holland. It, too, was published by Edition du Carrefour in Paris, in 1935.

Kisch's frenetic literary pace in the short period of his residence in Versailles must have made the prospect of a long ocean voyage to Australia too tempting to resist. In October 1934 the French communist writer and anti-Nazi activist Henri Barbusse asked Kisch if he would be willing to participate in an antiwar congress in Melbourne as a delegate of the Paris-based World Committee against War and Fascism. After the Nazis began implementing their internal and external policies, congresses of intellectuals and artists denouncing Nazism and fascism sprang up throughout the world, some organized by various pacifist organizations, some by the Soviets and their supporters in other countries. Kisch's participation in such international conclaves was a foregone conclusion. It did not take the "raging reporter" long to say yes to Barbusse's proposition. Little did he know when he agreed, relishing the thought of an invigorating journey by sea to a country he had not yet visited, that he was about to plunge into one of the most bizarre episodes of his entire career.

Australian Cause Célèbre

On 13 October 1934, Kisch enthusiastically set sail from Marseilles for Melbourne on board the steamship *Strathaird*. However, the meeting he was going to attend posed unexpected problems. Planned by Australian pacifists to coincide with the elaborate Melbourne centenary celebrations, the congress was meant to call attention to what the pacifists believed were covert Australian plans for new military preparations. The Australian authorities viewed the congress as a deliberate provocation on the part of a suspect body—the World Committee against War and Fascism—intent on embarrassing the country for its own political purposes. Since Kisch was being sent from France by the committee to be the key speaker at the congress—its star, in other words— the focus of the authorities naturally came to center on him. They felt that they had good reason to prevent his landing in Australia. He had previously been denied entry into England, where he was supposed to appear as a witness in a countertrial in London organized to expose the sham trial following the burning of the Reichstag. As a member of the British Commonwealth, Australia was hardly likely to welcome him with open arms. Indeed, the same day on which Kisch was issued a visa for Australia by a British consular official in Paris, the director of the Commonwealth Investigation branch informed the Australian Department of the Interior of his projected participation in the Melbourne congress. Moreover, once the Germans learned of Kisch's impending visit, their diplomats in Australia mounted a frenzied campaign to keep him out of the country, even presumably threatening economic sanctions.[48]

In order to keep the now unwelcome Kisch from going ashore at Free- mantle, the Australians fell back on a 1920 amendment to their Immigration Act intended to keep anarchists and communists from entering the country. A foreign-language dictation test, originally designed to limit the number of Asians entering Australia, could now be administered to anyone regarded as undesirable. Since the test involved a language that the examinee would most likely have no knowledge of, the essential unfairness of the amendment was all too obvious. In Kisch's case he was examined in Gaelic, which of course he did not know. A fellow delegate to the congress, the New Zealander Gerald Griffin, whom the Australians were also intent on keeping out of the country, was examined in Dutch. Kisch's account of his problems with Gaelic, and the aftermath of the dictation test, are described in detail in *Disembarking in Australia.*

Thus barred from leaving the *Strathaird* at Freemantle, frustrated and restless, Kisch decided to take matters into his own hands. On 13 November he jumped ashore when the liner berthed in Melbourne, but broke a leg in the process. He was eventually taken into custody while his case made its way through the courts. The outcome was predictable: Kisch was branded an undesirable immigrant and was sentenced to six months' hard labor for violating the Australian Immigration Act. Mounting public support in his favor, and the obvious embarrassment the case represented for Australia during the centenary celebrations, eventually resulted in a compromise. All charges and court costs against Kisch would be dropped if he agreed to leave the country at the earliest possible opportunity. Before he accepted the compromise, and during the time his case was before the courts, Kisch was out of jail on bail and managed to participate in several pacifist and antifascist rallies in different Australian cities. The police and internal security officers kept a sharp eye out for the slightest infraction that would have permitted them to take him into custody again; but Kisch often eluded them and avoided any outright provocation. He returned to Europe aboard the *S. S. Orford* from Freemantle on 11 March 1935, almost four months from the time he first landed on Australian soil on 13 November 1934. What had begun innocently enough as a projected brief stay in Australia for the purpose of addressing a congress in Melbourne turned into a nearly four-month cloak-and-dagger ordeal that greatly enhanced Kisch's fame and notoriety. His often entertaining account of his personal Australian adventure ("Weg zu den Antipoden," Journey to the Antipodes) makes up almost half of *Disembarking in Australia.*

Although the most engrossing part of the book is devoted to his trials and tribulations at the hands of the Australian authorities, there are other small chapters in which Kisch turned his attention to Australia itself, its people, customs, and history. Assuming the German reader's probable lack of familiarity, he included a fair amount of historical information as well as descriptions of specific Australian monuments, holidays, sports, aboriginal population, and industry. In view of the enthusiastic show of support he claimed to have received from workers during his tumultuous stay in Australia, Kisch made a point of addressing their status in the Australian economy and offers a quite readable chronological account of the Australian trade union movement from 1835 to 1935.

Unlike his previous collections of reportage, Kisch was not merely a journalist in Australia. His own ordeal in trying to get into the country in the first place aroused his understandable indignation. This was exacerbated even more by his conviction that, as had been the case in England, it was principally the machinations of German diplomatic officials that conspired to keep him out of the country. He saw himself no less a victim of fascism than when he had been imprisoned, and he was determined to use the treatment he received as the basis for an indictment of Australian politicians and parties who were only too eager to accommodate the Nazis and to stifle growing antiwar protest in the country. Some of this animus can be felt in "Journey to the Antipodes," but Kisch, as usual, is never strident or confrontational, and the informality and humor of the account make it good reading. Other sketches in the book leave little doubt, however, that he derived a certain satisfaction in debunking the myth of Australia as a land of contentment.

Disembarking in Australia also commands attention for the narrative strategy of "Journey to the Antipodes." Of the options open to him, Kisch vetoed a straightforward first-person account. Written not long after the events themselves, but obviously drawing on extensive notes made during the entire trip, "Journey to the Antipodes" is narrated mostly in the present tense by an omniscient narrator who refers to Kisch throughout, in the familiar style of detective and spy fiction, as "unser Mann" ("our man"). Although he makes extensive use of dialogue, in which he appears in his own voice, Kisch is careful to maintain the literary distance of his narrator, who at the same time is decidedly close to the subject of his narration. As the narrator declares early in the work:

> Nevertheless, we have more to do with the man than either he or we would like. We, that means we who are writing this book; the man is the hero of this book. "Hero"—that's the word we would have preferred avoiding, although we are employing it, of course, not in the sense of

hero but rather in the sense of "literary figure." We have no desire to present the man with whom we are going to be preoccupied as a hero. But it would be quite pleasant in this instance not to brand him to the contrary. That is because he is near to us, as a fellow countryman, like-minded, and so on. We show solidarity with him; indeed, we identify with him.[49]

A. T. Yarwood remarks that Kisch made a "tremendous impression" on the Australians, above all for his irrepressibility in the face of persecution. "Those who met him privately," writes Yarwood, "seem universally to have been attracted by his charm and spirit."[50] One of those so attracted was a twenty-five-year-old journalist named John Fisher, who covered Kisch's visit for the Melbourne *Herald*. Fisher, the youngest son of the Australian Labor prime minister, Andrew Fisher, became so taken with Kisch and sympathetic toward his views that he gave up his job with the *Herald* and accompanied Kisch back to Europe on the *Orford*. During the long passage, Fisher acquainted Kisch with much of the background to the Australian history and society written about so knowledgeably in those parts of *Disembarking in Australia* not dealing with Kisch's own adventures. Kisch in turn may have kindled Fisher's interest in the Soviet Union. In 1942, during World War II, Fisher arrived in Moscow to take up his duties as a broadcaster for the Australian Broadcasting Commission. He later became press attaché to the newly formed Australian Legation in Moscow. Although Fisher went on to a productive literary career as the author of seventeen books, his diaries covering the period of his official duties in Moscow from 1942 to 1945 have never been published.

The Spanish Civil War

Kisch's activities between April 1935, when he returned to Europe from Australia, and December 1939, when he sailed for New York after the outbreak of World War II, consisted primarily of his completion of *Disembarking in Australia*, participation in the first International Congress of Writers for the Defense of Culture in Paris (June 1935),[51] where he delivered a lecture, "Reportage as a Form of Art and Combat" ("Reportage als Kunstform und Kampfform"), participation in the second International Congress of Writers

Kisch as a member of the International
Brigades in Spain. To his left is the singer
Ernst Busch.
Courtesy Ullstein Bilderdienst.

in Madrid (1937), and his coverage of the Spanish Civil War for various, mostly left-wing, German-language newspapers.

Kisch was in Spain from early June 1937 until his return to France the following April. Although he was close to scenes of some of the most bitter fighting of the war, and with his own eyes saw the destruction visited on Valencia and Madrid from the air, above all by the German Condor Legion, Kisch produced less reportage from the Spanish Civil War than from previous foreign travel experiences. There are various ways to explain this. After his own military service in World War I, Kisch had no further exposure to war until the fraternal-political conflict in Spain. As a young reporter caught up in combat for the first time, Kisch understandably sought to commit to paper the savagery taking place all around him and so kept the diary that eventually saw the light of day as *Soldier in the Prague Corps.* In his later collections of reportage, Kisch was free of wartime pressures and able to compose at least his first drafts in the relative quiet of hotel rooms and other lodgings. Spain was another matter. The hard-fought battles of 1937 and 1938, from Brunete to Teruel, and Kisch's concentration on the activities of the International Brigades, kept him on the move much of the time. As a noncombatant, a journalist traveling from one part of the country to another as conditions allowed, Kisch would have had little reason to keep a chronological account of the fighting in diary form. Other factors also shaped the quantity and character of Kisch's writings from Spain. The nature of the civil war itself, between the left-wing, Soviet-supported republic and Franco's nationalists with their German and Italian fascist backing, engaged the energies and emotions of the world liberal community to a degree matched only by the Russian Revolution. The outpouring of support for the beleaguered republic led to the formation of the International Brigades, with volunteers of every conceivable persuasion—communists, socialists, antifascists, anarchists, just plain romantic adventurers with a cause to fight and die for—pouring into Spain any way they could from more than thirty countries.

Besides viewing his reporting from Spain primarily in terms of the fulfillment of newspaper assignments—which clearly bore on the style of his writing—Kisch became so caught up in the political drama of the Spanish Civil War that he projected an activist image in some ways reminiscent of his Red Guards days in Vienna. His reportage had two main thrusts. With one, he sought to bring home to readers the terrible destruction caused by German and Italian interventionists, notably the aerial assaults on Valencia and Madrid. It was only during the Spanish Civil War that airplanes were first used to bombard cities, and Kisch, stunned like so many others at the time by the damage such bombardment could inflict, sought to draw his readers into the sense of horror at what he saw with his own eyes.

The second main thrust of Kisch's Spanish reportage—one he shared with all other leftist commentators on the events in Spain—was to call attention to the national diversity and heroism of the International Brigades. To do so, he made a point of drawing close to the predominantly Central and East European brigades—the XIth, with its Austrian Fourth Battalion; the XIIIth, which was made up almost entirely of East Europeans; the XIVth; and the XVth, which was commanded by the Croatian communist Vladimir Copić and incorporated a battalion led by a Hungarian who called himself Major "Chapaev," after the famous guerrilla leader of the Russian Civil War.[52] These brigades were involved in the ultimately costly republican offensive in and around Brunete and Quijorna in July 1937. Although Kisch seems to have been in the Brunete area during the campaign, almost none of his reportage deals with frontline combat. Instead, the emphasis is on the behind-the-lines activities of the Brigades. The best example of this is the piece "Soldaten am Meeresstrand" (Soldiers on the Seashore), most of which is included in this book and represents an expansion of two shorter pieces—"Die 'Dissimulanten' von Benicasim" (The "Dissimulators" of Benicasim) and "Die Sanität der Internationalen" (The Medical Service of the International Brigades).[53]

In October 1937, after the battle of Brunete, Kisch visited the medical facility of the International Brigades at the seaside resort town of Benicasim, between Barcelona and Valencia. Benicasim was important to Kisch for two reasons. Behind the front, among the wounded, Kisch had more of an opportunity to engage the members of the Brigades in conversations about their backgrounds, their political views, and their motives for joining the fight in Spain. The hospital at Benicasim also happened to be under the direction of Kisch's younger brother, Friedrich, a surgeon.[54] The clinical detail of "Soldiers on the Seashore" not only recalls Kisch's observations of war wounded in World War I but also reflects conversations with his brother about the impressive treatment available to the International Brigades. Living for a time among the wounded at Benicasim gave Kisch the chance as well to consider the truly international makeup of the Brigades and their way of life behind the front.

It was while he was at Benicasim that Kisch made the acquaintance of two young Tiroleans, Max Bair and Johann Knotzer, who related to him the story of their journey to the battlefields of Spain from the small village of Puigg am Brenner. To cover the cost of his travel to Spain, Bair sold three cows, his most valuable possessions. With the money realized from the sale, he and Knotzer went to Paris, where their further passage to Spain was arranged. Kisch could hardly miss the human and political appeal of the Bair-Knotzer story. Two Austrian farmers, who had never looked or thought much beyond the confines of their village, imbued with such a sense of the moral rightness of the republican cause in Spain, set out for that strange, distant land in order to fight in a civil war, the scope and nature of which they had only primitive notions at best. And in the case of Bair, so strong were his beliefs that he was willing to sell the most valuable thing he owned at the time. The adventures of Bair and Knotzer formed the basis of Kisch's "The Three Cows," the longest, best known of his writings from Spain, and the only piece of his Civil War reportage to have been previously translated into English.

Apart from his travels with, and writing about, the International Brigades, Kisch also took part in the Second International Congress of Writers for the Defense of Culture—which was to take place in Spain in order to demonstrate the solidarity of the world literary community with the Republic—and in fact he attracted considerable attention with his attack on André Gide's highly critical *Retour de l'URSS* (Return from the USSR, 1936). The congress met in Valencia on 4 July 1937, moved on to Madrid and Barcelona, and was concluded in Paris on 16–17 July to accommodate writers who had been forbidden to enter Spain. The roster of writers participating in the congress reads, with only a few exceptions, like a who's who of the international literary left at the time: Malraux, Romain Rolland, and Louis Aragon, from France; Brecht, Thomas Mann, Feuchtwanger, and Anna Seghers, from Germany; Langston Hughes and Hemingway, from the United States; Ehrenburg, Mikhail Koltsov, and Mikhail Sholokhov from the Soviet Union; and the Chilean poet Pablo Neruda.

A large number of European and American writers sympathized with the Spanish loyalists against Franco's nationalists and visited and wrote about Spain during the Civil War. Some, like Malraux, took an active role in the fighting. A few—like Koltsov, a *Pravda* correspondent, and Koestler—cloaked their assignments as Comintern agents beneath their journalistic coverage of the war. One of the more notable writers was Hemingway, whose experiences in Spain found their way not only into his journalistic reports but also his fiction. Hemingway and Kisch would have run into each other at the congress, and it is illuminating to compare their Spanish reportage. Like Hemingway, Kisch returned to professional newspaper reporting during the Spanish Civil War, Hemingway writing for NANA (North American Newspaper Alliance) and Kisch for a number of German émigré papers, including *Deutsche Informationen* (Paris) and *Deutscher Volksecho* (New York), and such communist-affiliated organs as *Nordwestböhmische Rote Fahne* (Prague) and *International Literature* (Moscow). Both Hemingway and Kisch had a fair degree of latitude in what they could write about. With no obligation to cover the actual fighting on a regular basis, they were free to concentrate on feature and background stories.

Although they spent about the same amount of time in Spain (Hemingway over the span of four trips), neither Hemingway nor Kisch wrote a great deal of reportage based on their experiences during the Civil War. Hemingway sent twenty-eight dispatches to NANA, whereas Kisch wrote about eight or nine pieces.[55] Hemingway's reports are generally quite short, usually two or three pages apiece; Kisch's are longer and include the two substantial sketches "Soldiers on the Seashore" and "The Three Cows." But the trajectory of Hemingway's career went from reporting to fiction, whereas Kisch wrote fiction early in his career and then to all intents and purposes left imaginative literature permanently for reportage. Ever alert to the fictional potential of the material he was collecting in Spain, Hemingway eventually went on to write *For Whom the Bell Tolls* (1939) and the play *The Fifth Column* (1937), both of which have a Spanish Civil War setting. Both writers reported from the republican side, toward which they were obviously partial, Kisch for political reasons, Hemingway out of more complex motives. But Hemingway's support for the republic, which took the form of monetary contributions and propagandistic film work, was in fact tantamount to political commitment.[56]

The writings from Spain of both reporters reflect political as well as literary differences between them. Kisch's weightiest reportage from Spain centers on the International Brigades, the darlings of the international left. While sympathetic to the Brigades, and in their midst on more than one occasion, Hemingway did not align himself with them in the way that Kisch did.[57] Kisch is rarely ever as ideologically overt as he is in his reportage from Spain; Hemingway's dispatches for the most part steer clear of the ideological. Kisch also sought through his Spanish reportage to arouse the emotions of his readers against the forces of Franco and the German and Italian interventionists. Hemingway is colder in the sense of being largely unemotional, detached, more the mainstream uncommitted foreign correspondent. His writing is also terser yet more aware of nature, to which Kisch remains largely insensitive. Human interest lags in neither writer, but Hemingway did not produce anything like Kisch's "The Three Cows" within the framework of his Spanish reportage. Although both writers relished adventure and felt the strange allure of battle while in Spain, there is a greater sense of the proximity of war and its dangers in Hemingway than in Kisch. While Kisch shows the aftermath of the bombing of such cities as Valencia and Madrid, Hemingway's dispatches—especially that of 23 December 1937, from the Teruel front—have great immediacy. We see planes flying overhead, dropping bombs, strafing, killing and wounding civilians, damaging property; we feel the insecurity that Hemingway felt at the time and yet the commitment to stay the course for the sake of his reporting.

It might seem that Kisch and Koestler would make for a more natural comparison than Kisch and Hemingway. Like Kisch, Koestler had an East Central European–Jewish background and was steeped in German culture.[58] Although both writers embraced communism, Kisch never became as politically entangled in it as Koestler, nor did he ever feel the need, as Koestler, to repudiate it. Kisch went to Spain to cover the Civil War as a politically engaged journalist writing for predominantly communist or left-wing newspapers and journals, but Koestler used journalism as a cover for risky Comintern assignments. Koestler's activities in Spain involved him in considerable danger, including incarceration by the nationalists for four days followed by nearly another three months in solitary confinement. Although he could have been executed at any moment as a spy, he was eventually exchanged for a nationalist hostage held by the republic.

Neither Kisch nor Hemingway courted death in Spain the way Koestler did. Nor did they produce the type of literature based on their experiences that Koestler did; Koestler wrote a full-length book of outright propaganda, originally published in German in 1937 under the title *Menschenopfer unerhört* (Unprecedented Human Sacrifice). Koestler later dropped the propaganda chapters—to which George Orwell had objected in his review of the book— and kept only that part of the original work describing the ordeal of his imprisonment by the nationalists. The new version of the work, the only one Koestler permitted to remain in print, was published in book form in 1946 under the title *Dialogue with Death.*

World War II and Emigration to Mexico

With the imminent defeat of the republic in Spain, Kisch returned to France in April 1938 and was married in late October that same year. But the gathering clouds of war over Europe negated the possibility of any stability in Kisch's life in the small village outside Versailles where he had taken up residence. The German annexation of Austria, the occupation of Czechoslovakia, and the invasion of Poland convinced Kisch of the wisdom, indeed the necessity, of leaving Europe. His situation was all the more precarious because of his Jewish origin and his status as a prominent German antifascist exile in France.[59] Following the example of other German exiles scrambling to get out of harm's way, Kisch looked to South America for easy entry and obtained a visa to Chile. Moreover, his established reputation as a journalist and contacts in the United States dating back to the late 1920s brought his case to the attention of the League of American Writers and the American Committee for Writers in Exile and resulted in his being granted an American transit visa. Armed thus with his Chilean and American visas, Kisch set sail for the United States on the steamship *Pennland* in December 1939. His wife was to join him later. Kisch reached New York on 23 December. Perhaps planning to write an account of his passage from Europe to the Americas, he made daily entries in a notebook discovered among other possessions only after his death.[60] The diary reveals that Kisch's entry into the United States was anything but easy and recalls the difficulties he had trying to disembark in Australia. Well aware of who Kisch was, and the embarrassment he had caused them in 1934, the English authorities in Southhampton denied him landing privileges (which he had neither wanted nor sought) and stamped his passport with such an ostentatious landing prohibition that he was afraid the American immigration authorities would see it and in turn deny him the right to land. However, when he reached New York, he was detained aboard the *Pennland* not because of the British prohibition but because the Chilean visa, which he had obtained in Paris, was deemed insufficient for an American transit visa, despite the fact that the visa had been accepted by the American consul general in Paris. He was told that he would have to get another visa from the Chilean consulate in New York. On 26 December, he was at last allowed to leave the *Pennland*, after being aboard it for two weeks. However, after clearing customs, he was taken by tender to Ellis Island, where he had to share sleeping quarters with twenty-two other men but at least had access to a telephone from which he could make calls (but not receive them). Once a $500 bond has been posted by a distant relative who was living in New York, he was at last able to enter the United States legally. The Chilean consul in New York also agreed to confirm his country's visa.

Kisch left Ellis Island at the beginning of 1940 and was joined by his wife in New York in March.[61] When in July 1940 the war-time Czech government-in-exile of Edvard Beneš was officially recognized, some five thousand Czechoslovak soldiers were evacuated from France to Great Britain and subsequently served with the British in the war. Kisch was for a time enthusiastic about the prospect of joining them as a correspondent and, in a sense, picking up his career where he had left it in Spain. But his application had to be processed by British Intelligence, which sought references from Beneš personally. Although complimentary about Kisch as a writer, Beneš raised the specter of Kisch's communist ties.[62] The application, not surprisingly, was rejected.

With his American transit visa limiting his stay in the United States, Kisch had to make up his mind where he and his wife would live out the rest of their exile. The Chilean entry visa would have enabled them to settle in Chile, but Kisch decided instead to go to Mexico. There were, to begin with, historical-sentimental and literary reasons for his choice. Like any young person growing up in Austria-Hungary in Kisch's time, the tragic story of Emperor Maximilian and Empress Carlotta was still vivid. Then, Kisch was undoubtedly familiar with John Reed's account of the Mexican Revolution, *Insurgent Mexico* (1914). It was of more immediate and practical concern that Mexico City had become home to a colony of German antifascists, among them such writers and friends as Renn, Seghers, and Bodo Uhse. The thought of rejoining the German exile literary community he had been a part of in France seemed irresistible. Mexico also offered a compatible political climate. Under the liberal, left-leaning leadership of its most respected and arguably greatest president, Lázaro Cárdenas, Mexico had sided with the republic during the Spanish Civil War and, after Franco's victory, opened its doors wide to thousands of refugees from Spain. Moreover, Mexico had never recognized the Munich agreement legitimizing the German takeover of Czechoslovakia and permitted a Czechoslovak diplomatic mission to function throughout World War II. This would prove important when Kisch decided to return to Czechoslovakia after the war. And finally, Mexico was much closer to the United States than Chile; maintaining contacts with friends north of the border would be easier. If there was a negative side to exile in Mexico, it had to do with manifestations of anti-Semitism aroused by the large number of Jewish émigrés coming into the country from Europe. The government of Cárdenas and that of his successor, Manuel Ávila Camacho, did its best to contain anti-Semitism while still pursuing a liberal emigration policy. If Kisch was ever troubled by the resentment of many Mexicans over Jewish immigration, he gave no evidence of it. And as for the intrigues of representatives of Hitler's Germany against the anti-Nazi German exiles in Mexico, Kisch regarded them as ludicrous and mocked them.

Once in Mexico, which was to be their home for nearly six years, Kisch and his wife settled into a small apartment in an outer district of Mexico City on the corner of Avenida Amsterdam and Avenida Michoacán. They lived here until 1942, when they moved to an apartment on Avenida Tamaulipas, where they remained until they returned to Europe in 1946. Although Kisch had no idea in 1940 when, and if, a return to Europe might be possible, he had no intention of spending his time in Mexico brooding about the past or fretting over an uncertain future. Temperamentally different from Stefan Zweig, suicide never presented itself to him as an alternative. Apart from the resumption of his writing, he and his wife became active participants in the life of the German émigré community and took advantage of every opportunity to travel throughout the vast and fascinating country. Their financial situation imposed a certain frugality, but they were not destitute and drew a regular monthly stipend from the Joint Antifascist Refugee Committee in New York headed by Edward K. Barsky, a medical doctor who had fought in Spain.[63]

The cultural life of the German émigré community in Mexico City centered on the Heinrich Heine Club. Here the Kisches and such writer friends as Renn, Uhse, Seghers, Theodor Balk, Bruno Frei, and André Simon (Otto Katz), and the Viennese composer Marcel Rubin got together often for readings, concerts, lectures in German and Spanish, and theatricals. On the occasion of Kisch's sixtieth birthday on 26 April 1945, for example, a play by Kisch based on the Colonel Redl affair was performed by members of the club. Before long, the German exiles had their own journal, *Freies Deutschland* (Free Germany).[64]

The literary project of greatest urgency to Kisch after he settled in Mexico was *Sensation Fair*, the autobiography that he had begun planning as early as 1936. Not a formal autobiography in any strict sense, the book was to consist of twenty-one loosely connected sketches, in the style of his reportage, about his youthful past in Habsburg Prague. It was published in July 1942, in German, as the first volume of the newly founded anti-Nazi publishing association "El Libro Libre": Editorial de literatura anti-Nazi en lengua alemana ("The Free Book": Publishing House for Anti-Nazi Literature in German). This collection is arguably Kisch's most engaging. In focusing on his youth as a young local reporter in Prague, he effectively recreates a bygone era in superb detail and with much obvious affection. The book became an immediate sensation among his fellow German-speaking exiles in Mexico City. He gave public readings of it in 1941 and early 1942, and the Heinrich Heine Club devoted a special evening to it on 19 February 1942.

The warm reception of *Sensation Fair* in the German community in Mexico and among German exiles elsewhere encouraged Kisch to think in terms of a broader market. The modest volume on cheap paper put out by "El

Libro Libre" in Mexico City in 1942 obviously had little possibility of international resonance. Even before he arrived in Mexico, shortly after reaching New York, Kisch had hoped to improve his financial situation by again offering the collection to Alfred A. Knopf. It had been Knopf, after all, that had published *Changing Asia* in 1935. Moreover, *China geheim* had appeared as *Secret China* in London that same year. With his international reputation by then well established, Kisch originally proposed his memoirs to Knopf as early as 1936, and a contract is believed to have been signed on 14 July of that year.[65] But a reading, ostensibly by Blanche Knopf, the publisher's wife, of the outline Kisch had submitted led to the book's rejection on the grounds that he intended to incorporate previously published sketches. Convinced that a different reader would come to a different conclusion about the prospects for the book, especially since more than three years had elapsed since his original proposal, Kisch lost no time in contacting Blanche Knopf not long after he set foot in New York in 1940. To his deep disappointment, however, she refused to change her mind and informed Kisch in a letter of 2 February (1940) that any agreement between him and Knopf was null and void because he had failed to submit what had been expected of him.[66] Furthermore, he would be asked to return advances that had already been paid him. Whether Kisch actually had a contract with Knopf, and whether the manuscript had in fact been rejected for the reason usually given, cannot now be established with any certainty. There are apparently no surviving records related to *Sensation Fair* at Knopf's offices in New York, and my inquiries there proved fruitless. Nevertheless, it was accepted by another American publisher, Modern Age Books of New York, and was published in 1941. Although it was favorably reviewed, it attracted no great attention, to Kisch's disappointment. Perhaps the world of pre–World War I Czech-German Prague, and the twilight era of the Habsburg monarchy, were too remote to the American reader of 1941, who was about to be oppressively burdened with the grim realities of the present. Kisch subsequently expanded *Sensation Fair* by an additional twelve sketches, which are always included in newer editions of the book, and planned, but never succeeded in executing, a second volume of sketches along similar lines.

With *Sensation Fair* behind him, Kisch turned next to a book of reportage about Mexico. His curiosity about the land of his exile, and his previous exposure to Hispanic culture in Spain both before and during the Civil War, led him to travel widely about the country and to study virtually every facet of its past and present. The scope of his interest is reflected in the subjects covered in *Discoveries in Mexico,* which was first published in 1945 by "El Libro Libre." Visits to the Yucatán aroused his interest in the ancient Mayans and accounts for such sketches as "Versuch einer Beschreibung von Chichen Itzá" (Attempt at a Description of Chichen Itzá) and "Sportbetrieb bei den alten Mayas" (Sports among the Ancient Mayas). In "Interview mit den Pyramiden" (Interview with the Pyramids), he describes the ancient pyramids at Cholula, Cuicuilco, Tenayuca, Teotihuacán, Tula, and Xochicalco. From the period of the Spanish conquest he writes about Cortés's hunt for the gold of Montezuma, and two sketches are devoted to Maximilian and Carlotta. Mexican flora are taken up in the entertaining "Kolleg: Kulturgeschichte des Kaktus" (Lecture: The Cultural History of the Cactus) and "Was immer der Peyote sei" (Whatever Peyote May Be), about the narcotic peyote mushroom. The Mexican enthusiasm for chewing gum and cock fights forms the subject of "Der Kaugummi, erzählt vom Ende bis zum Anfang" (Chewing Gum, from End to Beginning) and "Der Mensch im Kampf der Hähne" (Man in the Cock Fights), respectively. In "Der Kaspar Hauser unter den Nationen" (The Kaspar Hauser among Nations) Kisch weighs the past and future of the Indian population in a modern Mexican state. One of the more interesting sketches in the book, "Indiodorf unter dem Davidstern" (An Indian Village under the Star of David), which is included in the present book, describes Kisch's discovery of a tiny community of Jews in the village of Venta Prieta, some sixty miles from Mexico City. And finally, in "Mexikoforschung bei den Nazis" (Nazi Research on Mexico), he discusses German scholarship on Mexico in the Nazi period and the reasons for the Nazi classification of Mexicans as an inferior people (brown skin and racial mixing).

The original edition of *Discoveries in Mexico* contains twenty-four sketches. For the new edition of the book published by Aufbau-Verlag in 1947, four more pieces of reportage were added. As with *Sensation Fair,* Kisch also planned a second volume, but this never materialized. However, six additional sketches that were supposed to go into the second volume have been incorporated into the sixth edition of the eighth (previously seventh) volume of his collected works published by Aufbau-Verlag in 1983. Two sketches—"Sportbetrieb bei den alten Mayas" (Sports among the Ancient Mayans) and "Teoberto Maler" (under the title "Ein Österreicher in Yucatán," An Austrian in Yucatán)—were printed in 1948 in the collection *Adventures on Five Continents*. A large quantity of writings on different aspects of Mexico discovered among Kisch's papers after his death enabled the editors of Aufbau-Verlag to incorporate four more completed and previously unpublished sketches into the 1983 edition of *Sensation Fair* and *Discoveries in Mexico* published as a single volume.

Return to Prague

With the war at an end, Kisch and his wife left Mexico on 17 February 1946 after waiting some nine months for all the appropriate visas to be processed.[67] They journeyed first to New York, where they spent a few days, and then on to England aboard the *Queen Elizabeth*.[68] From London, they flew to Prague on 21 March 1946. They first settled into a room in the old Hotel Alcron on Wenceslaus Square, but a few weeks later, thanks to friends, were able to move into a house in which, ironically, Adolf Eichmann, the principal architect of the Nazi plan to exterminate Jews, had lived during the war.

Kisch's return to the city of his birth at the age of sixty-one was something of a mixed blessing. As a writer with an international reputation, he was naturally welcomed back as a cultural feather-in-the-cap for the postwar Czechoslovak state. Hardly did he and his wife take up residence at the Alcron when he was literally besieged by journalists seeking interviews and invitations to lecture. He was enthusiastically greeted when he appeared at the Eighth Congress of the Communist Party of Czechoslovakia—the first postwar congress of the party—in Prague's Lucerna Hall on 28 March. But despite all the hoopla surrounding his return, Kisch was a vestige of a bygone era, of Prague's old, once brilliant, and largely Jewish German literary community. The world of German culture in which he had grown up in Habsburg Prague was now ancient history, and in a sense he was like a fish out of water. Whatever practical knowledge he had of the Czech language, he had written exclusively in German and doubtless at this stage of his career could not easily reinvent himself as a writer in Czech. That need not have been an insurmountable problem, either for Kisch or for his publishers, since he could have continued writing in German and been published in both German and Czech. In fact, he continued writing in German.

The satisfaction in Czechoslovakia over Kisch's resettlement there after World War II is manifest not only in his reception, but also in what may be referred to as his "Czechization." A cottage industry of translation of Kisch's works from German into Czech sprang up along with literary studies that played up his significance as a writer of Czech background. His unpublished manuscripts and other papers eventually came to be housed in the Museum of Czech Literature (now the Museum of National Literature) in Prague.

That Kisch sought to ingratiate himself with the postwar Czech authorities by proposing—either before his actual departure from Mexico or immediately upon his arrival in Prague—to write a book about the "new Czechoslovakia" is mentioned in all the communist Czech and German literature on him.[69] Noncommunist sources, however, suggest that the idea for such a book was proposed by officials of the Communist Party and that Kisch ever so politely declined the offer.[70] The truth, as usual, probably lies somewhere in between, but he seems to have planned a collection of reportage on the subject of postwar Czechoslovakia. Schlenstedt, following Balk, lists the topics Kisch planned covering in the book, and most concern economic and industrial themes—just the type of thing the party would have expected him to write.[71]

Kisch did not live long enough to complete the book. He wrote only six pieces of reportage after his return to Prague.[72] The first was a report on the execution in May 1946 of the Nazi war criminal Karl Hermann Frank. A visit shortly thereafter to the Jewish cemetery in Žižkov, where his grandfather, Jonas Kisch, is buried, resulted in the sketch "Friedhof, reichend von Industrierevolution zum Imperialismus" (The Cemetery, from the Industrial Revolution to Imperialism). Kisch covered the trials of H. Jöckl, the commander of the Terezín (Theresienstadt) "model" concentration camp, and of the World War II Serb royalist leader Draža Mihailović, but he left no account of them. In Belgrade he had the opportunity to meet again with Marshal Josip Broz Tito, whom he had known in Paris in the mid-1930s when Tito came to the French capital as a representative of the Comintern to take charge of the organization and transport of volunteers to fight in Spain. Once

Kisch (center) and other guests at Karlovy Vary (Karlsbad) on the occasion of the unveiling of a plaque on a house in which Karl Marx once lived, 1946. Courtesy Museum of National Literature, Prague.

back in Czechoslovakia, Kisch wrote two "industrial" pieces of reportage: one on his visit to Třeboň for the annual fish harvest, and an unfinished piece about the world-famous Czech shoemaking company founded by the Bata family. While in Zlin, the site of the Bata shoe works, mutual friends arranged a meeting between Kisch and the highly regarded Czech poet Petr Bezruč (pseudonym of Vladimír Vašek). This is described in the sketch "Ein Tag mit Peter Bezruč" (A Day with Petr Bezruč).[73]

Kisch's most impressive reportage after his return grew out of his participation on 21 and 22 September 1946 in a ceremony commemorating Karl Marx's sojourns at the former Pension Germania in the West Bohemian resort town of Karlovy Vary (Karlsbad). Invited to give a lecture on Marx and Karlsbad, Kisch expanded his talk into a thirty-four-page account of Marx's visits to the spa. Summoning up the investigative skills demonstrated in past reportage, Kisch drew on old correspondence, municipal and police records, photographs, and other sources to produce an exhaustively detailed yet readable account of a less well known chapter in Marx's life. The piece was published for the first time in 1953, five years after Kisch's death.

In 1948 Czechoslovakia became a Soviet-dominated police state. Yielding to communist demands, in February Beneš accepted the new cabinet proposed by Prime Minister Klement Gottwald, in which the communists, the largest political party, held half the positions. The machinery was in place for the coup by which the communists gained complete control of Czechoslovakia. Kisch was by this time seriously ill. After his first stroke in November 1947, doctors ordered him to give up smoking and drinking. Although he yielded somewhat on the latter demand, he was unable to stop smoking. Kisch had smoked heavily throughout his entire adult life, and there is hardly a photograph or picture that does not show him with a cigarette dangling from his lips. Because of his weakened physical condition he tended to spend most of his time at home. But the darkening political situation in Prague in early 1948 also discouraged him from going out. Rumors had began circulating about political arrests, and there were signs of outspoken anti-Semitism. Fate intervened, however, to spare Kisch deeper disillusionment, more difficult compromises, or conceivably worse. A second stroke on 24 March proved fatal. Unable to move and barely able to speak, he was taken by ambulance to the hospital on Katerinská Ulice in Prague's New Town, where he died on 31 March at 1:45 in the afternoon. Elaborate preparations were made for the public viewing of his coffin in the building of the Central Committee of the Communist Party of Czechoslovakia and for his funeral procession. On 5 April 1948, a dreary, cold, and damp day, with thousands of people lining the streets, the cortege solemnly wound its way through the city that Kisch loved and chronicled as perhaps no other literary son of Prague in the twentieth century.

Kisch and the Art of Reportage

Walter Benjamin, in his well-known essay "The Author as Producer," uses Tretiakov as an example of the blurring of the boundaries between literature and journalism and the need to rethink the entire matter of literary genres:

I should like to direct your attention to Sergei Tretiakov and to the type, defined and embodied by him, of the "operating" writer. This operating writer provides the most tangible example of the functional inter-dependency that always, and under all conditions, exists between the correct political tendency and progressive literary technique. . . . You may have a high regard for Tretiakov and yet still be of the opinion that his example does not prove a great deal in this context. The tasks he performed, you will perhaps object, are those of a journalist or a propagandist; all this has little to do with literature. However, I did intentionally quote the example of Tretiakov in order to point out to you how comprehensive is the horizon within which we have to rethink our conceptions of literary forms or genres, in view of the technical factors affecting our present situation, if we are to identify the forms of expression that channel the literary energies of the present. . . . We are in the midst of a mighty recasting of literary forms, a melting down in which many of the opposites in which we have been used to think may lose their force.[74]

Kisch's contribution to the development of reportage in the twentieth century must, I believe, be related to this "mighty recasting of literary forms."

From the beginning of his entry into the world of journalism as a local reporter in Prague, Kisch would not be content with conventional reporting. Once he dedicated himself wholly to the journalistic enterprise, he set out to enhance the prestige of his profession by transforming reportage into a literary genre without sacrificing truth or objectivity. In doing so, he was driven by his own creative needs and, as we shall see, by the impulses of the age. One of the sketches in his autobiographical *Sensation Fair,* "Debüt beim Mühlen-feuer" (Debut at the Mill Fire), is especially interesting for the light it sheds on Kisch's attitude as a young reporter toward truth versus invention in reportage. Having fabricated an incident in a report about the fire in a local mill in a way that reporters were often expected to do at the time, he felt a sense of self-betrayal. He vowed thereafter that no matter how difficult, he would pursue only the truth as a real reporter but that he would strive, as an artist, to present that truth in as engaging a manner as possible:

I defined for myself what the report really represents. It is a form of expression, perhaps even a form of art, although a small one.

Specific to the report is the fact that an actual incident shapes its subject. Couldn't one simply pretend that the incident had taken place? No. If the occurrence is invented, whether the reader notices it or not, the account is no report. Writers of novels and stories, and tellers of anecdotes, often maintain that the episode described by them actually took place. If the reader doesn't believe this assertion, not only does it not hurt the writer, it even elevates him. But a chronicler who lies is done for.

However, the treatment of the subject contains within itself a choice. Either one takes the incident as the point of departure for a product of the imagination (which I did yesterday with the mill fire), or one attempts to establish the connections and details in such a way as to make the incident every bit as interesting as the product of the imagination. (I should have discovered the scene with the homeless, not made it up.)

I had demonstrated my skill with the "either" part of the above, and my ineptitude with the "or" part, but I had to choose the second alternative.

Oh, not on any moral grounds! It was that Dantesque curiosity of mine. From childhood on, as a result of this curiosity, I used to bring back with me from every trip to a store or post office window such an abundance of things worth relating that everyone thought I was exaggerating. This suspicion upset me, since I didn't have to make up anything; I just saw and heard so many unbelievable things that happened to be true wherever I went. How could it be that experiences that were completely natural to me seemed to others to be impossible?

Yesterday, for the first time, I made something up, and everybody believed it . . . Should I keep on telling lies? No.

It was precisely because truth escaped me when I pursued it the first time that I wanted to track it down in the future. It was the sporting thing to do.[75]

The social and political ferment that engulfed Europe in the aftermath of World War I was paralleled by ferment in the cultural sphere. The twenties became a time of extraordinary innovation and experimentation in a quest for new values and new forms of expression in what was then perceived to be a world radically transformed by war. Among writers, the view was widespread that old structures were incompatible with changes taking place in the postwar period. A genre so closely identified with the bourgeoisie as the novel, for example, was regarded as another casualty of the war. Imaginative literature in general, while hardly destined to disappear from the literary horizon, was now thought of as largely irrelevant. In light of the destruction and devastation suffered during the war, a war in which new technology had been employed for the invention of machines and devices of death, reality was seen as so powerful and immense, so extraordinary and unbelievable, that it far exceeded the potential of human imagination. It also made artificial literary constructs a thing of the past or at the very least subject to intense reevaluation. Balk made the point unequivocally: "Reality became more fantastic than any artistic fantasy; the novels of Jules Verne have fallen into oblivion—overtaken by reality."[76] Benjamin alludes to the same processes of change in "The Writer as Producer": "How comprehensive is the horizon within which we have to rethink our conceptions of literary forms or genres, in view of the technical factors affecting our present situation, if we are to identify the forms of expression that channel the literary energies of the present."

The widely held belief, especially but by no means exclusively among writers on the political left, that fiction had been overtaken by reality underlay certain closely related literary developments in the period between the First and Second World Wars. The new objectivity, and optimism, that accompanied the economic stabilization achieved in 1924 by the Weimar Republic after the horrendous political and economic turbulence of 1918–23 came to be known as "die neue Sachlichkeit" (also translated as "the new sobriety," "the new purposefulness"). The term was contributed by G. F. Hartlaub, the director of the municipal gallery at Mannheim, who applied it to the exhibit of pictures of "tangible reality" that he organized in 1925. Opposed to the utopianism and abstraction of the expressionists, the advocates of the "new objectivity" directed their attention to their immediate surroundings, which they sought to portray in as down-to-earth and unembellished a way as possible, with particular emphasis on social and economic conditions. Before the movement showed signs of losing momentum in 1928, it had shaped the dramatic writing of Brecht and Ödön von Horváth and the "documentary theater" of Piscator. Characteristic also of the antiromantic and antiheroic tendencies of the "new objectivity" was the antiwar writing of the period. Erich Maria Remarque became an international celebrity with *Im Westen Nichts Neues* (All Quiet on the Western Front, 1929), but Arnold Zweig's *Der Streit um den Sergeanten Grischa* (The Quarrel over Sergeant Grisha, 1927) and Theodor Plivier's *Der Kaiser ging, die Generäle blieben* (The Emperor Went, the Generals Remained, 1932) were also widely read. Biographical writing became newly popular under the aegis of "new objectivity," and so too did the equally fact-based genre of reportage.

"New objectivity" had a distinct appeal to writers of leftist persuasion because of its easy accommodation of antimilitarism and its adaptability to an unvarnished "documentation" of the actual economic and political tensions of the time. Both for literary and political reasons, Kisch would thus have been greatly encouraged in his preference for reportage as a type of writing wholly compatible with the new emphasis on reality and concreteness.

In the new Soviet state writers and other artists in the immediate post-revolutionary period mounted a vigorous campaign to legitimize a new art that would be more appropriate to the projected socialist transformation and proletarianization of Russia. The dramatist and literary theorist Osip Brik declared:

> Indeed in recent belletristic writing we can observe the transition from plotted prose to so-called plotless prose. The distinction is this: in plotted prose the entire interest of the work is concentrated on the development of dramatic intrigue, most frequently of psychological collision; only secondarily, as background, do local details of everyday life appear. In plotless prose, there is either no intrigue or nearly none, and if there is, it serves just as the link for the union of separate observations, anecdotes, and thoughts into a single literary whole. The genre of memoirs, biography, reminiscences, and diaries is becoming dominant in contemporary literature and is decisively dislodging the genre of big novels and novellas which has prevailed in literature to the present.[77]

Art was now expected to deal with real life directly, to confront it head on, even to shape it. Through various forms of documentary writing and film, readers would be appropriately enlightened and their social consciousness raised. Ideally, their participation would thus be enlisted in the effort to resolve economic, social, and cultural problems, with which the "literature of fact" primarily occupied itself. The most aggressive proponents of a fact-based literature in the Soviet Union came from the *Novy Lef* (New Left) group in 1927–28. The goal of both the Left Front of Art and New Left was the eventual dissolution of literature as an independent institution, to be replaced by a new complex of forms generated by a merger of literature and journalism. To the propagators of factography the highest form of literary activity was factual reporting, by which they understood topical sketches, biographies, travel accounts, and documentaries of one sort or another.

In light of the emergence of "New Objectivity" in Germany and "factography" in the Soviet Union, and the successful siege by journalism of an embattled fiction in the aftermath of World War I, Kisch's work can easily be seen as having been shaped by the same currents to which those movements owed their genesis. Chronologically, in fact, his efforts antedate the development of both "Neue Sachlichkeit" and the "literature of fact."

Although Kisch in no way regarded himself as a theorist and was generally disinclined to make theoretical pronouncements, he did express himself on the responsibilities of the reporter and the nature of reportage, as he understood it, on several occasions. His first essay on the subject, a defense, if you will, of the reporter as opposed to other types of journalistic writers, was his short article "Wesen des Reporters" (The Nature of the Reporter), which dates from 1918. In it, Kisch declared:

> Every writer, even the non-realist, needs milieu study [Milieustudie], and every milieu study is reportage. Wholly senseless is the disparaging undertone that often accompanies the term "reporter" and contrasts with the colossal overestimation of the editorial writer, the art critic, the political commentator, and especially the feuilletonistic prattler. *In principle,* the work of the reporter is the most noble, the most objective, the most important. . . .
>
> I am speaking only of the reporter as such. He may exaggerate, and he may deliver unreliable reports. Nevertheless, he is always dependent on the facts, on the real. . . . The editorial writer in principle is always in the position of never having to leave his armchair in order to write about a particular subject.
>
> There is always some subject or other. He can treat it with brilliant expertise and overlay it with appropriate quotations. But quotations are drawn from publications, hence are secondhand. The findings of

investigation are firsthand because they are drawn from life itself. To be sure, the fact is merely the compass of his [the reporter's] journey; he also needs a telescope, that of "logical fantasy" [logische Phantasie]. That is because the *complete* picture of a particular state of affairs never presents itself from the autopsy of a crime scene or other scene of action, from the snatched-up remarks of the parties involved and witnesses, or from conjectures about the event or events. The reporter must himself fashion the pragmatics of the occurrence, the transitions from the causes to the effects, making sure only that the line of his presentation leads precisely through the facts known to him (the given points of the route). The ideal now is that the curve of probability drawn by the reporter coincides with the true line of communication of all phases of the event. . . .

It is in this respect that the reporter is differentiated from every other member of his species, in this respect that the degree of his talent manifests itself. . . . [78]

I believe this passage contains the kernel of Kisch's concept of reportage. The writer of reportage is not a mere chronicler of events, the author of a report. To be sure, he deals in facts, the facts of events in the past as well as in the present. He must be loyal to his facts; he cannot embroider them, nor can he invent them. But the facts are the raw material out of which the writer constructs his reportage. They are, as Kisch puts it, just the "compass" of the reporter's journey. The "telescope" of "logical fantasy" is the instrument with which the writer of reportage brings into view the circumstances in which facts, or events, occurred, focuses on the associations between facts that are not immediately visible, and on the cause-and-effect relationship between one set of facts and another. The "logical fantasy" of the writer of reportage determines the most effective arrangement of the constituent parts of the reportage, that is, the order in which facts and circumstances are presented. It also chooses the appropriate style of narration: the presence or absence of a narrative frame; the presence or absence of the authorial ego; the creation of a persona or personae; the reconstruction of dialogue; the use of tense; quotation from original sources, and so on. For example, in *Paradise America,* Kisch invents the persona of a certain "Dr. Becker," through whose eyes American society and culture will be viewed; in *Disembarking in Australia,* he borrows from the technique of detective fiction by creating another persona, the initially mysterious "our man," which permits Kisch to write about himself in the third person. In *Tsars, Priests, and Bolsheviks*, the reportage is far more expository than narrative. In the sketch "Two-Color Print of Tashkent," in *Changing Asia*, Kisch uses two different colors to contrast the old tribal and Islamic ways that have not yet changed under the Soviets and those that have; in another sketch, one of the best in the collection ("Ich, Chassjad Mirkulan," I, Khasyad Mirkulan), Tretiakov's "bio-interview" technique allows the subject of the sketch, an old woman who has moved with the times, to tell her life story. Sometimes Kisch uses the device of the omniscient narrator, himself fading completely from view; many other times in his reportage he is very much in view, now the principal protagonist of the piece, now the curious, witty, chatty, ironical, urbane observer of phenomena. But whatever the modality of narration or exposition, and notwithstanding the absolute respect for truth and objectivity, it is ultimately the consciousness of the reporter that determines the angle of vision. Distinguishing between the art of the novelist and that of the writer of reportage, Balk comments: "In the novel reality is reflected in the consciousness of its personages; in reportage it is reflected in the consciousness of the reporter." Unlike the writer of fiction, the reporter is not allowed to experiment with his people. "Concrete life," continues Balk, "experiments with them, offers proof through the particular case of the universal validity of a social law or laws. The reporter must limit himself to this concrete case."[79]

Viewed from another perspective, Kisch's concept of "logical fantasy" validated his use of compositional strategies and techniques common to imaginative literature. And it is in this respect above all that his reportage differs from the regular journalistic report. So long as he remains true to his facts, so long as "the curve of probability drawn by the reporter coincides with the true line of communication of all phases of the event," the writer of reportage is free to order his material and present it in whatever way he deems suitable.

Kisch's further defense of the craft of the reporter and his reflections on how reportage relates to other forms of literary expression appear in the preface to *Classical Journalism* and in his introduction to *The Raging Reporter*. Although generally disclaiming serious interest in literary theory, Kisch contradictorily portrays himself in the preface to *Classical Journalism* as someone "who has for years been preoccupied with theoretical questions concerning the nature of journalism, above all with the newspaper as the advocate of new intellectual directions."[80] That Kisch had indeed given more thought to the profession of reporting is abundantly obvious from the considerable amount of work that went into the preparation of the impressively comprehensive *Classical Journalism.* Ranging from Pliny the Younger to Richard Wagner, covering authors of many nationalities—but excluding anyone still living—and with specimens of virtually every journalistic genre, *Classical Journalism* well merits consideration as a tour de force. Besides the time that Kisch must have put into the very process of selection of the pieces to be included in the book, which he discusses in his preface, he also had to learn enough about the authors represented to write separate prefaces for the selections. These prefaces are noteworthy for Kisch's ability to grasp the essence of the individual author's contribution to journalism in relatively few words. However, Kisch's anthology is no mere compendium of meritorious specimens of the reportorial craft; it is a broad overview of the role of journalism in the great moral and intellectual issues of the time from classical antiquity to the early twentieth century.

Commenting on *Classical Journalism,* Tucholsky characterized the book as a "treasure house." "Kisch," he went on, "collected the most unknown pages of the best-known writers and the brilliant works of unknown writers, and all together make up the magnificent wildness of the day. . . . Newspaper in the best sense of the term. . . . Kisch has done something very good here; I'd like to send a copy to each and every journalist as a Christmas present."[81]

Kisch's most trenchant observations on the responsibility of the reporter come, perhaps appropriately, in his first major collection of nonlocal reportage, *The Raging Reporter.* Taking issue with any kind of tendentious reporting, Kisch maintains that

> The reporter has no bias, has nothing to justify, and has no point of view. He must be an impartial witness and must deliver impartial testimony as reliably as possible; at any rate, such testimony is more important (for clarification) than the clever speech of the district attorney or the defense attorney.

Even the bad reporter—the one who exaggerates or is unreliable—
performs useful work, since he is dependent on facts and must gain
knowledge from them, through evidence, through conversation, through
observation, through information.[82]

Notwithstanding the book's overwhelming success, there were those
who felt that Kisch was idealizing the case for the absence of bias, or
"tendency," on the part of the reporter. Tucholsky was his usual acerbic self in
taking Kisch to task for advocating a literary position to which he himself
was incapable of adhering:

> There's just no such thing. There is nobody who doesn't have a point of
> view. Kisch included. Sometimes, unfortunately, when it's that of the
> writer, then what he writes isn't always good. Very often, however, when
> it's that of the man who simply reports, then it is excellent, faultless,
> interesting. . . .
>
> Much [in *The Raging Reporter*] has been said well, and almost
> everything is entirely honest. But no matter how "objective" one may
> write or how far one may stray from the subject, it's all the same. Every
> report, no matter how impersonal, always first reveals the writer, and
> whether in tropical nights, ships' cabins, Parisian flea markets, and
> downtrodden sections of London, which every one can see through
> thousands of glasses—even if they don't have them on—you always
> write yourself.[83]

Kisch emphasizes that for the writer of reportage firsthand experience
is paramount. The writer must in a sense live his material:

> The good reporter needs a capacity for experience [Erlebnisfähigkeit]
> for the craft that he loves. He would still have experiences even if he
> did not have to report on them. But he would not write without having
> experiences. He is no artist, he is no politician, he is no scholar . . .

Although it was not long before Kisch himself succumbed to the allure
of distant horizons, at least in the period in which *The Raging Reporter* arose,
he pleads for the reporter's discovery of the world around him, of the
excitement of his own time and place:

The places and events he describes, the effort he makes, the affair of which he is a witness, and the sources he consults must not be so remote, so rare, and so difficult of access, if in a world that is flooded by lies, a world that wants to forget itself and therefore goes in merely for untruthfulness, he remains devoted to his goal. Nothing is more amazing than the simple truth, nothing more exotic than the world around us, nothing more fantastic than actuality. And there is nothing more sensational in the world than the time in which one lives!

Kisch's closing remarks in the introduction to *The Raging Reporter* are of particular interest for the photographic idiom in which they are cast. "New Objectivity" in Germany and the "literature of fact" in the Soviet Union coincided with the rapid development of camera art, both still and cinematographic, and indeed raised the camera to the level of an aesthetic model. As a mechanical device for recording actuality, the camera lens was a neutral observer, setting forth on film only what appeared before it without commentary. The documentary and montage work especially of the pioneer Russian filmmaker Dziga Vertov exerted considerable influence not only on cinematography but on literary thinking as well. A parallel was drawn between the camera and the writer of reportage. As Tretiakov put it with his characteristic militancy: "Each boy with his camera is a soldier in the war against the easel painters, and each little reporter is objectively stabbing belles-lettres to death with the point of his pen."[84] Balk also pointed out this relationship: "Reportage and film are young, very young partners in art. They have much in common in their dynamics. The close-up, the aperture, the economy, the montage."[85]

In explaining that *The Raging Reporter* was assembled from sketches written at different times then assembled for publication as a book, Kisch draws close to Vertov's montage technique:

The following time exposures were not made all at the same time. Subject and object were in the most varied circumstances and in the most varied moods when the pictures arose; position and light were as dissimilar as possible. Nevertheless, nothing can be retouched, since the album is being shown today.

Since *The Raging Reporter* was published in 1924 and Vertov's newsreels and documentaries were only then beginning to become known in Germany, it seems doubtful that Kisch was familiar with Vertov's work at the time he assembled the collection; his first trip to the Soviet Union did not take place until 1925. But as a propagandist for the primacy of a literature of fact in which the lead role would be assumed by the reporter, Kisch was in the vanguard of cultural (as well as political) revolutionary thought and would have been certain to regard the new medium of film as a visual parallel to print reportage. In this, as in other respects, he was of his time and ahead of it.

Bibliography

Editions of Kisch's works in German

The only complete edition of Kisch's works in German is the series jointly edited by Kisch's widow, Gisela Kisch, and Bodo Uhse, under the general title Egon Erwin Kisch, *Gesammelte Werke in Einzelausgaben* (Collected Works in Separate Editions) and published by Aufbau-Verlag, Berlin and Weimar. The series began to appear in 1960; to date, twelve volumes have appeared. A very good, well-illustrated two-volume collection of Kisch's works, edited by Walther Schmieding, and titled *Egon Erwin Kisch: Nichts ist erregender als die Wahrheit,* was published in 1979 by Kiepenheuer & Witsch, Cologne.

Selected Studies on Kisch

Balk, Theodor. "Egon Erwin Kisch und die Reportage (Zu Kischs fünfzigstem Geburtstag)." *Internationale Literatur: Zentralorgan der Internationalen Vereinigung Revolutionärer Schriftsteller,* no. 3 (1935), 3–16.

Internationale Literatur, no. 4 (1935). Contains a number of testimonials to Kisch from such promiminent figures on the political left as Henri Barbusse, Michael Gold, Sergei Tretiakov, Konstantin Fedin, Aleksandr Fadeev, Mikhail Kozlov, Leonid Leonov, Lion Feuchtwanger, Bert Brecht, Erwin Piscator, Arthur Holitscher, Anna Seghers, Oskar Maria Graf, Kurt Hiller, Max Brod, and others. There is also a short essay by Georg Lukács on Kisch as a "Meister der Reportage" (18–19).

Egon Erwin Kisch 1885–1948: Erinnerungen zum 90. Geburtstag. Ed. Oldrich Bures. Prague: Internationale Organisation der Journalisten, 1975. A Czech work, in German, with contributions by several Czech journalists and writers, among them Josef Valenta, Jan Martinec, Norbert Fryd, Jiří E. Marek, and Jarmila Haasová-Nečasová (Kisch's principal translator into Czech).

Felbert, Ulrich von. *China und Japan als Impuls und Exempel: Fernöstliche Ideen und Motive bei Alfred Döblin, Bertolt Brecht und Egon Erwin Kisch.* Frankfurt am Main: Verlag Peter Lang, 1986. A comparative analysis of Far Eastern motifs in the works of Döblin, Brecht, and Kisch.

Geissler, Rudolf. *Die Entwicklung der Reportage Egon Erwin Kischs in der Weimarer Republik.* Cologne: Pahl-Rugenstein Verlag, 1982. A German university master's thesis analyzing Kisch's transition from a writer influenced by the fashionable feuilleton to a politically engaged journalist in the period 1918–33.

Goldstücker, Eduard, et al. *Egon Erwin Kisch. F. C. Weiskopf: Leben und Werk.* Berlin: Volk und Wissen Volkseigener Verlag, 1963. Short biographies of Kisch and Weiskopf (1900–1955) as representatives of Prague's German literary community together with a few excerpts from their works.

Hamšík, Dušan, and Alexej Kusák. *O zuřivém reportéru E. E. Kíschovi.* Prague: Československý spisovatel, 1962. A modest Czech "life and work," strongly communist in orientation. It was translated into Polish by Marek Perlman under the title *Egon Erwin Kisch* and published by Wiedza Powszechna in Warsaw in 1966.

Hofmann, Fritz. *Egin Erwin Kisch: Der rasende Reporter. Biographie.* Berlin: Verlag Neues Leben, 1988. A straightforward, factual East German biography by someone who knew Kisch but devoid of serious interest in the genre of reportage and Kisch's contributions to it. Well-illustrated with photographs.

Horowitz, Michael. *Ein Leben für die Zeitung: Der rasende Reporter Egon Erwin Kisch.* Vienna: Verlag ORAC, 1985. A lightweight, popularly oriented biography of sorts. Nearly half the book consists of excerpts from Kisch's writings and reminiscences of him by friends and colleagues.

Jacobi, Lotte. *Russland 1932/33: Moskau, Tadschikistan, Uzbekistan.* Ed. Marian Beckers and Elisabeth Moortgart. Berlin: D. Nishen, c. 1988. Photographs by Jacobi accompany texts by Kisch.

Kozlová, Danica, and Jiří Tomáš. *Egon Ervin Kisch.* Prague: Horizont, 1984.

Kozlová, Danica, and Jiří Tomáš. *Egon Erwin Kisch: Journalist and Fighter.* Trans. John Newton. Prague: International Organization of Journalists, 1985. A small collection of Kisch's sketches in English translation preceded by a concise biography of Kisch viewed wholly in Marxist terms. The interpretation of Kisch's career and literary contributions is typical of the Czech scholarship on Kisch in the communist period. The volume is very well illustrated.

Pytlík, Radko. *Pražská dobrodružství E. E. Kische.* Prague: Panorama, 1985. A Czech study devoted primarily to Kisch's early years in Prague.

Schanne, Karin. *Anschlage: Der rasende Reporter Egon Erwin Kisch.* Stuttgart: Ernst Klett, 1983. A small, popular biography.

Schlenstedt, Dieter. *Die Reportage bei Egon Erwin Kisch.* Berlin: Rütten & Loening, 1959. A small but serious study of Kisch and reportage.

———. *Egon Erwin Kisch: Leben und Werk.* Berlin: Volk und Wissen Volkseigener Verlag, 1968. A good overview of Kisch's life and career from an orthodox East German perspective.

Siegel, Christian Ernst. *Egon Erwin Kisch: Reportage und politischer Journalismus.* Bremen: Schünemann Universitätsverlag, 1973. A well-researched but disjointed study of Kisch primarily as a political writer, with particular attention to reportage in theory and practice. Especially useful for its very thorough bibliography of works by Kisch and about him.

Text + Kritik: Zeitschrift für Literatur, no. 67 (July 1980). The entire issue is devoted to Kisch.

Tomáš, Jiří, and Gabriela Zemličková. *Egon Ervin Kisch: Novinář a bojovník.* Prague: Novinář, 1984. The Czech original of the Kozlová and Tomáš volume.

Utitz, Emil. *Egon Erwin Kisch der klassische Journalist.* Berlin: Aufbau-Verlag, 1956. An early and basically straightforward communist study of Kisch as a politically inspired journalist. It was translated into Czech under the title *Klasický žurnalista: Egon Erwin Kisch* and published by Orbis (Prague) in 1958.

Translations of Kisch in English

Changing Asia. Trans. Rita Reil. New York: Alfred A. Knopf, 1935.

Secret China. Trans. Michael Davidson. London: John Lane The Bodley Head Ltd., 1935.

Sensation Fair. Trans. Guy Endore. New York: Modern Age Books, 1941.

Tales from Seven Ghettos. Trans. Edith Bone. London: Robert Anscombe & Co. Ltd., 1948.

Three Cows. Trans. Stewart Farrar. London: Fore Publications, 1939.

Australian Landfall. Trans. John Fisher and Irene and Kevin Fitzgerald. London: Martin Secker & Warburg, 1937. Reissued 1969 by Macmillan of Australia,

South Melbourne. Another edition of the same book was published in Sydney the same year by the Australian Book Society.

Egon Erwin Kisch: Journalist and Fighter. Biography by Danica Kozlová and Jiří Tomáš. Selections translated by John Newton. Prague: International Organization of Journalists, 1985.

Notes

1. Her family name appears variously as Lyner, Lynner, and Liner.

2. Michael Horowitz, *Ein Leben für die Zeitung: Der rasende Reporter Egon Erwin Kisch,* 27. Kisch originally claimed that he had spent 260 days in military confinement but later reduced the number to the slightly more plausible 147. See Fritz Hofmann, *Egon Erwin Kisch. Der rasende Reporter: Biografie,* 40–43.

3. Egon Erwin Kisch, *Kriminalistisches Reisebuch* (Berlin: Verlag Die Schmiede, 1927), 104.

4. Max Brod, *Der Prager Kreis* (Stuttgart: W. Kohlhammer, 1966), 191.

5. Thomas Kramer, ed., *Reclams Lexikon des deutschen Films* (Stuttgart: Reclam, 1995), 383–84.

6. There is a reproduction of the page containing the report in *Bohemia* in Hofmann, *Egon Erwin Kisch,* 89.

7. Kurt Tucholsky, *Gesammelte Werke III: 1929–1932* (Reinbek bei Hamburg: Rowohlt Verlag, 1962), 643.

8. For a good overview in English of the events leading up to the January strike and this period in the history of Vienna in general, see Charles A. Gulick, *Austria from Habsburg to Hitler* (Berkeley and Los Angeles: University of California Press, 1948). The workers' movement and Vienna socialism are well covered in Helmut Gruber, *Red Vienna: Experiment in Working-Class Culture, 1919–1934* (New York and Oxford: Oxford University Press, 1991).

9. Egon Erwin Kisch, "Wien und die Rote Garde," *Mein Leben für die Zeitung 1906–1925: Journalistische Texte 1* (Berlin and Weimar: Aufbau-Verlag, 1983), 225. Kisch's other writings on the Red Guard, which afford a rather complete picture of its organization and the reaction to it in contemporary Vienna, can be found in *Mein Leben für die Zeitung 1906–1925: Journalistische Texte 1,* 226–52.

10. Horowitz, *Ein Leben für die Zeitung,* 47.

11. Franz Werfel, *Barbara oder die Frömmigkeit* (Frankfurt am Main: G. B. Fischer & Co, 1953), 407–8. The page numbers for subsequent quotations are given in the text.

12. Peter Stephan Jungk, *Franz Werfel: A Life in Prague, Vienna, and Hollywood,* trans. Anselm Hollo (New York: Fromm International Publishing Corporation, 1990), 123–24.

13. For a good collection of writings on the early twentieth-century Prague coffeehouse, see Karl-Heinz Jähn, ed. *Das Prager Kaffeehaus: Literarische Tischgesellschaften* (Berlin: Verlag Volk und Welt, 1988). The book also contains Kisch's sketch on the Montmartre, "Zitate vom Montmartre," which was originally included in *Aus Prager Gassen und Nächten.*

14. For a study just of Kisch's reportage during the Weimar period, see Rudolf Geissler, *Die Entwicklung der Reportage Egon Erwin Kischs in der Weimarer Republik* (Cologne: Pahl-Rugenstein, 1982).

15. On Kisch and his Prague theatrical activity, see Danica Kozlová and Jiří Tomáš, *Egon Erwin Kisch: Journalist and Fighter* (Prague: International Organization of Journalists, 1985), 28–29; and Angelo Maria Ripellino, *Magic Prague,* trans. David Newton Mainelli, ed. Michael Henry Heim (Berkeley and Los Angeles: University of California Press, 1994), 24.

16. Kisch's original sketch about Ferda Mestek de Podskal, "Dramaturgie des Flohtheaters" (Dramaturgy of the Flea Theater), is included in this book.

17. For the text of the sketch, see Kisch, *Der rasende Reporter. Hetzjagd durch die Zeit. Wagnisse in aller Welt. Kriminalistisches Reisebuch* (Berlin and Weimar: Aufbau-Verlag, 1972), 605–11.

18. Hofmann, *Egon Erwin Kisch,* 215.

19. Horowitz mentions (*Ein Leben für die Zeitung,* 67–68) that the official document can be found in the Museum for Czech Literature in Prague.

20. For a rather good general view in English of Russian-German cultural contacts in the 1920s and early 1930s, and the German interest in postrevolutionary Russia, see John Willett, *Art and Politics in the Weimar Period: The New Sobriety, 1917–1933* (New York: Pantheon, 1978).

21. See John Reed, *The War in Eastern Europe* (New York: C. Scribner's, 1916).

22. George F. Kennan, *Russia Leaves the War* (Princeton, N.J.: Princeton University Press, 1956), 68–69.

23. John Reed, *Ten Days That Shook the World* (New York: Penguin, 1977), 13.

24. The name appears in some English publications as Larissa Reissner. On Larisa Reisner, see Cathy Porter, *Larissa Reisner* (London: Virago Press, 1988); and the collection in English of her writings about Germany in the early 1920s, Larisa Reisner, *Hamburg at the Barricades and Other Writings on Weimar Germany,* trans. and ed. Richard Chappell (London: Pluto Press, 1977). The best Russian collection of her works is Larisa Reisner, *Izbrannoe* (Moscow: Khudozhestvennaya Literatura, 1980).

25. Egon Erwin Kisch, "Our Own Correspondent John Reed," *Mein Leben für die Zeitung 1926–1947: Journalistische Texte 2* (Berlin and Weimar: Aufbau-Verlag, 1983), 192.

26. Egon Erwin Kisch, "John Reed, ein Reporter auf der Barrikade," *Mein Leben für die Zeitung 1926–1947: Journalistische Texte 2,* 91–92.

27. *Hamburg auf den Barrikaden: Erlebtes und Erhörtes aus dem Hamburger Aufstand 1923* (Hamburg at the Barricades: The Hamburg Uprising of 1923) (Berlin: Neuer Deutscher Verlag). The ban is discussed in E. Solovei, *Larisa Reisner: Ocherk zhizni i tvorchestva* (Moscow: Sovetskii pisatel, 1985), 99–100.

28. For a more detailed account of the publication history of Reisner's reportage on Germany, and German editions of the works, see Larissa Reissner, *Hamburg at the Barricades,* 9–11.

29. Sergei Tretiakov, *Strana-perekrestok: Dokumentalnaya proza* (Moscow: Sovetskii pisatel, 1991), 315.

30. There is a brief discussion of the Kharkov conference in Willett, *Art and Politics in the Weimar Period,* 214–16.

31. Egon Erwin Kisch, "Der Charkower Schriftseller-Kongress," *Mein Leben für die Zeitung 1926–1947: Journalistische Texte 2,* 270–72.

32. There is an English translation titled *A Select Collection of Singular and Interesting Histories Together with the Trials and Judicial Proceedings to Which the Extraordinary Facts Therein Recorded Gave Occasion* (London: Printed for A. Millar, 1744).

33. Kurt Tucholsky, *Gesammelte Werke II: 1925–1928,* 62.

34. Michael Horowitz, *Ein Leben für die Zeitung,* 69; Dieter Schlenstedt, "Nachwort," Egon Erwin Kisch, *Paradies Amerika* (Berlin and Weimar: Aufbau-Verlag, 1994), 301.

35. Schlenstedt, "Nachwort," *Paradies Amerika,* 304.

36. Egon Erwin Kisch, "Erstes Gespräch mit Upton Sinclair," *Paradies Amerika* (Berlin and Weimar: Aufbau-Verlag), 36.

37. Kurt Tucholsky, *Gesammelte Werke III: 1929–1932,* 387.

38. Egon Erwin Kisch, "Hollywoods Natur, Kultur und Skulptur," *Paradies Amerika* (Berlin and Weimar: Aufbau-Verlag), 257–58.

39. Egon Erwin Kisch, *Asien gründlich verändert* (Berlin: Erich Reiss Verlag, 1932), 25.

40. *The New York Times Book Review,* 3 February 1935, 12.

41. *The New York Times Book Review,* 10 February 1935, 10. The remaining quotes are from the same page of the review.

42. *New York Herald Tribune Books* (Sunday), 10 February 1935, VII, 18.

43. Sergei Tretiakov, *Strana-perekrestok,* 8.

44. *Kasematten* is the German for "casemates," the term in English generally used with reference to the fortifications of a naval vessel. "Dungeons" is more in the spirit of Kisch's account of his imprisonment in Spandau.

45. There is a good discussion of the German cultural community in Paris from 1933 to the German invasion in Frederic V. Grunfeld, *Prophets without Honour: A Background to Freud, Kafka, Einstein and Their World* (New York: McGraw-Hill, 1980), 221–63.

46. Rost was imprisoned in Dachau during World War II for a little less than a year and published the diary he managed to keep there covering the period 10 June 1944–30 April 1945. For a German translation of the work, see Nico Rost, *Goethe in Dachau: Literatur und Wirklichkeit,* trans. Edith Rost-Blumberg (Berlin: Verlag Volk und Welt, 1948).

47. *Books Abroad* (Norman: University of Oklahoma Press, 1935), ix.

48. There is a brief discussion of these issues in A. T. Yarwood's foreword to the 1969 edition of the English edition of Kisch's *Landung in Australien,* which had first been published in 1937 under the title *Australian Landfall.* See Egon Erwin Kisch, *Australian Landfall,* trans. John Fisher (London: Martin Secker & Warburg, 1969), vii–xxi.

49. Egon Erwin Kisch, *Landung in Australien,* 8.

50. Egon Erwin Kisch, *Australian Landfall* (1969), xx.

51. Michael Gold, who had been at the Kharkov congress in 1930, also participated in the Paris conference of 1935. He was one of the delegates sent by the newly formed League of American Writers. His reports shed some interesting light on the conference. Three were published by *New Masses* in 1935. The first two (30 July, 6 August) deal mostly with the business of the conference; the third, which appeared on 13 August, describes Gold's contacts with other writers (Malraux, Paul Vaillant-Couturier, the Russian writer Babel, the Dane Martin Andersen-Nexø, among others; Kisch is not mentioned).

52. The literature on the International Brigades is considerable. For two good accounts, see Verle B. Johnston, *Legions of Babel: The International Brigades in the Spanish Civil War* (University Park: The Pennsylvania State University Press, 1967); and R. Dan Richardson, *Comintern Army: The International Brigades and the Spanish Civil War* (Lexington: The University Press of Kentucky, 1982). As these studies point out, the national composition of the units making up the Brigades shifted throughout the war owing to heavy losses in combat, the arrival of new volunteers, and the need to restructure the Brigades. Thus my characterization of certain battalions and brigades in terms of national components should be regarded as relative.

53. The expanded version of the two pieces appeared first under the title "Die ver-wundeten Kameraden der Internationalen Brigaden" (The Wounded Comrades of the International Brigades); it was published in the Soviet journal *Internationale Lite-ratur* in June 1938. The same version, under the title "Soldaten am Meeresstrand" (Soldiers on the Seashore), appeared first in the collection *Abenteuer in fünf Konti-nenten* (Adventures on Five Continents) in 1948.

54. The hospital was actually named the Comenius Field Hospital and had been sent to Spain, fully staffed, as a gift of the Czechoslovak nation.

55. Nine of Hemingway's dispatches from Spain are included in *By-Line: Ernest Hemingway. Selected Articles and Dispatches of Four Decades*. Ed. William White (New York: Charles Scribner's Sons, 1967). This collection is also available in paperback in a Bantam Books edition (1968).

56. See, for example, Stephen Cooper, *The Politics of Ernest Hemingway* (Ann Arbor, Mich.: UMI Research Press, 1987), 82–85.

57. In his classic study of the Spanish Civil War, Hugh Thomas notes, however, that Hemingway "took an active part in the war on the Republican side, exceeding the duties of a mere reporter by, for instance, instructing young Spaniards in the use of rifles. The first visit of Hemingway to the XIIth International Brigade was a great occasion, the Hungarian General Lukacz sending a message to the nearby village for all its girls to attend the banquet he was giving." See Hugh Thomas, *The Spanish Civil War* (New York, Evanston, and London: Harper & Row, 1963), 388n.

58. For a biography of Koestler, see Ian Hamilton, *Koestler: A Biography* (London: Secker & Warburg, 1982).

59. The plight of such German exiles, Jewish or otherwise, in France in the 1930s is very well described in Grunfeld, *Prophets without Honour.* See especially chapter 7.

60. The text appears in the two-volume collection of Kisch's reportage edited by Walther Schmieding: *Nichts ist erregender als die Wahrheit* (Cologne: Kiepenheuer & Witsch, 1980). See vol. 2, 111–14.

61. Kisch's release from Ellis Island upon the posting of the $500 bond is confirmed by the FBI file on Kisch, which indicates that he was under surveillance throughout the entire period of his stay in the United States and Mexico. FBI NY (New York) File No. 100-12552 (covering the period 24 July–8 August 1941) also mentions that in an interview with the Board of Special Inquiry of the Immigration Service Kisch admitted that he was a "left-wing writer" but denied "any and all communist affiliations." This would indicate that the FBI had been alerted to Kisch's arrival in New York and had reasons to place him under surveillance.

62. Danica Kozlová and Jiří Tomáš, *Egon Erwin Kisch,* 73.

63. Hofmann, *Egon Erwin Kisch*, 333.

64. In its file on Kisch, the FBI notes that the Los Angeles Field Division had copies of *Freies Deutschland* in its possession and that Kisch was a contributor to it. The publication is characterized as showing a "marked attachment to the Soviet Union." The banquet in honor of Kisch's sixtieth birthday is also duly noted in the FBI report. Kisch is identified in the FBI file as "one of the leaders of the group of Communist writers in Mexico. He is on very intimate terms with Anna Seghers (deleted) He is also closely connected with (deleted) and Ludwig Renn, all Communists or fellow travellers of the extreme left. He [Kisch] is a well-known Communist whose opinions are greatly respected by the Communists of Mexico."

65. Kozlová and Tomáš, *Egon Erwin Kisch*, 74.

66. Hofmann, *Egon Erwin Kisch*, 323.

67. The FBI file on Kisch notes that when he applied for an American transit visa at the United States Embassy in Mexico City, Kisch gave as the reason for wanting to return to Czechoslovakia a communication he said he had received from Klemens Gottwald, Deputy Premier of Czechoslovakia, telling him that he was needed there and asking him to return as soon as possible.

68. Kisch was still under FBI surveillance at the time. NY Office file 100-124525 mentions that on 24 February 1946 he and his wife were observed entering the home of a party whose name has been deleted in the copy of the file made available to me.

69. For example, Kozlová and Tomáš, *Egon Erwin Kisch*, 77–78; and Schlenstedt, *Egon Erwin Kisch*, 59–60.

70. See, for example, Horowitz, *Ein Leben für die Zeitung*, 84.

71. Schlenstedt, *Egon Erwin Kisch*, 59.

72. These six pieces were originally published in different editions of Kisch's works. They appear together under the rubric "Späte Reportagen" (Late Reportage) in the second part of the second volume (II/2) of Kisch's writings about Prague in the collected edition of his works published by Aufbau-Verlag in 1975. The volume also contains the collection *Prager Pitaval*. The first part of the second volume, also published in 1975, contains the collections *Aus Prager Gassen und Nächten, Prager Kinder,* and *Die Abenteuer in Prag.*

73. Bezruč's reputation as a poet rests on a single work, *Slezské písně* (Silesian Songs, 1909), about the people of his native Moravian-Silesian Beskyd Mountain region.

74. Walter Benjamin, *Reflections: Essays, Aphorisms, Autobiographical Writings,* trans. Edmund Jephcott, ed. Peter Demetz (New York and London: Harcourt Brace Jovanovich, 1978), 223–24.

75. Egon Erwin Kisch, "Debüt beim Mühlenfeuer," "Marktplatz der Sensationen," *Marktplatz der Sensationen. Entdeckungen in Mexiko* (Berlin and Weimar: Aufbau-Verlag, 1993), 6th ed., 131–32.

76. Theodor Balk, "Egon Erwin Kisch und die Reportage," 7.

77. O. M. Brik, "Fiksatsiia fakta," *Novy Lef,* nos. 11–12 (1927), 48.

78. Egon Erwin Kisch, "Wesen des Reporters," *Mein Leben für die Zeitung 1906–1925: Journalistische Texte 1* (Berlin and Weimar: Aufbau-Verlag, 1983), 205–8.

79. Balk, "Egon Erwin Kisch und die Reportage," 13.

80. Egon Erwin Kisch, ed., *Klassischer Journalismus: Die Meisterwerke der Zeitung* (Berlin and Weimar: Aufbau-Verlag, 1982), 5.

81. Kurt Tucholsky, *Gesammelte Werke III: 1929–1932,* 234.

82. Egon Erwin Kisch, *Der rasende Reporter* (Berlin: Aufbau Taschenbuch Verlag, 1994). All quotations from Kisch's introduction are from pages 7–8.

83. Kurt Tucholsky, *Gesammelte Werke II:1925–1928,* 50, 51.

84. Sergei Tretiakov quoted in John Willett, *Art and Politics in the Weimar Period: The New Sobriety, 1917–1933,* 107.

85. Balk, "Egon Erwin Kisch und die Reportage," 14.

Kisch in Berlin, 1930.
Courtesy Kiepenheuer & Witsch Verlag.

A Dangerous Literary Genre

Allow me to devote a few minutes to the sketch or reportage, that special form of literature that all bourgeois aesthetes hold in light regard. . . .

These wild attacks on the part of the vestal virgins of bourgeois criticism are less the consequence of novelty than of the dangerousness of our genre. Let me introduce an example. Three months ago I was in Ceylon. While on board ship, I read books about the island: official travel guides and advertising brochures from different travel bureaus, and in addition literary travel descriptions. When I got to compare all this literature with the living reality, I was overcome by fear and disgust. I saw an island where at least 30,000 children died of malaria and malnutrition between October and January, where 80 percent of all children are starving to such an extent that they are too weak to go to school, where people are whipped daily.

But what did I find in the travel books? They spoke about the beauty of the island of pearls, about the thunder of the surf, about the eternal rustle of the jungle, about the ruins of ancient imperial palaces, and about thousands of similar things; lush nature, vestiges of prehistoric culture—yet not a word about the abominable, terrible everyday life.

If we really sought to reproach the authors of all these accounts, they would merely declare that they are not lying, that all these splendid ancient palaces and the wonderful lush nature do indeed exist. Even more, they would protest against such a violation of their literary freedom: we even have the audacity to want to tell them what to write about! And then they would go on the offensive and declare that they are above all artists, whereas we are banal demagogues bereft of any imagination, dry rationalists, and so on.

But if a person who thinks in social terms sees the kinds of things I saw on Ceylon, he will sometimes be tempted simply to record them, to enumerate the horrors—that is, to truly fall into banality. No less strong is the temptation at times to break into tears, to cry out in view of all the human misery, and to earn the just charge of demagogy. Finally there remains the temptation to give these facts the possibility of direct, independent treatment, to set them down simply, without adding to them or omitting anything in the slightest— that is, to show oneself to be truly bereft of any imagination whatsoever.

It is hard, my friends, much harder than many of you think, to present the truth accurately, without sacrificing artistic form or vitality. Sketch or reportage, both describe work and life. But we know what drab, awkward material they often present in our time. The novelist who reaches his goal is a true artist.

But for us, people and life are supreme. Our literature must serve them and their awareness.

Egon Erwin Kisch, "Eine gefährliche Literaturgattung," *Mein Leben für die Zeitung 1926– 1947: Journalistische Texte 2* (Berlin and Weimar: Aufbau-Verlag, 1983), 396–97.

Germans and Czechs

[...] The *Prager Tagblatt* was indeed a commercial undertaking. Founded by the Huguenot Mercy family as an exclusively advertising paper, it gradually added editorial sections, which as a result of its monopoly of want ads (jobs, swaps, secondhand sales, and marriage proposals) it could expand with the considerable means now at its disposal. Still, the greatest amount of space in the paper was devoted to small-business news. The financial difficulties or bankruptcy of a tie shop, the commodities market, and the price of goose feathers and hog bristles were noted with minute exactness. Information of this type was grouped under the general heading of Political Economy, which gave every goose-feather and hog-bristle trader the right to think of himself as a political economist. And his wife fancied herself educated when she read articles by Heinrich Teweles adorned with Latin quotations.[1]

If advertisements continued to come in late in the evening, whole pages of other sections of the paper would then be tossed out to make room for them. When the author of such a sacrificed article complained about it, he would be told by the administrative head of the paper: "Our subscribers prefer to read ads a thousand times more than your pearls of wisdom."

Needless to say, there were also events that were immune to such danger and for which space and money were made available. During the Hilsner trial in the town of Pisek, the *Prager Tagblatt* got the jump on the world press by means of the newest invention. While all other correspondents had to wait for the single telephone line to become free, only those of the *Prager Tagblatt* drove off in an automobile to Prague and there wrote their report. They boasted of traveling at a speed of twenty kilometers an hour.

At the *Bohemia,* by contrast, patriarchal conditions reigned. The newspaper was eighty years old and devoted mainly to politics. Its views were regarded as representative of all the Germans in Bohemia, were reprinted by the provincial papers, and were phoned out to foreign newspapers. The Prague correspondent of the all-powerful Viennese *Neue Freie Presse,* Herr Hermann Katz, was at the same time the editor of the *Bohemia.* Prague correspondents of other Vienna and Berlin newspapers were also members of our editorial staff.

The internal politics of the *Bohemia* was a tug-of-war over whether the Germans or the Czechs were being discriminated against by the Austrian government, whether the new mailman of the community of Melnik should be a Czech or a German, and whether on the signposts in the Bohemian Forest the Czech place names should appear above or below the German. A scientific resolution of the nationality problem—with which such socialistic theorists as Otto Bauer and the Caucasian Josef Stalin, who had come to Austria especially for this purpose, were then seriously concerned—was of course out of the question. The *Bohemia* sought to give the sterile polemics a coating of culture by means of certain quotations, which it repeated over and over again. These included, for example, Mommsen's remark about the shape of the Czech skull or Friedrich Hebbel's verse:[2]

> Servile peoples also shake
> A structure all thought dead.
> The Czechs and Poles shake
> Their shaggy caryatid head.

As evidence of the insignificance and obscurity of the Czechs, it was pointed out time and again that in his *Winter Tale* Shakespeare situates the land of Bohemia on the seacoast. The forgery of the Königinhofer manuscript was brought up at every opportunity. Josef Willomitzer, the editor-in-chief of the *Bohemia,* had published a parody of the manuscript in book form, and the journalist Friedrich Mauthner had made it the subject of a satirical novel, *The Bohemian Manuscript.*

Incidentally, Willomitzer and Mauthner no longer belonged to the journalistic guild when I entered it. Willomitzer had died, and Mauthner had become known abroad as a great philosopher of language whose seventieth birthday academies and learned societies were preparing to celebrate.[3] It was in connection with this event that I interviewed his sister, the elderly wife of a physician, about Mauthner's childhood. "Yes indeed," the old woman told me, sunk in reminiscences, "Fritz was a gifted boy." But all of a sudden her features grew very stern: "He could easily have gotten his doctorate if he had tried."

German Prague spoke from these words. If you didn't have a title or weren't rich, you just didn't belong. German Prague! It consisted almost exclusively of the upper middle class, owners of lignite mines, directors of coal and steel companies and the Škoda munitions works, hops dealers who commuted between Saatz and North America, sugar, textile, and paper manufacturers, as well as bank directors. Professors and higher-ranking officers and government officials moved in their circle. There was no German proletariat. The twenty-five thousand Germans, who constituted only 5 percent of the population of Prague at the time, possessed two magnificent theaters, a huge concert hall, two colleges, five high schools, and four advanced vocational institutes, two newspapers with a morning and evening edition each, large meeting halls, and a lively social life.

The Prague German had nothing to do with the city's half million Czechs except what related to business. He never lit his cigar with a match from the Czech School Fund, any more than a Czech would light his with a match from the little box of the German School Association. No German ever set foot in the Czech Citizens' Club, and no Czech ever deigned to visit the German Casino. Even the instrumental concerts were monolingual, and the same for the swimming pools, the parks, the playgrounds, most restaurants, coffee-houses, and stores. The promenade of the Czechs was the Ferdinandstrasse, whereas the Germans preferred the Graben.

In Hussite times, the churches of Prague had instituted Utraquism, according to which Holy Communion was administered in both forms. Now they weren't even Utraquist in the matter of language. The Germans had their own churches, and the Czechs theirs.

The German and Czech universities, and the Czech and German technical institutes, were as remote from one another as if one were located on the North Pole and the other on the South Pole. Each of the hundred academic chairs had its counterpart on the opposite language side, but there was no common building, no common clinic, no common laboratory, no common observatory (one possessed the astronomical instruments of Tycho Brahe, the other those of Johannes Kepler), no common reference library, and no common morgue. For the botanical garden of one university a plant was ordered from the South Seas that could be seen blossoming in the botanical garden of the other university had a wall not stood in the way.

What was obvious to any Czech, and must have seemed unbelievable to anyone not from Prague—the more so when the role of the theater in the life of the city is taken into consideration—is that no Czech citizen ever visited the German theater and vice versa. If the Comédie Française or the Moscow Art Theater or some famous singer was giving guest performances at the Czech National Theater, the German press took no notice of it whatsoever, and the critics, who day in and day out juggled the names of Coquelin, Stanislavsky, or Chaliapin, never for a moment considered attending a performance by any of them in the Czech theater. On the other hand, guest performances by the likes of the Vienna Burgtheater, Adolf von Sonnenthal, or Enrico Caruso simply didn't register with the Czech public.

To make sure that these barriers between the two national ghettoes were never transgressed, the *Bohemia* stood watch on the German side with flaming sword. The attempt by some German and Czech actors, for example, to find a place to get together, was denounced as national treason; and the Czech press joined in the denunciation.

From the moment I went to work for the *Bohemia* the golden rules were impressed on me: No Czech word without the corresponding German translation, since we do not expect our readers to understand Czech. Even the cry "Slava" has to be explained in brackets as meaning "Long Live," and the same for "Hanba," meaning "Down with." The common Czech woman's name Blažena is our Beatrice, and Blažena our Theodora; but people so named wouldn't have recognized themselves under these Christian names. The bridge on the Podskaler Quay, which the town council had named the Palacký Bridge in honor of the great Czech,[4] is known to our readers only as the Podskaler

Bridge. The "Sokol," an organization with hundreds of thousands of members, is referred to only as the "Czech Gymnastic Society Falcon."

When Emperor Franz Joseph came to Prague to visit the Czech jubilee exhibit, entire columns of our paper were devoted to the receptions, the decorations, the ovations, and every turn of the wheels of the imperial carriage. But suddenly our description broke off with the sentence: "His Majesty then stepped onto the fairgrounds," since the exhibit itself was totally ignored by the German side. Only an unsuccessful balloon ascent during the exhibit was reported, naturally in ridicule. But the Czechs themselves made fun of it, and the Blind Methodius sang, "Don't piss up in the air, / Lest it land in your hair."[5]

The German Progressive Party was at best progressive on the Jewish issue but as intolerant as possible when it came to national and social relations, a true reflection of the Vienna liberals. Even when it came to art the liberal Vienna and Prague press appeared conservative and often reactionary. Against Richard Wagner they published his "Letters to the Milliner"; Oscar Wilde was condemned for homosexuality, and Rodin for cheap showmanship.

Although I mentioned that young writers and artists kept their distance from the official German circles and ostentatiously frequented the bilingual Café Central, it must be added that this progressive party paid them no heed at all. The intellectual youth also spurned the activities of the traditional colors-wearing, dueling and bar-crawling student fraternities. The members of these organizations were "German-Bohemians" or "South Moravians" (the term "Sudeten Germans" wasn't used at the time) and most were followers of Member of Parliament Georg Ritter von Schönerer.[6] This Ritter Georg wanted to link the fate of all German-speaking districts for better or for worse with the Hohenzollerns. He led an attack on the editorial offices of the *Neuer Wiener Tagblatt* because the paper had committed "lèse-majesté against our hereditary master" through a false report about the death of Emperor Wilhelm.

Anti-Czech hatred blossomed in the Schönerer Party wards long before the world was told that the Sudeten Germans were being politically oppressed by the Czechoslovak state and economically destroyed by the bosses of Prague. There was no Czechoslovak state in those days, and the bosses sat in Vienna and were German.

After the December uprising of 1897, a fleeting glimpse of which I had caught as a child from a darkened window, a boycott arose against Czech sports clubs. In that turbulent week the clubhouse of the German Regatta Rowing and Soccer Club on the Kaiserwiese had been set on fire by demonstrators, reportedly under the leadership of Herr Freya, the captain of the Czech sports club Slavia. All meets were therefore canceled, not only against Slavia, but against all other Czech athletic associations. This boycott lasted for a quarter of a century, even after World War I. The German soccer club known by the acronym DFC never played against the Czechs, but it so happened that the Czechs competed in Berlin, Vienna, or Budapest against a team that a week later took the field against the DFC. This gave rise to a mathematical science, dubbed "paper-form," which sought by means of goal and corner shot figures to calculate whether DFC or Slavia was the better team.

Only one German club did not participate in this boycott, the soccer club Storm, of which I was the left end. Once we played a league match against Slavia, which was better than we were, a lot better. We were determined to break off the game if any pretext to do so presented itself. Of course the match would then be counted as lost, but we would at least reach the final round with fewer goals scored against us. The hoped-for opportunity arose when, while I was making a long dash down the field, a small Slavia half-back named Beneš tripped me. Or maybe he didn't really trip me. In any case, he immediately withdrew from the field as soon as we began accusing him of it so as not to give us a pretext for quitting. It was a shrewd move, but later, after he had become president of the Czechoslovak Republic, one that he unfortunately repeated.

As insurmountable as the gap stretched between the German and the Czech press, secret bridges were nevertheless erected. One day a Czech member of parliament, the director of the Bohemian Regional Orphanage, stopped to talk to me in front of the building housing our editorial offices. He said he had some important information to give me, but first wanted my assurance that everything would be kept strictly confidential. When we met in a secluded wine cellar, he showed me the register of the public schools to which the wards of the orphanage had been assigned. They were without exception Czech schools. As a result, the orphans were being alienated from the German districts of Bohemia (30 percent of the total) and were being Slavicized.

I turned this information over to our political editor, who raised a bloody outcry. The Czech press immediately defended the actions of its orphanage. The director of the institution himself replied to the "vile attack from the German camp" and reprinted the annual report of the Vienna Regional Orphanage, from which it appeared that it was doing precisely the same thing with Slavic children. But this was only reprehensible in view of the fact that Vienna was abusing its position as the capital of the empire to Germanize children from non-German crown lands.

The polemics grew ever sharper, involved Provincial Legislature and Parliament, regional court and Supreme Court, and dragged on until the expiration of the Czech orphanage director's term. Before the entire affair started, his co-nationals had decided—for different reasons—not to nominate him again. But now he was unanimously reelected; it was impossible, after all, to desert a man who stood in the midst of the battle against the national enemy.

I myself wrote nothing on politics; I had no taste for any of this nationalistic wrangling. My soccer team Storm, against which the *Bohemia* had hurled its nastiest comments—before I joined the staff of the paper— continued to play against Czech teams. From the telephone operators at the post office I asked for the Czech connection and carried on conversations with Czech officials in their language right from the offices of the paper. My colleagues growled: "How can we demand that everyone speak German in government offices when our own gentlemen speak Czech!"

Perhaps the reader will now ask how a cub reporter could manage such deviations from the official position of his paper. Isn't even an experienced editor, who believes he is determining the direction of his paper, much more determined by it?

Yes, that is indeed the case. But mine was an exceptional position, which I owed only to the fact that I was young. The editorial staff was mostly elderly, and the old gentlemen let those who relieved them of work do pretty much as they liked.

Egon Erwin Kisch, "Deutschen und Tshechen," "Marktplatz der Sensationen," *Marktplatz der Sensationen. Entdeckungen in Mexiko,* 6th ed. (Berlin and Weimar: Aufbau Verlag, 1993), 79–86.

1. Heinrich Teweles was the editor-in-chief of the *Prager Tagblatt* when Kisch worked there as a young man.

2. Theodor Mommsen (1817–1903), the famous German historian, won the Nobel Prize in Literature in 1902.

3. Friedrich (Fritz) Mauthner (1849–1923) was an Austrian writer of fiction who became even better known for his extensive and controversial writings on the philosophy of language.

4. This is a reference to the Czech historian and political figure František Palacký (1798–1876).

5. The "Blind Methodius" appears in Kisch's *Sensation Fair* as a local Prague balladeer.

6. Georg Ritter von Schönerer (1842–1921) was the Vienna-born founder of the extreme nationalist and anti-Semitic German-National movement.

Unforeseeable Consequences

Once there was a little freckle-faced office girl from the small town of Podie-brad who came for a weekend to Prague in order to enjoy herself away from the ever-watchful eyes of the inhabitants of her hometown.

She found the kind of entertainment she was looking for at the Hippodrome, a riding academy that every evening turned into a nightclub of a cheaper variety. For twenty hellers one could ride ten times around the ring, and three such rides cost fifty hellers. A "quartet" consisting of three musicians provided musical accompaniment. The female guests, mostly young girls, sat astride, jerked the reins, and tried, by clicking their tongues and bouncing up and down, to spur their apathetic nags into a bold gallop and themselves into feeling like Amazons. Of the six horses the one most sought after was Bella, a one-eyed bay with a white spot on her forehead and two on her croup, which made her look as if she had lost her underpants and became the butt of many jokes. The male guests sat around the arena, drinking beer and reviewing the ladies as they rode past, their skirts blowing high.

In this mounted nightclub the freckle-faced girl from Podiebrad found favor in the eyes of a friend of mine, with whom I had just entered. Since he had to leave for a few hours to tend to some business, I was supposed to look after the girl so that no one else might make off with her.

This wasn't very entertaining, since, first of all, I was just baby-sitting, without being personally involved, and, secondly, since there wasn't much to talk about with her. Nevertheless, I had to converse with her, otherwise she would have kept on riding, and that would have cost money, twenty hellers a ride.

She was well aware of the fact that she was boring me and she tried to arouse my interest. But the revelation that she was employed at the post office in Podiebrad wasn't enough to make any big impression. So she brought out supposedly heavier artillery: she said could understand some German. Courteously I made an expression of mixed surprise and doubt.

Jawohl, she corroborated her statement, and again repeated that she understood some German, *jawohl,* and that she had to, since "telegrams in German often come for our Prince Hohenlohe. Day before yesterday, for example, a telegram came for him from the emperor in Germany, ninety-four words long."

"Really?" I asked. "What was in the telegram?"

"I took it down myself, *jawohl,*" she said, proud partly that she finally was able to get me interested, partly that she herself had taken down the imperial telegram. She considered that an important detail.

"So tell me, what was in the telegram?"

"It was in the German language, *jawohl.* It came over the Prague relay station. Ninety-four words, not counting the address, all in German, and I didn't make a single mistake in taking it down, *jawohl.* Even the postmaster said so himself, and he rarely ever praises anyone. Do you know Postmaster Beranek in Podiebrad? No? He's an old grouch, always finding fault with everything."

"So what was in the telegram?"

"The emperor scolded our prince. I guess the emperor's an old grouch like Postmaster Beranek."

"But why did the emperor scold your prince?"

"I don't know. Probably doesn't know himself. Sometimes Postmaster Beranek goes around scolding the whole morning and himself doesn't know why. I'd like to go riding again, if you don't mind, sir."

I let her have three more rides. A tip to the head groom and I obtained for her the special rider's luck of getting to mount the coffee-colored, one-eyed, bare-bottomed Bella. I bought three tickets for myself. Maybe while I galloped alongside her like a squire I could find out something about that telegram.

We were standing in the ring getting ready to mount our horses.

"How was the telegram signed?" I asked.

She had raised her right foot into Bella's stirrup. This was one of the moments most awaited by the spectators. If circumstances allowed, pink fustian bloomers with white frills would be plainly revealed. As if aiming to please the audience, Bella pulled back a little, causing her companion to hop after her on the left leg while the right one hung high and visible in the air.

I wasn't going to let that distract me, and I repeated my question as to how the telegram had been signed. As she tugged up the other half of the deep-pink bloomers together with the white frills in order to get into the proper riding position, she answered: "Wilhelm Comma Imperator."

Her answer overcame my suspicion that the story of the imperial telegram had just been invented for the sake of impressing me. She would scarcely have ever heard this title before coming across it in the telegram, and she could not have known that a comma goes between Wilhelm and Imperator.

The "quartet" made up of three brass musicians kept on playing the Piccolo song from the *Walzertraum* operetta. Like a jockey I dug my heels into the flanks of my apoplectic nag to make it keep to the same tempo as the spirited Bella. It didn't work. I then switched to the tactic, so useful for a hedgehog when confronted by a rabbit, of bringing my horse to a halt. After each circle Bella had to pass by me; I could then get next to her for a few steps and ask her rider about the telegram. All she could recall was that it contained the words "unforeseeable consequences"; *jawohl,* no other employee could have taken it down as faultlessly as she, and those aren't simple words, are they?

True indeed: "unforeseeable consequences"—coming from the mouth of an emperor—are no simple words.

With the "quartet" still laboring away at the *Walzertraum*—"Piccolo, piccolo, tsin, tsin, tsin, / All wisdom lies therein"—the coffee-colored, one-eyed, front- and rear-spotted Bella was long gone.

"What did the telegram refer to?" I asked when we were again seated next to each other at a table. She said she didn't know exactly. When she put the matter to the postmaster, he shook his head and grumbled: "God knows what it's all about! Our prince must have lent the emperor money and now he wants it back. That's why the emperor is carrying on like a madman. You should never lend anyone money."

To me every word of that telegram was important, yet the girl kept on repeating that it contained ninety-four words, which I couldn't do anything with one way or another. There also wasn't much to be done with Postmaster Beranek's hypothesis that it was probably all about borrowed money.

Where could I learn more about the matter? I knew one man who could get the telegram—the assistant postmaster of the main Prague post office. He nurtured the ambition of becoming a minister, either minister for postal affairs, in which case he promised to run his office with the strictest national impartiality, or minister for German minority affairs, in which case he would work assiduously to protect German interests against those of all other nationalities.

Toward these ends he delivered, on the one hand, technical lectures on the reform of the postal system, and, on the other hand, fiery speeches against the preferential treatment shown employees of Czech extraction and always brought our editor-in-chief the texts of these speeches with remarks in parentheses such as "loud applause," "approval," and so on. He sucked up to our editor-in-chief because, as a member of the German National Council, he had political influence. But he never exchanged a word with any of the other editors and barely acknowledged their greetings.

I told our editor-in-chief about the telegram. He smiled tolerantly at my enthusiasm. Stroking his wood-colored beard all the way to the nipples, he asked me if I seriously believed that an emperor would deal with affairs of state in an ordinary telegram. "Either something is intended for public consumption, in which case it is announced officially, or something is not intended for public consumption, in which case it is not wired openly."

"But when the emperor speaks of 'unforeseeable consequences,' it has to be something important," I objected.

"Of course it's something important," he said, "a family affair or some financial matter that doesn't concern anyone else."

At that point all I could do was shut up, embarrassed.

"There's one lesson you've got to learn for the rest of your life, my young friend, and that is that affairs of state are *not* conducted the way your little corner shopkeeper thinks."

The editor-in-chief said this with a gesture of emphasis that ran the entire length of his oaken beard. I had occasion to recall his lesson, but with a slight modification that I had to make just a few hours later, namely, that the little word "not" had to be dropped from his maxim. In these few fours I had learned that the telegram in question referred neither to a family affair nor to any financial matter, but to affairs of state on the very highest level.

I had finally wrung from the editor-in-chief permission to use his name in approaching the assistant postmaster about the telegram.

"But only so that you can realize how wet behind the ears you are when it comes to politics," he said. "But don't forget to convey to the assistant postmaster that I personally do not believe in the political importance of the telegram. I shouldn't like to come across as another political babe-in-the-woods."

Naturally I forgot to convey this message, but substituted another for it instead. I said that our editor-in-chief indeed attached the greatest possible importance to the telegram and that he would be particularly indebted to the assistant postmaster if he would just . . . and so on, and so forth.

The assistant postmaster first interrogated me as to whether anyone else besides the editor-in-chief knew of my visit to him, and if anyone else in the building had seen me. Only after he was reassured on these points did he agree to meet me at his apartment at two o'clock. There he dictated to me the following brief sentence: "The Emperor Wilhelm protested by wire to Prince Hohenlohe in Podiebrad against his publishing in the newspapers without his express permission, characterizing this as tactless in the extreme."

Where this tactlessness had been committed was not to be inferred from the telegram. But since publication was usually done through the press, the assistant postmaster himself, as I soon discovered, had added the words "in the newspapers."

The matter had nothing to do whatsoever with a newspaper article but with the announced publication in book form of documents representing the political legacy of the deceased chancellor of the Reich, Chlodwig zu Hohenlohe-Schillingsfürst. The documents had been prepared for publication by Prince Alexander Hohenlohe, the chancellor's youngest son, with the collaboration of the Strasbourg historian, Friedrich Curtius. It was this forthcoming publication that had aroused the wrath of Wilhelm II and had led him to complain vehemently to the head of the House of Hohenlohe.

But I knew even more. I knew that the telegram had also spoken of "unforeseeable consequences," and I added these words to the report that appeared in our paper on 8 October 1906.

What kind of consequences could there be that this sworn defender of God against all pessimists had described as "unforeseeable?" It was to this question that the governments and newspapers in London, St. Petersburg, and Paris sought an answer the day after the freckle-faced girl from Podiebrad had shouted these two troublesome words to me from Bella's back.

Originally, the Deutsche Verlags-Anstalt of Stuttgart had planned to publish the Hohenlohe memoirs in an edition of a thousand copies. But in response to our announcement, orders came pouring in from all over. An American bookstore firm cabled an order of two thousand copies. Three printing houses were employed just to meet the unparalleled demand. Entire chapters were telegraphed abroad. The world learned in black and white of the danger that Emperor Wilhelm posed the world, and how swiftly and totally he intended to liquidate Bismark's rapprochement with the Russians. War seemed unavoidable.

In the French Chamber of Deputies, Clemenceau demanded an immediate increase in the military budget with the cry: "Against the 'unforeseeable consequences'!" The House of Commons demanded that a counter–triple alliance be formed against the Triple Alliance, that the time had come to carry out the much-discussed Triple Entente. The English company of Armstrong was commissioned by the tsarist government to produce armor-plating for four modern battleships. At a meeting of the Duma, deputies waved the Union Jack and the tricolor of France, shouting "Da zdravstvuyet Antant-Kordial!"—"Long live the Entente Cordiale!"

I met the friend whose place I had held down at the Hippodrome. He excused himself for saddling me with the girl. "You must have been bored something awful. I didn't know what a dumbbell she was."

Dumbbell? The foreign offices of the great powers thought otherwise. Downing Street took her for a diplomat of pacifist persuasion. The Quai d'Orsay counted her among those strata of the Prussian official aristocracy who remained faithful to Bismarck's policy. The Ballhaus-Platz in Vienna came nearer to the truth: they suspected an indiscretion on the part of Czech civil servants. But when the *Fremdenblatt,* the organ of the Austrian Ministry for Foreign Affairs, called for a purge of Bohemian officialdom, it scarcely had the Podiebrad post office in mind; and when it demanded the disclosure of the entire affair down to the last detail, it had no idea that all it would uncover was pink fustian panties with white frills.

The international furor had to be defused. For that reason the German government declared in the *Norddeutsche Allgemeine Zeitung* that His Majesty's telegram to Prince Philipp zu Hohenlohe-Schillingsfürst was a private telegram, and that it had been only the unauthorized publication and tendentious rendition of it by *Bohemia* that had led to false conclusions abroad. In order to put an end once and for all to further complications, the authentic text was hereby revealed: "It is with surprise and indignation that I read of the publication of the most intimate private conversations between your father and me concerning the departure of Prince Bismarck. How could it happen that such material was made public without your first obtaining my permission? I must characterize this action as in the highest degree tactless, indiscreet, and utterly inopportune, since it is unheard-of that events concerning a still-reigning sovereign should be published without his consent."

"Did you see the official text?" my editor-in-chief asked me sharply.

"No," I answered, since the political editor had given the official explanation to the typesetter without saying even a word to me about it. After all, what concern was it of a local correspondent?

"There's nothing in it about your 'unforeseeable consequences' that have got the world so upset," fumed my editor-in-chief. "A pretty sight we are now!"

I got a copy of the official text from the composing room. No journalist and no reader could have noticed anything unusual in the wording of the text; nobody could doubt its authenticity.

But something had to strike me, a doubt had to arise, for . . .

. . . for as silly as the statement of Postmaster Beranek of Podiebrad had been that the telegram had something to do with borrowed money, he wouldn't have made it if it had contained the words "concerning the departure of Prince Bismarck."

When the girl from Podiebrad had repeated to me what her postmaster had said, it seemed utterly insignificant to me at the time. And now it was because of that that I discovered a deliberate insertion on the part of the German government. Why couldn't the other thing the girl said that seemed unimportant to me turn out to be important—her information on the number of words in the telegram? I did some counting, compared them, and wrote: "The text intended for publication contains, including the newly added restrictive clause 'concerning the departure of Prince Bismarck,' just eighty-two words and punctuation marks. By comparison, the telegram we reported on consisted of ninety-four words and punctuation marks, excluding the address but including the crucial and now eliminated comment on the 'unforeseeable consequences' and"—and here the pink bloomers with the white frills flashed in my manuscript—"the signature, Wilhelm Comma Imperator."

My gloss provoked a new furor. "Aufgedeckte Fälschung!" resounded from all the presses. "Official forgery!" "Falsification commise par le gouvernment du Kaiser."

The official German press responded with attacks on foreigners who were instigating war. The *Norddeutsche Allgemeine* carried an editorial declaring: "The anonymous figure on the Moldau foments war—the war of others—in a pinkish slant against war. Bella gerant alii [Let others make war]. Disguised, it rides out to take the field against Germany, but through the slit in the visor the eye of the enemy of the state is recognizable."

I whistled through my teeth when I read this. Did the imperial court and government see the bloomers beneath my report? Why would they otherwise have chosen as the color of the slant the color of the undies revealed by my informer at the Hippodrome? Instead of the German word for "wars," why did they use the Latin *bella,* the name of the horse in the Hippodrome? And why did they speak of a figure riding; why did they mention the slit?

But the terminology seems to have been just coincidental.

Parliaments and editorials had to keep on guessing as to the identity and intentions of the source. They were still guessing when a new and amusing sensation occupied the world's attention. A Berlin shoemaker named Voigt, attired in a captain's uniform, stopped a detail of soldiers on the street, marched them off to the town hall of the suburb of Köpenick, and ordered the mayor to hand over the municipal funds, whereupon he disappeared with the money.

> Der Kaiser depeschiert,
> Der Schuster kommandiert,
> Und ganz Deutschland marschiert.

(The emperor sends a wire, / A shoemaker issues orders, / And all Germany marches.)

So sang Blind Methodius, who usually sings just of Prague local events. His song echoed throughout the world and was sung in all languages.

Incited by the laughter of foreign countries, the German police devised a real war strategy to capture the captain from Köpenick. At the same time the investigation into the identity of the person who had published the emperor's telegram was pursued as vigorously as ever. At the request of the German consulate, the Prague police undertook a search of our editorial offices. Several manuscripts in my handwriting were confiscated and are no doubt still stored in the Hohenzollern family archives in Potsdam along with the record in which the responsible editor and I refused, on the grounds of editorial secrecy, to make any statement concerning the source of the information.

Among those who wanted to find out who had furnished us the content of the imperial telegram was none other than the assistant postmaster of the Prague Post Office, who had furnished us the content of the imperial telegram. He was convinced that we already had the text of the telegram in hand when we asked him for it. Otherwise how could we have known about "unforeseeable consequences," or the signature "Wilhelm Comma Imperator," or the number of words, or that the clause about Bismarck was not in the original? He feared that a trap had been set for him in order to cover the tracks of the real informer.

But it wasn't this that was to put an end to his career. Through the influence of the editor-in-chief, he was put up as a candidate in the parliamentary elections. But when the opposition party revealed that he belonged to a roundtable known as "The Mormons," whose members swapped wives at night, he gave up his candidacy and went into retirement. I never saw him again, nor did I ever again run into the Podiebrad postal employee with her freckles and pink fustian panties with white frills.

But I did see Bella again, the coffee-colored, one-eyed horse from the Hippodrome with her white front and rear end. The unforeseeable consequences did after all materialize; the World War had erupted. Bella served our machine-gun unit. When I recognized her, she was grazing near company headquarters.

"Bella," I cried out. She turned her head around with a start and gazed at me with one big eye and one empty socket. Was she expecting me to ride her back to the time when she carried a merrier burden than cartridge fittings and the band played for a different purpose than to rush one headlong into death?

Ah, Bella, those happy evenings have passed. I can't do anything for you now but whistle the old song.

I whistled it, and Bella broke into a trot, and, to the rhythm of "Piccolo, piccolo, tsin, tsin, tsin," raced around in a circle, the way she used to do when all the world's wisdom still lay therein.

Egon Erwin Kisch, "Die unabsehbaren Konsequenzen," *Marktplatz der Sensationen. Entdeckungen in Mexico,* 6th ed. (Berlin and Weimar: Aufbau Verlag, 1993), 144–53.

Magdalene Home

I was reminded in the most curious way of an article I wrote—or, better said, tried to write—in my youth, thirty years later.

In the year 1933, German writers who had left their country after it fell to the Nazis as booty founded in Paris a cultural center of the antifascist emigration. They called it the Schutzverband Deutscher Schriftsteller [the Defense Association of German Writers]. Every Monday several hundred German refugees gathered in the building of the Société de l'Encouragement de l'Industrie to hear lectures and readings. Exhibitions of art banned in Nazi Germany were held, and theater and cabaret performances were arranged on big Parisian stages. A "Library of Burned Books," consisting of several thousand volumes, was also established, and the Heinrich Heine Prize was created for the purpose of honoring every year the first literary work by an émigré writer. A journal, *Der Schriftsteller* [*The Writer*], which superficially imitated the similarly named organ of the National Socialist Chamber of Literature, went by mail to all writers living in Germany. Partly anonymous and supportive, partly not anonymous and ostentatiously derogatory, but always informative, they confirmed receipt of the publication.

The editorial board of this journal kept close track of the literary columns of the Nazi press. This was not a fruitful kind of work, since in the Nazi press everything else played a far more important role than literature. But suddenly a shift toward more energetic literary promotion seemed to be in the offing. The city of Hamburg announced a prize of a thousand marks for the short story that "best expressed the indigenous humor and wit of the German sea-coast." Fifty or a hundred marks used to be the maximum for this sort of thing, and a thousand marks for a short story was an astonishingly high sum for Germany.

A few weeks later I read that the honored story was titled "Magdalene Home"; the prize winner was the humorist of the *Hamburger Fremdenblatt*, Hanns ut Hamm.

In and of itself a Magdalene home, an institution for the reform of prostitutes, is hardly a source of indigenous humor and wit, least of all for the Nazis, whose cultural program rests on a belief in the miracle working of such homes—retraining centers, education camps, concentration camps. How can a home for fallen girls who are still German girls serve as the subject of satire?

It so happens that once upon a time, through the conjuncture of circumstances, such a home revealed its comic side to me, but my description of this conjuncture of circumstances did not bring me any prize.

It came about this way. I called up the Prague home for wayward girls and asked the mother superior if I could visit the institution to write an article about it.

A cry of alarm was her answer: "An article? You said, an article?"

I could only assure the mother superior that she had heard correctly.

"For heaven's sake," the groan came from the other side, "nothing has happened here! Why on earth do you want to write an article about us?"

I calmed the mother superior, telling her that all I had in mind was to describe the furnishings of the institution and the educational activity, in general terms, without any exterior motives.

"Oh, I see!" A great weight fell from the mother superior's shoulders. "But I can't issue any visitors' permits without first asking Her Excellency, the president. I'll let you know tomorrow afternoon."

The following afternoon all I learned was that the day after tomorrow there was to be a board meeting to consider my visitor's permit. And the day after the day after tomorrow I was duly notified that the day after the day after the day after tomorrow I might appear at the institution at eleven in the morning.

I was punctually at the gate, which was filled with the imperial beard of a porter, and asked to be admitted. The imperial beard asked me imperiously: "Do you have a permit?"

Whereupon I replied that I had been sent for.

"Are you perhaps the gentleman from the press?"

I was indeed, which gave him cause for unconcealed surprise. "It's for you that I'm standing here," he said, "and the ladies are waiting for you, too."

By "ladies" he most certainly did not mean the wayward girls, for with the ladies who were awaiting me, the board of the institution, there could be no talk either of girls or of anything wayward. They were the female scions of families whose nobility reached back to the days of the Bohemian Amazon war. Big-boned, big-bosomed, big-handed, and big-footed, they rose up before me, and as if so much bigness were not big enough, they had huge ostrich plumes, so-called *pleureuses,* stuck on their heads.

In the midst of this stately virility stood an embarrassed and timid creature, clad in a long black gown; he was the pastor of the institution. In profile he seemed fat, for he carried one belly in front of the other; but when seen head-on, he would have to be described as thin, since his shoulders and his body were narrow. This paunchy-thin priest first introduced himself to me with a kind of curtsey, then Her Excellency, Madam President, the other ladies of the board, and finally the mother superior, who had been so terrified by my telephone call but who had also been relieved of a heavy burden.

We all sat down at a round table. By way of a welcome, the priest rose from his seat, which he had barely occupied, placed in front of himself an alarmingly huge manuscript and began a speech that had been written for me and was directed at me: "Esteemed Editor, may I tell you, in the name of our institution, how gratified we are that a representative of public opinion has grasped the seriousness and benevolence of our moral activities" (at this the ostrich plumes nodded to each other appreciatively), "and wishes to print in his newspaper an article about our institution. At its meeting on 22 February of this year, which had been convened according to statute, our board unanimously approved of this. Before your tour of inspection, my dear sir, I should like to inform you, in just a few words, of the goals and aims of our institution."

His words may have been short enough, but the speech itself was long. It was half a forceful Lenten sermon and half an instructive lecture. It began with the concepts of temptation and seduction. Vice, so I was informed, does not approach earthlings in forbidding form; no cloven hoof and no horns and no odor of pitch and sulfur betrayed the emissary of Lucifer. On the contrary. Vice approaches its victim in a pleasing form, flattering and hypocritical, in order to lure her into its trap.

After the pastor had made this revelation to me, in a loud voice as if he were holding forth in the nave of a church, he stared at me. His look asked: Would you ever have thought such a thing possible?

Till then I had never really given any thought to the methods of vice and, consequently, had also not imagined that it would be recognizable by horns and a devil's tail and its presence made known by the stench of hell. But because I saw the gaze of the speaker, who had momentarily paused, directed at me in expectation of an answer, I replied by shaking my head in disbelief, as if saying: Is what is being reported here about the perfidy of vice really true?

Yet, it had to be true, since all the ostrich plumes around me nodded in agreement. And so I let every doubt slowly vanish from my face.

Satisfied, the pastor resumed his speech: "But this agreeable form of vice is nothing but a deception, nothing but a disguise, nothing but a mask. Woe to its poor victims, woe especially to the young girls who willingly allow themselves to be led astray by it and give themselves . . ."

His female auditors grew alarmed, but fortunately the speaker went on to say that they give themselves to . . . temptation. "Woe to them," he cried out, "thrice woe! For tell me, what wages do they reap from it? Their only wages are contempt, and this contempt is wholly justified; for they wished to escape from poverty, which is truly no shame, and they wished to escape from work by the sweat of their brows, which is commended to us all by the Scriptures."

At this point the speaker nodded his own approval, and the female ultra-nobility nodded along by the sweat of their own brows.

The stream of speech continued: It was the girls' own pride that led them into evil. Instead of winning the respect of their fellowmen as servant girls or factory workers, they preferred self-indulgence and voluptuousness; instead of wearing the honorable garb of need with pride, they would rather adorn themselves with cheap finery and baubles. But by the same token they cannot be spared disillusionment, "bitter disillusionment, especially in old age"!

I was dumbfounded. Who would have imagined it? But since the ostrich plumes again nodded in affirmation, I suppose I had to believe it too, whether I wanted to or not.

"Even more justified than our contempt for the fallen girls is our contempt for those who seduce them. To whom are we referring?"

My look indicated that I had no idea to whom he was referring.

"We are referring to those depraved men who become involved with girls only for their own pleasure, without any intention of marrying them."

This time it was I who, through vigorous nodding, proclaimed complete agreement with the condemnation of such men. It was a consolation for me now to hear that immorality had found its opponent: "Our institution rises"—and here the speaker's voice rose—"like a fortress"—the speaker's voice rose higher—"like a bulwark"—the speaker's voice rose still higher—"like a bastion against the depravity of today's world. Of course,"—at this point the speaker's voice sank from the heights of the fortress, the bulwark, and the bastion onto the ground of plain facts—"of course, we have not yet achieved victory. The fault lies not with us, the fault lies with the girls themselves. Only a very few come to our walls out of repentance and of their own will. The police and juvenile courts have to bring them to us by force. Imagine, brought by force to the place of their salvation! Some of them who ask to be taken in on their own claim that they are doing it out of a penitent heart, but the truth is otherwise. They seek out our home only because they want to live for a while without having to worry about where their next meal is coming from or because they are ill. Some also come because they believe, falsely, that they are safe from the police with us. What is there to wonder, then, that after they are discharged from here they again throw themselves into the arms of the above-described vice. What am I saying—'arms'; better to say talons, claws, the devil's clutches!

"But never again will we let ourselves be deflected by such a failure from the path of moral improvement, for Christ had taken pity on the penitent from Magdala and had led her up the steps of holiness.

"We want to do the same as our Lord did, and our motto is 'ora et labora' ['pray and work']. 'Ora' stands first, commandingly. We hold prayers here in the morning and at noon, at vespers and in the evening, and during the work hours, which our charges must strictly observe. No misguided leniency prevails in our house of penitence. We impose the strictest punishments, for it is also written: 'Whosoever loves his children, chastises them.' And so we educate with strength and prayer and labor, that labor the fruits of which we sell for pious churchly purposes. Amen."

With that the pastor ended his speech and looked around the circle, which rewarded him with applause from all the ostrich plumes. Then he fixed his eyes on me. I did everything I could to convince him that I was shaken by his revelations.

Her Excellency, Madam President, now took the floor to announce that we would next make the rounds of the workrooms, living quarters, and chapel. "We have also put together an exhibition of feminine needlework expressly for our honored guest." The honored guest was none other than myself. Her Excellency, Madam President, expressed the hope that the honored guest would recognize in this crocheting, knitting, and embroidery the energy of the supervisory staff and would appropriately praise it.

"By all means, by all means," I promised.

With these final words of mine, the reception ceremony ended according to plan and we proceeded through a long corridor, the ladies of the board in the lead, followed by the pastor, and then me. On the way, the pater whispered to me that this was the first time that he had ever spoken before the press. He handed me his manuscript and explained to me how important it was for the speech to be published *in extenso* and to make sure that his name was printed correctly.

When we entered the workroom, some thirty girls got up demurely from their seats and expressed a pious greeting in a drawn-out chorus. "Forever and ever, amen," we answered.

"Here you see first . . . ," Her Excellency, Madam President, began explaining to me, when Fanny Melker recognized me.

"Hi, Egon," she called out.

"Egon's here," resounded on all sides as the girls came running up to me. The hatcheck girl from the Café Montmartre embraced me and kissed me out of sheer joy at seeing me again. Leaning over her, the tall Mitzi, known as Cookie, stretched out her hand. "Let me have a cigarette, will you, we don't get any here." "How's my gunner," shouted Liesl, the darling of the artillery, "is the rascal all cured yet?" Another one ordered me: "Say hi to the guys at the Brasilia Bar and tell them that Hansi Waschblau will be back with them in two weeks at the most."

As embarrassed as I was by these greetings, the ladies of the board were considerably more so. They might just as well have found shelter for fallen girls in a cuckoo house.

The first to regain her speech was Her Excellency, Madam President. In a tone as frosty as the cold of Greenland, with outrage as lofty as a mountain peak, and contempt as deep as the sea, she turned to me and said: "My dear sir, you need not trouble yourself further, since all the rooms here are so similar."

I was herewith dismissed, but I wrote down everything as I experienced it. My report made for bad blood, bad blue blood. Some aristocratic families canceled their subscriptions to our paper. But others enjoyed the joke, and a Berlin publishing house accepted it for an anthology of world humor.

It was this visit to the Prague home for wayward girls that I was reminded of a generation later by the title of the prize-winning Hamburg story, announced in all the German newspapers. For a moment it occurred to me that Hanns ut Hamm's work might in some way have been influenced by my experience. But I immediately rejected the notion, for whatever else anyone could get out of the description of my visit back then, in no way could it be the indigenous humor and wit of the German seacoast.

After the prize-winner received his certificate and the thousand marks from the Nazi jury in the banquet hall of the Hamburg Senate amid many fine speeches, and the masterpiece of humor was read aloud to thunderous laughter, "this delightful specimen of unfalsified humor of the seacoast reminiscent of Fritz Reuter's stories and still coarser works" appeared in the newspapers of Hitler's Germany.

My friends, I simply didn't believe my own eyes. It was literally my Prague home for wayward girls. Hanns ut Hamm merely transposed it to Hamburg and the Low German dialect, and introduced one small but effective change in my text—instead of the fallen angels greeting me as "Egon," he has them calling out "Hanns" instead.

I wanted to give those colleagues of mine who had remained in Germany something to think about by writing about this award bestowed on me by the

Nazis in our newspaper *Schriftsteller.* But the *Schwarze Korps* [*Black Corps*], the organ of the SS, got the jump on me. They had discovered the source of the story and threw a fit. Certainly it wasn't the matter of the literary theft that made the blood of the *Black Corps* boil on 6 May 1939 but rather the "shameless smuggling of a typical alien train of thought into National Socialist folkways."

The idea of National Socialist leaders gathering solemnly for the purpose of "honoring some rootless and decadent scribbler whose books had already been appropriately burned on our first stake" filled the *Black Corps* with acknowledged feelings of the deepest humiliation. It demanded that the new author of my old article be immediately taken into custody "so that Hanns ut Hamm should learn *once and for all* the price of slipping into Egon Erwin Kisch's worn-out shoes and starting to Jew around in Low German dialect . . ."

After the results of this prize competition, the efforts to create a Nazi literature were again abandoned.

Egon Erwin Kisch, "Magdalenenheim," "Marktplatz der Sensationen," *Marktplatz der Sensationen. Entdeckungen in Mexiko* (Berlin and Weimar: Aufbau-Verlag, 1993), 6th ed., 241–48.

The Chief of the Prague Detectives

"Old Lederer," the chief of the Prague police detectives, filled out his pension application in the security department on 30 March 1909, delivered it today, and from tomorrow on will no longer accept any assignments. For the first time in thirty-eight years (except for periods of illness that he had to endure last year). He has done his service and is now going into retirement. The announcement will arouse the interest of all those who know him—and the number of those who know him is immense. Only a few perhaps view his departure from his post with regret. He was intensely disliked. An aura analogous to what centuries earlier surrounded the hangman also enveloped him, the "informer," the "spy," the "snoop." People always used the same words to describe him when they drew a companion's attention to old Lederer strolling along the sidewalk at night, holding his cane and hands behind his back, bent forward, eyes on patrol. They had worse names for him in the dives. But no one dared throw them in his face. People respected the old man.

As soon as they saw him from a distance, repeat offenders and professional sleepwalkers disappeared around the corner in the greatest possible haste. And when, around four or five in the morning, he put in an appearance at such pubs as The Sign of the Wreath, The Three Little Stars, The Gold Doubloon, Chocolate's, At the Frog's, and Banzett's, regular guests of both sexes who were sleeping on the tables, on the benches, or on the floor jumped up, as if the commanding general of a guard detachment had surprised them playing cards. The drowsy eyes of the night owls looked timidly at the

Dreaded One, and with feigned obsequiousness he was greeted on all sides with "Ruku líbám, milostpane" ["Good day, sir"]. Everyone knew him. But he also knew everyone. His gaze cut through the smoke-filled premises. Immediately he spotted someone who had been expelled from Prague permanently. He nodded to him and without permitting a word of opposition, he takes the Prague enthusiast along with him to the next officer on duty. Or he observes someone he's never seen before: "You're R.S.!" He had formed a mental picture of R. S. from the words of a wanted poster and now recognized the person sought. That was his specialty; was it intuition or routine?

His unpopularity in criminal circles would have assured him sympathy in the circles of those citizens who lived according to the law had it not been for the fact that Detective Inspector Lederer also couldn't resist getting involved—because of the call of duty—in a sphere where interference on the part of inquisitive officials is justifiably treated with hostility by the general public: the sphere of politics. It was on account of this aversion to "informing" in politics that old Lederer had to suffer the most. During the recent cemetery riot he was recognized in the vicinity of Spinka by a group of Czech-national socialists and was threatened. The Social Democrats undertook legal proceedings against him, and on one occasion the zealous secret policeman was given a good beating even by the German side. And, to add insult to injury, on German soil. That was on Sunday, 12 July 1897.

The Austrian authorities had banned the Eger National Day[1] but achieved nothing by doing so, since the participants marched in droves on the nearby Bavarian town of Waldsassen in order to hold discussions and make decisions there without being heard or disturbed by any "district commissar." But among the higher-ups there was an even greater interest in the gathering on the other side of the black-and-yellow border post and so—enter Herr Lederer in Waldsassen, a cornflower in his buttonhole, as the persistent Universal German. But he was recognized, and he, who had wanted to find out something, found more than he could handle. He also made countless trips on political spy missions, but on these occasions must have been spared a mishap à la Waldsassen, since only that one tragicomic incident became known. Among other things, Inspector Lederer functioned as the eye of the law on trips by visiting rulers throughout the entire Austro-Hungarian Monarchy and snooped along the tracks of Wilhelm the Talkative, King Edward, and King Milan the Erstwhile Merrymaker of

Serbia.[2] The Order of the Sun or Lion was even bestowed on him in gratitude for protecting the ruler of Persia from possible harm.

He had performed good service in the ferreting out of criminals. Admittedly, he knew as little about modern criminal procedure—about fingerprint identification, anthropometry, cephalic measurement, measuring crosses, scars and pockmark quantification, and the rest of the instruments of the Bertillon system—as his clients did about honesty.[3] But he knew his Prague, Vineyards, and Žižkov burglars by the way the burglary was carried out. And he knew how to find them. Especially in the Josefstadt, which before its cleanup had been the home of the Prague Mafia, Lederer was familiar with every hideout—he had been the head of the police station there for many years—and knew every single inhabitant, male and female, in the countless bars by name.

But even in better society the detective inspector's intuition didn't desert him. He was no one to be taken in by elegance and a worldly manner. Thus on one occasion he randomly arrested a well-dressed gentleman in a coffeehouse simply because he was guzzling champagne and throwing money around. The gentleman protested. But old Lederer couldn't be put off. In the security department they wanted to haul him on the carpet for arresting someone without probable cause. However, when the provenance of his money was investigated, it turned out that the arrested man was operating a bogus telegraph office in Nusle, from which he remitted and withdrew money. This man's name—Plocek—has since entered the annals of postal fraud.

"I saw at once that he hadn't worked hard for his money," old Lederer said when he received the bonus for his catch.

He was on the scene of all murders committed in recent years: the Omladinist[4] Mrwa; the jeweler Gollerstepper; the girls Hruza and Klima in the Polna woods; the hotel keeper Wolf; the pair of lovers Takacz-Hanzely in Krtsch; the schoolgirl Smrček; Schaněl, the doorman of the Museum of Trade and Commerce; the prison guard Kaucky; and the newlywed Frau Novotny in Böhmerwaldgasse. He was always one of the first on the trail. Sometimes with luck; sometimes without luck. His name became a commonplace in the reports on Prague criminal cases. It is therefore fitting to take note of the fact that today's date is that of the day when old Lederer stops attending to his duties.

Egon Erwin Kisch, "Der Chef der Prager Detektive," "Aus Prager Gassen und Nächten," *Aus Prager Gassen und Nächten. Prager Kinder. Die Abenteuer in Prag* (Berlin and Weimar: Auf-bau-Verlag, 1975), 43–46.

1. Eger is a commercial center in West Bohemia, Czech Republic, near the Bavarian border. The Eger National Day commemorated the town's incorporation into Bohemia in 1322 by John of Luxemburg and was a rallying point for Czech nationalism.

2. A reference to Milan Obrenovich, who ruled as Serbian king from 1882 to 1889. His scandalous private life became public knowledge.

3. The Bertillon system was the first modern system of criminal identification. It was named for the French criminologist Alphonse Bertillon (1853–1914), who developed it.

4. A member of Omladina, the "Young Czech" political party.

Scenes from Dives:
In the Omnibus on the Night of the Murder

She fled her mad pursuer from the back alleys of the Old Town into the flood of light, into the Ferdinandstrasse, which she usually never dared enter in the middle of the night. Here she thought she was safe from her jealous lover's attacks of rage. But hardly had she set foot within the orbit of the incandescent lights when the butcher knife penetrated her throat unerringly and fatally. Her body described a wide arch as it plunged to the pavement and twice lurched up convulsively. Before passersby grasped the horror of what had happened, the murderer had already plunged the knife six times into his own chest. Both bodies were taken to the morgue. In the gray-yellow face of the dead woman, over which the green headband had slipped, a policeman recognized Kotab from the Omnibus pub in the Small Ring. Another officer had been sent to the dive and there corroborated that the murdered woman was indeed Karoline Kotab. Now the atmosphere of murder and death has intruded on the apathy of this bar.

A long room barely two and a half meters wide, the light vault of the ceiling—one can truly imagine himself seated in the inside of an omnibus. Once that may have been an honorable name, in the period when traveling in a carriage was something elegant. Nowadays the name would have to be different, if it were going to have a noble ring to it—at least "automobile." The walls must have been brown earlier; now they are covered with black, cloudlike spots, the fallout of dirt and smoke. The narrow room has space for just two thin tables, set at a distance from each other of barely a foot; all the guests sit next to each other, like at a bar. The musicians are down below. A baldheaded violinist with hollow cheeks and twitching eyelashes; a thickset accordion player with hair combed down way over his eyes; and an elderly guitar player whose nose and cheeks have shiny places. The row of extra guests follows hard on the band. Pockmarked, brutalized women. And men whom you can see creeping behind them in the alleyways at night.

For a moment conversation dies down when I enter the premises. But I greet a one-legged party girl by her nickname, the Czech greeting "Tě bůh, Revoluce" ["Hi there, Revoluce"] legitimizes me sufficiently, and conversation picks up again. A pockmarked beauty sobs to a side: "She was a hussy; she deserved what she got ten times over. But it's a shame about Jarda."

"Who knows if he's dead," a gigantic recruit comforts the girl. His overcoat is much too small for him; a one-year volunteer is probably still pining for it.

"He's dead," says a frail man without a brow. "They've already taken him to pathology; I know it for a fact."

"All you ever know is crap, you twisted pretzel," the soldier yells at him, and the man without a brow shudders nervously.

"A pity about him! I just can't help crying." The pockmarked one says it.

"You must have mixed your tears with salt in a tub, you're so sensitive you are, dearie," the unbelievably fat waitress Žanda calls to her. She was trying to direct the conversation into a more cheerful channel.

But the pockmarked blonde wouldn't let herself be yanked out of her sentimental mood. "He was a great guy . . ." And then, after a tear-filled pause, she began humming: "Co dělá má žena [What's my wife doing] . . . That was his song!"

"Yeah, that was his all right," confirms the one-legged Katty Revoluce and then shouts to the musicians: "Violin player, play your instrument!"

Accordion, guitar, and violin strike up and everyone present joins in singing the murderer's favorite song:

> What's my wife doing,
> When I'm not at home?
> What's my wife doing,
> When I stay away.

She sits by the window
And calls to the fishermen:
"My husband left today!"

"She always said that one day a lover would get even with her for all the others."

Her head leaning on the edge of the table, Frau Broum, the most defiant of all the women assigned to the Prague morals police, had until now been sleeping soundly. She's called Remiška now, since her present lover is that Herr Remiš who with expert hand and a pocketknife held flat makes a living in Prague nightclubs cutting out sculpted flowers on calling cards and beautifully curved signatures on writing paper and postcards. Frau Broum-Remiška rises from sleep: "Night before yesterday I grabbed a butcher knife away from Jarda, since he wanted to stab Karla in front of the Green Frog. I just happened to be hanging around there then, and when I heard her screaming, I ran over—and in no time I had the knife. Show the knife, Žaninka."

Žaninka, the popular waitress Žanda, who was called by this diminutive pet name, opens the cigar box and holds up a large butcher knife. "Yesterday he wanted it back from me. He was going to go to work today, he told me. Then come pick it up early, I said to him. OK, he answered, if need be I can get by with my jackknife."

"He was a fool for getting involved with her," the pretzel man says, "she was a lot older than he was. She was twenty-six and he was twenty-one."

"Who told you he was twenty-one, you scoundrel?" Remiška yells at the shrinking pretzel man. "He was twenty-five. I ought to know. I'm from the same village. That was his misfortune, that he came from Laz. Melichar, the pub owner from Leonhardiplatz, also comes from Laz, and all the other Laz people were with him on Christmas Eve. Kotab worked as a waitress there at the time, and that's where they fell in love. Jarda dished out four guldens there! He even paid for me. I won't forget that. He was a great guy!"

A very young fellow with a vacant expression, who was sitting near the door snuggling up to some girl, remarked: "When Jarda gets better, I'll help him out in court."

"How you going to do that?" Herr Novaček, the proprietor of the Omnibus, asks him.

"Well, I'll go to the court and say that Jarda's a fine fellow. A good word means a lot."

"You ass, they'd really take you seriously! You'll be out of there as soon as you show your face." Laughter breaks out on all sides. The girl blushes; she's embarrassed by her lover's stupidity. The fellow wants to appease everyone now and says quite naively: "Well, if that's the way it is, then I won't go."

An enormous guy, the director of the puppet theater in the Josefi Market in the Old City Ring, calls the waitress over: "Žanda, let me have a look at the knife."

"Oh yeah, I'll hand over the knife to you, all right, you big bull! Right away we'd have another funeral."

"By the way, when is the funeral?" Everyone wants to know when the funeral is going to take place. "The whole Omnibus has to turn out, and Nana Gulasch has to carry the banner."

Nana Gulasch, a gray-haired drunk, who had just come in, yells back at the soldier: "I'll tear you to shreds and carry you as the banner."

"You yourself'll be lying on a slab before then," the soldier replies. "Then you can really have a look at the lovers."

Everyone laughs, and the pockmarked sentimentalist, whose tears had already dried, tosses a cigarette butt at Nana Gulasch. "You can take it with you for Jarda."

The mood has changed. People are laughing and making fun of the murder and the supposed suicide of Turek. I pay and get up. Remiška points to my beer mug, from which I had taken only a swallow from the least-used place, back near the handle.

"Can I finish it?"

"Sure."

She thanks her benefactor.

Egon Erwin Kisch, "Die Mordnacht im 'Omnibus,'" "Szenen aus Spelunken," *Prager Kinder,* in *Aus Prager Gassen und Nächten. Prager Kinder. Die Abenteuer in Prag* (Berlin and Weimar: Aufbau-Verlag, 1975), 221–25.

On Pubs and Their Guests:
Dramaturgy of the Flea Theater

In cheap nightclubs you often come across people who do not earn "honorable" bourgeois livelihoods but nevertheless do not earn their money in some dishonest way. People born with some talent who aren't suited for the track of ordinary life. So they derail themselves, and the course of their lives runs along side roads. But just imagine that in some peaceful street you suddenly encounter a railway. You'd shake your head angrily; at the very least you'd stare in wonder at it. That's what the derailed people understand. And because they have no desire to be the cause of any angry head-shaking or astonished stares, these bashful originals go among people as little as possible during the day and venture out into the light of day, so to say, only at night. At night the philistinism of humanity is not so assertive; people tend to show those of odd professions an inquisitive understanding. Often you can find a whole assembly's worth of colleagues of such rare talents together—silhouette cutters, market hawkers, chantant directors, fair acrobats, instant portrait artists, conjurers, weather forecasters, couplet singers, mind readers, harmonica virtuosos, eccentric dancers, and similar artists.

By all means the most interesting of these Prague figures is *Ferda Mestek de Podskal,* since he has not sustained his adventurous life just by one of these curious ways of earning a living but rather has pursued all imaginable professions. "You've already been everything, Ferda," his friends sometimes remark after he's recounted some episode from his life in his usual jovial way. At which he protests quite matter-of-factly: "No, no! I haven't been a midwife yet."

Since no genealogical handbook gives the birthdate of this whimsical aristocrat, here you have his curriculum vitae short and to-the-point:

Ferdinand Mestek, whom the Prague Flaming Guild later honored with tax-free hereditary nobility and the title "de Podskal" for his contributions to art and learning, was born on—or, better said—in water. He came into the world as the son of the Prague master tailor of the same name on 17 March 1853 during the great flood when the tides of the Moldau River had overflowed the Podskal workshop and residence of Mestek the tailor. Fortunately, soldiers of the corps of engineers, using a pontoon, succeeded in rescuing the tailor, his wife, his five daughters, and the hereditary prince, whose birth had been announced by cannon shots from the XIX Bastion. (The assertion that the occasion for these shots was the flood is a perfidious slander.) From this the first day of his life, little Mestek began to hate water, which had sought to destroy his still-innocent existence, and to this very day still can't comprehend that many people regard this uncongenial fluidness as something to be enjoyed.

After the flood, Mestek senior hastily rented a new apartment at the corner of Ferdinandstrasse and Charvatgasse and began hemming seamlessly. His one and only son was also supposed to take up tailoring, but Ferda aimed higher. He wanted to become a scholar and at an early age grew interested in zoology. He crawled into the garden of the convent of Our Lady of the Snows, roamed all around the grounds on the Vyšehrad, and examined the entire Scharka for all manner of animal life—mice, hedgehogs, salamanders, caterpillars, slowworms, and beetles—with whose help he turned his father's apartment into a menagerie. At night he shut the animals up in a wooden box; during the day he allowed them as much freedom of movement as possible (please note his presentiment of the Hagenbeck[1] system). Only once did he forget to put away a hedgehog in its night quarters. It crawled into the bed of one of Ferda's aunts and onto auntie herself. A terrible outcry, a sound thrashing, the closing down of the little zoo, and stern warnings were the consequences of the unfortunate omission. Since Ferda nonetheless did not respect the ban and kept on dragging various mammals and reptiles back home with him, he was given a sound thrashing by his father every morning. This punishment became a daily exercise. "Why are you beating me; I didn't do anything," he howled once during the bastinado. However he got this answer: "That doesn't matter; you'll be up to more pranks even before the day is out." That was a prediction that held good for Ferda Mestek's whole life. Hardly a day passed without him committing some prank.

When Ferda was ten years old, his father died, and he became an apprentice to the goldsmith Held, on Purkyněstrasse. He was delighted, since learning how to work gold seemed miraculous to him. But it didn't amount to anything. His activity was limited to looking after the master's children, chopping wood, and helping out Frau Held in the kitchen. It was from this period that he derived his knowledge of cooking, which he often boasts about. But no one ever has taken him up on any of his invitations to a home-cooked lunch. He had plodded along this way for seven years, but as well-versed in the Bible as he was, he believed that seven full years had to follow. Without knowing a word of German, he set out in 1875 to travel through Germany. He went to Bavaria, then Baden, followed by Alsace-Lorraine, finally reaching even France. He found respectable employment along the way as a cattle drover, a swing pusher, and a carousel operator. He no longer had to make the trip home on foot; he could now travel by rail and was in fact transported from Paris to Prague via Schub. After returning to Prague, he found a position as an enameler with the Lokesch Company on Ziegenplatz. And when the Bohemian garnet industry reached its stride, he got a job in a garnet cutting shop on the basis of his seven-year work with a goldsmith. Although he had concealed the fact that he did only servant's work at the jeweler's, his lack of experience was quickly discovered and he was graciously dismissed.

But then a position came his way which with one blow made him popular in the fast set of the bottom ten thousand of Prague. He became the dancing master at the Hetzinsel Restaurant and there organized, among other things, winegrowers' festivals with beer, masquerades without masks, ladies' evenings just with men, men's evenings just with women, but at the big rags-and-tatters balls there were real rags and tatters present. At Mestek's big affairs at the Hetzinsel, three bands played, sometimes simultaneously, and whoever was not drunk on beer or love all but lost his senses from the philharmonic concert of the three egoistically playing orchestras. The men were active, the ladies heated up, and the garden was big and shaded; why should the Hetzinsel dances have lacked customers?

But dancing master Mestek de Podskal himself began dancing the quadrille, which from time immemorial Amor is used to arranging. Herr

Mestek became the seducer of a pretty servant girl from Moravia, and married her, and she may have been the one who pulled him away from the fickle and temptation-rich trade of dancing master and induced him to become an honest and settled merchant. And so he became—a fairgrounds grocer and roamed at Frau Anna's side from city to city, from fair to fair, selling a cold lemonade in bottles as a cure-all for cholera, an infallibly helpful soap for gout, and other kinds of things which he knew how to push with all the persuasiveness of an old-time snake-oil salesman. After the swindled customers and the authorities put an end to his flourishing trade, he returned to Prague.

He then established himself in the ghetto as a hawker. It happened to be the time of the Jewish Passover holiday. Mestek saw macaroons displayed in the baker's window and hence also displayed macaroons. But nobody bought them. He asked around and learned that the Jews bought macaroons only in shops approved by the head rabbinical council, and that the macaroons had to be baked according to ritual regulation, which means that only unleavened macaroons could be sold. But Mestek the grocer was not one to be easily deterred. He asked a particularly promising lad from the Josefstadt named Friedl Brod (Brod is now a waiter and renowned because of his skill at drumming entire operas with his fingers on two metal plates) to get him such a certificate. Little Brod then skillfully removed one from the door of a bakery and brought it to his client, who quickly put it up. But the swindle was detected even quicker and the notice removed. "Alas, not before twenty Jewish children had committed the mortal sin of eating some of my macaroons," Ferda remarks sadly when he recounts the episode.

But the merchant Mestek could console himself over this setback insofar as his business flourished despite it. All his goods found a ready market, and even the bakery items, which were already five weeks old, went like fresh bread. Nevertheless, there was a catch to the whole thing. All his customers bought on credit; no one paid cash, and the company of "Ferd. Mestek" went bankrupt.

"Ferdo," his wife Anna, deeply grieved, said to her husband, "Ferdo, you have nothing but bad luck in this world! If you ran a funeral parlor, I swear, no one would ever die. And if you already delivered a coffin on order, the next day the dead person would return it and say 'I just seemed to be dead.'"

From this day on Ferda Mestek de Podskal resumed his career as a traveling salesman. He first became an innkeeper at various expositions, and he is very proud of the fact that at the military show in the Vienna Rotunda in 1894 Emperor Franz Josef once visited his establishment "and drank the swill I was serving as Pilsner beer." The end result was always that Ferda Mestek's business went kaput. Finally, he was no longer able to raise the rent necessary for his participation in further expositions.

He thus became an impresario, and as the travel companion of an assortment of monstrosities and shows acquired a dubious renown for the merry swindles that he pulled off from one end of Europe to the other.

The big impresario began with something small—with fleas. Who put this flea in his ear, we have no idea. Any more than the great Delft microscopist, Antony von Leeuwenhoek, in E. T. A. Hoffmann's *Master Flea* can come up with a satisfying answer to George Pepusch's question as to why after his death he opened a flea theater in Berlin instead of lying quietly in his grave in the Delft Cathedral the way a proper corpse is supposed to or at least pursuing his original profession of manufacturing magnifying glasses and lenses. Or any more than Mephisto can illuminate the honorable guests in Auerbach's cellar as to the reasons for the king's loving the young flea as his own son. These little, bloodsucking creatures seem, therefore, to possess a demonic power that enables them to subdue strong natures. Hence Ferdinand von Mestek most likely decided also to become a flea tamer.

Back in his room, with all the precision of the goldsmithing acquired in the kitchen, he fabricated a series of filigree carriages, omnibuses, bicycles, and even cannons, since it was his intention to bring an artillery battery into play, as only well-trained artillery can help bring about the victory of a respectable flea theater as well as of a respectable army. After putting together the resources he needed for his stage, he began to hire his staff. He placed an ad in the paper to the effect that he was prepared to pay ten Austrian kreuzers for each flea. However, he was looking for "only human fleas from a good family." In order to make it easy for vendors to find their way to his residence, he put a huge poster with the words "Fleas purchased here" on the front entrance of the house as well on that of the Hetzinsel Restaurant, where from the time of his engagement as a tolerant dance arranger of balls he stood in high esteem. The plaque on the front of his house was the occasion for the first battle Ferdinand de Mestek had to endure in his new profession. The other tenants of his building felt offended and assembled in groups in the courtyard, on the stairwell, and in the hallways to take a firm, and menacing, stand against living in the same house with fleas and being taunted by everyone that they were living in the "flea palace." They also complained that Mestek had no permit to train fleas and no theater concession, that he was paying no tax for keeping domestic animals, and that what he wanted to do represented outright cruelty to animals. The landlord placed himself at the head of the outraged, but the waves of revolt broke on the torrent of words of Mestek's wife. Frau Anna, who later, thanks to her intercession on her husband's behalf among various officials, earned the name of "scourge of the authorities," drove everyone into flight with the power of her speech.

Shortly thereafter, the flea sellers showed up. New problems! Mestek had expressly stated in his ad that the creatures should be kept in dry bottles, but very few heeded his request. Most of them brought their booty in liquor bottles. Ferda Mestek declared that these specimens were intoxicated from the smell of the alcohol and had become prey to alcoholism for all time. He had no use for boozers in his troupe. Other sellers had brought their living goods in Seidlitz Powder boxes. Mestek diagnosed that these creatures would suffer from diarrhea the rest of their little lives, and he refused to purchase them. Since they had no desire to drag the vermin back home again, the disappointed sellers let the clever merchant have the creatures that they had arduously tracked down, for nothing.

A woman from the market brought twenty-five living fleas in a properly dry bottle and asked for a bounty of two guldens and fifty kreuzer. Well, that was not such a tough problem for the future circus director. He put his plain glass pince-nez on his nose and, ostentatiously shaking his head, began examining the creatures one after the other:

"My dear woman, where on earth did you get these? They're all just females! I can't use them. The females have hindquarters like Lippizaner stallions. That's why they can't jump. You'll have to take them back."

The old woman was completely taken aback and was so upset she didn't know herself if she was male or female. She chased the twenty-five fleas around the house, she said, and saw that they could jump . . .

"Of course they can jump. All fleas and all humans can jump, but that doesn't mean they can perform in the circus. Female fleas aren't qualified for the circus."

At this point there wasn't any more the old woman could say in favor of the fleas, and she just expressed her genuine astonishment that, without exception, she had captured fleas of the gentle sex. Well, one thing may be true: from time immemorial only female beings have clung to her husband and especially those who weren't any good. "Couldn't you at least give me a couple of kreuzer for the lot of them?"

Finally, Ferda Mestek offered to pay ten kreuzer for the entire herd so that the woman wouldn't have made the trip for nothing. The saleswoman took the ten kreuzer, Ferda Mestek the twenty-five beautiful fleas and laughed up his sleeve.

Then a maid came with two bottles of the contents requested in the advertisement. She works for Fräulein von T., and the fleas come from her. "They're elegant little animals," the visitor eagerly extolled them, "the most aristocratic creatures; they drink only blue blood . . . Once I put one of them on my own arm. You think it bit me? It didn't occur to it. Well, you know, our mistress is scented with perfume and has tasty blood, since she's always sucking on mints and lives just on sweets, and . . ."

Ferda Mestek looked at the creatures. "They've gone completely daffy from the perfume. They're not even moving!"

"What's wrong with you?" cried the quickwitted donna. "They're just sleeping now. You ought to see how they behave at night. They carry on so much in my lady's bed that no one there can catch a wink of sleep, such rascals they are."

"I'm afraid I can't do anything with them if they're so cosseted that they sleep all day long. My biggest source of income comes from the afternoon performances, after all."

"Fine," replied the ostensible lady's maid of the noble Fräulein von T. and handed the presumptive flea tamer the other bottle. "The ones here haven't been coddled; they're my own, you know. Just have a good look at them; don't they look like Pinzgauer horses? You could hitch them up right away to the heaviest carriage, that's how strong and healthy they are. Sometimes they shake my body so that I'm afraid of falling over."

Ferda Mestek was quick to gallantly assure her that he liked the contents of the second bottle a lot better and that he was indeed ready to round up additional wild fleas of the same provenance. He could manage that handily, and compared to him Buffalo Bill was an outright bungler in the art of the hunt. The girl was satisfied, but no sooner had she begun to unbutton her blouse when Frau Anna appeared on the scene. At which point the fearless hunter grew small, very small, a lot smaller than a flea.

The next vendor who arrived, the proprietress of an inn, brought the smallest quantity: only two of the carnivores of the insect world. But they became the heroines of Mestek's flea theater: the Siamese twins Lo and Hedda, of whom the older had black eyes and the younger deep-blue ones, which Ferdinand Mestek de Podskal never failed to mention at his any of his appearances.

When in the evening the future theater director counted the heads of his darlings he saw that there were three hundred of them; he had therefore hired more personnel than he had originally intended. But the wages were small, the workers good, and Herr Mestek was thoroughly pleased. He was just about to leave the room to take down the company sign from the front door when a drunk staggered into the building, swinging a bottle of fleas in his hand.

"The acceptance period has already ended," Ferda immediately dismissed him.

But the drunk didn't withdraw. "Man," he yelled, "I captured eighty-five of them, so I've got to get eight guldens fifty kreuzer. I'll let you have them for eight guldens, a real deal for you."

"Too late, my dear friend."

"Hey, fellah, I chased around the whole night before I got the company together. A hundred times I had to drink up for strength and now you're spurning my soldiers? You've got to recruit them; you advertised for them."

"If you had just come earlier."

The tippler began bawling that he was being cheated, that he had put in a lot of effort and deserved compensation, at least a gulden, or otherwise he'd tear the place apart.

"Not a red cent," Frau Anna joined in the conversation.

"Shut your mouth," the souse bellowed, "and don't mix into business matters I've got to settle with the director, you stupid bitch!"

Frau Anna resolutely grabbed the offender and started to push him out of the room. She succeeded in doing it, but she wasn't able to prevent the drunk from hurling the bottle on the floor with all his might. The glass shattered and the company deserted in all directions. A flea chase began compared to which that of the pious Johannes Fischart was an idyll, but the woman again triumphed—Frau Anna captured most of the loafers beneath her skirt.

The future tamer removed several sand fleas and dog fleas from the troupe that he hadn't recognized as such inferior specimens in the big crush, divided the troupe into solo, orchestra, and chorus members, set aside a bottle as a domicile for the extras, and then began the feeding and training of the little beasts of prey.

We know that the members of a human theater are difficult to handle. What does that imply then for a troupe that without exception descends from the family of *pulcidae irritans?* They are even more an erratic, biting stage bunch of an utterly bloodsucking nature. Nobody is spared their jabs and they are addicted to drink. But Director Mestek knew how to get along with them.

He first addressed the matter of their feeding. He shook the fleas into a bottle containing dried wood shavings at the bottom and had a wide neck at the top. This wide opening was closed with the flat of the hand; then the bottle was carefully turned upside down, whereupon the little beasts of prey literally began eating out of the hand. They dug their proboscises into the hand and didn't let go until they had drunk their fill. After leaving the trace of a bloody stab, they again fell back on their four-poster bed of wood shavings.

When the feeding was over, the artists entered another container, which the director designated a "rehearsal stage." This was a shallow glass bell, so shallow that the animals had to knock against it if they wanted to give free reign to their jumping impulse.

"Pretty soon I'll get the beasts to stop jumping," Mestek muttered grimly into his beard when he was locking them up in their low-vaulted cell. "After all, I can't go jumping after the little dears. They're so small, and they jump so high. If they were as big as dogs, my heavens, they'd be able to jump over the Powder Tower."

A few days later the dressing began. With a smallest available dustpan, moistened lightly, the tamer lifted the well-fed little animals out of the bottle one at a time and took it carefully between two fingers of the left hand while holding a trap at the ready in the right hand. This was a tiny loop of silver-plated copper wire attached to a long needle. As soon as the flea began working its way out of the embrace of the fingers, Ferda tossed the wire lasso around its neck with all the virtuosity of a cowboy. With a pair of tweezers, he then carefully tightened the loop above the proboscis, and for the rest of its life the little beast of prey was fettered like prisoners sentenced to Siberia for life to their chains. Ferda Mestek could rein in his troupe in the truest sense of the word.

The roles were now distributed. Some of the little creatures were harnessed to the small carriages and omnibuses. Others (the gunners) were hitched up to the foot of the gun carriage. An old saying goes, "To make a saddle for the rump of a fly is the masterpiece of masterpieces." When he forged saddles for his flea riders, Mestek made such a masterpiece.

The two duelists—this number, which now belongs to the repertoire of all the more serious flea theaters of the world, was discovered by Ferda Mestek —received their small paper sabers, which they had to knock out of each other's "hands."

The dainty damsels received ballet tutus made of silk paper and one of them even an upside-down tutu, so that she appeared to be dancing on her head, which Ferda Mestek vehemently asserted was indeed the case.

He had to employ yet another director's trick when the creatures designated as draft animals did not want to pull their vehicles. He tried moving a magnet underneath the thin tabletop, and it worked. The little carts moved forward together with the reins of solid wire and the harnessed fleas. And it looked exactly as if the fleas were pulling the carriages. During performances Ferda could astonish the audience in no uncertain terms when, at his command, the little vehicles drove zig-zag, or when the draft animals from the insect world stopped at the command "Halt!" and strictly followed the orders "right" or "left." Who could imagine that some kid off the street was perched beneath the table with a horseshoe magnet in his hand? It seemed much likelier that the tamed fleas were endowed with unheard-of intelligence and trained to respond to every nod of their master!

It so happened that at that time the huge American circus, Barnum and Bailey, had rented the big Invalidenplatz in order to put up its tents in time for its impending appearance. Now Ferda Mestek had in mind giving it some competition on the small Invalidenplatz. The idea was that everyone who was planning to visit the Barnum and Bailey circus should first stop by his flea circus. "I'll ruin the American barkers in no time."

But the police official in charge of the district unfortunately did not appreciate the fact that local art was to be given preference over foreign art. "What is it you want to put up?" he asked the master of all fleas.

"A flea theater."

"So it's a theater! Theater concessions for Prague can be granted only by the regional committee after permission has been obtained from the directors of both district theaters. Good-bye!"

Ferda began complaining that he was afraid of a considerable loss of time. "No, no, I'm not going to put up a flea theater. It's going to be a flea circus."

"A circus? Don't you know that the most famous circus in the world is opening on the large Invalidenplatz? You'll just go bankrupt."

"Oho! I'll show the Americans how better I am at humbug."

"Aha, so it's humbug you're up to, is it? Well, you're going to have to answer to me! Most important, you have to set up twenty meters from the edge of the Liebener Landstrasse so that the passageway is kept clear, understand? You'll give me that in writing."

What good did it do poor Ferda to protest that this was going to be his ruination, and that he had been counting on the curiosity of passersby. With a bleeding heart he had to sign the document.

Ferda then built his wooden stall on the very edge of the Landstrasse. The sign read: "The Biggest American Flea Circus in Europe." Beneath it were the words: "Royal Provincial Flea Theater." A poster announced: "352 Artists and 700 Reservists. Performances All Day Long! Two different orchestras: A women's flea orchestra under the direction of Fräulein Anastasia Stich and a Gypsy flea orchestra under the personal direction of Baron Springer."

The first guest who entered the newly erected temple of the muses was the district police official. He was brandishing the note the way Shylock did his. ". . . twenty meters from the edge of the Liebener Landstrasse," he read out menacingly.

"And . . .?" asked Director Mestek naively.

"Is that twenty meters? You're right next to the street, you know!"

"Pardon, sir, did you mean *this* edge? I measured from the other edge over there and the street is exactly twenty-two meters wide. I really could have put up my circus on the Landstrasse. But I thought you'd have plenty on your hands with traffic jams. And I have no intention of causing any high police official any inconvenience when he has been so obliging toward me. I therefore made you a present of the two meters, sir."

The eyes of the Law were laughing tears. "Mestek," the official finally said, "Mestek, you're a first-class con artist! Now I actually believe you'll give P. T. Barnum a run for his money."

The stall remained on the Landstrasse and the theater could begin operations. Like every better stage manager, Mestek also hired a group of applauders; for ten free passes he engaged ten street urchins to deliver genuinely enthusiastic applause. He placed himself before the portals of his homemade palace and summoned people bombastically:

"Mundus, vult, decipi! Three Latin words meaning Come, See, Admire! Never before has learning produced such a triumph as is revealed behind this plain wall. What an astonishing wonder of training, what magnificent fruit of energy can be seen here! Only one man can do all of this, me, Ferda Mestek de Podskal, who possesses nothing other than his noble name and the shining honor of his coat of arms: three boxed ears on a field of red. I have succeeded in educating as human beings the smallest animals, commonly designated in the secular world as 'fleas.' No, I should say instead educating them as artists. They do gymnastics and juggle like the best acrobats and jugglers in the world of humans; they ride as passengers in automobiles and carriages, the chauffeurs and coachmen of which belong to their same tribe; they fence—these bloodthirsty creatures— with foil and Italian saber against each other to the death; they chase out of the ring in full gallop before the audience and ride academy-style on magnificent stallions; they dance modern dances; they exhibit their talent as bicycle stunt riders, tightrope walkers, and high-wire daredevils.

"The star of our ensemble, however, our prima ballerina, is Mademoi-selle Nudelmaier." (At the cue "Nudelmaier" the ten members of the claque within the theater began wildly applauding.) "She was offered the highest wages by other enterprises; even Barnum and Bailey tried to get her so they would have at least one good number in their fraudulent show. But Mademoi-selle Nudelmaier is faithful, as only a ballerina can be, and it would cost her a fortune to break her contract. When she appears, the audience is truly enchanted. They throw her flower arrangements, bouquets, and oranges on stage; recently an admirer in his enthusiasm even threw her a brick because he didn't have anything else with him at the time.

"You hear the heavenly music coming from inside the theater? You think it's a phonograph playing? Wrong! That's our female orchestra, which, under the personal direction of the flea damsel Anastasia Stich, plays during the performance. Fräulein von Stich conducts the most difficult symphonies, Lieder, and dances, pieces that are so weighty that the master weight-lifter Rasso could never lift them off the ground. And the way her hair is done! In the Secessionist style. And her clothes and hats! All the latest cut, Parisian fashion."

After Ferda Mestek de Podskal had thus introduced to P. T. Public the stars of his troupe, he began—exactly according to the model of his competitor, Barnum—to make announcements about his organization and the social facilities of his enterprise:

"We have our own huntsmen, who often have to endure the greatest dangers, since they have to bring their game home alive. Their craft requires special agility, as they have to catch the fleas in flight.

"We have our own sanatoria, our own hospital, our own flea doctors, and our own disability and old-age insurance as well as marriage and death funds.

"While Barnum and Bailey, who arrived from America expressly with the intention of competing with us, boastingly announce that they have engaged 300 artists, we claim no fewer than 352 performing artists as our own, and 700 reservists who are at our disposal. We also have 90 wet nurses with sweet blood; they have to sleep with the fleas and are handsomely paid, since they do not even have Sunday off and so that they cannot say that they are being sucked dry in our service.

"Keep on coming in, ladies and gentlemen, as long as there are seats left. The entry fee is just six kreuzer, half-price to military personnel above the rank of quartermaster. No need to push, ladies and gentlemen, I beg you, no pushing! Please, one at a time, nicely now."

That was the speech he gave, a Prague Theophrastus and Hagenbeck, a Cagliostro and Till Eulenspiegel together, though in flea size. Woe to him who followed the siren call with great expectations! All he saw was some fleas hopping around just like other fleas. When anyone asked about the famous fleas, Herr Ferda or Frau Anna immediately pointed to this or that member of the troupe. The sanatoria, the female orchestra, and so on are in the ring, but entry there is forbidden because of the mortal danger. A peasant went up to Mestek and demanded his money back.

"I went around twice and didn't see a damned thing."

"What? You went around twice? You owe me another ten kreuzer."

The peasant began complaining, but Frau Anna threw him out, and Ferda announced to the public outside that the man wasn't satisfied with one tour and without paying any more would have gladly gaped at the wonders another ten times.

An elderly woman remained in her seat after the "show" closed, waiting for the next and the one after that, all the while sobbing her heart out.

"Are you crying because you're touched at how talented these tiny creatures are?" the flea director asked proudly as he approached the old woman.

"Oh, no, that's not what I'm crying about. I'm crying because of the money I had to pay to get in . . ."

Egon Erwin Kisch, "Dramaturgie des Flohtheaters," "Von Beisln und ihren Gästen," *Die Abenteuer in Prag,* in *Aus Prager Gassen und Nächten. Prager Kinder. Die Abenteuer in Prag,* 493–509. Although a scarcely believable character, Ferda Mestek de Podskal was no invention by Kisch. For a little more background on the character in English, see Angelo Maria Ripellino, *Magic Prague,* 221–22.

1. A reference to Karl Hagenbeck (1844–1913), a well-known authority on animals and an animal dealer. In 1907 he established a zoo in Stellingen, near Hamburg, which became the model for zoos in which animals are exhibited in moated, open-air enclosures rather than in cages and pits.

Kisch at the front during World War I,
March 1915. The man to his right is a
Russian prisoner.
Courtesy Museum of National Literature,
Prague.

Episodes from the Serbian Front, 1914

The day before yesterday I wrote as far as the word "flank." I covered the largest part during the halts in the march; the last sentences I tried to write shorthand on the front line. The men around me fixed their gazes on the near ground; I looked there too, nervously wincing after I wrote each word, anxiously watching in the direction of the enemy.

Silver streaks were whistling around us; every moment one of the shells that were chasing each other struck the small mound of earth that everyone had piled up with his hands for protection. Almost everyone's life had been saved by the ration kit he had shoved in front of his face. The sacks have holes in them, bullets lodge in the winter underwear stored in the sacks, others ricocheted against the full cans of food. How slowly, how laboriously, in what a dangerous situation I wrote the last three sentences the day before yesterday! It was—and is—as if I had to record the peak of cruel, human experience. Two days have passed from the afternoon of the day before yesterday, when I had to interrupt my writing because of an artillery shell that whistled directly over my head and cut down the branch of a tree behind me. Two days whose torment still remains in our limbs and nerves.

To continue: At ten-thirty in the morning our regiment lay under cover on the Austrian bank of the Drina River. Now it was our company's turn to be transported across over pontoons. After groups of twenty men each were counted out, the first lieutenant ordered "Let's go!" and ran over the slope to the river. The company followed in after him with hesitation, because as soon as we were visible, the swarm of enemy shots, which until now had whizzed over the embankment, increased immeasurably. Some of our men drew back under cover when they felt the long trajectories crackling, but a threatening command drove them forward again. The first lieutenant jumped into the boat, which was guided by scouts. Then only about ten men out of the twenty that had been counted off took their places in it. We lay flat on the bottom so as to be shielded by the metal sides of the pontoon.

A terrible, lacerating whimpering, bawling, was audible. I looked over the side of the boat and saw hundreds of our soldiers on the Serbian shore. They were standing in the water up to their knees, thighs, and stomachs, their hands thrust high in the air; their shrieking was a single endless scream, like a madman's raving.

I felt nothing other than a choking incomprehension of this witches' sabbath. I had just one thought: now you yourself are going to cruise over so that in a little while you can be standing in the same place, like the others there, dazed, crippled, or pleading for help.

They were the wounded. They were crying for medics to come to their aid and to be taken back. Hills and woods, which edged the sandy shore of the riverbank, kept on spewing out the injured and those who were supporting them— that species of good Samaritans that emerges in war and helps the wounded to dressing stations in order not to have to advance with the line of battle.

Although we had pushed off at least ten minutes before, we had barely covered twenty meters. The scouts had done almost no rowing. "Should we continue rowing forward?" asked the leader of the scouts. "Obviously!" barked the lieutenant. "You have your orders, don't you?" "Well, yes, but . . ." "They're only wounded," one of us reassured the gondolier, who nevertheless in his dread viewed the scene over there as a retreat and feared the immediate appearance of pursuing Serbs. Resigned, the scout pushed the oar ahead, but his two assistants passively resisted with the back oars with the result that the boat still did not move forward. Only when the first lieutenant brandished his revolver and shouted "Get going!" did we head closer to the shore.

We got only to within about twenty-five paces, since the wounded escapees had plunged into the water to that point and, screaming, wanted to swing onto the pontoon in order to secure a place for the return trip. The boat was so besieged there was no way we could get out. A man without a shirt, who was recognizable as an officer only from his breeches and leather gaiters, kept on shouting: "I have to get back, I have an important message." "You're lying," someone yelled at him. He then disappeared in the direction of another pontoon.

It was impossible to get control over the others who were trying to seize our boat, so we alighted from it and were now wading in water just above the hips. The current was strong, our equipment heavy, and we were all afraid of going under before we set foot on Serbian soil.

In line with the colonel's command we wanted to turn right, but Major General Daniel, who was running around here with the chief of his general staff, Baron Pitreich, ordered us to beef up the left flank as soon as possible. We advanced through a thicket. "Kisch, go back and the lead the rest of the company here on the double." So I rushed again to the shore.

Men from the 11th were just then disembarking from all the pontoons. The ones from the 15th company were taking up prone positions on the shore. "That was bad, that business with the lieutenant, wasn't it?" an infantryman said to me. "What do you mean?" "Well, he was shot in the chest in your presence." "In my presence?" "He caught it just when you spoke to him and turned away to run to the embankment." "Is he dead?" "Don't know."

Meanwhile, we were all set to move out. We advanced on the double through the forest, perpendicular to the course of the Drina, in the direction of the line of defense.

Bullets by the thousands were whistling through the thicket and past tree trunks. Blood, red-stained shirts, cloths, bandages, abandoned ration kits, weapons, boots, and knapsacks were strewn all around. The wounded were dragging themselves past, and so not for a single second did I doubt that I was headed in the right direction. I was thus all the more surprised when we, who had kept on putting more distance between ourselves and the river, were suddenly standing again on one of its banks. But then it struck me that the current before me was no longer the disastrous Drina, but the Sava River. We then shifted to the right and soon were at the line of skirmish. An infantryman, as it happened, reported to the squad commander, a major from the 91st, that the position of Captain Sychrava from the 91st was seriously weakened as a result of continuous losses and had become so precarious that he absolutely had to have reinforcements if he was to hold his forward position. Before the major could answer, our company commander reported that he was prepared to provide the necessary reinforcements. It seemed obvious that the major would order us to the rescue of the threatened detachments.

Finally: "Lieutenant, for the time being consolidate the left flank at the rampart and wait and see whether we advance." The infantryman was still waiting for an answer. "Tell Captain Sychrava that if he can't hold his position he should retreat to this rampart, which I will defend with all my strength . . ."

We regarded each other in amazement. Have a look over the wave of earth there, "this rampart"—row after row of corn. Not a square meter leveled, as if someone had been afraid to disturb nature. The clearing amounted literally to just half a meter.

The infantryman was about to return to his endangered comrades with the report when the major called him back and instead entrusted a very young cadet candidate to deliver the negative message. But hardly did the cadet plunge into the corn when he tumbled to the ground with a scream. He had taken a shot in the head just above the ear. He was quickly bandaged. In the meantime it was the infantryman after all who was commissioned to deliver the orders. It never entered his mind to run into open terrain; instead he used the protection of the rise.

While all of this was going on, a lieutenant who, as it happened, belonged to the major's staff, had initiated a conversation with the cadet. "That's a real mousetrap there, isn't it?" Only now did I connect in my mind the parameters of our position and realize how right he was—a mousetrap. On the left was the Sava, behind us was the Sava; on the right was the Drina, and in front of us the dense, tortuous cornfield with the enemy within, who was firing endless rounds into the woods between the Sava and the edge of the field. The thicket was barely twenty-five meters wide, and once inside it we had to protect ourselves on two fronts, since its trees were a clear target, while we were firing randomly into the sea of corn.

The shots of our own people rattled ahead of us. We might have had to shoot them if we had begun firing from here. "Forward!" the lieutenant ordered spontaneously, but we had advanced barely thirty steps into the corn when soldiers from the 102nd came toward us as if hounded by the Furies. They were racing to the shore. We stopped in our tracks, and it took the threatening shouts of superiors to propel us a few more steps forward. But then we ran into an entire line of defense in retreat, a cadet in the lead. "Halt!" our lieutenant shouted to him, but he kept on running. "Halt, or I'll fire!" Now he stopped. He trembled like an invalid. "I am commanding you to advance!" "It's not possible, Lieutenant sir; we're under such heavy fire, and we're out of ammunition." He stammered from fear and his knees buckled. "Turn around and again, move out!" "I'm on my way, sir, on my way." But it was to no avail. His men had not waited for the resolution of the argument and, unnoticed in the high corn, reached cover, taking our people along with them.

There was thus nothing to be done. In the opaqueness of the cornfield, and given the general mood of depression, the company simply couldn't pick itself up and move forward. The first lieutenant ordered the columns of Lieutenant Valek and Cadet Weiser to advance, the rest to stay as reserves. We had barely gone sixty paces when Captain Sychrava returned with part of his company. He had held out as long as possible. He was utterly disoriented. He kept on repeating the names of his noncoms, the men he saw fall around him, and he cursed and cried.

We took up a position on the crest of a low hill overgrown with corn. Since the Serbs were lying on the other side of the slope, their shots went too high, and that was why, until then, we had taken so relatively few hits. Already on our advance we kept coming up against the corpses of Serbian soldiers from whom blood was still gushing, a sign that they had been killed only a little while before and that their comrades couldn't be far back. The frontal fire was extremely intense, and from the bank building near Serbian Rača we received (lighter) left-flank fire. Moreover, bullets from detachments of our own division regiment positioned somewhat to the right behind us whistled much too near to us, since they couldn't aim in the cornfield.

The enemy could not be permitted at any cost to take possession of the rise, since that would have meant that the entire division be wiped out in the woods or driven into the water. For that reason we cut down the corn up to the rampart and had in the area in front of our company at least enough of a clearing to deter anyone from pouncing on us suddenly with their rifle butts or tossing grenades at us unseen. Then we returned again to the protection of our cover and dug in.

Since I had no field spade, I scratched out a little hole for myself with my bayonet laboriously and awkwardly. An orderly from the brigade command, an acquaintance of mine, ran past: "Don't knock yourself out; we're not staying here." So I let the bullets whistle all around me, and I felt sorry for the idiots who were digging in by the sweat of their brows only to have to leave the cover as soon as it was ready.

But it was getting very late, shrapnel shells and grenades were now racing parallel to the trajectories of the rifle bullets, and we still hadn't left. (The orderly hadn't deceived me. We were supposed to advance until we linked up with the reserve infantry division, which was to extend us on the left. But it was beaten back and hadn't even made it to the shore.) So there I lay in my hole in the ground shoveling a little mound of earth with my hands while the others, idiots that they were, had long since erected a castle around them. But when more and more shots began coming from the left, I laid my mess kit over me, and a few minutes later the first round clanked against the tins of food in it. I then turned my cap around, since my visor got in my way and kept me from pressing my head flat against the ground so as to protect myself against the firing. Shells kept on screaming overhead and landed against a side of the cover, throwing up soil in our faces so violently we thought we were done for.

The abandoned trenches of the Serbs, which were built in peacetime, are to the left of my miniature cover. Fortified with concrete against shrapnel shells and even grenades, and outfitted with embrasures, they were virtually impregnable. These were no "mutton thieves" or "sheep humpers" who were arrayed against us on the Sava: there's a Serbian-French grammar in a trench, a Serbian-French dictionary alongside it. Elsewhere the notebook of a pupil in the sixth secondary school class with an hourly schedule of classes. The moment the Serbs left the protection of their cover, they were greeted by the hail of our shrapnel. A long-dead Serb is sitting propped up against a drum, blood slowly trickling from an eye, as if from an eyedropper. Another one is lying on his back with outstretched arm, next to him fresh fruit shaken out of his ration kit. We are all thirsty and hungry for the fruit, but nobody dares touch the dead man's property. A Serb first lieutenant, his hand on his saber, is also lying on his back; he was hit on the chin from below.

We got used to our cold company. A young platoon leader from the 91st keeps on making jokes about it. He stands erect, as if going for a walk on Rosenberg Pond and not through the litter of cartridges. "We'd be through with the

Serbs soon enough, but the corn . . ." A whimper completes the sentence. This whimper struck us like a torn nerve, however quickly it passes. I turn away; you're nervous enough from the noise and danger. And now we've got to listen to the screaming of someone wounded! Thank God, though, he's quiet. Quiet to the point of attracting attention. I peer over the parapet, a small, natural traverse. He's lying there, not breathing any longer . . . A moment later someone from the 91st limps past, his foot all bloody. "You see, he's walking," says the captain, "and he whined as if he had been struck dead." "That's not the platoon leader, sir." The captain looks over the parapet and shivers.

Lieutenant Valek returns from a forward position with members of our fourth platoon. He's been wounded in the shoulder blade; First Lieutenant Manlik caught one in the arm.

Three regiments of us are lying against the rampart, huddled close together. (The 73rd is in reserve over there.) There are more than 10,000 men here, and we fire everything we've got from afternoon till evening. Each one of us has at least 140 rounds. Let's say we each shot only a hundred times, that would still be a million rounds fired. And over us whistle the volleys of our artillery. Serbia must be strewn with our lead products. Maybe one of them hits an old woman picking apples near Ub. And to the millions of our shots are joined millions of Serbian rounds, Serbian shrapnel, and Serbian grenades, since six Serbian divisions are reported to be positioned opposite us. These statistics can hardly convey the din, for which the expression "infernal roar" would be a euphemism. But by now we're completely apathetic.

I was thirsty and there was nothing to drink. I had some chocolate in my ration kit. I got up and emptied out the bag. It was all wrapped up in laundry and not easy to find. Two splendid bars of Cailler in their original wrapping. I took them out and stuck them in my shirt. A first lieutenant was standing behind me, two infantrymen next to me, since the fire had grown weaker. Just at that moment a grenade whizzed by within inches of our heads. The branches of a tree came crashing down on us, and as we threw ourselves to the ground, I saw the chocolate fall to the left of me. Captain Mimra yelled to me: "Pass on to the artillery scout: blast the Rača bank building!" I repeated the order and passed it on. That lasted for half a second. When I went to retrieve the chocolate, it was gone. I roared at the men around me, I cried from anger, I thought about how I was going to let the thief have it if I got hold of him. Instead of thanking fate for every second that a bullet didn't hit me, all my thoughts were on nothing other than the chocolate that my mother had packed at home and that someone else would now be enjoying. Yeah, I cried from anger and just wanted to lay my hands on the crook.

Legions of wounded men kept on staggering by. How it is going to be when we move up? What would the morning bring us on those heights over there? These fears were disturbed by a message whose terror made me a thousand times more uneasy.

It was two in the morning. The company commander called me over. "I have the feeling there's going to be a retreat." "Impossible, sir, there's not a single bridge up." He gestured with a hand, and I understood that it wasn't a *feeling* about something but the *knowledge* of it that had prompted his remark. "Pay attention now: if the retreat proceeds from the left flank, stay with Captain Mimra as a link between him and my company."

I ran to the captain, past men who were streaming toward the Drina. There were already orderlies there from other companies. I heard the captain getting them ready. "First Lieutenant Scher will begin." The left flank was the first to move out. I lay there anxiously for three quarters of an hour. There were thousands of soldiers here and at the most twelve small pontoons to transport them across that for sure held no more than forty persons each. The pontoons were steered by only a few scouts, some of whom were cowardly and some wounded. Is this how we were supposed to get out of the mouse trap? The scenes of the initial crossing were sure to be repeated, if not surpassed!

Whenever a new detachment pushed forward from the left flank, without the men who were lying concealed and firing on the line of attack realizing what was happening, the company commanders received notification to which they responded with the command for more intensive firing. Our people, who regarded this command as an expression of special danger, trembled from fear, fired like wild men, and burrowed their heads deeper beneath their covering.

At a quarter to three in the morning, *we* were the left flank. Captain Mimra yelled to me: "The fifteenth, move out!" Now I had to run to all our platoon commanders to repeat the order to them: "15th Company 11th Regiment, retreat." Easily said, but difficult to do in the nearly total darkness of this night, in the excruciating noise, and while other regiments and other companies were hemmed in together on our line of attack. None of our comrades were to be left behind, and so I ran from one flash point to the other to transmit the order and to ask about the platoon commanders. I had informed two of them when the retreat got under way in earnest.

The company commander was waiting in the old position: "15th Company move to the right." To the forest. In the direction of the Drina. Through bushes and undergrowth the whole time, constantly hitting the ground because of the artillery comets that grazed our caps, until we had soon lost our way or at least believed that we had. "This way, Lieutenant," yelled one man. "Over here, Lieutenant," called the others. By now there were only five of us still together, and so we decided to head toward the Sava and to make our way along its bank toward the Drina. But when we came to the river, which was at least somewhat illuminated by the reflection of the pale moon, we had no idea in which direction the Drina lay. One of our party wanted to throw a box of matches into the water to determine its course. "Not the matches, that'd be a shame," the others complained. Instead we threw a picture postcard into the river and saw that we had to go left. Squads of soldiers broke out of the bushes and joined up with us; others overtook us, and still others approached us and tried to convince us that we were headed the wrong way and that the right way led in the opposite direction. But we knew in which direction the picture postcard had flowed, and our only doubt was if we really were at the Sava and not perhaps at the Drina above the crossing point. But we soon saw the mouth of the Drina.

A scream made up of a thousand elements, a single scream from a thousand voices and without end split our eardrums. Just as we had foreseen with hearts pounding when we received the retreat command, chaos reigned at the crossing relay. The closer we got to the tumult, the louder it became. The crossing point was recognizable from the masses of men gathered there. The howling and our own fear paralyzed us. Slowly, as we got caught up in the pushing and shoving, we began to make each other out in the pale light of the moon.

Men were throwing knapsacks and weapons onto the sand, sitting down on the ground, and hurriedly fiddling with their boot laces. Most were standing loaded down with full equipment in water up to their hips in order to reach the pontoon even before it came ashore. They were the ones who sought to attract the attention of the scouts with frenzied howling and insane gesticulating, and who were fighting with those around them, since they, with even more exaggerated gestures, hoped to find consideration.

Others had the idea of wading straight across the river, so that troops in water up to their necks were moving forward as a solid group. I threw my lot in with them and pressed forward, half pushed. Since my rifle made it difficult for me to balance myself with my hands, I slung it over my head by the straps. We kept on stepping on knapsacks and rifles. In midstream we had to come to a stop, since some of our men had begun turning back; you couldn't go farther, it was too deep, the current was too strong.

All of a sudden the yelling and shouting of the masses cohered into a single cry:

"The Serbs are already on the bank!"

The horizontal hail of bullets indeed began increasing. The shots no longer flew over our heads but punched holes in the water. Some of our men ran back to the right, since it seemed that the Serbs were coming just from the left; some wanted to swim across to the Austrian shore. Five steps diagonally from me I saw an officer swimming energetically. As far as I could make out, it was Lieutenant Batek. I called his name, but he didn't hear me. I wanted to swim up to him when his head plunged beneath the water and didn't resurface again. Either a bullet had struck him or a sudden heart attack brought him death in the Drina.

Everywhere the same picture: upwards of thirty men drowning, screaming, breathing their last, flailing about with their hands, diving out of the water, trying to stay in the air and pull themselves up on nothing; feet were poking through the water . . . As I write these lines, my hand is trembling and I have to pause.

Several nonswimmers were clinging to swimmers, who, in an effort to shake off the burden, were thrashing about them with the result that swimmers and nonswimmers alike sank into the depths. If someone nearby had lost the ground under him, those of us who were still able to stand in a row stretched out our hands to him and pulled him to us. I pulled in two myself. One of them ran right back to the shore. The second one tried to catch his breath a while but sank down and disappeared on the bottom.

A movement toward the right passed through the ranks. Three pontoons were passing by. All excited, I rushed in the same direction as the others to the extent that it was possible to rush when the water was neck-deep at best and in some places reached as high as the mouth. The pontoon I got to had come to a stop and stood parallel to the shore. While everyone in a renewed battle of despair tried to swing into the boat on the side turned toward them, I trudged over to the more distant side, which was actually closer to the Austrian shore, and clung hard to the gunwale.

Another fellow was just as clever and was hanging on there. I implored someone who had already climbed in to the boat: "Pull me into the boat, man." He grabbed hold of me but was unable to pull me over the high edge, since I myself was in no position to help him in any way. With a glance at my neighbor, who similarly couldn't get into the pontoon with just one person pulling him, no matter how hard he tried, I advised my rescuer: "First help the guy over there and then me." He did it, and my neighbor got in.

The pontoon in the meantime had filled up. Voices grew loud: "Push off! Don't let anyone in!" I said to my rescuer: "OK, now I'm coming in." But he wasn't helping me any more, nor was the other occupant of the boat, whom he had supported, and least of all my previous neighbor from the outside, who owed me his life after all.

Meanwhile, the entire vessel, including the side I believed I already laid claim to, was grasped by more than sixty desperate hands. "We can't row this way," yelled the scouts, and that was the signal for an attack on us "outsiders." Rifle butts were smashed down on the fingers of those hanging on the outside or their hands were pummeled by fists until they finally let go. The poor souls then fell into the water, gurgled, surfaced, some two or three times, then sank beneath the surface.

The task of shaking me off the side of the boat was assumed by a young fellow, whose face I shall never forget. A dusky-blond tuft of hair fell wide over his temple from beneath his cap; he wore the parrot-green marking of the 91st, and he had large, light blue, kindly eyes, with which he deigned not to give me a glance but instead looked quite matter-of-factly at my fingers, which were clinging tenaciously to the gunwale.

He calmly bent down and began indifferently pulling my hands away, as if he were shelling nuts. He finally succeeded in prying open my right hand, but hardly did he begin working on the left when I again got a firm grip with the right one. Now he was stuck. He pondered the situation for a moment, grabbed hold of the little finger of my left hand, then the ring finger, the middle finger, the index finger, the thumb.

I was anything but mute while all this was going on. I implored him, promised to be eternally grateful to him, appealed to his sense of comradeship, swore on his mother's life, and pointed out that the boat wasn't going to capsize because of me. But he was not to be swayed from the calm pursuit of his intention to drown me and again lifted my fingers. There was nothing to be achieved through pleading. "Bastard," I roared, "I know who you are all right, and if I make it over, you're going to be hanged for murder; throwing me down isn't going to help you either, since the others will denounce you as a murderer!" No impression. He had almost freed my left hand and was holding it tight in his own left hand to keep it from grasping the side of the pontoon again. Then with his free, right hand he prepared to continue the procedure on the fingers of my right hand.

The other occupants of the boat were already furious that I was doing my best not to get drowned. "Knock him into the water!" Having no wish to make a nuisance of myself any longer, I plopped into the water.

I tried to swim. But I couldn't make any headway, since my rifle, which I had forgotten about, slipped down around my neck, and the strap was now choking me. Besides, the heavy army boots and the rest of my gear were dragging me down. I couldn't manage to pull the rifle strap over my head. The pontoon, meanwhile, had turned around and was now in deep water. My desperation enabled me to leap up; I grabbed hold of the boat in the rear, concealing my head.

A terrible fright was gripping everyone aboard. Serbian bullets whistled, and the moaning and screaming, screaming, screaming indicated that they were hitting their targets.

One of the Serbian shrapnel shells, which until then had dropped their loads or their red-hot detonators in the Drina to the right and left of us, burst over our boat. Noise, groans, moans, curses, and then panic. "The bottom's hit!" "Stuff the holes quickly!" "Get the tent sheets!" "Plug them with coats!" I heard a thousand similar cries, but couldn't see anything. Another pontoon glided alongside and was struck by two shrapnels one after the other. It capsized; I turned my eyes away.

Our vessel was driven off course by the current; some two hundred paces farther north we reached the Austrian shore. Sappers and some infantrymen helped it ashore; but before I pulled myself forward from the rear of the boat, everyone had left it, everyone had run away from the hail of bullets, abandoning the wreck.

I attempted to clamber to the shore, but the water was too deep, the current too strong, and so I called for help. Some of those who were hurrying up the slope turned around, but not one of them came back. I recognized a comrade from the same company. "Neumaier!" I shouted. He turned around. "Who's calling me?" "It's me, Kisch." He came down, extended his rifle to me, I grabbed hold of it, and he pulled me to the shore. It was steep and slippery, and I lost my footing. My weakness caused me to lose my balance and tumble backward into the water. Neumaier leaped back after me, but I had already managed to get up under my own power. We were standing in water up to our necks. He stood behind me, held me tight around the hips, and thrust me forward over the embankment until I felt the ground beneath me.

A column that reminded me of Falstaff's recruits, wretched and miserable, was trotting single file along the slope. Naked soldiers, soldiers in their underwear, soldiers in full gear, soldiers wrapped only in tenting were trotting apathetically. Others shoved their way in between Neumaier and me.

A huge tree to the left. That's where the medical aid station of the 102nd was located, I remembered, which we saw on our advance. Dr. Klein, Dr. Turnovsky, or Dr. Wollin will help me somehow. So I turned in that direction and within five minutes was at the tree. It was a tree like a hundred others, without a trace of an aid station. Wasn't it the next tree there? In no time at all I had lost my way and was wandering alone through fields of clover, while on both shores an uninterrupted debate was raging between cartridge magazines, and shots, streaking in pursuit of their solitary target, were the only sign of humanity.

Thirty paces ahead of me, a sentry called out to me from the bushes: "Halt, who's there?" I didn't know any password or other means of identification, since I had been part of an integrated platoon. But the man in the bushes insisted on it; perhaps he would have shot me. Fortunately I remembered that that morning the sentries had been recruited from the 73rd, and so I passed myself off as a friend by speaking the Egerland dialect.[1] Two men led me to a lieutenant, who yelled at me: "You miserable shirker, you ran away from the front!" He still didn't know about the general retreat, since no troops had passed by his remote field watch. He finally let me go and showed me the way to Velino-Selo. Ten minutes later I reached the road to Velino-Selo. Thousands of soldiers were camped there. They had taken their shirts off to wring them out and then put them on again.

At last a building, a small military police barracks, soldiers in front of it getting cleaned up. I emptied out my ration kit; the reserve portion of rusk lay like runny mush on the bottom of the little bag. My letters and cards were stuck-together scraps, the same for the old pieces of newspaper that I had kept for any emergencies. My diary was quite smudged and blurred, since it had been written with an indelible pencil. The pencil was also of no more use to me as its supply of lead had dissolved. The tin case in my pants pocket had opened and my identity card had become illegible. It was all the same to me; I could be buried as X or Y!

I came across my savior at the military police barracks. He was smoking. "Neumaier, let me have a drag." "Certainly not," and with that he turned me down.

On the outskirts of Dolni Brodac, our old camp, soldiers were waiting around, asking anyone passing by about the whereabouts of acquaintances, excitedly greeting special comrades. There was also a group of officers sitting there, among them my first lieutenant, who had been in the capsized pontoon but had managed to save himself; a first lieutenant who had been shot in the arm; a lieutenant who caught four bullets in the shoulders; and others.

They asked me if I knew about some wounded officer. "Kirrmann's dead." "We've heard the same, but we don't think it's true." One of them said that he had seen him clobbered. They then fell silent. They mentioned the names of other fallen officers. "What happened to Lieutenant Batek?" I asked, recalling my swimming companion from the Drina. "Missing in action." Captain Mimra was lying in a fever in his tent, from pneumonia.

The company lined up so that losses could be tallied. "Our platoon's been badly thinned out," I remarked mechanically to my deputy commander, who always stood next to me at roll call. Someone else answered. Corporal Czeschka was also missing. He had been put up for a decoration two weeks ago for swimming across the Drina under enemy fire in order to rescue our patrol. How he had looked forward to getting the medal, in spite of our ribbing. More than twenty of my buddies were missing. The losses are said to be even heavier in the other companies, to say nothing of the other regiments of our division!

The whole morning long I wept for no reason at all and without warning; in the afternoon I laughed as if I had become a kid again. Despite exhaustion and heat I couldn't manage to fall asleep. Everyone's in the same mood.

I dropped in on our fourth battalion, which had suffered especially heavy losses. A group of men was sitting sad and disconsolate. "You know, our white horse is dead too." Yes, I already knew that our beast for carrying ammunition had drowned.

Some noncommissioned officers who were unable to buy any rank stars in all the hustle-bustle of the mobilization in Pisek, had painted them on their shirt collars with indelible pencil. In the water of the Drina, these stars grew very large. Everyone was laughing his head off over it: "Have a look, what a big star he has; must be proud that he made lance-corporal." I too giggled to myself in satisfaction.

Egon Erwin Kisch, "Schreib das auf, Kisch!" Das Kriegstagebuch von Egon Erwin Kisch (Berlin: Erich Reiss Verlag, 1930), 97–115.

1. I am omitting two short lines of dialect here: "Seid's diats Dreisiebzger? I tirt gern mit enkern Kummadanten riadn" ("You from the 73rd? I'm glad to be talking to my own buddies," 113).

Kisch in his library, 1931.
Courtesy Ullstein Bilderdienst.

Preface to *Classical Journalism*

To anyone who has for years been preoccupied with theoretical questions concerning the nature of journalism, above all with the newspaper as the advocate of new intellectual directions and with inquiries into the energy and duration of the journalistic filtering process, the commission of this publisher, editing an anthology of renowned journalists may seem an easy undertaking. But even the procurement of the raw material (books and especially volumes of newspapers from abroad) encountered serious obstacles, and still more difficult was the selection of names and works. All intellectual struggles of the modern period, from the Reformation to psychoanalysis, from the Irish struggle for independence to expressionism, have been waged in the columns of newspapers. Of the names that have come down through the centuries, not one is missing among the authors of such articles, scarcely any one of the philosophers, ethicists, poets, artists, revolutionaries and reformers, politicians, and military commanders. A hundred and fifty of these major figures, to whom the newspaper was especially important and who were especially important for the newspaper. In the final analysis, it was doable. But which of their articles to choose? It had to be one that was decisive for the author, for the idea represented, and for history, and one that also demonstrates the essence of his manner, through style, form, and occasion. Accordingly, it was difficult to select, transcribe, and then translate (where necessary) this somehow most striking essay from the hefty collected works of an author who led his times and shaped them or from the tomes of old issues of newspapers. But it was still much more difficult and painful to have to tinker with this now reanimated organism—to remove something from it so that the anthology might itself not become a multivolumed tome, from which an anthology would then have to be compiled in turn. However, no sooner had a contribution by one of the major figures been targeted, when the editor, who now had at hand the entire work of the author and was excited by it, found, in the course of what he presumed to be his private reading, a better or more representative article. When this occurred, the original contribution had to be dropped.

The range of material was limited only by the decision not to subsume under the rubric of classical journalism any author who is still under current discussion, that is, still tarrying among the physically living. The great publicistic issues of the World War, the revolutions, the transformation of states, and peace, as well as the philosophical and artistic issues of today should be reserved for an analogous work possibly titled "Contemporary Journalism."

Anyone who has ever entered the field of journalism, or has ever propagated on behalf of any cause, has—in the comprehensive history of intellectual struggles—a predecessor who can serve him as a model or a warning. Can he discover him? That is a task whose difficulty has been characterized here with some justification. But if he wants to, in this anthology he must experience both the trial and the stimulation through his unknown master.

The establishment of just such continuity is urgently needed. Quite apart from the fact that the journalist, if only because he is forceful and often repeats himself, must speak to masses of a certain sort, the danger of writing himself dry and rigidity of form is greater for him than for any other intellectual producer. He must, therefore, procure for himself a new tool or at least sharpen the old one anew. This renewal demands reflection, rest, and a supply of energy, and it makes no difference from which source of the spirit it is acquired. But does that not mean, viewing it positively, that if devotion to artistic achievement can be connected to such renewal, one can learn how before—in the same situation—a master had tried to resolve the problem? Only history provides information on how the game went.

History provides information . . . It is history that has added its verdict to every pleading. And that should make an anthology of classical journalism a primer of the nation. People must learn that the spiritual can be encountered only through the spiritual, not through the judgment of a court, an assassination, or lies. People must learn that it is not the better cause that achieves the earthly victory, but the better-argued cause. And that it counts for nothing if one is unconquered on land and on sea; the war of humanity can only be lost when one is conquered in spirit.

Prague, June 1923

Egon Erwin Kisch, ed., *Klassischer Journalismus: Die Meisterwerke der Zeitung* (Berlin and Weimar: Aufbau-Verlag, 1982), 5–7.

The Case of the Chief of the General Staff Redl

In the year before the outbreak of the World War the compulsory suicide of
Colonel Alfred Redl, the chief of the General Staff of the Prague Corps, and
the leaking soon after of his espionage activity caused an unprecedented stir,
which was well founded politically in view of the tense European situation
and criminally in view of the perpetrator's rank and sphere of influence.
Rumors, protests, accusations, suspicions, and conjectures followed in rapid
succession down to the winter of 1914, when the deployment of the Austro-
Hungarian army was judged a failure.

Since the purpose behind the command for voluntary demise had been
to drive the monstrous incident from the world silently, even after this plan
had long since proven unfeasible, not a word was reported about the powers
for which the colonel of the General Staff had carried out his espionage, what
he revealed, where he delivered the military documents, how much money he
received for them, and who in the final analysis had given the heinous order
for a person to take his own life, who observed this hara-kiri, and how the
impact of this incident on court and army manifested itself. Indeed, as concerns
the discovery of the deed and the conviction of the perpetrator, only accounts
became known that contradicted one another or were intended to conceal the
truth.

The Austro-Hungarian General Staff, above all its office of military
intelligence, was reproached from the most divergent sides with bearing the
guilt for the fact that such a highly placed military person had for years been

able to practice the trade of a spy undetected, and that through the order to commit suicide, the full clarification of this politically, militarily, and historically important criminal affair was impeded. In particular, the head of the office of military intelligence at the time, August Urbański von Ostromiecz, was often named in this connection. As Colonel Urbański's transfer to nonactive duty was reported by the press a year after the revelation of the case, it was understandable that people could believe in at least some guilt on the part of the office of military intelligence. Lieutenant–Field Marshal Urbański is now living in Graz at the home of his wife's grandmother, Frau Reinighaus, whose son was married to the wife of Field Marshal Conrad von Hötzendorf. It was there that I proposed to the chief of the office of military intelligence of the General Staff that by means of an authentic presentation with the aid of records, I could silence all rumors connecting the unresolved Redl case to the office of military intelligence.

Moreover, I had also obtained material from conversations, files, and remarks of officials who at the time held senior military or police positions. Besides Urbański's communications, there were the accounts and other remarks by the present section chief of the Czechoslovak Ministry of the Interior, Dr. Novak; the present acting general auditor of the Czechoslovak army, Dr. Vorlicek; the general military advocate of the Austro-Hungarian army, W. Haberditz; Colonel Emil Seeliger; the retired auditor Dr. Hans Seliger; and the former deputy to the assembly, Count Adalbert Sternberg.

In view of the latent danger of war in which Austria-Hungary found itself from the time of the annexation of Bosnia, Urbański, who in 1908 took over the office of military intelligence of the General Staff, must have been constrained to expand the spy service. Under his predecessor, General von Giesl, the former Major Alfred Redl assumed the direction of the service to which the joint active and passive Austro-Hungarian espionage—that is, the organization for the ferreting out of foreign military relations and the defense against foreign espionage at home—was subordinate. The bureau was organized along modern criminological lines. Every secret visitor was photographed in profile and full face without realizing it, since two paintings on the wall had openings for the lenses of cameras that were operated from the adjoining room.

In similar fashion fingerprints could be obtained from every visitor without his or her being aware of it. While making a telephone call the officer with one hand offered the male or female visitor a pack of cigarettes or a box of chocolates, both of which were sprinkled with invisible red lead. The lighter and ashtray, which the smoker had to pull toward him, were also prepared this way. If the visitor refused both cigarettes and chocolates, the officer on duty had himself called from the room; if the guest was inclined to espionage, he couldn't resist taking in hand the file that was lying ready on the table and was marked "Secret! Restricted inspection!" This document was also of course strewn with silk powder.

In a small box on the wall that one could easily take for a medicine chest, a sound tube was installed that served as a listening device for the stenographer in the adjoining room but could also set a metal stylus in motion that faithfully captured the conversation on a gramophone record. Every classified book or fascicle of documents could within a few seconds be separated, projected on the wall, photographed sideways, and again tied together so that in the shortest possible time it was again in place, as if untouched, from where it had been "borrowed." There were albums and card files with photographs, manuscripts, and typescript samples of all the people in Europe suspected of espionage, especially those in such espionage centers as Brussels, Zurich, and Lausanne.

From 1900 to 1905 the General Staff officer Redl had acted as an expert in all Vienna espionage trials, pitilessly disallowing any mitigating circumstances, demanding the highest extent of the legal penalty. In the year 1902, thanks to his energetic conduct, he had obtained the sentencing of the former officer Alexander von Caric to four and a half years of hard labor and the sentencing of the international spy Paul Barstmann and the Italian engineer Pietro Contin to four years' incarceration. When in 1904 Redl undertook a house search in connection with the auxiliary district commander of Lemberg, Major von Wienckowsky, who was in prison on charges of espionage, he lured the six-year-old child of the prisoner into an intimate conversation and in this way succeeded in learning where papa was in the habit of hiding his secret papers. Noteworthy for Redl's insensitivity is a Viennese episode of this period. A man named Jonasch had given a photographer the drawing of a fortification plan to be photographed. This was reported to the police, and when Jonasch came to pick up the pictures, he was taken into custody. He had already spent nine years in prison on a fraud charge. At the time of his arrest he admitted at once that he wanted to sell abroad the photographs as the map of the Trento fortress, but all they were was the usual "diagram of a modern fortress" that he had an artist copy from a widely accessible text on fortifications. When this confession proved to be correct, the police wanted to release the man. But Redl, who had to be consulted on all matters of espionage in advance, protested and insisted that Jonasch be delivered to justice. "I ask you, what harm does it do him if he sits through a few weeks' investigative detention? And it's always better for us to be able to point to a large number of espionage cases . . ." The man in fact had to spend five months in the slammer before the proceedings against him were suspended.

Perhaps these tactics of Redl's succeeded in strengthening counter-espionage, beyond even Redl's imagining. For soon after, as prescribed for the career of a member of the General Staff, he was assigned to military service command with the rank of lieutenant colonel. A year later, General von Giesl, who now commanded the 8th Corps of the Prague garrison, requested that his former espionage expert Redl be reassigned him. A section of the General Staff had been established in the 15th Austro-Hungarian Corps command; the head of it carried the title of a "chief of the General Staff," while the title "Chief of the Imperial and Royal General Staff" was appropriate for the commandant of the joint Austro-Hungarian General Staff Corps. After long-standing service in the capital, Redl was now transferred to Prague with the ranks of colonel and General Staff chief. He was needed here; the man with the underworld connections was needed here. Bohemian constitutional law, which was directed against Viennese centralism, had thousands of supporters; the antimilitarist action against the National Socialists had demonstrated how this powerful party was determined to work against the army; the leaders of the Czech Pan-Slavists had formal dealings with the Russian, Serbian, and Bulgarian governments; and the General Staff officers of the Slavic states were invited as guests to the Sokol congress, an obvious nucleus of the future Czech army. Provincial Czech papers had to be constantly confiscated, since they carried episodes of the greedy mismanagement and merciless treatment at Archduke Franz Ferdinand's Konopischt Castle. "Out of Vienna" was the outspoken slogan behind which antidynastic sentiments and "high treason" conspired.

While Redl now had to organize a military informers' service in Prague, back in Vienna Redl's counterespionage measures were being expanded to an extraordinary extent. Hence the state law guaranteeing the confidentiality of correspondence was abolished by the office of military intelligence in view of the impending war danger. Mail was also inspected; in a locked, secret room about a thousand letters a day were opened, and it was there as well that investigations were initiated in the case of suspicious contents. The officials who carried out this illegal mail censorship themselves didn't know that they were acting on behalf of the military. They believed that their official duties served primarily the discovery of exceptional cases of customs violations and smuggling. Concerning this inspection of private mail by means of the "black box-room," which was first established when he had been posted to Prague, Redl knew as little as anyone else in Austria before the war. By means of these unrestrained arrangements for counterintelligence measures against enemy spying, espionage trials reached unheard-of proportions. Found guilty of espionage, among others, were the Russian military attaché, a certain Colonel Martschenko, and his successor. Both were consequently recalled, the former after he learned from the personal behavior of Kaiser Franz Josef —who snubbed him at the court ball—that his secret activities had been uncovered.

In March 1913 two letters being held in the main post office in Vienna in poste restante with the code "Opera Ball 13" were opened as suspicious. They were from Eydtkuhnen and contained, with no accompanying explanation, sums of money in Austrian currency, 6,000 crowns in one, 8,000 crowns in the other. In no way could it be assumed that such sums would be sent poste restante if legitimate money were involved. (The total budget available to the office of military intelligence for espionage purposes amounted to 150,000 crowns, while the Russian chief of intelligence in Warsaw received five million rubles for these purposes.) The address on the letters had been typed.

Immediate steps were taken to seize whoever came to claim the letters. Two detectives were assigned to permanent duty in the police guardroom of the post office. The guardroom was connected to the post office counter by means of an electric bell; at the signal that the letters were being picked up, the detectives were to grab the person who came for them. Weeks went by, months. The official who had ordered the surveillance of the letters, police chief Dr. Novak, was transferred to a ministry and had turned the matter over to his successor (the future chancellor of the republic, Dr. Schober). No one asked for the letters containing such money.

On the evening of 24 May 1913, a Saturday, around closing time, the signal suddenly roused the agents from their weeks-long rest. Before they came through the passageway of the post office from the Fleischmarkt to the Dominican Church to the poste restante window, where the clerk slowly— although not conspicuously so—had handed over the letters with the "Opera Ball" code to the party who had come to claim them, the individual was gone. They raced after him, and even caught sight of him, a well-built man who slammed shut behind him the door of a car that had been left running. They also saw the car driving away from there. It was a taxi.

Neither of the detectives had an automobile that might have been used for the pursuit. Of what use was it to them that they had been able to see the number of the fleeing car? Of what use was it to them that on the next day they would be able to interrogate the driver as to where the "fare" had come from and where he was headed? The stranger for sure had not come from his residence, nor did he drive to his residence! A criminal with such a sum of money gets off in the street or at a café or in front of some passageway, then takes a new cab. The two detectives were certain of only one thing: that a close disciplinary investigation would be undertaken against them, the outcome of which could not be in doubt.

But then there began for them and the Austro-Hungarian Army a chain of unbelievable coincidences, what's called "hunter's luck."

While the two agents deliberated whether to interrogate the driver of the taxi on their own that very night and in collusion with him cook up a story about the strange flight of the stranger, or to report their misfortune to the state police, a taxi drove past them on the Kolowratring. They saw the license plate; it was the same car that had carried their prey away from the post office twenty minutes before. They whistled, yelled, and ran. The taxi stopped. It was empty.

"Where did you take the man from the post office?"

"To the Café Kaiserhof."

"Take us at once to the Café Kaiserhof."

On the short ride there the detectives snooped around the inside of the car and found the case of a pocketknife; it was made of a light-gray fabric. When they entered the Café Kaiserhof together with the taxi driver, the suspect was nowhere to be found. They rushed to the nearest cab stand. Yes, a man who looked like him just drove off. Where to? We're in Vienna, so there's one person sure to know—the water man. Actually he's no water man, since there aren't any coach horses at the cab stand to be given the bucket, but he shines the coaches and busies himself primarily opening doors. He naturally heard where the gentleman ordered himself taken: "To the Hotel Klomser."

Off to the Hotel Klomser! The hotel doorman was grilled in the foyer. "Just now two men arrived in a car, businessmen from Bulgaria." "And before them a man by himself?" "By car? Don't know. A quarter of an hour ago Colonel Redl came in. Dressed in civvies, he was. But I don't know if he left by car."

Colonel Redl? The name filled the police agents with awe. They knew him well. He didn't give them a second's peace, did not acknowledge the necessity of a night's rest when they served as his beaters on a spy hunt. And how he tracked down his quarry when in the courtroom as the leading expert, as director of the Austro-Hungarian espionage service, he showed the guilt of the accused spy in the most glaring light! How strange it would be if the person who claimed the parcels of money was really a spy and by chance lived in the same house, maybe even right next door to the chief of counter-intelligence, in the very lion's den!

But the time isn't ripe yet for such speculation! Senior Civil Servant Gayer of the state police had surely been apprised already by the Vienna main post office that the letters containing the money had been picked up. He had to be informed by all means as to how the pursuit turned out. And also asked if he approved of Colonel Redl directing the investigation in the hotel, since this is where, coincidentally, the colonel happened to live. At any rate the hotel had to be brought under immediate surveillance. While one of the two agents went to the telephone, the other spoke to the hotel doorman. He handed him the knife case so that he could find out to which guest it belonged.

Just then a man in uniform came down the steps from the first floor and placed the key to room no. 1 on the table in front of the doorman. "Did the colonel lose the case from his pocketknife?" the doorman asked.

"Yes," answered Colonel Redl and thoughtlessly shoved the little light-gray cloth case into a pocket. "Where could I have . . ."

He suddenly broke off his sentence. He had last used the pocket knife on the ride from the post office when he opened the envelopes containing the money. That's where he left the knife case behind. He looked at the man who was standing next to the hotel doorman and was going through the letters lying on the table with apparent interest.

Colonel Redl did not complete the question as to where he had left the knife case. Colonel Redl grew quite pale. He knew that in a few hours he would be dead.

He went out to the street, looked around a bit, and then made his way down the Herrengasse on the right. Before he reached the Café Central on the corner, he looked around again to see if anyone was following him from the hotel. No one. But the two men who left the pub of the Klomser Restaurant surely struck him as suspicious.

One of them later instructed the hotel doorman to call the number 12-348, the secret number of the state political police. "Say that everything's in order; the knife case belongs to Colonel Redl."

When the two agents reached the corner of Strauchgasse, Colonel Redl had disappeared. He was nowhere to be seen, either in Strauchgasse or Wallnerstrasse. Could he in the meantime have reached the Haarhof, which leads to Naglergasse? No, not even running. Then he must have disappeared in the building of the old stock exchange, from which there are three exits, two of them through the Café Central and one toward Freyung. Hats off to a man who two minutes ago had been unexpectedly unmasked, who for two minutes has known that his life has been forfeited, and who was already cold-bloodedly probing the possibility of escape!

Meanwhile the telephone buzzed from the Hotel Klomser to the state police, from the Schottenring to the Stubenring, where the office of military intelligence of the Imperial and Royal General Staff was located. Colonel Redl! The officers of the field agent group were visibly shaken. Their commander, their teacher, their role model, their adviser, was the person being sought. Captain Ronge, Redl's successor as director of the spy service, drove at once to the main post office in order to ask the counter clerks to describe the man who picked up the letters. There was also a slip of paper there on which the person had written the code of his poste restante letters. Meanwhile, the other men in the office of military intelligence began looking for specimens of Redl's handwriting. There was no lack of them: for example, a "Memo on the Recruitment and Screening of Operatives, written by Alfred Redl, Imperial and Royal Captain on the General Staff," fifty paragraphs long; an "Outline for the Obtaining of Operatives' Material"; "Standards for the Discovery of Spies at Home and Abroad"; a thick brochure under the title "Reports for the Years 1900 to 1905." All this material was laid out on the table. But when Captain Ronge returned from the post office, the slip of paper in hand with the notation "Opera Ball 13," there was no need for any handwriting comparison. To be sure, the words were written down faintly, but there could be no talk of any attempted disguise. The handwriting was that of Colonel Redl.

The detectives meanwhile pursued their prey. In the passageway to Freyung they again caught sight of him. But he had also seen them. And he knew that he couldn't give two of them the slip. He pulled papers out of his pocket (as it turned out later, very incriminating papers that he absolutely had to get rid of if he wanted to defend himself) and tore them to shreds. He threw the scraps of paper onto the ground in the passageway. One of the detectives, he assumed, would stop to pick up the scraps, while he could probably manage to escape the other one. But both of them continued pursuing him. On Freyung they stopped a car and ordered the driver to follow them slowly. Then one agent returned to the passageway, collected the scraps of paper, and took them to the police. From there they went at once by car to the office of military intelligence, where they were reassembled. They turned out to be postal certifications: a receipt for a remittance of money to a certain lieutenant of uhlans Stefan H., and three receipts for registered letters to Brussels, Warsaw, and Lausanne—all three addresses were known to the office of military intelligence as those of spies. That it was espionage on behalf of Russia that the addressee of the letters had been carrying on was known for months, since Eydtkuhnen was indeed a German-Russian border station. Since Russia conducted its espionage service in tandem with France, the Brussels address (a branch of French espionage) was no more surprising. But the Lausanne address was that of Italian espionage headquarters located there.

The matter had to be dealt with. Should one proceed immediately with arrest? With military or political arrest? Should the kaiser be immediately informed? Or should that await the further course of the investigation? Should the criminal be allowed to escape earthly justice?

Colonel Redl passed Tiefen Graben and Heinrichsgasse on his way to the Franz-Josef quay. Every now and then he looked around; his shadow was following him. On the quay he turned left. He was doubtless heading for Brigittenau. He had arrived there from Prague at four that afternoon in the chain-drive car that he bought from Daimler in August 1911 for 18,000 crowns. A handsome car, with the initials A. R. intertwined in gold letters on the door. The middle slash of the *A* wasn't a horizontal stroke but consisted of two slanted lines; it looked like a *V.* There was also a crown over the monogram, if only the five-pronged civic crown, but who noticed that? He had left the car with the body maker Zednicek, on Brigittaplatz, for him to trim the lower sides of the chassis with shiny leather and reline the entire interior with Bordeaux-red silk. Everything was to be ready within four days, since the colonel wished to return to Prague that Tuesday in the renovated automobile. He instructed his driver to buy two new tires at Prowodnik's and then be ready to leave Tuesday morning. Then he hailed a taxi, which took him from Wallensteinplatz to the Hotel Klomser, where his servant, Josef Sladek, of the 11th Infantry Regiment, had arrived at noon on the Prague train.

Stefan H., a young cavalry officer from Stockerau, and Redl's lover, came to the hotel room in the afternoon on a visit. A long argument took place, the nature of which would come out later in Redl's letters. In the hotel Redl had again won over his young friend. At five-thirty Lieutenant Stefan H. left, followed ten minutes later by Redl—in a hurry. He had to get to the post office. To pick up the money. He had put it off for months. Now was the time. He wanted to buy his Stefan a car. To drive cross-country together.

"To drive cross-country . . ." And now Redl was hastening along the Danube canal, with a weird retinue, and thinking how good it would be to be sitting in his touring car—even without the shiny leather covering on the lower parts of the body and without the Bordeaux-red lining—and how pleasant to be able to drive cross-country. To drive cross-country. He had to realize, however, that he couldn't think about that now, and he headed home across the Schottenring.

The director of the office of military intelligence, Urbański von Ostromiecz, drove up to the Grand-Hotel. The "chief" was sitting in the restaurant surrounded by a number of people. "Did you bring me something nice?" Conrad von Hötzendorf asked his friend. The band played a potpourri from the new operetta, *The Count of Luxembourg*.

"May I respectfully request a private conversation with Your Excellency?"

"So urgent, is it? Well, if that's the case, let's go."

The chief of the General Staff went through the restaurant with the chief of his office of military intelligence.

In an adjoining room Urbański began to deliver his report. Conrad was already prepared for something bad. But when he heard what the matter was about, he turned as white as a sheet. He didn't utter a word. He tried to imagine the implications of the crime being described to him. Once the case becomes known, the roof will fall in; as it is, the troops hate the General Staff, the "chosen ones." What would they say abroad! And the enemy! What a triumph! Everything's rotten anyway, people are only too glad to say about the monarchy. And in the German Reich, just imagine the anxiety, the distrust! And what will happen among the oppositional national minorities when a match hits this powder keg! Especially now, when the situation is more than critical, it's going to stretch things to the breaking point. And the chief of the General Staff thought: "This silly music; if it would just let up for at least five minutes!" He sat down, got up again, then announced his decision:

"The scoundrel has to be caught. We have to hear from his own mouth how far the treachery reaches and then—he has to die at once!"

The fatherland, the armed forces, and—above all—the General Staff had to be spared the shock that would be inevitable once something like this became known.

"By his own hand, Excellency?"

"Yes. No one must be told anything about the cause of death! Do I make myself plain, Colonel?"

"At your command, Excellency!"

"Everything has to be taken care of tonight!"

"At your service, Excellency!"

"You will immediately put together a commission, Colonel! Consisting of Höfer as head, the chief of the auditing office, you, and the head of spy operations. Only four men. All reports must be forwarded directly to me."

"At your service, Excellency!"

While Colonel Redl, observed, headed in the direction of Brigittenau, and then gave up this intention, an old acquaintance of his, who had telegraphed from Prague that he was coming, was waiting for him in the lobby of the Hotel Klomser. It was First Public Prosecutor Dr. Viktor Pollak, the attorney general with the prosecutor general's office of the Supreme Court of Appeal. Redl and Pollak knew each other professionally. When Redl, as military expert, had piled up incriminating material on incriminating material against a defendant accused of espionage, it was Dr. Pollak, as the highest public prosecutor, who in his irrefutable, vehement summation gave this expert opinion its devastating (to the defendant) effect. This cooperation forged a personal and human as well as professional relationship between these two men. They were partners and friends. Today they went together to the Ried-hof Restaurant in the Josefstadt. The senior public prosecutor had no idea that the dinner was being observed. He knew nothing of the fact that his friend, with whom he was just then clinking glasses, was such a serious criminal, the likes of which he had never encountered in his many years as a public prosecutor. What did catch his attention, however, was his table companion's nervousness, agitation, and taciturnity.

Colonel Redl considered his options. How could he escape death? Should he confide in his friend, the senior public prosecutor, seek his advice, plead for his intervention? And to what end? To flee abroad? To seek shelter in a sanatorium on grounds of mental disturbance or by presenting himself as a victim of sexual aberration?

Making compromises between these various possibilities, he did not openly confide in his friend but indeed threw out hints, did not concede his homosexuality, but spoke instead of moral confusion; did not admit being a spy, but implicated himself vaguely in some serious crime; and spoke in a confused way so that his friend could conclude from everything that he was suffering from a mental disturbance, and demanded immediate help getting back to Prague unhindered, where he could unreservedly confide in his superior, the corps commandant.

Senior Public Prosecutor Dr. Pollak listened, deeply alarmed. He had people imprisoned probably a hundred times for lesser causes and for more minor infractions proposed immediate arrest or denial of a reprieve. But in these circumstances, he thought, I'm an individual, in a personal relationship, and Redl is my friend.

He declared himself ready, at Redl's request, to call up the chief of the political police. To his surprise, Councillor Gayer, with whose home he wanted to be connected, was still at the office so late at night.

"I am here at dinner with Colonel Redl of the General Staff," he began.

"Yes, in the Riedhof."

"And how did you know that?"

"By chance. And you wanted?"

"Colonel Redl has apparently suffered a mental disturbance. He's talking about moral lapses and crimes he's committed. He's asked me to facilitate his undisturbed return trip to Prague. Perhaps you could assign him an escort?"

"I'm afraid there's nothing more to be done this evening. But do calm the colonel and tell him to contact me directly tomorrow; I'll be glad to do whatever I can."

The Senior Public Prosecutor was unable to obtain more than this assurance.

In the meantime, Colonel Urbański and General Staff Captain Ronge drove to the residence of Superior Auditor Kunz, the chief of the auditing office. But he was not in Vienna. They then proceeded to a coffeehouse and looked in Lehmann's directory for an auditor of officer rank living in the ninth district. They found the name "Wenzel Vorlicek, Imperial and Royal Auditor-Major."

Poor Major Vorlicek! A hackney cab was just then waiting in front of his house. Inside, his bags were packed. He had received permission for an unscheduled leave for the purpose of taking his seriously ill sister-in-law to Davos. The sleeping-car accommodations could be obtained only with some difficulty, and he finally got them for that day and had already reserved a room in Davos by telegraph. His train left from the West Train Station at

11:20 P.M. Now the chief of the office of military intelligence and the head of the field operatives' section entered his lodgings and brought him the order to participate in a commission that would be tied up with an investigation for weeks. The sister-in-law wrung her hands in despair, the major himself was distraught. Couldn't anything be done? No; he just had to get a move on. The order came from the chief of the General Staff. Vorlicek had to yank off his civvies, put on his uniform, and jump in the car.

They rode to the deputy chief of the General Staff. Major General Höfer was pulled from bed and told that he was to serve as head of the commission. The four men then rode off to the Ministry of War first to get updated on the status of the affair. They learned of the dinner at the Riedhof, of Dr. Pollak's request, and that the police could facilitate Redl's supervised return to Prague. Furthermore, the two men were in the Café Kaiserhof after their dinner, and from there the Senior Public Prosecutor had again telephoned Councillor Gayer concerning the possibility of Redl's being brought by ambulance to a sanatorium. But by way of an answer he was just put off until the following day. At eleven-thirty at night Senior Public Prosecutor Pollak took his leave of Colonel Redl in front of the door to the Hotel Klomser.

Around midnight four officers rang at the door of the Klomser. The hotel doorman didn't want to let them into the room, in accordance with hotel regulations. But the firm manner of the men convinced him that any objections on his part would be futile. They knocked on the door of room no. 1. When they heard a hoarse "Come in," they opened the door. Colonel Redl, in casual attire, was sitting at a table writing.

He got up, unsteady on his feet. He was as white as a sheet.

"I know why you've come," he managed to say. "I've forfeited my life and was just about to write a farewell letter."

A letter of Redl to his brother lay on the table; the one he had begun to write was addressed to General von Giesl, the commandant of the Prague Corps. A pocketknife and a small piece of string lay on the washstand. ("A dagger-like knife" and a "garroting cord," said Minister of National Defense Georgi in Parliament the following week, when the military authorities were accused of having ordered Redl to commit suicide.)

The commission asked Redl about his accomplices.

"I had no accomplices," he answered.

As to the question concerning the scope of his treason, the details and duration of it, his answer was that all evidence could be found in his Prague service apartment in the corps command building. The commission seemed satisfied with this. Before leaving the room, one of them asked: "Do you have a firearm, Herr Redl?"

Colonel Redl: "No."

The member of the commission: "You may request a firearm, Herr Redl."

Redl (faltering): "I request, respectfully, a . . . revolver."

No one had one on him at the time. But he was told that he would receive one. One member of the commission drove home to pick up his Browning to hand it over to "Herr Redl."

Then the four officers waited on the corner of Herrengasse and Bankgasse to prevent the traitor from escaping death through flight. They couldn't see the window of no. 1, since the room faced the courtyard. They took turns going for black coffee. Then the Café Central closed. Hours went by. Nothing, no noise, no excitement, no shot gave away the fact that the espionage drama had found its temporary resolution. One by one the members of the commission drove home in order to change into civvies, since the coming and going of the four staff officers had already begun to attract attention in the quiet Herrengasse. The hours passed by. Nothing. One couldn't go up to the colonel, after all, and say: "Get on with it; we want to go to bed."

How late was it?

Respectfully reported: five o'clock.

The chief of the General Staff was to be called early with the report of the "ending" of the affair. Two of the officers had to take the first express train to Prague—the 6:15—to undertake the search of Redl's quarters there. A detective from the state police was thus summoned by telephone—one of the two who were involved in the pursuit of Redl and who that very night took a special vow of office to say nothing about the matter. Knowledge of the whole affair was to be limited to ten people, among them the highest personages of the monarchy. And never was anyone else supposed to be made privy to the fact that a chief of the General Staff had been a spy.

The detective who had been summoned received exact instructions on how to determine what had happened to Colonel Redl. In case he found him dead, he was to reveal nothing in the hotel, lest the extraordinary deed become known that the corpse was discovered by a police agent. With a note inviting Colonel Redl to a rendezvous, the detective betook himself to the Hotel Klomser and said that he had been ordered by the colonel to personally deliver to him at five-thirty in the morning this answer to a letter. The doorman, mindful of his futile protest against the nightly visit of the four officers, let the messenger in. He returned, barely two minutes later, and approached the people who had sent him and were waiting for him on the street.

"The room was open," he reported excitedly, "so I went in. The colonel was lying next to the sofa, dead."

This concluded the staff officers' street service—exactly twelve hours after the letters had been claimed at poste restante. So that the corpse would be found before daybreak, a call was put through to the hotel under a fictitious name requesting that the colonel be summoned at once to the phone. But then the party calling hung up immediately.

A few minutes later the Hotel Klomser informed the police of a suicide committed on their premises. Commissioner Dr. Tauss and Superior District Medical Examiner Dr. Schild then arrived to inspect the scene. They confirmed the suicide. Redl had shot himself in the mouth standing in front of a mirror. The bullet pierced the roof of the mouth, penetrated the brain obliquely from right to left, and remained in the left cranial bone; blood drained from the left nostril. He had slumped dead next to the sofa; the Browning lay alongside the corpse. Two sealed letters were found on the writing table, one to the elder brother of the deceased and one to Baron Giesl von Gieslingen, the commandant of the Prague Corps, and an unaddressed, open note with the words: "Recklessness and passion destroyed me. Pray for me. I atone for my errors with my death. Alfred."

A postscript was appended: "It is 1:45 A.M. I am going to die now. I ask that my corpse not be autopsied. Pray for me."

It was clear that this was a matter of suicide, and the police—equipped with orders concerning at least this—wanted the official act concluded quickly and unobtrusively. But they failed to take into account Redl's servant, Josef

Sladek of the 11th Infantry Regiment (whose slogan was "In true-blue loyalty"), who had no intention of accepting the verdict of suicide. In poor German, and visibly shaken, he first told the police and—when they pushed him aside—the hotel personnel, who were all ears, that the Browning did not belong to his master, that his master had no intention whatsoever of committing suicide, had gone shopping the day before and on the day of the "suicide" made all sorts of preparations in order to return to Prague on Tuesday in his specially renovated auto. Therefore, the colonel was shot to death and the revolver belonged to the murderer.

As uncomfortable for the hotel personnel as all the notoriety must have been, there was something there that lent credence to the servant's suspicions: the strange man who had come to the hotel at five-thirty in the morning to bring a message to the colonel. If he had really been fulfilling the function of messenger, then he must have seen the corpse! Why then didn't he say anything about it?

And what had the four officers been doing in room no. 1 at midnight?

The commission, which had been joined in the meantime by an officer from the command post, tried in vain to silence the rumors and suspicions. Sladek in particular was impossible to calm. Then one of the officers had the idea of convincing the annoying servant that the colonel was guilty of abusing his authority with respect to subordinates and took his own life when the truth came out. At that point the servant grew silent. For he knew something that neither the police commissioners nor the General Staff people who had orchestrated the suicide knew about: Redl's homosexuality. Then again, neither the police commission nor the stalwart Sladek had any idea of the true cause of the mandated suicide: espionage.

The personal effects of the deceased were then packed up and sealed and the corpse taken in the evening in a van to the mortuary of the garrison hospital.

The Imperial and Royal Telegraph Bureau released a report of the suicide of the chief of the Prague General Staff containing such items as "the highly gifted officer, who was surely destined for a great career, had in a attack of mental confusion . . . ," "he recently suffered from extraordinary insomnia . . . ," "in Vienna, where his official duties had taken him . . ."

The head of the office of military intelligence, Urbański, and Auditor Vorlicek traveled to Prague. The two gentlemen arrived around noon. Urbański dined with Corps Commandant Baron Giesl, who had already been made aware by telegraph that his chief of staff had committed suicide. However, it was only during the lunch with Urbański that General of Infantry Giesl learned the motive for the deed. The day before he had received a long letter from his brother, the Austro-Hungarian envoy to Belgrade, who reported that the Serbian government regarded war as inevitable. Both brothers were in constant correspondence with each other, since in "eventuality 3" (war with Serbia) the 8th Corps was assigned the advance across the Sava between the mouths of the Drina and Sava Rivers. The general's shock was all the more terrible as he had to face the fact that his spokesman and favorite had betrayed and counterchecked everything. After lunch they went to Redl's quarters, which were located in the building of police headquarters next to the offices of the corps commandant. The apartment was locked and had to be broken into. The same for the writing table and cabinets.

"By a locksmith?" I asked the former head of the office of military intelligence, who told me about this official trip.

"Yes, I believe so. It was Sunday afternoon and there was no soldier or craftsman available."

"Your Excellency doesn't know any more about where the locksmith came from?"

"No. Some locksmith, I imagine, from the neighborhood."

Lieutenant–Field Marshal von Urbański had until then responded to all the interviewer's questions with admirable patience and ready kindness. But now for the first time he seemed unwilling. The interviewer tried to excuse his silly question.

"Couldn't the locksmith have revealed the forcible opening of the apartment and cabinet drawers?"

"Meaning?" Urbański said ironically.

"I believe, Excellency, that he even told the press about it."

"I see!" Lieutenant–Field Marshal Urbański smiled in disbelief.

And at this point the interviewer interpolated a personal experience. On Sunday, 25 May 1913, the German ball club Storm played a soccer match in Prague against S.K. Union-Holeschovice. The account in the *Prager Tagblatt* the next day read as follows:

GBC Storm I against SK Union V (Holeschowitz): 5:7 (half-time 3:3). Storm dominated play from the beginning, which was evident in the number of points it scored. However, its defense was weakened by Mareček's and Wagner's absence to such an extent that Atja alone was unable to repulse all of Union's breakthroughs.

In short, an unfavorable result. The manager of Storm was doubtless most upset over the unannounced absence of Wagner, for whom he had done a favor shortly before, as managers are sometimes in the habit of doing for the stars of the leading team. In return Wagner had promised to report on time, but as early as Sunday failed to show up. The aforementioned manager (by profession the editor of a Prague newspaper and the Prague correspondent for a Berlin paper) did not have a friendly look on his face when Wagner came to visit him in his office on Monday.

"I really couldn't make it," the dilatory end tried to apologize.

"It's all the same to me." The manager remained disapproving.

"I was already dressed when an orderly came to our shop and asked for an assistant to come to the corps headquarters to break open a lock."

"Don't tell me any stories! Something like that takes five minutes. And we held up the kickoff a whole hour!"

"But I had to break into some officer's apartment and then open up all the drawers and closets . . . There was a commission from Vienna there that was looking for some Russian papers. And for photographs of maps."

"Really? And whose apartment was it?"

"Some general, I think. A very elegantly furnished place, all right."

"And the general wasn't there?"

"No, he died yesterday in Vienna."

Died yesterday in Vienna? The manager, who was an editor by profession, was no longer angry at the inexcusable end and conscientious locksmith's assistant. He no longer said, "Don't tell me 'any stories'" but instead had him tell the story all over again in detail—how the colonel from Vienna handed every photograph to the corps commandant and how he in turn shook his head in despair and said: "Terrible, terrible! Who could have imagined it possible?" And how very strange the apartment looked, as if it were a woman's, with nothing but toiletries and perfumes and curling irons, but the most perfumed letters of all were only from men, whose names were noted down by the gentlemen from Vienna.

The editor knew at once that it was the apartment of the Chief of Staff Redl, whose suicide together with an enthusiastic biography had been communicated that day by the Imperial and Royal Telegraph Bureau and was printed word for word in the afternoon papers. And he had no reason whatsoever to be discrete about the matter, since he hadn't been asked to keep any secrets, which no one had entrusted him with anyway. He began writing a report to his Berlin paper, since in Prague any announcement would most certainly be confiscated. Or should he try it after all? A consultation with the editor-in-chief. A compromise was reached: they would risk confiscation of the evening edition and would present the news in the form of a denial. "Prominent parties have requested that we publish a refutation of the rumors surfacing particularly in officers' circles that the chief of staff of the Prague Corps, Colonel Redl, who as everyone knows committed suicide in Vienna the day before yesterday, perpetrated a betrayal of military secrets and conducted espionage on behalf of Russia. The commission sent to Prague, consisting of a colonel and a major, who in the presence of the corps commandant, Baron Giesl, had on Sunday opened the service residence and cabinet drawers of Colonel Redl, had to investigate misdemeanors of a quite different character, and so forth and so on." Every reader obviously understands such denials, as when they say: "X is no cardsharp." But the report was difficult to suppress, perhaps because the public prosecutor for press matters believed that the denial originated with corps headquarters, whereas at corps headquarters they believed that it came from Vienna. So the evening paper appeared as scheduled, the wire service carried the report to Vienna, reporters raced to the Hotel Klomser, twenty emergency motions and interpellations were submitted in Parliament, and all Austria knew the real circumstances behind the suicide, which the leading foreign circles for whom Redl spied had immediately known anyway and which certain parties at home wanted to keep secret even from the emperor.

The arrest of the spy and a court trial with the examination and cross-examination of witnesses, records, and so on—all of which were bound to be revealing—had been dispensed with. For an entire night the hotel had been kept under surveillance, and special vows of secrecy had been imposed. And now the whole world knew about the matter. All because an end had missed a match. Against Union-Holeschovice.

The first thing that amazed the members of the commission when they entered the deceased's apartment was the pervasive feminine taste. The furniture was done in various shades of red; silk quilts and a pink plush throw graced the four-poster bed; alabaster was everywhere in the form of smoking accoutrements, night-table top, and figures (only the large bust of Napoleon on the writing table was made of bronze); a profusion of delicate knickknacks; and all three rooms filled with the strong scent of perfume. Conspicuous also was a huge vanity with hair-coloring materials, tubes, pans, curling irons, manicure sets, pomades, perfumes, and the like.

Only when the writing table was broken into and it was determined that the countless pastel-colored billets-doux of erotic content were in a man's handwriting was the mystery resolved: Colonel Redl had been homosexual.

Unfinished letters, crumpled and tossed into the wastebasket, attested to Redl's passion for the young uhlans officer in Stockerau. The latter had fallen in love with a girl and wanted to marry her, while Redl, with the most anguished appeals, tried to win him back.

"My dear, dear Stefan! I received your letter of the 22nd of this month and cannot believe that you really want to leave me after so often swearing loyalty and gratitude to me. I can only repeat to you that you will just make yourself miserable through this marriage. In the beginning, everything seems lovely and full of wonders, but when the mysteries are past one discovers what a woman really is. Under no circumstances tell her anything about me! Women interfere in everything, and the one thing they understand is what they are not supposed to understand. I warn you again not to leave me. I am in despair and do not know what to do. I would like nothing better than to go away with you somewhere (Davos?), and can immediately arrange a leave for you. I also think I can manage to buy you the promised Austro-Daimler (touring sedan). If you could come to Vienna, dear Stefan, write me at once, we'll then . . ."

This letter had been begun three times, but all three versions were thrown out. Redl made up his mind that it would be better to implore his friend orally not to leave him. He drove to Vienna, where he was joined by Stefan from his nearby garrison. The conversation in the hotel appears to have been concluded with Redl's promise to purchase the Austro-Daimler touring sedan. And it was to that end that he then drove to the post office, which was under surveillance at the time.

Immediately following the revelation of Redl's suicide, the young uhlans officer presented himself to the military court authorities; he voiced his suspicion that his friend had been reported to the authorities for homosexuality and because of that had taken his own life. It came out that he had absolutely no idea of his lover's espionage activity. Nevertheless he was sentenced to three years' hard labor for unnatural sexual relations.

The colonel's intimate relationship with the young officer had generally been well known, but no one found anything unusual in that, since Redl introduced the lieutenant everywhere as his nephew. In reality he was the son of a servant from Moravia and while still a student cadet was seduced by Colonel Redl. It was Redl who assumed the expense of his transfer to the Moravian-Weisskirchen cavalry cadet school, bought him two riding horses, and lavished other gifts on him as well.

Ample evidence was found of Redl's treasonable activity: receipts for transmittals of funds from Russia; receipts for exchanges of rubles; and above all photographic plates. With the shutters of his apartment windows closed, he had photographed manuals of a restricted nature, mobilization instructions, and similar items, which are composed throughout the world on the model of the German General Staff manuals—Field Marshal Moltke's masterpiece— but adapted, of course, to local railway, ship, road, and transport conditions. Redl had also photographed for his clients instructions pertaining to armaments and food supplies, rail transportation, and the implementation of troop movements as well as current orders from Minister of War Krobatin, Archduke Franz Ferdinand, and the chief of the General Staff, Conrad von Hötzendorf, dealing with organizational issues within the 8th Corps.

Although it widely maintained at the time, no evidence was in fact found establishing that Redl had betrayed concrete war preparations, as, for example, deployment plans, border fortifications, maps, artillery designs, or the names of Austro-Hungarian spies abroad. The traces of treason discovered in various hiding places in his apartment reached back just a year and a half, the length of his activity in Prague. During this period Redl's espionage had earned him nearly 60,000 crowns, some ten times his salary. From the absence of older pieces of evidence Minister of Defense Georgi deduced during his deposition before Parliament that the treason extended only over a two-year period of time. He had to admit, however, that for at least ten years Redl had pursued a life of inordinate extravagance, possessing, for example, two automobiles. Redl had indeed managed to convince people that he had considerable private means and had come into a large inheritance. Nevertheless, several years ago he had purchased an estate in Neustift-Innermanzing, had an elegantly furnished apartment in Vienna, on Wickenburggasse, apart from his place in Prague, maintained horses, and was in the habit of giving champagne parties. His crimes, therefore, must date at the least from the time he was the director of the Austro-Hungarian field operatives section in the office of military intelligence of the General Staff, if not indeed from the time of his military service with such frontier regiments as the 9th Infantry Regiment in Przemysl and the 30th Infantry Regiment in Lemberg.

In any case, Redl's behavior in Austria's greatest military discharge and espionage trial, the Hekailo-Wienckowski-Acht trial, was so strange that ten years later, after Redl's suicide, the few who had any knowledge of the matter had to suspect that he had played a double role at the time and destroyed people's lives in a way more frightful than one can imagine. In the year 1903 preliminary proceedings were undertaken in Vienna, as we know, against Colonel- Auditor Hekailo, the court examiner of the 43rd Territorial Reserve Division in Lemberg, who was suspected of having falsified receipts for purposes of embezzlement. During the strictly secret hearings Hekailo, who was on his own recognizance, fled. Only after his flight became known additional victims came forward, and their testimony made clear that Hekailo had embezzled the entire dowry of a captain of horse and the assets of his ward. A few months later Captain Alfred Redl of the General Staff appeared in the offices of the future military advocate general, Wilhelm Haberditz, who was conducting the investigation of Hekailo, and made the surprising announcement that on the basis of irrefutable evidence obtained by him, Redl, Hekailo was a spy in the service of the Russians and had probably delivered the deployment plan of the Austro-Hungarian armies to the Russians at the border town of Thorn. Through a letter sent to a friend in Galicia after his flight, Hekailo's whereabouts in Curitiba in Brazil and his assumed name

"Karl Weber" became known, and extradition proceedings were instituted. The relevant document, which of course addressed only the reprehensible crimes of swindle and embezzlement, was immediately drawn up, and the request for extradition from the Ministry of the Exterior was communicated by telegraph to the Brazilian government. But when Hekailo was about to be taken into custody, he produced a Russian passport bearing the name "Karl Weber" and placed himself under the protection of the Russian consulate in Curitiba. The decision had already been made to send a high-ranking officer to Brazil to identify the prisoner when word arrived from the Austro-Hungarian consulate in Curitiba that Hekailo had dropped his denials as soon as his trunk was opened and the jacket of his dress uniform was found right on top. Since it was now evident that the prisoner was an Austrian military person, the Brazilian gendarme officers compassionately left a loaded revolver in his cell. But Hekailo made no more use of the weapon than he did of the repeated opportunity offered him by the Brazilian lieutenant-colonel of artillery, who escorted him on the way from Paraná to Rio de Janeiro, to throw himself into the sea. In Rio Hekailo was put on board a steamship headed for Trieste. He was stowed in a cabin in steerage and must have suffered terribly in the tropical heat, since he was barely recognizable on his arrival in Vienna. According to plan Hekailo was interrogated first about his different embezzlements. The old emperor took a lively interest in the trial and was kept informed of every phase of it by his intimate friend, the chief of the General Staff, Count Beck. It was the emperor himself who urged that the investigation of Hekailo be extended as well to his espionage activity. Eventually they were able to confront the accused Hekailo with the proof of his treason. It consisted in the main of photographs and letters Hekailo had sent the Russian chief of the General Staff in Warsaw under the cover address of a governess in his employ. According to Redl's testimony, the acquisition of this evidence against Hekailo had cost 29,000 crowns, which had to be paid by the Ministry of Defense. Captain Redl had been called as an expert witness at Hekailo's hearing. Hekailo, who doubtless must have known that he couldn't be punished for espionage on the basis of the extradition request and the existing national treaty with Brazil—which is why he had not availed himself of the opportunities to commit suicide—appeared quite candid in the course of the investigation and confessed straightforwardly what he himself or with the help of third parties had delivered to the Russians, including the standby orders for the Lemberg garrison. But he claimed absolutely no knowledge of the general deployment plan. When Redl, with conspicuous overzealousness, repeatedly pressed him to admit betraying the plan, Hekailo on one occasion replied aptly: "Captain, sir, where would I have gotten the deployment plan? Only someone from the office of the General Staff in Vienna could have sold it to the Russians."

Under pressure Hekailo also named his accomplice, Major Ritter von Wienckowski, the commandant of the Stanislau auxiliary district. The very next day Major-Auditor Haberditz, armed with the broadest authority, went to Stanislau accompanied by Redl and Auditor Dr. Seliger. Immediately following Wienckowski's arrest in his office, a search of his residence was undertaken. At the outset the commission found nothing of importance there. The major's six-year-old daughter was playing with her German governess in the children's room. The pretty child was at first very shy and stared at the intruders, frightened. Only when Redl took her hand and began chatting with her in Polish did she become more at ease. Redl asked the child a few questions, such as, for example, how much two and two equals. He pretended to be very surprised that the child gave the right answers and praised her a lot, which made the child very happy. "Are you also so bright that you know where daddy keeps his papers?" "Of course," the child laughed and ran into the major's study, crawled under the huge desk, and pointed to the left corner. The heavy piece of furniture was then turned over. A concealed knob was discovered and when it was pressed, a secret drawer opened, full of incriminating documents. The commission could be satisfied with the results of its detective work, but this satisfaction was diminished by the reprehensible way in which Redl had used an innocent child to betray her own father. Moreover, the commission had no idea that Redl was a much worse criminal than Wienckowski.

How much serious material was found in this house search can be judged by the fact that the records of the investigation at the end weighed 120 kilograms. They were stored in a large crate and guarded by military sentries. Both majors inspected it only at night. Once, when Major Haberditz happened to be absent, Redl asked Dr. Seliger to let him examine a highly classified emergency mobilization plan that was among the records. Referring to his instructions, Dr. Seliger denied the request, whereupon Redl left upset. A short time later Redl suggested to Major Haberditz that he could arrange to send him, Redl, to Russia, since there were still some unclear aspects of the affair in Warsaw to be resolved. The head of the commission rejected the idea on the grounds that the proposed inquiry was not relevant to the case. Following the arrest of another accomplice, Captain Alexander Acht, the personal adjutant of the Lemberg military commandant, the commission returned to Vienna, where the interrogation of the prisoners was resumed.

A striking change then occurred in Redl. Whereas at the outset of the case he had worked so zealously for the conviction of Major Wienckowski, he suddenly began exerting himself just as zealously on behalf of his innocence. This went so far that Haberditz, who was running the interrogation, once had to reproach him privately and placed further cooperation with him in question. This led to a rather vehement argument, after which Haberditz demanded of the head of the office of military intelligence, Colonel Hordliczka, that Redl be removed from the case as consulting expert. Colonel Hordliczka agreed with him for the most part and promised to influence Redl appropriately; he couldn't, however, commit himself to Redl's dismissal, since the transfer of the leading defendants was due to Redl and he didn't want to deprive him of the fruits of his efforts. Major-Auditor Haberditz appeared satisfied, and Redl now became much more restrained and refrained especially from making further obstructive objections.

Indeed, one day he even proposed obtaining from Warsaw a specimen of mobilization instructions allegedly copied by Major Wiencikowski in his own hand, since Austria-Hungary had a very reliable Russian officer on the payroll at the Warsaw General Staff, for whom it was an easy matter to pull out of dossier "H" a small section of the document in question. However, Major-Auditor Haberditz was deeply shaken when about three weeks later Redl dryly and with an icy glance delivered the news that the aforementioned Russian General Staff officer in Warsaw was observed trying to remove items from dossier "H." A search of his desk uncovered bills for Austria, and the man was summarily hanged two days later.

After Redl's exposure his double-dealing at the time seemed pretty much elucidated: it was he himself who sold the Austro-Hungarian deployment plans to the Russians and then must have told the Russians that he absolutely had to have an espionage success for Austria. He needed this success the more so because the betrayal of the deployment plans to the Russians had become known and he desperately needed a scapegoat. The Russians then handed him the chief accused, Hekailo. They could do this the more easily since Hekailo not only was worthless to them after his flight to Brazil but had even become a liability. The Russian General Staff cheated him out of half his payoff and must have feared publicity over the matter. But when the investigation spread to regular Austrian officers in whom the Russian General Staff was still interested (Wienckowski and Acht), there would have been no lack of reproaches and threats from the Warsaw office against Redl. That was the reason for Redl's sudden intercession on behalf of the innocence of Major Wienckowski and the second officer and his attempt to convince the court officials to stay the proceedings against the two. But he didn't succeed, so Redl then had to demonstrate his continued "loyalty" to the Russians in another way and at any cost. That's when he committed his greatest villainy, by setting a cunning trap for the Russian General Staff officer in Warsaw who worked for Austria, thus abandoning him to the gallows.

Hekailo, Wienckowski, and Acht were sentenced to prison for eight to twelve years; Wienckowski died in the Josefstadt prison.

Another instance, wherein Redl caused the death of a Russian colonel who conducted espionage for Austria, is worth mentioning because of the speed of the denunciation. The successor to the throne, Franz Ferdinand, had been in Petersburg on a visit and had agreed with the tsar on various political questions. He was accompanied through Russia on the way home by Lieutenant-Colonel Müller, who was then serving as the Austro-Hungarian military attaché in Petersburg. During the trip the archduke instructed the military attaché not to provoke the tsar by unnecessary espionage. Lieutenant-Colonel Müller parted company with the successor to the throne in Warsaw. While in that city a Russian colonel of the General Staff, Kiril Petrovich Laikov, sought Müller out and offered to sell him the entire Russian deployment plans. Despite the archduke's admonishment, this was an opportunity that Lieutenant-Colonel Müller could not let pass, and he arranged the purchase of the plans. After a brief hunting trip, Müller returned to Petersburg and on the first day back encountered an icy, almost offensive rejection from people with whom he had previously been on friendly terms. Only when he read in the newspapers about the suicide of Colonel Kiril

Petrovich did he think he understood the cold reception of his former friends. It had somehow come to light that Laikov had offered to sell him the mobilization plans, and people now assumed that Müller had tempted the unfortunate man into making the offer. But that wasn't what the tsarist military had against him; what upset them most was that he had betrayed his spy to Russia. Müller, who was dismissed from his position the same day, was, however, innocent. Former member of Parliament Count Adalbert Sternberg had spoken about the affair with the wife of the Russian grand prince Pavel and with the Austrian successor to the throne, Franz Ferdinand, and concluded from the discussion that it was Redl who had betrayed Laikov to Russia and had abandoned him to certain death.

Sternberg even went so far, by the way, as to credit Colonel Redl with the blame for the World War. "This scoundrel," he said of Redl, "denounced every single Austrian spy, for the case of the Russian colonel was repeated several times more. Redl betrayed our secrets to the Russians and hindered our learning the Russian secrets through spies. Thus the existence of seventy-five [Russian] divisions—more than the entire Austro-Hungarian Army—remained unknown to the Austrians and Germans in 1914. Hence our desire for war and our defeat. Had we a clear view of things, our generals would not have pushed the court dignitaries to war."

This assertion that it was indeed Redl who had betrayed all Austro-Hungarian and even German spies who were active in Russia was often made by people involved in the affair. Such claims have a high degree of credibility, as does the assumption that Redl had also betrayed concrete preparations for war. In his deposition during the official inquiry, the Austrian minister of national defense, Lieutenant–Field Marshal von Georgi, denied this, but he was just as wrong in this respect as he was in his determination of when Redl had entered the service of the enemy. Georgi had been so duped by the General Staff Corps, which was still trying to exonerate one of their own when the individual had already been convicted of the greatest military crime. Redl had to reveal everything that was asked of him; that was clear to anyone who could imagine how Redl must have been recruited for espionage service and how very much he was in the hands of his clients from then on.

A man of Redl's capabilities and rank could not be seduced into espionage the way military greenhorns usually are. With the latter, the method was almost always the same: a young lieutenant, who was dying of boredom on duty in Cattaro, Drohobycz, or Rasuljaca, one day received an invitation from a Swiss or Dutch newspaper to write a series of articles about the life of the local inhabitants and the countryside. They had heard about his literary talent, and so on. So he took a stab at it, sent something in, received an author's copy of the newspaper—which was printed mostly for this purpose—was deliriously happy to see himself in print, received an honorarium of 200 francs and the great compliments of the "delighted" editorial staff. Other reports were then requested of him, or he was offered an editorial post with a princely wage, including vacation trips to Lausanne or the Hague. If he rejected the offer, he was subjected to considerable pressure: representatives of the Austro-Hungarian legation had already made urgent inquiries after the writer of the articles, but the people behind the paper were kept strictly secret, "as they did not want to lose the valuable contributor." This told the poor lieutenant enough. If he did not demonstrate further compliance, he would be betrayed. "Unauthorized reports to the press," perhaps even "betrayal of military secrets"—couldn't everything, after all, be regarded as a military secret?

Higher-ranking officers who were posted to border stations as punishment or had been driven to alcohol and gambling by desolation and monotony usually became dependent on loans offered by moneylenders who were secretly in the service of a neighboring state. A whole gang of such profiteers carried on this deplorable practice at the beginning of the century in Galicia and Bukovina, and it was they who managed to recruit Hekailo, Wienckowski, and Acht, among others, for espionage service.

A third technique of recruiting spies involved approaching people who were guilty of smuggling or other crimes and taking them into spy service by assuring them that they would not be punished. The most famous spies in the history of war belong to this category. Frederick the Great sent special couriers to arrange the release of the master thief Andreas Christian Käsebier from the prison in Stettin so that he could use him to get information about the situation in the besieged city of Prague before the Battle of Kolin. The king of spies, Karl Ludwig Schulmeister, otherwise known as Charles or Meinau, the great spy of Napoleon I, entered the service of the French military secret police in 1805 when his Strasbourg smuggling business was uncovered. In a certain sense Redl can also be regarded as such a victim of his previous life. It may also be fair to imagine that as head of the intelligence service he became spiritually infected. Is there any more two-faced occupation than recruiting spies and exposing spies, giving spies assignments and handing over spies for punishment? Since—Lasalle notwithstanding—work rubs off stronger on the workers than the workers on the work, the thought must have come to him as to how much better he could do this sort of thing than the poor fellows he easily exposed and who nevertheless earned a lot more money than he himself did. Yet, ambitious as he was, he never would have become involved in such a career if he hadn't become the victim of blackmail. As head of spy recruitment he would obviously be under surveillance by the agents of hostile powers, who wanted to know what contacts he was making. These agents soon found out what Redl's superiors and subordinates didn't know—that he was keeping forbidden company with men. Various circumstances suggest that the Russian military attaché whom Kaiser Franz Josef had snubbed at the court ball was the same one who pressed Redl into spying for Russia, though long before, to be sure. Once the Russian had discovered the homosexuality of his opponent, Redl was lost. The revelation of this abnormality was bound to cost him his head, while as a common criminal he could make his way up the ladder step by step, reaching as high as chief of the General Staff or maybe even higher.

The order of the Vienna district commandant who took personal charge of the funeral arrangements for the late Herr Alfred Redl, colonel in the Imperial and Royal General Staff, had already been issued. The band was rehearsing its funeral marches in the Rossauer barracks, three battalions were practicing the general volley on the grounds of the square, and the armed forces and government institutions were ordering funeral wreaths when on Wednesday morning the district commandant released a circular communiqué: "The funeral of the late Herr Alfred Redl, former colonel, is taking place without ceremony. The instructions issued yesterday on order of the district commandant are herewith canceled. Bürkl, colonel, military police."

The body was autopsied and then taken by van to the Central Cemetery. No officer accompanied it. The funeral expenses, which were borne by the brother of the deceased (who in the meantime had changed his name) and later Redl's estate, amounted to 467 crowns, including coffin, transport costs, and grave. Alfred Redl lies buried in the Vienna Central Cemetery, in grave no. 38, row 29, lot 79.

All documents, books, and photographic plates in any way related to Redl's treason were packed up in a large trunk, which the head of the office of military intelligence took back with him to Vienna. Further investigations were assigned to the auditors Dr. Leopold von Mayersbach and Dr. Vladimir Dokoupil; the notary Dr. Uhlir, who ordered the inventory made, was named court commissioner by the Malá Strana (Prague) local court. The inventory consisted of 15,184 crowns 47 hellers in cash; stocks in the amount of 5,966 crowns 38 hellers; bank deposits amounting to 2,685 crowns 90 hellers; valuables assessed at 2,618 crowns, and furniture appraised at some 3,584 crowns. Additionally there was a huge quantity of embroidered undergarments (including 195 shirts), a wardrobe with ten uniform coats made of silk and fur as well as rubber and riding coats, civilian winter coats and ulster coats, 25 pairs of Pejachevich trousers, 400 pairs of glacé kid gloves, 8 officer's sabers, 10 pairs of patent-leather shoes, and so on. Only one firearm was auctioned off: the Browning pistol with which Redl had killed himself and which was of course acknowledged as his property. His library consisted of 125 volumes on military subjects. The saddle storeroom, which was filled with caparisons, chest straps and harnesses made of patent leather, silver spurs and stirrups, as well as the photographic darkroom with Zeiss cameras, Tessar lenses, film cassettes, frames for copying, reflectors, electric developing lights, and tripods, were the most sumptuous parts of the apartment. Although the place was outfitted by specially appointed decorators from a company in Vienna, it was tasteless in the extreme. Nor did the knickknacks attest to any particular good taste of their owner: an alabaster female figure in ermine, for example, would drop its fur coat and stand naked when a concealed button was pressed! All the furnishings of the apartment together were legally appraised at a value of 33,167 crowns 75 hellers. Moreover, a full-blooded white horse, two crossbred riding horses, the two automobiles (about which jokes were passed during their auction, such as, for example, that the cars could drive to Warsaw without a driver), and Redl's property in Neustift-Innermanzing were reckoned as additional assets.

Great demands were made on this wealth. The uniform-outfitting company Szallay in Vienna was owed 9,038 crowns; the horse pool of the Imperial and Royal General Staff, 3,200 crowns; and the books, which came from the Vienna publishing house of L. W. Seidel, had not been paid for. Redl's brother claimed 4,400 crowns, including interest for outstanding loans; and furniture, laundry, auto, photographic, and shipping firms; a dentist; the Hotel Klomser (which by the way asked only 450 crowns for lodgings, wear and tear, and damages); and the servant also turned up with their own demands, so that the liabilities amounted to some 45,000 and far surpassed the assets. Hence on 30 November 1913 the Prague district court declared the Redl estate bankrupt. Since Redl's successor, Colonel Ludwig Sündermann, had to take over the service apartment, the auction of Redl's belongings was held in a room rented for that purpose on the Chotegasse in the Malá Strana. The results failed to live up to expectations. The creditors had to settle for a payment of only 14,938 crowns 30 hellers, that is, 17 percent of what was owed them.

A Prague high-school student who had bought a package of film at the auction discovered that one of the rolls had been exposed. He developed it in the presence of a teacher in the school lab. The picture of a classified supplement to the classified service manual J 15 (war timetable) came to light. The film was handed over to the corps commandant, who then passed it on to the office of military intelligence of the General Staff in Vienna.

The letters, which bear no evident relationship to the treason, are to this very day in the possession of the official bankruptcy receiver. They are love letters from men whose lack of any intellectual substance is all the more striking in view of the tendency of homosexuals generally to express more sensitive, self-analytical feelings. However, Redl's lovers were young officers and soldiers. "I grasp the pen with joy . . ." begin most of the letters and end with requests for money. A collection of some three hundred calling cards filled a drawer of his desk; all aristocratic names. He seemed to play up especially his connections to the Bohemian nobility, the attainment of noble status being his particular ambition. For the time being, though, he had to content himself with placing a civil crown above his initials on his car doors.

Two or three letters were from a Prague party girl, Ludmila H., who passed for the lover of the chief of the General Staff. But she was a "fausse maitresse," there just for the purpose of countering any growing suspicion of

Redl's homosexuality. There were also letters from her, asking for money, forthrightly declaring that out of consideration for her friendship with Redl, "in which you always demanded the maintenance of decorum," she was unable to pursue the most lucrative sources of income open to her . . .

No evidence was found attesting to any intellectual activity on Redl's part. The library on military subjects that he had ordered not long before his death had not been paid for, nor were the pages of the books ever cut open. He owned no other books and was seen at the theater only for operettas. His friendship with Dr. Pollak, the chief prosecutor of Austria, seems to have been built just on their common interest in criminal matters.

Redl was built tall and broad, his mustache was curled, and the blondness of his carefully parted hair helped along with color. He was regarded as the most energetic member of the General Staff corps, as the promptest handler of files (in Germany already in peacetime Ludendorff enjoyed the same distinction). This diligence was all the more noteworthy in light of his spying, the intrigues involved in concealing this activity as well as in concealing his homosexuality, and the affairs with his secret male friends and his public lady friend.

There is no doubt that Alfred Redl, the court official's son (his father was head of the Imperial and Royal garrison court in Lemberg),would have attained high honors had he been able to keep his clandestine activity from being discovered for another year or so, and had he survived the World War.

While Kaiser Franz Josef regarded the entire affair as a misfortune that had befallen the monarchy and about which there was nothing more to be done, the successor to the throne, Franz Ferdinand, had a different point of view. Perceiving the matter as typical for the army, he endeavored, in every way possible, to shift the blame, and he started inquiries that lasted until his death. Of three letters that we had the opportunity to inspect, the first refers to Redl's suicide. It declares: ". . . His Imperial Majesty immediately approached me and said, raising his voice: 'It is un-Christian to aid and abet in a suicide. Suicide in itself is un-Christian, but when one extends his hand (in order to facilitate it), it is outright barbarity! No other name for it! How can one permit a man to die without extreme unction? Even if he was a swine ten times over! Anyone who gets hanged receives the blessings of religion on the gallows, and that swine should have been sent to the gallows! I would have gladly let him swing, but to order a person to kill himself is un-Christian!' I took the liberty of pointing out that the suicide had not been ordered, but His Imperial Majesty interrupted me ill-temperedly: 'Let's not split hairs! It's bad enough that nobody stopped the suicide.' His Imperial Majesty was also extremely put out over the fact that no one knew anything of Redl's tendencies, and he repeated that it was a scandal that such a person had been proposed for the Crown (the Order of the Iron Crown, 3rd Class)."

A second letter of some high military figure deals with the reorganization of the War College and the General Staff that the archduke wanted to carry out in the wake of the Redl affair:

"As I was personally informed by the military office of His Imperial Majesty the Archduke and successor to the throne, His Imperial Majesty wishes to implement a complete reorganization of the War College. The cases of the War College students Jandric (espionage), Firbas (espionage), and Hofrichter (murder by poisoning), but above all that of Redl, demonstrate that morals at the college must be dreadful. Drastic measures must be taken. The resentment of His Imperial Majesty is directed especially against the chief of the Corps— and Division—General Staff and the bureau chief of the General Staff. He demands the removal of all the gentlemen from these posts and the regeneration of the entire General Staff. It is absolutely essential to bring the nobility into the General Staff; the prejudice that the aristocracy can serve only in the cavalry must be opposed."

The archduke failed to appreciate the reasons for the degeneration of war college cadets and members of the General Staff. The examinations and requirements for admission into the war college were extremely hard; the syllabus was so basically contradictory that in general only pathological ambition could achieve success. Special competence for one or another subject (for example, drawing, strategic, mathematical, or linguistic talent) was more obstructive than advantageous, since such a special ability for the most part comes at the expense of another area of activity. With the same expenditure of self-denial, energy, and ambition necessary for acceptance into the General Staff, one might just as well become an acrobat, for example. The archduke could not comprehend that such ambition might just as easily lead to criminal activity for the sake of career or money, and placed the blame instead on plebeian origins.

When the archduke finally had to acknowledge the impracticability of his radical measures, he turned his anger now more intensely against the office of military intelligence, as witness the following statement in one letter: "I cannot comprehend why an office of military intelligence even exists when an officer owns one or two automobiles and holds orgies without attracting the least attention."

The head of the office of military intelligence, Lieutenant–Field Marshal von Urbański, was the special target of the archduke's attacks. Although the chief of the General Staff and the minister of war pointed out that the office of military intelligence had performed its duty only too well in that it had trapped Redl himself, who was so familiar with its technique of unmasking spies, the successor to the throne remained unconvinced and persisted in his accusations. Urbański requested a court inquiry into his behavior, but this was rejected.

Lieutenant–Field Marshal von Urbański speaks with great bitterness about the persecution and insults he had to endure at the hands of the successor to the throne. At my request, he set down the course of this entire affair in the following memoir:

> In view of the many points of contact that existed between the military
> office of the successor to the throne and the office of military intelligence
> in that time of latent danger of war, I and my personnel felt the pressure
> of the successor to the throne very grievously. His Excellency Conrad
> von Hötzendorf tried to comfort me by mentioning the often sudden
> changes of mood of the successor to the throne, and the coming big
> maneuvers, where there would certainly be an opportunity to finally
> explain to the successor to the throne that I was in no way guilty of
> anything. I was accused above all of having offended the Christian-
> Catholic religion by approving of the suicide [of Colonel Redl]. The
> compelling motives for the suicide were acknowledged by all members
> of the commission. I was not the most senior among them, but the anger
> of the successor to the throne fell precisely on me! I should have
> recognized Redl's passion, I should have noticed his alleged extrav-
> agance, and especially his automobile ownership. Redl was a bachelor,

enjoyed all the perquisites of a colonel of the General Staff, and an apartment and stable in the corps command building in Prague were made available to him free of charge. He could avail himself, therefore, of a handsome income. I knew, moreover, from his list of qualifications that years ago he had come into a small inheritance, and in accepting him I noted "has his own means." In the time that he was my subordinate, Redl had no automobile; I could not be held responsible for his way of life later on during his military service in Vienna or when he was chief of the General Staff in Prague.

The successor's concentration of the rage against my person was nothing short of pathological, but it was soon to get worse. During the big maneuvers of 1913 that took place in the vicinity of Tabor I took charge, as in previous years, of the "attachés' quarter," that is, the assembling of all foreign officers who were present at the maneuvers as guests. The successor to the throne, by the way, behaved quite oddly, suddenly stopping the battlefield activity and over the head of the utterly amazed chief of the General Staff and those commanding the maneuvers issuing an entirely new set of orders, which now assigned a role to an ad hoc assembled "cavalry corps," which today would be regarded as exceptionally comic. At the introduction of the foreign officers, the successor to the throne was noticeably cool to me, contrary to his customary behavior on such occasions. He did not extend his hand to me the way he used to and did not speak to me, which the foreign officers interpreted as an affront to me. Things continued this way after the maneuvers for several months until an incident stirred the wrath of the successor to the throne anew. From Redl's estate, a Prague student had obtained a camera containing a roll of undeveloped film. When it was processed, it revealed a page from a mobilization handbook. A newspaper carried the report along with the sensational announcement that the roll of film contained an important order from the successor to the throne to the commander of the 8th Corps in Prague. A few hours later a telegraphic command from Konopischt Castle demanded the "legal investigation of the matter and the punishment of the guilty to the full extent of the law." Although I could exert no influence organizationally on the course of the legal investigation of the Redl case being conducted in Prague, I felt compelled to offer the advice that the court assign damages arising from Redl's traitorous activity to the armed forces administration; my ultimate goal was for Redl's entire estate to fall to the armed forces. From the ethical point of view, I found it wholly unacceptable for heirs to enrich themselves on the money acquired in a criminal way. I was particularly concerned that things connected to Redl's espionage activity, despite the keenest inspection, could still be available by chance and through an auction fall into improper hands, where they could cause new harm. The military authorities could then dispose of the estate as they saw fit, getting rid of unnecessary things, devoting money or the equivalent to some charitable cause, and so on. For reasons unbeknownst to me, the court did not accept my recommendation; in the end, Redl's entire estate passed into the hands of a notary for disposal at auction. When I learned of this, I brought to the attention of the corps commander (again in the form of counsel) that before being handed over to the notary the estate ought to be subjected to a thorough inspection in light of Redl's activities as a spy. The corps commander, following this advice, ordered a commission be established to review the estate. And still it happened that nobody thought of giving the camera, the most important corpus delicti, a closer look. Despite the fact that all these details were known to the successor to the throne, he was more than ever convinced of my guilt, and no intervention on the part of the chief of the General Staff or of the minister of war, nor the results of the legal examination were of any help; it was all in vain, you were up against a wall! The Prague auditors were taken into custody, but I couldn't be gotten rid of so fast until a trained replacement had been found.

In January 1914 I was officially informed that in the course of 1914 I would receive a brigade command. I immediately had to arrange for the replacement of the military attaché in Bucharest, Colonel von Hranilovic, and instruct him as my successor, since the chief of the General Staff attached great importance to our working together at least half a year in view of the wealth of material.

Easter 1914 was approaching. Our envoy in Cetinje, Freiherr von Giesl (Junior), was in a sanatorium in Berlin following a serious operation. The political waters were getting more treacherous, and the absence of our envoy in this tinderbox was felt keenly. His Majesty the Emperor wanted Giesl to return to his post as quickly as possible. Though barely fit for travel, Excellency Giesl rushed back to Cetinje. Around this time, my office was receiving rumors from several sources that

assassination attempts on our envoy were being planned by the Montenegrans for the purpose of confusing the situation, and that these attacks
were to take place, in fact, during his journey while he was still in
Austrian territory. I received instructions to ensure that Excellency von
Giesl reach Cetinje unharmed, as the consequences otherwise were unforeseeable. I set out for Bocche di Cattaro. Envoy von Giesl was
transferred from a steamship to a torpedo boat while still at sea and
landed at the naval station, from where he was delivered to his post safe
and sound. During the ship's stop in Spalato I had learned that the post
of brigadier in Spalato would soon be free. The prospect of leading a
tranquil provincial existence after years of grueling work at headquarters
so excited me that on the very day of my arrival in Vienna, on 10 April
1914, I asked the minister of war to put in my name for the brigade
command in Spalato. To my very great surprise, the minister of war
revealed to me that he had a firm order concerning me from the successor
to the throne, which he was admittedly not carrying out, but the Ministry
of War had indeed intended to give me the brigade command of Semlin
(on the Serbian border), where I would have the opportunity to
"rehabilitate" myself! The old grudge all over again; but there was
nothing for it—the obstinate nature of the successor to the throne could
not accept any outside judgment.

On 29 April 1914 the last act of this persecution, which can only be
explained in pathological terms, finally took place. At a signal from the
chief of the General Staff, I appeared unsuspecting at a conference, as I
did every day. Obviously upset, Excellency von Conrad told me that he
had to read me an order from the successor to the throne. The document
read as follows: "I have come to the irrevocable view that the drive and
intellectual vigor of Colonel von Urbański have suffered to such an
extent that he can no longer be considered for active service and must
undergo a thorough medical review."

I composed myself enough to reply: "I trust that in this unequal
contest I shall remain the more noble member."

The comedy then continued. A compromise was concluded with the
doctor. I was, thank God, quite healthy, so we agreed on a "nervousness
of medium severity, which doubtless would be remedied in the course
of six months." This wise medical opinion was also acceptable to both
doctors of the medical review commission, whereupon the head of the
commission approved Colonel von Urbański's request for a six-month

leave with pay. This was the agreement worked out between the chief of the General Staff, the minister of war, and me, since open defiance of an order from the successor to the throne seemed quite hopeless. The times were not propitious to these officials' making a state issue of me. I assumed no further duties and wound up all my personal affairs in order to spend the time until the resolution of my fate on my wife's property near Graz. But even there I was to be denied peace and quiet. The news of my sudden exit had already become common knowledge in Vienna; it was commented on in the press; politicians of various shading on both sides of Parliament, especially those who frequently opposed the successor to the throne, tried to get information from me; military people demanded clarifications. An archduke, among others, invited me to see him. With his request that I tell him the whole truth, unvarnished, about the disciplinary measures taken against me, I tried to avoid the issue by referring to the official secrecy that forbade me to discuss the subject. The archduke replied that he was not asking out of curiosity. But then he came out with something that amazed me because of its openness: "In the final analysis I am sure it's all the same to you whether in the foreseeable future you wear the emblem F. J. I. [Franz Josef I] or W. II [Wilhelm II] on your cap . . . Yes, we Habsburgs are well aware that our throne stands on unsteady ground, and that the army is our only support. And when its confidence in the dynasty is shaken, then we're done for. Arbitrary acts attributed to the successor to the throne, of which your own case seems to be one, are just too suited to undermining confidence in the army . . ."

I was only too well aware that there existed a faction at the court eager to denigrate the successor to the throne's suitability for the succession; my own case should strengthen the argument for his inaptitude.

My discussion with the head of the military chancellery of His Majesty the Emperor, Freiherr von Bolfras, was more serious. When the medical leave decision concerning me reached his hands, he asked to see me and greeted me with the words: "My dear Urbański, did you steal a silver spoon? Is that why they're so anxious to get rid of you all of a sudden?" When I informed Excellency Bolfras of the reasons for my transfer to nonactive status, he declared categorically that he could not submit the memorandum to His Majesty. There were good reasons why the emperor would have a fresh recollection of me in recent years.

In 1908 I had been active in Uesküb as *adjoint militaire d'Autriche-Hongrie* of the reform constabulary for Macedonia. When the revolution in Turkey erupted, I had to endure the first onslaught of Serbian wrath on the occasion of the impending annexation of Bosnia and Herzegovina. His Majesty personally heard out my views concerning the probable consequences of the annexation. In the following years, my office supplied the daily reports concerning the current military developments, the Balkan war, the Tripoli campaign, and so on. These reports had to be in Schönbrunn at four in the morning, when the emperor began his workday. During my direction of the office, two Russian military attachés from their embassy in Vienna had to leave their posts when they were charged with espionage by the office of military intelligence. In short, the emperor had good reason to keep me in mind. For Christmas 1913 he had, after all, awarded me the Order of Leopold, an indeed rare distinction for a colonel, and in January 1914 decided that I was to receive a generalship some time during the year. And now suddenly this retirement. The emperor will most certainly inquire as to the reasons. But if one were to tell him truthfully that it was an arbitrary decision of the successor to the throne contrary to all the views of responsible parties, then, in light of the well-known tense relations between the emperor and the successor to the throne, a serious conflict would be unavoidable, and this could not be risked because of the emperor's ailing condition. Thus the memorandum remained in a drawer of Excellency von Bolfras' desk. It lay there unprocessed when the successor to the throne died suddenly and my career then entered another phase. The chief of the General Staff had long resisted any cessation of the maneuvers in Bosnia and even more the planned ceremonial entry of the successor to the throne and his wife into Sarajevo shortly thereafter. My office was also receiving repeated warnings concerning almost certain hostile Serbian plots. Yet despite all this the successor to the throne insisted on going ahead with his politically motivated visit to Bosnia. Because of his position, the chief of the General Staff had to attend the maneuvers, but he had no wish whatsoever to take part in the subsequent agenda. That is why a trip of the General Staff into Upper Croatia was arranged so that the chief would have to leave the successor to the throne immediately after the conclusion of the maneuvers. On the way to Lika, the point of departure for this trip, the news of the Sarajevo assassination caught up with him along with the order that he return at once to Vienna.

Immediately after his arrival in Vienna, Excellency von Conrad informed me that my affairs had now taken another direction. A few days later I received a letter from the Ministry of War of similar content along with the proposal that I take a three-month leave of absence in order to recover from all the upsets and insults that I had been put through. In the meantime, war broke out, I went into combat as the commander of a brigade and soon received the command of the same division, which I led to the end of the war.

So concludes the memoir that articulates the defense not only of its author but also of the entire General Staff. It not only approves of the behavior of the "chief," who had ordered the suicide of one of his subordinates, but also attempts to exonerate the traitor-spy Redl, of whom Urbański also asserts in discussion that he, Redl, had no knowledge of anything crucial and betrayed no actual war preparations. The memoir is indeed a record of the "true-blue spirit of the corps," whereby the corps brethren of the Austro-Hungarian General Staff regarded themselves as the highest class of the military caste and took orders (death included) only from their superior. They despised the troops, disregarded any sense of justice when any one of their own was concerned, and paid no heed either to the successor to the throne or to his military chancellery; they tolerated absolutely no interference in the affairs of their corps. The Praetorian guard was always more powerful than the regent. Even the international scandal of the Redl affair provided Archduke Franz Ferdinand no pretext, despite all his efforts, to get rid of a colonel he didn't like (albeit groundlessly). On the contrary: the officer was even honored with the Order of Leopold and was nominated for promotion to general. Indeed, the document effectively retiring him from service had not been submitted to the emperor for his signature, and its ostentatiously rapid withdrawal after the murder of the successor to the throne rings of the scorn of survivors. Naturally the behavior of the archduke, by its very rage, indicates that his power was opposed by the power of the General Staff, and that his arrogance was opposed by the arrogance of the double-breasted bottle-green tunics. The General Staff allowed none of their own people to be called before a military court, nor was an auditor permitted to convict a member of the General Staff; hence Redl's suicide.

Colonel Redl had obviously known of all crucial measures for mobilization on the part of the army and all actual preparations for war, since members of the brotherhood kept no secrets from one another. And Redl had to reveal what was asked of him, even if greed hadn't compelled him to provide the best information. He was chief of the Austro-Hungarian General Staff and a Russian-Italian-Serbian spy. He could be coerced with a single word.

The criminal case of Redl may appear unique. But it will always be repeated in one form or another, for nations themselves are the instigators of this crime, which nations themselves punish with death by means of the noose, exile to Devil's Island, or the order to commit suicide.

Egon Erwin Kisch, *Der Fall des Generalstabschefs Redl* (Stuttgart: Klett-Cotta, 1988). Originally published in 1924 by Verlag die Schmiede, Berlin.

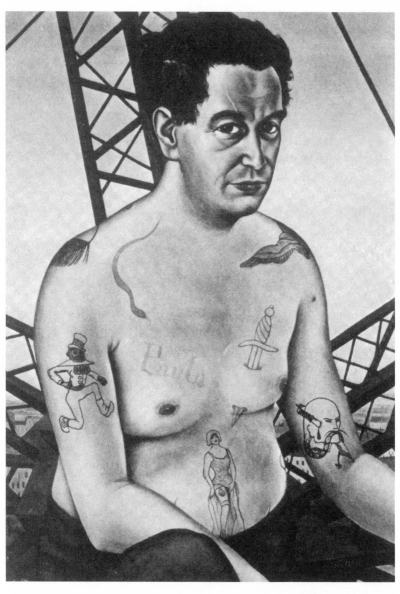

Painting of Kisch by Christian Schad.
Courtesy Kiepenheuer & Witsch Verlag.

My Tattoos

My roommate Heinrich, whose forty duels and thirty-five saber matches have turned his face into a herringbone pattern, his scalp into mincemeat, and his body into the illustrated section of a textbook on surgery, scornfully shakes the aforesaid mincemeat when I stand at the sink with bare chest. "It's unfathomable to me," he says, "how a person can let himself get so messed up!"

The retired postal clerk Anton Schissling, who is plagued by his conscience because he overcharged someone fifteen pfennigs once selling stamps, also considers my tattoos unwise. In the steam bath he swore that he would never ever let something like that be done to him. "If I ever commit murder, or anything like that, the police all over the world would be able to identify me."

Much the same sentiment is expressed by Harelip Willy, who really does have something to do with the police; he was convicted of counterfeiting in Rome and Stockholm, of check fraud in New York, of fencing stolen goods and swindling in Berlin—altogether he got eighteen years. When he limps in—fortunately you hear his clubfoot striking the pavement from afar, and the birthmark on his cheek sparkles from fifty meters away—I dodge him quickly, since he's forever mocking me: "Haha, I'm not so stupid to get tattooed just to make it easier for the police!"

My company commander, who has worn a medallion around his neck as a good-luck charm from the day he was born, found it inconceivable that a person would allow himself to be tattooed. "Even the thought of having the same thing on my body my entire life would drive me mad."

My ladyfriend Lu has universal principles. "One shouldn't tinker with the body God gave us." At which point she turns up her sweet little pug nose, for which she paid Professor Josef a hundred and fifty dollars last year without batting an eyelash, while she finds it outrageous that the young doctor in the Charité asks five marks for piercing her little daughter's ears. "Two tiny holes for the earrings! Isn't that a gyp?"

Herr Sigmar Wreschowinsky is angry at me for not following his advice on a tattoo remover and, what's more, letting myself get tattooed yet again. "You'll regret it for sure! I also committed such stupidities when I was a horse dealer in Frankfurt on the Oder and when I had a booth at the fair in Perleberg; and even when I had already worked my way up to traveling salesman in the ready-made-clothes business, I had models of blouses tattooed on my chest, since the customers, servant girls, like making their selections best of all in the flesh. But now I've had to have everything scraped out, although I'm diabetic. Is it fitting for a Berlin art adviser to run around with a tattooed body; how does that look?"

My first tattoo is already old; its subject attracted a lot of attention, although in this respect I'm innocent. I was sitting in army detention next to a lithographer, who offered to tattoo a still life on my back. What he actually did was engrave on me the perfect likeness of our colonel, head first and tongue stuck out, sliding down my back, deep down my back . . . It was no doubt the personal wish fulfillment of my cellmate that he applied to my reverse side without my noticing what he was up to. The other prisoners nearly split their sides laughing at my ignorance; they stood around the artist and kept on emphasizing how well the wine bottle, the roast goose, and the flower vase were turning out. When the work was finished, I expressed my regret that I couldn't examine it, since, unfortunately, we had no mirror in our cell. During the night the picture swelled up—it was injected with boot polish—to such an extent that I had to report to the infirmary. The regimental doctor at once recognized whom the picture represented and reported it. All the officers came in in a body and I had to unveil the artwork before them. But not a one of them believed my declaration that I had no idea what was being painted behind my back on my back. The lithographer, moreover, couldn't lie about it being the colonel who was prominently displayed, all puffed up red, on my hide. The colonel himself caught the resemblance and was so outraged he suffered a stroke. The tribunal revoked my officer's candidacy and lengthened the term of my imprisonment.

But I soon had to be released because the colonel died and a portrait of him was needed for the funeral ceremonies; the one on my back was the only one available. An artist copied the drawing while I stood on my head. The copy was a failure. And when the widow wanted to see the image of her late lamented, she came to me, kissed the dear features and moistened them with her tears.

In 1906, in a shop under the Galata Bridge in Constantinople, I allowed a character to tattoo me on the right arm. I did it because:

1. I had just left military service and so could let myself be tattooed, where and how I wanted, without any officers reading me the riot act;

2. I wanted to find out if tattooing was less painful without boot polish; and

3. mainly because the poster convinced me. It was in English and German.

This Yankee impressed me! He knew how to make the most of his experiences at sea! He understood the psyche of seamen and longshoremen of all nations! Such extravagance with exclamation marks and superlatives—pure American! It was a spur-of-the-moment decision on my part, and the next moment there I was, standing face-to-face with the former chief petty officer and tattooer of the flagship *Columbus* (USA)—America! I asked him to show me his finest models so I could choose whichever I wanted, according to my own taste, just the way it said on the poster. To his very great regret, Herr Alfred Löwenfeld of Prossnitz had sent the album to a ship's captain for approval half an hour before—what rotten luck! So today he had just a single model to show me, the famous Negro performer Bimbo. I had a look at Bimbo; a disgusting Negro variety theater artist with a mouth like a chimpanzee's butt and a necktie that looked like a rotten strawberry. Before I could attempt to leave, Alfred Löwenfeld had already grabbed my arm; the next thing I knew, the outline of the revolting figure was transferred from the decal onto my arm, a murky India ink was poured from its little bottle into a well, and an electrical apparatus turned on. With something that was half syringe, half needle, which was fed from the apparatus with electricity and from the inkwell with India ink, he traced the outline of the Negro in such a way that blood and ink mixed. He wanted to do the trousers in black, but I vehemently resisted the idea. My protest was to no avail, though, when he bordered the black bulging eyes in green. He was right—otherwise you couldn't see the eyes in the black face—so I let poisonous-green circles be engraved on my arm.

During the operation the old American chief petty officer from the flagship *Columbus* told me that up to the previous year he ran a grocery store in Prossnitz but went bankrupt. He left there in the dead of night, intending to go to Palestine, where he believed he had a nephew. But he got so seasick on the way that he had to disembark here in Constantinople. "And then I met a Norwegian who had this tattoo parlor. I thought that this'd be something for me and 'cause the Eskimo convinced me that business was good, I told him I was supposed to become a partner in an export business in Jerusalem, but if he gave me his business I'd let him have mine in trade and my steamship ticket as well. He agreed, and I went with him to a notary, since he wanted to have a proper document to the effect that I was surrendering my shares in the Jerusalem firm to him . . ."

"What did you say the name of the company was?"

"I don't remember it any more—some address or other—it's all the same, isn't it? To make a long story short, he sailed away on my ticket. For safety's sake, I saw to it that he can't come back, and I've remained here since. But no customers came into the shop—I ask you, who's so dumb nowadays to get tattooed? It was a bust; the crook took me for a ride. He just left me this rusty piece of equipment, which I can cause the loveliest blood poisoning with." He was just then engraving the rotten-strawberry necktie, so that carmine, blood, and India ink produced a splendid indecency. "You can imagine the trouble I'd have with the authorities if one of my customers died of blood poisoning! Nobody'd come into the shop if I hadn't had that poster made up—every now and then some nitwit falls for it!"

The creation of Bimbo had come to an end. It hurt, a lot more than injected boot polish. Guaranteed painless, I thought painfully. It'll wear off in eight days, Mister Lionsfield assured me; I just had to keep my arm raised the whole day and apply a lot of Vaseline to it. In fact, the swelling went down after a longer treatment by an outstanding dermatologist; only the green eyes flare up every year. But it's precisely because of those penetrating eyes (and no one knows better than me how they penetrate!) that women adore the tattooed Negro. Even years later they ask me: "How is your Bimbo doing; does he still get inflamed so often?" When I'm in company I don't like such inquiries, as people then want to know who this Bimbo is, and then I'm obliged to exhibit the black monster with the green eyes.

The tattoo on my left forearm portrays the head of a Chinese Mandarin with an elaborately tooled scimitar stuck in his temple. A butterfly perches on the decorated handle; the dead man's pigtail is laid on his mouth; blood drips from the temple; bloody too are his neck, the point of the knife, and the little ribbon around the masterfully plaited pigtail. Even the butterfly on the sword handle is in two colors, its wings done in red and blue. I picked out this drawing in the China House of Trieste's Cività vecchia from the many hundreds of pictures in the pattern book presented me by the renowned tattooer of the Adriatic. For a moment it seemed to me that the yellow-skinned master was surprised, that his slanted eyes squinted even more, and that there was irony in his question: "Why do you want even this?"[1] "I like this picture," I replied, whereupon he rubbed in the India ink, dissolved the merveilleux-red in a second little well, and with the needle now began engraving under my skin, precisely, soundlessly, the head with the blood stains, the fine plaiting of the pigtail, the veins of the butterfly, and the metal-work of the sword handle. Only when he was done, after carefully scrutinizing his work, he turned to me—again with that insidious smile of his—and asked if I knew what the tattoo represented. I didn't quite understand what he meant by the question. "That's the picture of a murdered Chinaman." Idiot, I thought, what else can it be! There was nothing more to get out of him, and I had no doubt that I had picked out the insignia of some secret Chinese order, a Boxer Rebellion society, or even some terrorist organization.

I was disabused of this delusion only several years later when some friends who happened to be London shipowners and I made an excursion to Pennyfields, the district of the West India docks. We made for the old crook Tschang Tu-tao, who not only owned a "Chinese Seamen Licensed Boarding

House" but also a less-licensed opium den as well as a business in Chinese bric-a-brac: pictures of birds on silk and bronze chimeras, jade idols, carved ivory boxes, little pagodas of porcelain or black amber—souvenirs or amulets that emigrants from the Middle Kingdom had left behind here as a deposit for a night's lodging or in lieu of payment for a ball of opium, or mementos of "Jack Tar," the English sailor, who had to sell them after disembarking on the Thames, since his seaman's sign-on bonus didn't suffice for the obligatory rounds of gin. My friends had learned at the ship exchange that a schooner from Peking today unloaded six geishas, who were staying at Tschang Tu-tao's. We wanted to have a look at them before Scotland Yard took an interest in their immigration.

We climbed up the staircase to the first floor, where in one room some thirty Chinamen were squatting on the floor, pipes in their mouths, whiskey glasses and teacups in front of them, their yellow faces turned toward the charcoal stove. The girls were sitting with them. At our entrance all the men leaped up, surrounded us, and started yelling: "Firemen? You want firemen?"[2] No, we didn't need any stokers; disappointed, the poor devils crept back to their places next to the girls. They were to be deprived of these too. Tschang Tu-tao came out from behind the counter and led us—without really asking what it was we wanted—to the second floor, past several rooms from which the sweetish-stinging smell of the opium merged with the already scorching heat of the house. Smokers were lying all around, lovingly rolling a soft mass into balls, holding them over the oil lamp, and then smearing them into the thick-stemmed pipes.

The head of the establishment deposited us in the "saloon" and took our order: real tea, served by the aforementioned geishas. He disappeared below, where the conversation stopped; the job-seeking "firemen" probably were learning the reason for our visit and that they had to let the girls go in order for them to serve the white gentlemen. The sudden silence was frightening. The tea maidens entered, shy and servile, bowed low three times, their hands touching the floor, began helping us out of our jackets and vests, and—suddenly the girl who was helping me stopped and stared speechless at the tattoo on my left arm. Aha, I thought, now she's noticing what a he-man I am. But she soon let out a shriek and began laughing. The other girls came over, shrieked as well, and laughed and laughed. Snorting, they raced out the door, down the stairs, and into the boss's office. The ominously pregnant stillness turned into uproarious laughter.

Nonplussed, we waited for the girls to return. We called our host, but he didn't come. We heard only the laughter, in bass and treble. We put our jackets back on and were about to leave when Tschang Tu-tao appeared, trying his best to maintain a serious expression. We asked him about the meaning of my etching. After a long hesitation, he came out with it: every man who was accepted into the service of the imperial Chinese women's quarters—whether Asian or European, it made no difference—was tattooed at the time he was castrated with the severed head, as a warning of the punishment that awaited him should he violate his duties, and as identification in case of attempted flight. Even in imperial China men tattooed with the "win," the sign of the eunuch, were objects of secret scorn; in the republic they were openly ridiculed, and nobody had anything to do with a "win-ho." Thirty quince-yellow faces smirked on the staircase as the girls pointed me out to their countrymen: "There he is, the 'win-ho.'"

The prettiest tattoo I've ever seen belongs to Admiral Horthy:[3] a dragon in green and gold that takes up the whole left side of his chest. Horthy used to put in an appearance every day at the Polesaner Marinebad spa, the upper left of his undershirt lowered so that everyone could admire the drawing. He let young naval officers and spa guests gather around him and, almost always in the same words, would then describe the details of the tattoo. Besides the dragon, he was tattooed on another part of his body. Egged on by officers of the admiral's staff, I asked him on 10 June 1918, after dinner on the *Viribus Unitis,* during the sole journey of the Austro-Hungarian dreadnought flotilla, to show me his other tattoo. He complied with my wish. A few hours later an alarm was sounded. The *Szent István,* the biggest and newest dreadnought in service, which was steaming behind us portside, had been struck by a torpedo, was wrecked, and sank. Everyone had to get up on deck in order to keep a lookout for enemy U-boats. Horthy refrained from coming to the help of the shipwrecked crew on the grounds that he couldn't expose the flagship to the danger of being torpedoed as well. Upset, he walked back and forth, and when he saw me, he came up to me. "I shouldn't have shown you the tattoo, Lieutenant; whenever I show it to anyone, some terrible disaster strikes." The disaster was indeed terrible—the number of dead was never released. Only fourteen corpses were recovered, which we buried two days later in the naval cemetery.

Archduke Franz Ferdinand was tattooed on the right hip, and with an Ibis serpent, which the Egyptians regard as a good-luck charm. Crown Prince Rudolf had the same tattoo above his heart, but with the serpent's head pointed inward instead of outward. That is why the totem did not protect the Crown Prince from the fatal shot; Archduke Franz Ferdinand used to tell people that the Arab who made the tattoo perhaps intentionally engraved the opposite symbol on the infidel. Incidentally, he'd say, his own tattoo was not perfect either; the serpent flicks its tongue upward, but it doesn't matter, since the tattoo is in a harmless place—a soft part of the right side of the body. The autopsy of the assassinated successor to the throne later revealed that the fatal bullet penetrated "above the right hip bone, right through the middle of a tattoo."

Albert Londres relates in his book *Le Bagno* that French convicts in the deportation stations engrave entire wigs on their shaved heads and glasses around their eyes.[4]

Tattooing is often done out of boredom in the military and in prisons. During the elections to the national assembly of the Yugoslav kingdom, a candidate vehemently railed against his Croatian-Agrarian opponent, who previously had belonged to "His Majesty's most obedient opposition" and was now posing as a republican, while he, the speaker, had been fighting against the monarchy from the time he was a young man, and so on and so forth. The agrarian was dumbfounded and could barely utter a word; when he was finally able to, he unbuttoned his collar, opened his shirt a bit, and declared that he acknowledged the greater determination of the esteemed previous speaker and was prepared to withdraw from the election if the opposition candidate would similarly stand before the assembly with bared chest. In this way he won, for on the other's chest was tattooed a magnificent imperial Austrian eagle.

Egon Erwin Kisch, "Meine Tätowierungen," "Der rasende Reporter," *Der rasende Reporter. Hetzjagd durch die Zeit. Wagnisse in aller Welt. Kriminalistisches Reisebuch* (Berlin and Weimar: Aufbau-Verlag, 1972), 87–96.

1. The line is in English in the original.

2. In English in the original.

3. Miklós (Nicholas) Horthy (1868–1957), Hungarian admiral and statesman. He commanded the Austro-Hungarian fleet in World War I. After the failed communist coup d'état of Béla Kun in 1919, Horthy took power as regent in 1920 and ruled Hungary until the end of World War II.

4. Albert Londres was a Parisian journalist whom Kisch held in high esteem. The only work of his to be translated into English, as far as I know, is an exposé of prostitution and "white slavery" in South America, under the title *The Road to Buenos Ayres,* trans. Eric Sutton (London: Constable & Co. Ltd., 1928). Theodore Dreiser wrote an introduction to this edition.

The Bombardment of Scutari and the Fire in the Bazaar, 11 May 1913

The column of smoke, into which the column of fire had transformed itself today, is our destination.

The steamer leaves the Montenegran shore and rolls through the mouth of the Rijeka River until the river bed widens immeasurably. We are in Lake Scutari. It is entirely covered with vegetation, with trees standing in water up to their crowns, with foliage plants that are flush with the surface, and with tall reeds. Through this thicket of water flora narrow lanes have been cleared and marked off with wooden pegs. This is the route the ship has to follow—crisscross, zigzag, and around sharp curves. In the distance the mountains of Albania, among which the earthly cloud appears today. We pass Lesandro, where before 1877 the largest Turkish fortress stood, past Grmosur, where the Montenegran prison stands. Two hours later, we reach Virpazar, change vessels, and sail on the *Neptune* toward Scutari. The Krunya Mountains, steep, dark, and jagged, loom on the right, and beyond them the Tarabosh, the village of Ckla, where this week Crown Prince Danilo received the truce negotiators of Essad Pasha, the villages of Zogaj and Sirocki Vir, over the roofs of which, from the last position on the Tarabosh, thousands of shots rain down to the very present, the mountain chain of Bardanjol, and behind them the Bertica Mountains.

Two smokestacks and the stern of a sunken steamship rise from the water. From the top of a strong mast triangles run into the lake—a sailboat that has been riddled with bullets from the mountains. Farther out the mast of a wreck. How many people are lying on the bottom? The Turks set up miles of barbed-wire installations right to the shore and far out over the shore into the sea in order to prevent the unobserved entrance of ships.

The citadel of Scutari overshadows us, the Mrnjacvica ridge over the Bojana River. The blue-red-white symbol of victory of Montenegro flies from the pinnacle. The old town is down below, from which the last flames of the fire leap up, enveloped in clouds of smoke.

The *Neptune* drops anchor, very near the place where Lake Scutari flows into the Adriatic as the Bojana. Big barks with dirty Albanian boys push their way to the ship; scolding and tugging, each of them tries to attract as many disembarking passengers as he can into his own bark to row them to the Bojana for the fare of one piastre. The route follows along large corn-storage facilities until it suddenly turns into the main street of the Tepé, the old bazaar quarter.

Here is the site of the terrible conflagration. For months the bazaar, this city of small shops and stands crammed into corridors and stuffy rooms, had survived the fire of heavy artillery from the Tarabosh and Bardanjol, at a time when there was no water supply and no fire-extinguishing equipment. But yesterday, on the second day after the siege had ended, a burning cigarette butt or the spark from a charcoal stove transformed the eight hundred shops into a single pitch torch. The flames blazed so high that they startled us on the other, distant side of the lake.

Now everything that was alive yesterday is dead; everything that was merchandise is rubble. A cordon of soldiers blocks the entrances to the smoking remains of the vault. Nothing of the rooms remains except the side walls. Between them lie stones, smashed tiles, melted tin containers, carbonized leather, burst cabinets, sooty fragments, stinking tobacco, rugs full of holes, tattered lace, ruined cooking utensils—a worthless hodgepodge of things that yesterday were meant to attract buyers and today aren't worth being picked up by the most desperate beggar. The conflagration spared nothing; even the metal fastener on a purse lying on the flagstones was warped, and the melted pieces of copper next to it had been hard-earned money.

Everywhere it glowed under the ashes, and the air, as if it couldn't believe that the vaults of the bazaar are no longer blocking its exit, as they had for hundreds of years, falters in its old cage. Clouds of smoke rise from the volcanoes of rubble and the smoldering remains of wood, but they don't want to drift away, they remain between the perpendicular walls. All the streets, thirty-two blocks of houses, have been burnt so low that nothing can be seen but the brick facades, and often not even these but just desolate places where wooden houses once stood. People whose possessions are going up in the smoke here are being admitted into the area of the fire. No laments are heard. Women search in vain in the funeral pyre for some treasure from their shops; children are sitting on the new black mounds playing with oddly melted metal objects. A Turk sits cross-legged in front of one of the fire-spitting mounds, looks into space, and takes deep drags through a cigarette holder. A tin of tobacco and tissue paper lie at his feet, ready as a quick replacement. His face is quince-yellow; caffeine and nicotine, as well as the rival temptations of his wives, plowed the crow's-feet at the corners of his eyes and the wrinkles extending from the base of his nose to his mouth. Nevertheless, his ancestry and faith bequeathed him his hollow-eyed look. Destiny is preordained. It has been so inscribed in the Book of Life from the very beginning that the Tepé of Scutari would be burned down, yesterday, on such and such a day of such and such a year after the Hegirah, on the day that it falls into the hands of the unbelievers.

A fire hose stands exhausted. It sought to perform its fire-extinguishing task. Just it, all by itself. Smoke constricts the throat, stench penetrates the nose, soot gets in the retina. A charred dog bares its fangs . . . Away from the area in which the elements wanted to demonstrate that they were capable of answering the devastating activities of man with more devastating ones of their own.

From the choking air the way leads through a Moslem cemetery that recalls the renowned tombs of that other, Asiatic Scutari. Even if the city of the dead of Albanian Scutari is smaller, it is no less stunning. You go through a heliotrope-colored forest of blossoms; they are irises that grow on the Turkish graves and cover the engraved Koranic suras.

The main street of the city. Low houses, completely riddled with bullets or half collapsed from the concussion of the cannonading, but still inhabited; ornate windows; a stream carrying dirt and excrement past houses; yet roses have grown up about the staircases, and acacias give off a fragrant scent. Under the elms: coffeehouses, narghiles on tables, their tubes joining together all the guests into a single larger than life-size animal with many heads. The shops have no windows, only horizontal boards on which the owners and their guests are crouching. Tobacco shops predominate. In front of brown mounds of cigarette tobacco sit merchants, and a hanging scale is their sole piece of equipment. In open bakeries strange pastries and white bread are being baked by hands that inspire little confidence. Shoemakers work in full view of the public, small shopkeepers with figs, goat cheese, dates, firewood, onions, corn, and the petals of the sumac tree, which grows only here and whose blossoms are used for tanning and blackening hides, fermenting vinegar, and flavoring tobacco. The track of a narrow-gauge freight railway runs through the entire city, but it isn't in service; the route has been all shot up. Eighty-five hundred artillery shells rained down on the city during the siege.

In the enormous plaza formed by three barracks wings and, on the other side of the street, by the hospital still under construction, stand Montenegran troops lined up for prayers. With a command for the shout "Živeo" ["long life," in Serbian], which a thousand voices repeat, they then fall out. Turks and Albanians leaning against the lower walls of the road look on in amazement.

There are eight thousand Montenegran soldiers in Scutari, most clad in brown-green field uniforms, but one also encounters at every turn the bright-red *dushanka*[1] with the appropriate blue canvas pants; many rifle-bearing reservists with red, white, and blue service ribbons; patrols on foot and on horse; emaciated and ragged Turkish soldiers in moss-green uniform; Montenegran officers with gold epaulettes and flat gray caps, with the "grb";[2] Turkish officers with their sabers and tall fur caps; wealthy Albanian women with pink-and-silver-embroidered blouses, gold-embroidered headbands, wide, flowery tunics, and barrellike pantaloons; harem wives dressed all in black and veiled; husky Turkish peasant women with white canvas men's trousers beneath their short skirts; Shqiptars, Arnavuts, Malissors, light Ghegs, and coal-black Tosks,[3] the men attired in white fustanella, a kind of pleated woman's skirt, stockings made of tanned sheepskin, and pointed shoes; Gypsies in rags and Gypsy women in carpet material. From a geography book titled *The Land of the Shkiptars,* the illustrated figures come to life and walk about and speak, speak all dialects spoken from the Adriatic to the Pindus, from Scutari to the Gulf of Arta, but Turkish, Greek, Serbian, and Italian can also be heard. For a gold coin you get all kinds of paper money back: piastres, dinars, liras, crowns, and so on.

There are two hotels in Scutari, but no accommodations to be had inside or out. While I negotiate with the doorkeeper, the deposed Turkish chief of police and municipal head of Scutari, Suleiman Bey, comes in and invites me to spend the night with him. "Oh, je suis charmé, mon président!" "Vous me connaissez?"[4] He didn't notice me yesterday at the court dinner of King Nikita's in Cetinje[5]—or at least took no heed of my physiognomy—and now doesn't seem terribly pleased that it is an acquaintance, and moreover someone from the Konak,[6] to whom he has by chance offered a night's lodging. Why? And what was he actually doing in this third-rate inn? (In any case, only later do I recall these moments of suspicion.)

We head for his villa on the outskirts of the city through scenes of destruction. On the way, the animated, corpulent gentleman tells me that three days ago, after the capture of the city, he was taken under Montenegran escort to Cetinje but had been received by the king in a very affable manner. After declaring his loyalty, he was invited to a court dinner and later given the authorization to return to his home unimpeded. Although his villa has been occupied by Montenegrans, the garden drawing-room, with its two beds, remains free. I ask him if he's married. "Marié? Moi et marié! Non, monsieur, pas de tout!"[7]

In these streets, where he was once greeted with timidity and respect and is now conspicuous because of his uniform laden with gold, he is regarded with contempt and scorn. Suleiman Bey points to a coffeehouse where Montenegran officers are sitting over their mocha. "Here we used to grab a coffee in a rush if we had a moment's time. Now these pigs sit there the whole day long!"

He makes it quite clear that he feels awful that the enemy now reigns in his sphere of power. "Mais, que faire,[8] at the end there were only eight Turkish battalions here; Constantinople left us in the lurch."

The city is already behind us; we approach a villa surrounded by walls. The garden drawing-room was turned into a lumber room—crammed full with furniture from all the rooms of the house. The two beds really are there. My host wants to be helpful when it's time to get undressed. Aha, I think, the renowned Oriental hospitality, and only with determination am I able to extricate myself from his kindness. I fall into bed exhausted. But the chief of police, who just today made the same tiring excursion over the steep roads of Montenegro and the same journey across the waves of Lake Scutari, doesn't seem the least sleepy. He sits down on my bed and strokes me on my cheeks and throat, which can't possibly have anything to do with the renowned Oriental hospitality. Suddenly he jumps up and goes to the door to have a look who's coming up the stairs. "Montenegran officers, of course," he grumbles, "the boors stamp like horses."

He wants to lock the door behind him, but I ask him to leave it unlocked. I ask him quite firmly, since I use the moment to remove my Browning from my pants, determined to defend my innocence. Suleiman Bey must notice this, since with a shrug of the shoulders he puts the key down and indignantly gets into his bed.

He doubtless regrets having offered me a night's lodging.

Me too.

Egon Erwin Kisch, "Bombardement und Basarbrand von Skutari," "Der rasende Reporter," *Der rasende Reporter. Hetzjagd durch die Zeit. Wagnisse in aller Welt. Kriminalistisches Reisebuch* (Berlin and Weimar: Aufbau-Verlag, 1972), 129–34. For Kisch's other writings from the Balkan War of 1913, during which Serbia seized parts of Albania, see "Geschichten von der montenegrischen Grenze" (Stories from the Montenegran Border), "Abenteuer in Montenegro" (Adventures in Montenegro), "Von Cetinje zum Skutarisee" (From Cetinje to Lake Scutari), "Im zerstörten Skutari" (In Ruined Scutari), and "Die Leichen von Bardanjol" (The Corpses of Bardanjol) in Egon Erwin Kisch, *Mein Leben für die Zeitung 1906–1925: Journalistische Texte 1* (Berlin and Weimar: Aufbau-Verlag, 1983), 134–53.

1. The upper part of the traditional Serbian national costume; it was trimmed in gold.

2. The Serbo-Croatian term for coat-of-arms or insignia.

3. "Shqiptars" refers to Albanians ("Shqiperia" is the Albanian term for Albania); "Arnavut" is the Turkish word for an Albanian; Malissors, Ghegs, and Tosks are different Albanian tribal groups.

4. "Charmed, my dear sir." "You know me?"

5. Nikita I (1841–1921), who ruled as king of Montenegro from 1910 to 1918.

6. "Konak" in Turkish can mean "administrative building," "government house." What Kisch is probably referring to is that he and the Turkish official have met in an official building now occupied by the enemy, which of course would be disagreeable to the Turk.

7. "Married? Me married? No, sir, not at all!"

8. "But what can you do?"

The Burglary and Murder in the Hotel Bristol

On 22 May 1918, at five o'clock in the afternoon, in the Hotel Bristol, on Vienna's Ringstrasse, Miss Julie Earl, the companion of Baron and Baroness Vivante, who resided in the hotel, was discovered murdered. It was determined that an hour and a half before, the nephew of Baron Vivante, Emo Davit, had been there. After his visit, Miss Julie had brought into her room the jewelry of her employer, which had been in a box. Moreover, a young man carrying a laundry basket passed by on the stairs. While the murder commission was carrying out its inquiries, Davit "accidentally" appeared in the Bristol. He was taken into custody, followed eight days later by his friend Kurt Franke.

All Vienna is floored by the sophistication of the burglary and murder in the Hotel Bristol. The police succeeded in determining . . . Cold-bloodedness, superb preparation down to the smallest detail . . .

I ask you. Emo Davit and Kurt Franke held rehearsals for a half a year. What was there to rehearse? The impact of the blows of a club and their effect on the skull, the wrapping up and dragging off of an intact corpse in a laundry basket? No, something like that can't be practiced. There could only be try-outs of equipment. I imagine that on his first trial run the small Franke left the club on the ground, perhaps also the gloves. At that point Kurt received a few slaps from Emo and no longer committed the same error. In later practice sessions he then stuck the gloves and club into the rucksack in a quite mechanical, professional way.

It would be nicer had these things remained at the scene of the crime! Such an exceptional instrument of murder, purchased by Davit in a specialists' shop rife with Trieste dialect—one would be overcome in a flash.

During the night Davit awakes with a start: did he forget to scrape off the trademark from the club? He leaps up and does it.

One thing is certain: he must be arrested immediately after the murder while his alibi is still warm. When his apartment is searched, nothing must incriminate his accomplice. He has to put back Franke's bankbook. If the savings deposits of someone else are found in Davit's drawer, then that other person becomes suspect. And once Franke is suspect, everything is lost.

I can't allow myself to be seen again with Franke. I will associate with everyone I can, for a full half a year develop friendships and go home with colleagues; but no one must see me with little Franke!

But what if Miss Julie doesn't die right away? Then we'll cut her throat with a razor and stuff her into the laundry basket. Ha-ha, everyone'll think she made off with the jewelry!

Another consideration, before they're done . . . The surprising realization arises, after all, that a person sometimes bleeds when his throat is cut. Had they been aware of that, they'd have had to deliver one more (fatal) blow with the dummy hand grenade or draw the noose tighter.

The murderer has a huge red spot on his trousers, and his helper, who, "unsuspecting," is to turn himself into the police, lends him without hesitation the overcoat with which everyone saw him come into the hotel. (Baron Vivante's wardrobe hangs in the adjoining room).

The club remains lying, and it still bears the Pohl trademark. Davit's gloves? They were also left behind alongside the corpse. Davit stays with the stolen box on the Kärntnerstrasse, Franke heads back to the hotel. There is a murder alert in front of the room. He therefore goes down the stairs again. The notebook of the arrested Davit contains a drawing of the layout of the murder scene. A detailed map with arrows. Whether one believes it or not— that looks suspicious.

According to concurring newspaper reports, the map was found only on the fourth day. Oh well, who would be in such a hurry to hunt for the notebook of a burglary and murder suspect? It might, after all, contain private matters.

But perhaps the sketches of the scene were in fact found on the day of the murder and whoever found them simply did not reveal them to the press. But if the police had tracked down the sketches on the first day, then they certainly would have known that Davit was involved and it was then just a matter of looking for his accomplice.

Easily said: "Just a matter of looking for his accomplice." But there was nary a clue to go on. Davit had associated just with the trainee Franke, had left the office with him daily and almost daily had come with him to the office, had been with him day and night (although nearly twice his age), until it attracted attention to the point where people began teasing him and gossiping about homosexuality. And Franke's bank savings book was with Davit. It would have raised serious doubts as to the ingenuity of the arrested if indeed his best friend turned out to be his assistant!

And this accomplice! A real shrewd article! He had dressed himself as a jockey (didn't one read about it in blaring headlines?). I imagine a jockey this way: a hemispherical silk cap, one half red, the other green, a satin shirt in the same colors, egg-yellow, tight breeches, polished boots with spurs, a riding crop in the hand. But he didn't have riding boots, or a crop, or short pants, or a sports outfit, just his oldest office suit. He did, however, have a cap, yes indeed, a cap, and a rucksack on his back so that the people on the street would stop and think: Ah, a jockey!

After the deed: He repays his parents an old debt, lends some family nine hundred crowns, flings money around so that he doesn't make himself suspicious by exaggerated frugality, says that he and Davit earned a lot in the food business, discusses with journalists interviewing him whether he should take the murder upon himself out of true friendship, and hides part of the loot—in Davit's office.

Summoned to the police for some reason about which the press is noticeably poorly informed (probably from reports of his acquaintances, to whom he's been more than suspicious for five days), he calmly surrenders the key to Davit's apartment without waiting to be asked for it. We learn that it was hidden in the intensely sought overcoat. When he is now asked about the murder, he confesses everything: "The jewelry is in my apartment!" he declares. Now they start moving fast! The investigating police official hits on the idea of sending detectives to the apartment of Davit's accomplice and they find the loot there. It is then borne in triumph to the security office.

The Austrian minister of internal affairs is here; his presence is urgently required, since everything is in order in Internal Austria. He passes out commendations right and left that almost reach the level of those conferred by the press on the police and the murderers.

Only the murder weapon is still missing, the razor. Where can it be? It is in Franke's apartment. With diabolical cold-bloodedness he placed it on his washstand, but the Sherlock Holmeses found it—the secret is revealed.

Egon Erwin Kisch, "Der Raubmord im Hotel Bristol," "Der rasende Reporter," *Der rasende Reporter. Hetzjagd durch die Zeit. Wagnisse in aller Welt. Kriminalistisches Reisebuch* (Berlin and Weimar: Aufbau-Verlag, 1972), 180–83.

Yiddish Literary Café

The puritanically strict observance of the closing hour in London, the lack of continental-style coffeehouses, and perhaps also the isolated situation of the by no means untroubled British Isles may account for the fact that the network of the international coffeehouse bohème, which extends from the lily castle of the prince of Parisian poets, Paul Fort, to the various literary cafés of Berlin, Munich, Vienna, and even to the other bank of the Seine as far as the great boulevards, did not find its way across the English Channel. Out in East London, however, in the midst of every conceivable kind of poverty, there exists a haunt of literature. It bears a national stamp: the people there speak only Yiddish, that mixture of Middle High German, a few Hebrew words, and Slavic phrases that is written in Hebrew letters.

In order to tell the passerby that Jews from Galicia, Bukovina, Ukraine, and Palestine congregate here, the place is called "New Yorker Restaurant." A low, vaulted room, on the ground level. The aroma of baked fish wafts pleasingly from the buffet to the noses of all the customers to whom the aroma of baked fish is pleasing. Manuscripts are generated at two or three tables; uncompromisingly huge, black ties are the decided fashion here. A few smooth-shaven faces with the typical mime's wrinkles around the mouth stand out conspicuously in this full-bearded section of the city. They belong to actors from the Yiddish Pavilion-Theater on the opposite side of the street.

Even the proprietor of the café has literary inclinations; he is the amateur dramaturge of the theater, sometime collaborator with the Saturday supplement of newspapers, and "Ezesgeber"—that is, literary adviser to the Yiddish publishing house. The worst thing about him is his association complex. If he hears about the newest offense of the suffragettes, or an amusing street debate, or God knows what else, he's always ready to recite a fable of Krylov, the Russian Aesop, one, he believes, that perfectly fits the situation.

Everyone greets the gentleman with the goatee when he comes through the door, but only a few can tell you his name. People know him just as "Avroymele"; this is the pseudonym he uses to sign his satirical articles. His résumé is paradigmatic for the settlement of intellectuals in Whitechapel. He is the son of a timber merchant from Bobruysk and had to complete most of his secondary-school studies with private tutors because the existing quota for Jewish pupils in Russia had been exceeded. Hence no assimilation was possible for him in his youth. He went to Berlin as a medical student, got engaged to the tragedienne Klara Bleichmann, who made guest appearances with her parents' Yiddish troupe in the Pulhmann Theater on Schönhauser-allee and in the Concordia Theater on Brunnenstrasse. So as not to have to wait years for the delivery of his Russian identification papers, he married in London and remained in Whitechapel.

The Yiddish literary historian at the next table, of whom we can see just his neck with two boils, is drinking his "nut brown."[1] He discovered in the library of the British Museum the four-act Yiddish drama of an author named Wolfsohn that appeared in 1796 in Posen, and is now doing a study of it when not here drinking his "nut brown."

We cannot deny the owner and director of the Pavillon Theater, Mister Joseph Kessler, our approval of his production of Gordin's drama *E yiddisher Koenig Lear* [A Jewish King Lear]. This doesn't surprise the general manager at all, since he's used to it; serious critics acknowledge daily that the actor Mister Hochstein is an advantage and that the actress Mistress Wallerstein has a lovely face.[2] He regrets that we saw Mister Hamburger, the comic, only in a tragedy; he's apparently preferable in a comedy. We agree that the orchestra conductor is gifted: in the intermission and in melodramatic places he played the harmonium with one hand while attempting to control the orchestra with the other. The audience expressed its sympathy in the middle of the leading scenes through sincerely admiring whistles.

We talk about the theater and they ask us about Osip Dymov, Rudolf Schildkraut, and Sholem Asch.[3] And if we knew Adolf Ritter von Sonnenthal, and if he was really as splendid as they say.[4]

In no time we meet all the regulars, those for whom writing is an excuse, and those for whom it is a lucrative way of earning a living. A pockmarked, burly colleague—his head rests like a cube on a prismatic neck—is introduced to us. They make jokes about his laziness and say that he discovered the Yiddish distich in order to write just two lines. Urged by a Yiddish publisher to write an essay about Israel Zangwill, he began with the words: "Zangwill is a Catholic writer through and through . . ."[5] From that time on he has not been burdened with any more requests.

The spindly local composer of songs is there as well. His specialty is rhyming Yiddish and English words, as for example in the refrain of a couplet about a buttonhole maker:

> I am a yiddisher
> Buttonhole-finisher . . .

All of Whitechapel sings his song about the "unfortunate worker:"

> Fun de kindheit, fun dei yugend
> Finsterst ob dein welt in shop,
> Und kein heim dos hostu nit,
> Mied dei herz, dei kopp.
> Oi! seh! men behandelt dich punkt wie a hund.
> Fun dei schwere horewanie leben reiche in paleste . . .

(From childhood, from youth, / Your whole life is spent in a dark shop, / And you don't have a home you can call your own. / Ah! See! People treat you like a dog. / From your hard labor rich people live in palaces.)

A nineteen-year-old lad has run away from the Lodz Seminar; he doesn't want to be a "bocher" and doesn't want to become a rabbi.[6] Instead, he wants to create, to conquer the world, to write books, to "become a second Max Brod."

There are three Yiddish dailies in Whitechapel that come out in the large format of the London newspapers: *Die Zeit, Yiddishes Journal,* and

Express. They all differ in their political orientation, but join forces in fighting vehemently against anti-Semitism and the agitation of the well-represented missions houses, and for the amendment of the immigration law. One of the many Yiddish weeklies, the anarchistic *Arbeiterfreund,* is edited by a German Christian, an honorable book printer from Mainz who learned Yiddish expressly for the purpose of agitating in this ethnic neighborhood of London for Tolstoy and Luccheni, for philanthropy and direct action, for mutual help and political assassination. In the English anarchy described by Mackay,[7] Prince Peter Krapotkin, now quite old and living reclusively in nearby Brighton, plays no greater a role than Karpovich, who provided the impetus to the Russian Revolution of 1917 with his fatal shooting of Minister of Culture Bobolepov and now leads a faultless bourgeois existence as a London masseur. On the occasion of the centenary of Bakunin's birth, great-grandfather Cherkesov spoke at an anarchists' meeting and told about his youth, about the revolution, and how—in 1848—he had fought alongside Bakunin on the barricades of Dresden.

The Yiddish corner café on Whitechapel Street also has regular Christian guests, among them journalists sent here from Fleet Street like foreign correspondents representing the big London papers to cover the life of the Whitechapel ghetto.

The bohemian café couldn't do without its literary waiter. To be sure, he doesn't have an army of newspapers at his disposal, but that is why, in the circle of the self-educated, "Waiter Jow" is a respectable personality, an authority in matters of learning. For Master Jow is a university-educated man. He studied philosophy in Bern, came to London in order to continue his studies, had no money, became a waiter, and remained one. And nobody in Whitechapel's Café Megalomania can tell if he despises or envies those of his guests who combine the historical restlessness of the Jews with the nervous rootlessness of the Bohemian.

Egon Erwin Kisch, "Jiddisches Literaturcafé," "Der rasende Reporter," *Der rasende Reporter. Hetzjagd durch die Zeit. Wagnisse in aller Welt. Kriminalistisches Reisebuch* (Berlin and Weimar: Aufbau-Verlag, 1972), 265–68.

1. A particular combination of coffee and milk.

2. The line in the original German contains a few Yiddishisms, which I italicize here: "... seriosen Kritiker bescheinigen täglich, dass der *Versteller* Mister Hochstein ein Vorzug ist und die *Verstellerin* Mistress Wallerstein ein *schmeckediges Ponem* hat."

3. Osip Dymov (1878–1959), a once popular but second-rate Russian dramatist; Rudolf Schildkraut (1862–1930), a German-Jewish actor who emigrated to the United States in 1911 and was a star of the Yiddish Art theater in New York until 1922; Sholem Asch (1880–1957), a well-known Yiddish novelist and playwright.

4. Adolf Ritter von Sonnenthal (1834–1909), a brilliant Austrian actor long affiliated with the Vienna Burgtheater.

5. Israel Zangwill (1864–1926), an English writer of Jewish background and an ardent Zionist who wrote mostly about modern Jewish life.

6. "Bocher" refers to a young man, a Talmud student.

7. Kisch is referring to the novel *The Anarchists* (1891) by the writer John Henry Mackay (1864–1933).

Kisch dressed as a dervish among Moroccan children, late 1926 or early 1927.
Courtesy Museum of National Literature, Prague.

Vatican in the Sahara

The most venerable and holy sharif and sheik Sidi El Hadji Ali ben Sidi El Hadji Aissa, caliph of the monastic order of Tidjania, founded the monastery of Tamelaat more than a hundred years ago, and his name and title can be read on his tomb.

This is a mausoleum the size of a cathedral. The stone vault soars at least twenty meters above the coffin; sculptured ornaments of stone and authentic Arabian arabesques decorate the inner walls, a crystal chandelier descends over the deceased, another one over those praying; the wrought-iron barred windows bulge outward in a wide curve; the sarcophagus is, as usual, draped with the offerings of pilgrims, with silk, gold, carpets, and rosewood; the wall is ornamented by colorful frescoes and a family tree of the great *marabout,* which is important to the present monastery dwellers, since they are almost all his descendants.

The monumental tomb is enclosed by the mosque, in which old men and children sit with legs crossed, text tablets in hand, and in unchanging melody continuously wail out suras of the Koran. While this is going on, people wander about the monastery, which is a vast city, a remarkable city with ruins of fortifications at its corners and with two gates: one for the pilgrims who come from Tem Assin, the nearest community, and the other for those on their way to Blidet Amar, the last oasis of the Ued Rirh.

Most of the ground-level houses have decayed; the "brickwork"— cracked lumps of clay stuck together with camel dung—remained. Grass grows rampant in open courtyards, where goats and cattle pasture. Even palaces, one-storied houses, have collapsed, and from the street you can catch sight of brightly painted apartments with stalactite vaults.

In days past, when no Gallic cock gave a hoot about the desert and only the crescent reigned, the Za-uja Tamelaat must have been more inhabited. Nonetheless, grandchildren and great-grandchildren of the founder multiplied abundantly and it is still the most important Mohammedan base in Algeria, the most influential monastery of the Sahara, and still wealthy.

The worldly power of Islam has been broken, the *Rumi* [foreigner] holds power in his hands: his are the regiments of the Spahis, the battalions of Senegalese, the Tirailleure [riflemen], Zouaves, and Foreign Legionnaires. It is he who purchases palm gardens and drives out, shoots, imprisons, or deports the hereditary owners; it is he who imposes taxes and drafts soldiers For four years Mohammedan Africa had to fight for the Entente, despite the fact that the standard of the Prophet was unfurled against it in a Holy War. The *Rumi* has power over life and death.

But he does not have power over love and hate! He knows that, hence the foreign occupation of the Territoire Militaire, the garrisons all over consisting of colonies of people of different races and languages, the many minarets that have been turned into observation posts so that binoculars and floodlights can comb the sandy plains for Djihs (armed native troops), and the ban on carrying weapons, buying ordinance, conducting telephone conversations or sending telegrams in the Arabic language. All these measures weren't entirely successful; there were uprisings during World War I that flared up simultaneously in many places and which might have been dangerous, as the Rifkabyles in Morocco demonstrated emphatically.

Who organizes this resistance? There's no need to look farther than the holy monasteries, since they represent the sole independent authority, one not subject to supervision. There is no Muslim who will admit this; only in matters of faith, he maintains, does the influence of the Za-ujas make itself felt, and they are nothing more than places of devout meditation and theological instruction.

Before sunset the foreigner can view the Za-uja in peace; however, according to Islamic religious precepts Jews daring to enter the mosque or the Za-uja must be killed. In small monasteries, in Tolga or Rab-Abbar, for example, I saw a labyrinth of courtyards, people singing psalms, children, pale youths, men with white beards, all with their legs crossed, holding ancient editions or magnificent manuscripts of the Koran, committing the words of the law to memory loudly and rhythmically; they seemed to scrutinize the intruder with burning eyes.

They sit the same way here, in the mosque of Za-uja Tamelaat. But in the narrow, often arched alleyways, I run across men who are obviously more than readers and learners of the holy suras. They wear silk turbans, wound five times around with braid, and gold-laced sandals; their burnooses are made of fine blue-gray cloth. They walk quickly, and pay no attention at all to the European, who is usually regarded with curiosity in the settlements in the Sahara and scrutinizingly in places of prayer.

Those finely clad esoterics are the grandchildren on the male and female sides of Sidi El Hadji Ali ben Sidi El Hadji Aissa. Their names grow up out of the painted family tree on his tomb, and they have the hereditary right to live here as *marabouts,* to make decisions in matters of faith, and to inscribe amulets. Together with their wives from the tribe of the founder, it is their responsibility to make sure that the holy seed does not die out. They teach the holy learning to those who endeavor to function as priests in the wilderness, in the oases, and in the black villages. The three-hundred-member lay brotherhood of the Tamelaat works for them in palm planting, sheep herding, and in their houses. The esoterics also appoint the foremost of the *marabouts,* the pope of the Sahara.

He is, to be sure, not present. In his house, which presents itself as the Vatican of the Sahara by means of a wider stone portal, an arched courtyard, a throne room with brightly painted vaulting, and an audience chamber with old clocks on engraved consoles, one can at best encounter the son of the pope. The latter suffers from tuberculosis and lives, because he trusts doctors more than the medical precepts of the Koran, in Biskra, where a house on Tolga Desert Street belongs to the monastery.

It is there that one can speak with him. Bedecked in turban and burnoose, Sidi Laid ben Sidi El Bashir Tidjani ben Sidi El Hadji Ali, the grandson and successor in office of the first sheik of Tamelaat, a man of about fifty-five, sits cross-legged on his sickbed.

Seated on the ground around the bed are the followers and friends of the Master. The man with the white flowing beard and the golden spectacles squatting to the left of the invalid is Si Mohammed Tahar, a product of the school of Tamelaat who now prays and preaches in Taïbal, a Taaleb of great fame in the empire of the eternal sands. The turban of the black-bearded man in the black burnoose is decorated with black cords. He also acquired his knowledge of heavenly matters from the Za-uja Tamelaat, and he now demonstrates his knowledge of earthly matters in his capacity as the wealthiest carpet merchant of the Maghreb. The other guests are one son, two nephews, and two pupils of the Master, and two pious gentlemen from Biskra.

A carved table inlaid with mother-of-pearl is brought in, and everyone drinks mint tea from small glasses.

Politics? What politics? Oh no, the Za-uja has nothing to do with politics. Absolutely nothing. Only with meditation and learning.

When the sultan of Tuggurt laid siege to the Za-uja, Sidi El Hadji Ali marched against the enemy praying and without arms. And this is what happened: at the head of the band of besiegers, the palm trees caught fire and collapsed, burying under them all the sultan's troops who did not flee in time. No, the monasteries conduct no politics. On the contrary (on the contrary?), we are more kindly disposed to the French than other sects. Our mother monastery is the Za-uja Kurdan, between Langhuat and Ain-Mahdi. A French woman used to live there who married the sheik of Tidjani and, after his death, his successor. When the *Rumi* arrived, she came to their aid, talked the Arbi out of resistance, and averted much bloodshed. Her original name was Aurélie Picard, and she came from Orleans.

She has been dead a long time. No, we conduct no politics. Please have another tea with us, *efendi!*

Egon Erwin Kisch, "Vatikan in der Sahara," "Wagnisse in aller Welt," *Der rasende Reporter. Hetzjagd durch die Zeit. Wagnisse in aller Welt. Kriminalistisches Reisebuch* (Berlin and Weimar: Aufbau-Verlag, 1972), 540–43.

Runaways, Little Vagabonds, and a Small Poet

Sometimes the heavy guns had to be spared, ammunition used frugally, food supplies now and then abandoned; strategic plans could backfire, tactical measures fail, but the tsar always had soldiers to send to the front against the Germans and Austrians—the human reserves were inexhaustible. (Did anyone—does anyone—ever think of the children when talking about Mazuria or Przemysl?) Later on—the February Revolution; the October Revolution; the civil war against Denikin, Wrangel, Koltchak, Petlyura, Yudenich, the Entente, the Czechoslovaks, the Finns, the Balts, and the Poles, with mass executions, reprisals, assaults, and forced conscription, during which everyone thought about the enemy and nobody about their children. And then came the famine. Armies of adolescent tramps stole and begged their way through villages and cities, spent nights in the steppes and in fields, crept into railway cars, perched on the bumpers, and squeezed in between the axles in order to get to more prosperous regions as stowaways—to Tashkent, the bread-basket city; to the legendary sea of light, Petersburg; or right to the mother of Russia. Moscow has nine railway stations, and from every arriving train the widely traveled street-smart boys, experienced beyond their years, know how to dart past the police and conductors, find comrades, and with them spread out through the streets, begging, stealing, picking pockets, and spending the nights in garbage cans, boilers, pits, and construction sites and behind billboards. There were thousands of such miniature vagabonds, and now there are still hundreds, despite the fact the everything was done to try to counter this present and future danger. The SPON (the acronym for Sotsialno-pravovaia okhrana nesovershennoletnikh—Social-Legal Protection for Underage Children) is in charge of Moscow's four assembly points (priyomniye punkty) for street children, two for boys, one for girls, and one for very small homeless children between the ages of four and seven. They stay in these facilities for at least two months, two weeks of which they are kept in physical quarantine while the remaining six weeks are devoted to their psychological and social observation, after which a determination is made as to what should be done with them. Usually they are turned over to one of the 407 children's homes in Moscow. A hundred of these are for normal children who can attend public schools; sixty-five are for normal children for whom schools have been set up in the facilities; twenty-four have school workshops for asocial children; fifteen with apprenticeships for vegetable, garden, and field cultivation, are also for asocial children; fourteen of the homes maintain courses for professional training for the gifted and preparatory study groups for the workers' universities; ten serve as residences for boys and girls already employed; three are reserved for the blind, eight for the deaf and dumb, two for the feebleminded, one for those with venereal diseases, one for the plain physically weak, one for drug addicts, and one for epileptic street children. Moscow also has 109 homes for homeless normal children of the individual districts; there are thirty-six open-air schools with residential and pedagogic buildings in the outlying districts, and seven *posyolki,* "children's cities," with 4,150 inhabitants, dwellings, workshops, stables, barns, schools, fields, and gardens, maintained by the children themselves. The largest of these children's cities is Pushkino, near Moscow.

There is also a night hostel for children, to which they can come at six in the evening, take baths, get clean clothing, and then be on their way again come morning if they don't choose to enter the neighboring house that serves as a daytime hostel or let themselves be taken to an assembly point. Thirty-five thousand underage children now live permanently in these Moscow homes.

Children taken into custody by the police and convicted as criminals by the youth court are also handed over to the communal shelters. There actually is no youth court, but rather a "Commission for Underage Children's Affairs." There is also no conviction, just a "legal discussion"; and there are no youthful criminals, just "underage lawbreakers." Everything having to do with courts, crimes, and punishments is avoided. Only the most serious cases, involving perpetrators between the ages of fourteen and sixteen, are adjudicated by a regular people's court empowered to sentence them and send them off to the workhouse for underage children ("Trudovoy dom dlya yunoshchey lishchennykh svobody ot 14–16 let"). The commission, which is made up of an educator, a physician, and a people's judge, is charged with paying less attention to the offense than to the character and influence of the environment on the child. It meets daily and deals immediately with those brought before it, after which any in-house records are brought forth. On the basis of these records, and the nature of the incident that led to the arrest, a resident educator draws up a report; then files, records, and educator disappear, and the underage lawbreaker enters. A conversation then ensues. "Hello, Mitya, so here you are again! What have you been up to now?" "I pinched an orange." "*One* orange? I thought it was a whole bag of oranges that was being weighed at the time. On Tverskaia, wasn't it?" "Yeah, at a stand." "When was it?" "An hour ago, maybe two." "At eleven-thirty, then. Weren't you in school?" "Nah, I didn't go today." "Just today? It's better to be in school, isn't it, than to be hanging around the streets in such cold? What do your father and mother have to say when you don't go to school?" "They go to the factory and don't give it a thought." "So you have to think about it yourself. Do you want to become a thief?" "I'm no thief." "Of course not if you just walk off with a few oranges; that doesn't make you a thief yet. But that's the way to become one, especially when you don't go to school. Promise me that you'll go to school on time now." "It won't work. The teacher's going to punish me 'cause I haven't been there for eight days." "He won't say a word to you. We'll give you a note saying you weren't able to come. Agreed?" "Yeah." "Can you give your word of honor that you'll go to school tomorrow, so that we won't be writing the note for nothing?" "I give you my word of honor that I'll go back to school starting tomorrow."

The next defendant, around thirteen years old, ragged, wearing mismatched shoes, almost without a brow, wide chin, protruding ears, stole a pair of galoshes in the marketplace. He's relapsed, has already run away twice from institutions. "Guess there's nothing to be done with you, eh? You don't want to go to any commune or school, isn't that so?" "Can't do what the others can." "You've got to learn how, then." "Can't learn it. I'd like to go back to the country." "You can go to a field settlement." "Rather tend cows and oxen. My uncle'll take me on right away." "Where is your uncle?" "He's a peasant near Leningrad; he lets me sleep in the barn and feeds me." "When would you plan to go?" "Today even, if I had the money." "Well then, we'll buy you a ticket and put you on the train this evening." "For real?" "But you have to promise us that you'll go to school there." "I can promise, but I won't learn anything, I'll tell you that straight off, since nothing goes into my head."

The next: a girl, barely fifteen, mangy Astrakhan cap, short hair, wrapped in tatters, works as a prostitute, homeless, raped by her landlord two years ago, is brought in for stealing laundry and asks not to be handed over to the *sud,* the court. She is assigned to the appropriate girls' home. "Should a militiaman accompany you there?" "No, I'm glad I'm going." "Here's money for the tram." "I don't need it. I'll walk. Can I have some tea as soon as I get there?" "Yes, we'll arrange that at once." They telephone the home, so that the new arrival will be given tea and a sandwich as soon as she gets there, and the girl leaves.

A thirteen-year-old with a red necktie, the insignia of the Pioneers, comes in next. He stole a bunch of notebooks from a state department store. "What's this, you wear the red scarf and still steal?" The young boy (weeping): "I haven't taken my oath yet." "And when you do take your Pioneer's oath, will you keep on pilfering things from stores?" "Either I'll steal or I'll take the oath. You can't be a Pioneer and a thief at the same time." "And what would you do with you if you were sitting here in my place?" Accused (reflecting): "I'd give me a reprimand. More I don't deserve, since that was the first time I did it and probably won't do it again." "You see, and we are commending you. Because when someone realizes that a thief cannot be a Pioneer, he'll surely become a useful person." Handshake.

The Opeka, the commission for legal counsel for the young, is meeting in another room. Children appear here as plaintiffs against their parents or guardians. A girl complains about her stepfather, who tries to assault her; an apprentice levels charges against his master, who exploits him and makes him work more than eight hours a day; a father spends his own wages on drink, and those of his wife as well, while his family goes hungry; a father doesn't let his son join the Pioneers; another father thrashes the twelve-year-old plaintiff for no reason at all. In most cases, the identity of the plaintiff isn't supposed to be revealed. The inspector whom the children's commission maintains in every street block has to informally investigate the matter and where possible step in *in flagranti*. This demands special skill, for in many instances, as for example that of the stepdaughter, the tragedies can barely be witnessed by a third party. If an accusation proves to be valid, the accused is summoned, given a warning or turned over to the people's court, which deals more sternly with fathers than the youth court does with the sons.

II

All bundled up in order to brave the ice, snow, and wind through the night, lice- and flea-ridden, which can't be helped, since they gladly use for clothing any rags they pick up, filthy and sooty, the way they can't help being when they sleep for months on end in garbage bins, discarded boilers, on piles of bricks, and behind billboards, a worn-out bag and a battered bowl in hand, so come the little street rascals to the shelters, brought by the social inspectors, the police, or passersby, or on their own initiative. Nobody asks them any questions, and a few minutes later these images of misery are transformed into children, romping in the bathroom stark naked, jumping into the tubs, snorting under the shower, and rubbed down with soap and brush by a bath attendant their same age. As soon as they're dry, a barber cuts their hair off down to the scalp while their beggars' bags and bowls are disinfected and tossed into the dump.

Each one of them receives clean underwear and a black suit buttoned high at the neck. So outfitted, he is then received. Now he is asked his name, age, place of origin, experiences, and problems, whether he can read and write, what he wants to be, and what he's been doing. The ill are taken into the infirmary; many of them are suffering from eye diseases, have scabies, rashes, and dirty wounds that they sustained brawling or during a burglary. Two to three percent are tubercular and not less than one percent syphilitic. The healthy ones are domiciled in one of the huge dormitories, which accommodate fifty beds each. Each Moscow shelter takes in almost six hundred children apiece, and in 1921, when famine raged on the shores of the Volga, so many orphans fled to the shelter of the white walls of Moscow that as many as two thousand children had to be accommodated in a single home. There was enough space there. One of the shelters is located in a complex that shared the typical fate of tsarist buildings: first it served as a barracks, then, after it became dilapidated, it was used as a mass asylum for the widows of civil servants. At the beginning of the war, these women were put out on the street, since the huge rooms they were living in were needed for an army hospital. The wounded and sick repaired the walls and made the place habitable. After the revolution, it was assigned to children. Local laborers, working evenings voluntarily and unremunerated, whitewashed the walls and fixed it up again. Community work.

The boys who are accepted here range in age from eight to sixteen; there are eight schools. Some of the children know the geography of Russia from Yekaterinoslav to Odessa, the mechanism of door locks, the history of consumer goods carried by freight cars, how receivers of stolen property arrive at their figures, and the natural history of all edible animals and plants. But they don't know the alphabet or multiplication or a single honest skill. Others, however, enjoyed education, but their parents died during the intervention and civil war and the children lapsed into banditry. Still others, barely twelve years old, learned the trades of their fathers, whom they had to help from a very young age, and are shoemakers, basket weavers, tailors, or cabinetmakers. Circumstances just forced them to take a break from their trades, but if the educational process succeeds, they can soon resume their former work. Several of them understand different languages (Turkestan, Polish, Tatar), and one of the children "speaks German." The little fellow says "Komm rin!" ["Come on in!"]. Well now, and what more do you know? Then he clenches his fist and shouts: "Verfluchter Kerl!" ["Damned kid!"]. This isn't any insult, just the second half of his knowledge of German; he didn't learn any more when he was begging his way around the Volga Republic. Either a friendly "Come on in!" or an enraged "Damned kid!"

With the rest, you have to speak Russian if you want to find out what a child knows about Russia. You point to a picture of Lenin and ask who it is. "Lenin was the leader of the workers and peasants and he made them free; thanks to him, they have something to eat and are learning how to read and write." "Fine. Now tell me who that woman is on the wall?"

"That's Rosa Luxemburg, who wanted to do in Germany the same thing as Lenin, but the tsar shot her to death there." "And Liebknecht?" "That was Rosa Luxemburg's husband and also a good person." "And who's the man over there with the big beard?" "That's Karl Marx. He was Lenin's teacher and he told him how to do everything." "Did you ever hear anything about Christ?" "Of course. The peasants believe he's a god, but there is no god."

There are three pianos and a pianino in the home, and a self-taught musician is tinkling the keys on each one of them. Most of the youths, however, lie on their stomachs on the tables in the clubhouse playing checkers. A sixteen-year-old and one barely eight are having a chess game, and the younger player is going to beat his opponent in four or five moves. The walls are decked with huge brightly colored and hand-lettered pieces of cardboard: these are wall newspapers. They come out monthly and deal with the current problems of the home in a satirical and serious way, but always very naive. (Wall newspapers, by the way, can be found in every factory, every apartment house, and every store in Russia. The forgotten art of the *journaux d'affiche* of the Great French Revolution is coming into its own again.)

The largest room of the home has a stage, on which the pupils put on a play every week. On Monday the premiere of Tchaikovsky's opera *Stenka Razin* is taking place, but without Tchaikovsky's music; the text is going to be recited. During the intermission a balalaika orchestra is going to perform the "Internationale," the "Marseillaise," and some folk songs. The musicians are rehearsing right now, as a matter of fact, but take a break because they have a visitor and play in honor of their German guest. Their instruments are made out of unfinished planks of wood crudely fitted together, and the triangle is an old horseshoe. Their teacher is a professional musician and he corrects them, but it's hardly necessary, since the boys demonstrate an unbelievable musicality. And even the two members of the orchestra who can't participate because there aren't enough instruments to go around sit in their seats, a deadly serious look on their faces, and pluck the nonexistent strings of a nonexistent balalaika.

In the art room boys paint under the supervision of a teacher, who instructs them in the use of the brush, paper palette, or crayons, and clay modeling. Very small children busy themselves with assembling things and with picture books. The lockmaking shop, an electrical operation, is already empty; the four-hour labor period is over. But some children are still at work in the cabinetry shop. They got permission for this because they want to finish their toboggans as fast as possible; they're in a hurry—tomorrow or the day after they're due to leave the home.

Two months is the maximum length of residence, after which each child has to be assigned to one of four hundred facilities for underage children. These facilities consist of labor communes, which run independent agricultural or industrial operations; clinics for the psychopathic or the ill; children's cities; various labor schools; or a huge home for children. Discipline exercised by elected children's councils reigns in these homes and is so stern that the teachers sometimes have to intervene in favor of those being punished. For eight days now a small offender has been sitting alone in the dormitory during meals. His colleagues bring him his food, but without speaking to him, and if you ask him what he did that was so awful, he cries that he didn't start the fight at all, and that the next time his turn comes to be judge he'll show them and slap an even longer period of punishment on them. The four members of the rations commission, whose combined ages don't equal forty, assemble the menu for the week from a list of eighty dishes. The editorial committee of the wall newspaper takes itself very seriously, especially one of the members of it, who for the second time now has been elected for a three-month term of service. This twelve-year-old colleague tells how hard it was to edit the anniversary issue for the centenary of the Decembrist uprising and still carry jokes and caricatures without undermining the ceremonial character of the issue. The Pioneer Club is the elite of the institution, and its members don't admit anyone into their circle they consider undeserving. They sit just like a board of governors in their little conference chairs; the president has a bell in front of him, and from time to time a Komsomolite makes some factual observations. They discuss questions of self-management and deliberate the case of a boy who took a set of crayons from his neighbor—did he just borrow them or did he steal them? A red banner, flanked by two drums and two trumpets and bearing the inscription "Pioneer Club of the A. I. Herzen Home for Children" stands in a corner. Next to it is an illuminated crèche depicting battle on the barricades. All the masonry is plastered with drawings—motifs from the life of the institution, pictures of factories and peasant farms scribbled next to each other so precariously that a cow can easily fall into the chimney or a drive belt get caught on a peasant's house. This subject—the union of the industrial proletariat and the peasantry, the so-called *smytchka*—is used often; hammer and sickle shake hands, and what the party propagates is the subject of all the drawings. One even sees tractors idealized in gold; bread, money, and fruit flow from its parts. Electrification and its beneficial effects are strewn on the patient paper in glaring shades. Not only does a picture of Lenin appear, appropriately, in Lenin's Corner, but the walls are full of them, and where genre pictures hang depicting, for example, a policeman or a fat man sitting with his wife and son on the bank of a river fishing, the policeman and the angler have Lenin's features. Constituting a different kind of wall decoration are the letters, written in still cruder hand, of peasants attesting that the children who helped them bring in the harvest during the summer were useful little helpers.

There is no guard in front of the house and the door is open all day. However, a different boy each day performs the duty of a "Swiss Guard"; he is not supposed to let anyone in or out of the house who doesn't have the approval of the children's council. Leaving the commune on one's own is regarded as desertion, and whoever has done so is dishonorable and has broken the bond between himself and his criminal, homeless contemporaries, who have renounced crime and found a home.

III

The doors to the facility on the Deneshni Pereulok open differently from those of the other Moscow children's homes. No boy performs here with amusing earnestness the service of watchman entrusted him by his colleagues; no, it's an old professional lady doorkeeper. This is a closed institution: "Home for Juvenile Addicts."

The typical heirs of a terrible era, children have become hooked on drugs that adults used as a refuge from the grim reality of war and famine. The revolution banned alcohol, so before long a still arose in every twentieth house in the Russian provinces; the grain that was so urgently needed became booze instead. Patrols of Red Army men destroyed hundreds of stills, thousands of vats of poison, but in vain; new ones were fired up again and throughout the steppes you could get "Samogon," illegal vodka. In 1921 the regime permitted the serving of beer and later also Turkmenian and Caucasian wines. The illegal distilling industry receded but didn't disappear. The state itself produced spirits, 30-percent alcohol, and the illegal distilling industry receded further but still didn't disappear, since it began producing 40-percent alcohol. The state now also turned out 40-percent alcohol. The illegal distilling industry retreated some more but didn't disappear completely, since the legal bottle cost one ruble sixty kopecks, while a bottle of Samogon cost only a ruble. The alcohol war thus dragged on—and still drags on—in the country and will end with the victory of organized, anti-alcohol youth, who are destroying the moonshine stills of their elders.

There were new poisons in the cities. Russia was still sealed tight by the blockade, the country was still closed off on all sides by interventionists, yet smugglers had penetrated everywhere. From Poland and Germany they came with cocaine and morphine, and the Chinese hawkers who were crawling all over the place openly sold toys and secretly peddled opium. Almost all the Chinese in Moscow are passionate opium smokers and had brought sufficient quantities with them from their homeland so as to be able to sell some. The cocaine peddlers gave away doses of the white powder to strangers in dives and on the street; they knew that the next day the strangers would return, would pay all the better for a new dose, and would remain regular customers. An epidemic arose and spread like wildfire, since every drug addict tries to get everyone around him to share the same "happiness," to recruit proselytes. And so the street children also found their way to the white poison. Of five hundred inmates in a single home for juvenile delinquents, forty-six proved to be cocaine addicts or at the least cocaine users. Since a gram of "coke" costs eight or nine rubles (a ruble is more than two German marks), and some children consume three grams a day, you can figure out how much they have to beg and steal in order to reach their quotas. Even now there are ten-year-old children who down three bottles of vodka daily, which similarly demands a hefty budget, and this is augmented by what they shell out for *papirossy* [cigarettes]. One hundred percent of the Moscow street children are cigarette smokers. Six-year-olds, who often puff away thirty cigarettes a day, are compelled either to steal the cigarettes or buy them with stolen money. The strong measures of the authorities were not dictated solely by considerations of health but also by concern for public safety.

It is to the Deneshni Pereulok, to that home whose doors open differently from those of the other Moscow children's homes, that the poisoned children are brought. They are taken here by the police, who discovered them intoxicated in some corner; ordered here by the courts, whose medical experts diagnosed them as addicts; or transferred from the children's night hostel, where it was the staff who made the determination.

The juvenile alcoholics suffer from stunted growth. They have the reddish, bloated faces of adult drunkards. The cocaine addict loses weight, can go five or six days without eating or sleeping, and sells his clothes in order to get his hands on a new dose. The opium smokers are lost in dull intoxication, which after the immediate effect wears off continues on as apathy.

In the home for drug addicts, every young person gets two cigarettes a day after lunch and supper; a reduction of the ration would make smoking seem even more desirable and the internment even harder. (The educators and physicians employed by the home are not permitted to smoke on the premises, whereby they demonstrate that they themselves are not the hopeless slaves of habit; hence the existence of a residence in which children are allowed to smoke, but adults are not.) The effort is made to cure the children of alcohol, cocaine, morphine, and opium addiction not through a gradual withdrawal, but through a radical one; no narcotics are kept in the facility. This means that in the first three or four weeks the children are wildly unruly, cry for hours on end, and in fits of rage smash windowpanes and try to escape. Despite all precautions, they repeatedly succeed in making a getaway. After four weeks in the home they mostly forget the poison and can be assigned to a labor commune a month later, unless they have to be taken to a neurological-psychiatric children's clinic. During the summer, the half-cured are taken to the town of Talgren, a village for juvenile drug addicts, located thirty kilometers to the north of Moscow in the vicinity of the children's city of Pushkino. Here, working autonomously in workshops and on farms in a pretty landscape, they lose the rest of their longing for the precociously acquired coke and other vices of a big-city character.

In the house on the Deneshni Pereulok you could scarcely tell from the occupants that any possibility for treatment existed; these are not the inmates of children's homes with whom the state can make a public show. There isn't any Pioneer Club here (the Russian Scouts take oaths against alcohol and nicotine just like the youth organizations); there isn't any self-government; there is also very little instruction or workshop guidance. The boys run all over or just hang around, inhaling cigarette smoke. Some of them have bandages on both hands, which they wounded smashing windows or biting themselves during withdrawal. You can't get much out of them, and they don't ease up even at the experimental-psychological examination that they're supposed to undergo once a week. They think nothing of begging a visitor for cigarettes or gloves, and you have to watch out that they don't steal from you. In this regard, the child drug addicts overwhelmingly make up the most talented stratum of Moscow vagabonds; this is partly a result of the nerve-stimulating toxins and partly attributable to the fact that the uncontrollable urge to obtain the expensive narcotics makes them inventive, skillful, and daring.

Their talent manifests itself not only in the experimental-psychological examinations but also in the pictures hanging on the walls, most of which depict the way of life of the homeless and are more individualistic than children's drawings usually are. Some paintings already reveal the influence of their schooling. One, for example, contrasts the wretchedness of life in an asphalt boiler with the good fortune of a child who has been accepted in a detoxification home; it carries the inscription "Whoever wants to become a good citizen of the U.S.S.R. has to renounce cocaine and place himself under the care of a narco-clinic."

There's also a poet here, the twelve-year-old Beglov, known as "Gypsy," whose verse has already been published, inter alia, in the journal *For a New Life,* which is put out by the Moscow Commissariat for Public Health. I read the poems in the office and express the desire to translate one of them into German, with the personal authorization of the poet. The teacher is immediately prepared to fetch the youngster, but she comes back alone; Beglov, it seems, is in bed and has no intention of getting up, and if anyone wants to translate anything of his, he can do so in the absence of the poet. This fills with me respect, for there is hardly a writer on earth who doesn't come running up when the chance presents itself to become famous in a world language. So I betake myself alone to Beglov's bedroom. There he is lying down, black-haired, his face in the shape of a triangle with two light-blue circles. He advises me not to translate the poem I had selected. "Do instead the poem 'Nyu-khoder' (The Sniffer); just between the two of us," his light-blue circles blink, "it's a lot more honest." He asks for three cigarettes as an honorarium, which unfortunately I'm not permitted to give him, and so the poem must be published herewith unauthorized:

The Sniffer

The whole day today I dragged myself 'round;
I ran and stole and fought with other crooks.
I didn't really freeze, but in the evening felt cold,
So into my cauldron for asphalt I crawled.
I curled up inside my little round house,
And on my old straw had a good night's sleep.
But now I'm awake, can't be glad any longer;
It's time to be off to steal what I can.
I slept pretty well, regained all my strength,
Five rubles are easy for Beglov to get.
I buy me some coke and sniff it deep in.
As soon as it's over, the card game begins
And what do you know—the last kopeck has gone!
I head back to my house, the round one, that is.

—Gregor Beglov, known as "Gypsy"

Egon Erwin Kisch, "Von Ausreissern, kleinen Vagabunden und einem kleinen Dichter," "Tsaren, Popen, und Bolschewiken," *Zaren, Popen, Bolschewiken. Asien gründlich verändert. China geheim* (Berlin and Weimar: Aufbau-Verlag, 1980), 150–63.

Kisch and Charlie Chaplin in Hollywood, 1929.
Courtesy Museum of National Literature, Prague.

Working with Charlie Chaplin

"Chaplin? We can stop in on him on the way, if you'd like."

Of course I'd like; he is one of the righteous for whose sake America must be spared the fate of Sodom and Gomorrah.

Another of the righteous is the one who's asking me if we want to stop by Chaplin's place. His name is Upton Sinclair.

We were then in a large Hollywood film production center where Sinclair had driven his Nash in order to pick up a film. For his wife. Sinclair was talking about her problems. She was filled with a constant, desperate fear of succumbing to cancer although she rationally understood that her anxiety was groundless. Seeking help through suggestion and hypnosis, she became attracted to a hypnotist known publicly as "Nostradamus" and privately as "Roman Astoja." He's really a Pole who developed occult talents. The reel that Upton Sinclair wanted to pick up contains pictures of the trances in which Roman Astoja pierces his tongue and arm with nails. He told me that the film also shows Astoja being buried live and soccer being played on his grave.

Soccer on the fakir's grave . . . what an idea for a film, I thought suddenly. For Chaplin! The soccer player Chaplin senses transcendental power, is entombed alive according to his wishes, and scratches his way to the surface during the game just in time to repulse a dangerous shot.

I didn't voice this idea, since it really wasn't appropriate to the seriousness of our subject. I didn't say a word.

But Sinclair answered. It was now that he interrupted the occult conversation with the suggestion: "Chaplin? We can stop in on him on the way, if you'd like."

I replied that I had long ago expressed the wish to be taken to him, but even yesterday I had learned from film bigwigs that all their efforts to meet him failed and that everyone in Hollywood who boasted of being his best friend had at most seen him once having dinner in Henri's Restaurant.

"Oh, he's frightfully besieged," says Sinclair. "More than a hundred people a day come with all kinds of requests to see him, to express their admiration for him, to interest him in some project, or to borrow money from him."

Sinclair stops his car at the corner of Longpré Avenue and La Brea Avenue in front of a group of small red-roofed houses. The last thing you'd take them for was a film studio, since film studios in Hollywood are gigantic walled complexes with iron-barred gates and gatekeepers, and with every gable wall plastered with film posters. Here, however, "Chaplin's Studio" is engraved on a tiny metal plaque. We go into an office, that is, to a young woman who alternates between answering the phone and taking care of correspondence. We walk past her into a courtyard that really is a courtyard and where film sets are located. Elsewhere it wouldn't be a courtyard, and if it were it would be called "Stage No. 35," entry would be prohibited, and a watchman would be majestically posted in front of it.

Two men greet Sinclair. There really was a film being shot, they tell him, and one of them says: "The boss is coming!"

The boss! The old man! The chief! We turn around to the boss. To Charlie Chaplin. Were he at least dressed in the appropriate attire of a boss, a chief, the "old man," he could at any other time—when he is not the boss, chief, or "old man"—be that sad vagabond with the comic routines whom we love so much. But now he approaches in the loose-fitting, mended trousers, the patched-up oversized shoes, the disarranged necktie, and the worn-out jacket. He is in fact coming from work; he is a boss who works.

"Hello, Upton," he calls from afar. "Good to see you again!" Sinclair says something about the guest he's brought along. "That's fine," replies Charlie Chaplin in the flesh, and we shake hands. He curses; his work isn't moving ahead. He's shooting a new film, *City Lights*. But "damn it, we've hit another dead end, and can't go on. You want to help me, boys?"

Yes, we boys want to help Charlie Chaplin.

He's not entirely the Charlie Chaplin of the movies. It's true he's coming straight from work, but he's not still at work, or, better said, he's no longer playing a role. His hat, that crushed, melon-shaped little hat, is missing, and so too are the bamboo cane and the small black toothbrush under the nose. Besides, his boots are not so overwhelmingly large and not so overwhelmingly funny as they seem on film; they are misshapen, patched-up, torn, somewhat too big, but still ordinary shoes, and only the art of their boss invested them with their cosmic proportions. Now, rushing to the projection room with us, who are supposed to "help" him, his boots are unobtrusive and the boss is anything but flat-footed. He is wearing horn-rimmed glasses. Without them he can't even sign his own name, he's so farsighted.

From his hair two streams of a fountain of silver cascade over the middle of his brow. Even the hair growing on his neck is gray, where it's growing out. ("You ought to have it cut, Charlie," I said to him cautiously a few days later. But he makes no secret of his dyed hair. "You see, I'm not bothering with it any more. What gets white isn't going to be colored any more. That's the end of it. At forty I'll be entirely white again, the way I was at thirty-five." "And what is your wife doing now?" "I don't know," he remarks with a gesture of indifference, "but I've got two children, and they're both with her.")

Now we're in the projection room. While the reel is being loaded, Charlie Chaplin plays the song "Violetera" on the harmonium and sings Spanish words to it that he makes up. He then invites me to come to his house, where he'll play the organ for me till my eyes and ears give way. "Eh, Jungens?"

The Jungens confirm, as the boss wishes, that he indeed has a powerful organ at home that he knows how to play in an ear-shattering way, whether his visitor likes it or not.

"I play fantastically well," laughs Chaplin. "But you don't know crap about my music."

The Jungens, who by the way address the boss as "Charlie," are in fact two men named Harry Crocker and Henry Clive. Harry Crocker is a young American with a sweater and a sense of humor. In *Circus* he played the tightrope dancer in evening dress and Charlie's lucky rival; also the clown that Charlie lathers up and other roles as well. Henry Clive is older, forty-eight, and has a serious career as a magician in American provincial variety shows behind him. The third of the Jungens is called Heinrich, much like the other two [Harry, Henry], but isn't here today, but that's an exception. We're not going to have any further visit to Chaplin's studio without Mister Henry Bergmann sitting, pot-bellied and broad-gauged, in an appropriate chair. At night Bermann-úr (as we prefer to call him, since he's a real Magyar[1]) is himself a boss, the owner of a Hollywood Boulevard restaurant for the prominent and those who want to see them. Chaplin made the restaurateur Henry and also endows him with his regular evening visit, for which Bermann-úr returns the favor by visiting Chaplin every day.

Besides the harmonium, a black leather armchair and four wooden easy chairs make up the furnishings of the projection room. Chaplin insists on my taking the armchair, but seems very pleased when I decline. He squats on it with legs folded; it must be his usual place.

And now we're going to let the film roll. For the moment, only a quarter of it is ready, four hundred feet, some of which will be reshot and some cut. The film starts.

I burst out laughing at the place with the watch chain (see below). But someone puts his hand on my knee and tells me to be quiet. Who is it who disputes my natural right to laugh madly at one of Charlie Chaplin's mad moments? It's none other than Charlie Chaplin, and he's sitting right next to me. The film isn't ready yet, and since we're supposed to "help," my laughter is out of place, just as when poor Charlie laughs in *Circus* when he's supposed to be learning the clown's jokes.

"Terrific," we whisper, after this section of film has been run through and the lights in the projection room come on.

The boss parries: "Can you tell me what you just saw?"

Of course. With pleasure. A girl is selling flowers on a street corner. Then Chaplin comes along . . . .

"Oh, not yet."

First a man comes accompanied by his wife and buys a flower.

"A man? What man?"

A man who looks a little like Adolphe Menjou.

"Yes, an elegant gentleman with a lady. That's important. What else?"

Then Chaplin rounds the corner. He sees a fountain on the wall and takes off his gloves in order to have a drink. That is, not the gloves all at once, but one finger at a time. One finger is missing, and Charlie looks for it without success.

"See, Charlie!" shouts Harry Crocker triumphantly.

"No, it's not clear. We'll shoot it over again." (He explains to me that it's a mistake first of all to pull off the glove finger that isn't there, look for it on the ground, and only then remove the glove fingers that are still intact.)

Now Charlie takes the drinking glass in front of the wall . . .

"Did you recognize what I represent?"

???

"Am I not this time something different from before?"

Yes. You have a small bow tie and the gloves. This time you want to be a rather foppish tramp, isn't that so? The business with the cup indicates the same thing.

"Would you please explain that too?"

Chaplin takes the cup that's hanging on a chain. As the chain comes to rest on his stomach, Chaplin notices that it would make a splendid watch chain and tries to free it from the wall (see above) while he drinks. But he fails and, in resignation, waddles over to the flower girl. She offers . . .

"Stop, stop. There's something else going on."

Chaplin looks at me piercingly, anxiously, almost imploringly. "There's something else going on."

No, I absolutely can't recall anything else in the scene.

"A car comes, don't you see?"

Yes, a car comes. A man emerges from it and goes over to Chaplin. Chaplin greets him as usual.

"And what is the car doing?"

"I don't know," I confess.

And Upton Sinclair ventures: "I think it's going away."

"Damn, damn," Chaplin mutters, "the whole thing's ruined." His colleagues are also depressed.

I relate what else happens. The girl hands Chaplin a flower, it falls to the ground, both bend over to retrieve it, Chaplin picks the flower up, but the girl continues looking for it despite the fact that he holds it out to her. Then he realizes that the girl is blind. He buys the flower and goes on his way.

In order to convince himself that he wasn't wrong, he sneaks back again . . .

"No, no, he doesn't sneak."

He returns the second time very quickly, as if hurrying by, but draws to a halt while gradually muffling the sound of his steps. Then he turns around, slowly, on tiptoe and sits down next to the girl. But she had just sprinkled the flowers and empties the bucket—right in Chaplin's face. He creeps away and then comes back for a third time. And again buys a flower. The blind girl wants to pin it on him and in so doing feels the flower he bought before in his buttonhole. She understands that the man has come back because of her. Chaplin explains to her that his other buttonhole is free, but she insists that a person can't wear flowers in both buttonholes. Then he asks her to keep the flower. She fastens it to her bosom . . .

". . . and . . ."

. . . she's in love!

"With whom?"

With Chaplin!

"Damn, damn!"

??

"Doesn't anyone pass by?"

Not that I know.

"Damn, damn! You mean to say you still didn't notice a car and a man?"

No.

"And you, Upton?"

Didn't notice a thing.

Despairing, Chaplin buries his head in his hands, a picture of abject misery against a black leather background. His colleagues are also sad. But what happened? What are they all so upset over if I, a stranger who just dropped by, doesn't get the gag?

Oh, but it's more than a gag; it's the basic idea of the film that's fallen flat because it's absolutely unclear—my summary means nothing less. The street is an elegant street, symbolized by the first buyer and his lady. The flower girl takes the man getting out of the car for the person who buys the flower and returns because of her. The car—and we didn't notice this at all—was standing at the corner of the street during the whole scene.

No sooner does the blind girl pin the second flower on herself, in accordance with Chaplin's wish, when the man comes back and gets into the car. The awakening love is directed to *him,* the wealthy man with the car. And Chaplin now has to notice this misunderstanding and throughout the entire film play the role of the wealthy admirer; he has to steal the money to pay the doctor for the operation the girl needs to cure her blindness, get arrested, and see the girl again after serving his prison sentence. And the girl will *see* him for the first time—and laugh at him, since she has no idea who he is and because he looks so funny, as Chaplin indeed looks . . .

But if the public doesn't immediately grasp the tragic *qui pro quo*—Chaplin's shock, the obviousness of his raw poverty and his instantaneous decision to resort to fraud and theft on account of the girl's confusion, on account of his love, on account of her love—if the public doesn't have a basic grasp of all this, then everything surely is ruined.

"We have to shoot the whole thing all over again," says Chaplin.

And now begins the serious, difficult, agonizing work of dramaturgy and direction on this detail. It goes on for almost eight days, and only when everyone was in high spirits at night did Charlie suddenly interrupt the mood: "How would it be if we did it this way with the flower girl . . ."

Books have been written about actors, mimes, directors, and about popular dramatic art; why is it that no one has tried to record Charlie Chaplin at work, either by taking notes or with a Dictaphone? Charlie Chaplin, after all, writes, directs, and produces; his impact on the history of the stage is without parallel, and he has become a truly legendary figure.

For eight whole days the scene was rehearsed, with each of us taking turns I don't know how many times playing the flower girl (least of all Virginia Cherril, who is going to play the role in the film), the gentleman in the car, the chauffeur who opens the door. But Charlie Chaplin was always Charlie Chaplin; he threw himself into every effort, now hopeful, now hopeless.

"How would it be if . . ." That's the way it always begins. Someone jumps up, full of his idea, and directs the others.

The dramatic impossibility of the opening situation is soon grasped: how can the spectator accept the fact that the flower girl takes Chaplin for the gentleman getting out of the car when he doesn't yet know that she's blind? Therefore her blindness should be shown ahead of time. Chaplin, however, rejects this idea; he has to make the tragic discovery simultaneously with the audience.

Can the scene with the car somehow be strengthened so that the spectator can at least recall it later? How would it be if . . . The man gets out of the car and says (in the subtitle): "Chauffeur, wait here." Chaplin courteously closes the door of the stranger's car, the girl takes a few steps in the direction of the car . . .

Or: the man walks behind Chaplin at the same pace, pauses, lights a cigarette, so that Chaplin takes as intended for himself the flowers extended to the stranger.

Shouldn't the man with the car be somewhat less blasé, rather a conspicuously good-looking younger person who jumps out of the car enthusiastically? Even though the flower girl doesn't see him, the audience does and senses that he's someone definitely important to the girl. The spectators thus have before their eyes what the blind girl only imagines.

How would it be if the girl, who is already understood to be blind, were to say to Chaplin with reference to the second flower: "Give it to your chauffeur"?

How would it be if Chaplin were to help the man in the car and the flower vendor were to try to hand him the second flower through the window but instead bumps against the window pane, which is really the open car door behind which Chaplin is standing?

"Splendid, splendid," Chaplin exclaims and rehearses it. The way he plays it really is splendid, but he suddenly jumps into his armchair and collapses in it. "It won't work. I can't act the lackey when a moment before I was shocked by the girl's blindness and fell in love with her."

How would it be if the man were to say to his chauffeur "Home," or "the Ritz-Carlton," and the girl imagines herself in a magnificent palace or in the lobby of the hotel . . .

"For heaven's sake, no visions!"

How would it be if the blind girl were to follow the car with her gaze, as if looking right through Chaplin or the air . . . And Chaplin suddenly notices that she takes him for the wealthy man. The car itself has to be shown as it turns the next corner and then another and another. And all the while the flower girl keeps on gazing at it. No person, after all, can see a car turn one corner after another, but the flower girl is blind, *she* can . . .

So it goes, as I said, for days on end. On the set of the street corner, where the business with the car can be worked out, or up in the bungalow, where a strategy session is held, or in the dressing room, or in front of the huge statue of three allegorical figures, the purpose of which Chaplin asks us to keep secret until the statue and its secret are revealed to the whole world.

A story could be told about each of these locales. Take the dressing room, for example. It really isn't a dressing room but the most socially presentable area of the entire studio. To the left, there's a little room with a mirror and dressing table; the bathroom is on the other side. One afternoon we were all drinking tea when a very famous woman, Chaplin's best friend, was announced. He went to greet her and I walked over to the side room to comb my hair.

There was a comb lying in front of the mirror; it was white, but not terribly clean—there was a tuft of combed-out, dark hair stuck in it. I pushed it out, threw it on the floor, and put my hair in order. But then it occurred to me that one could see the tuft of hair on the immaculate parquet floor and realize that someone had used the boss's dressing room without permission. Maybe the little bunch of hair was there for a definite reason. So I picked it up and placed it back on the comb.

Harry Crocker came in also to fix himself up a bit. "Have a look," he said, pointing to the black "something" that was again on the white comb, "that's the mustache. He's had it for fifteen years already, the exact same one; a New York theater barber made it for the boss. No other mustache can stand up to months-long shooting in any kind of weather. And we can't find the New York barber any more. When the mustache is worn out, Charlie says, he's going to perform clean-shaven." I must surely have turned pale. Kids, just imagine: Chaplin without his little mustache, and all because of me.

Over and over again the conversations with Chaplin turned on the unity of aesthetic and social purpose. He, whose work embodies this unity, who is almost socially outlawed as a "radical" and "Bolshevik," constantly expresses doubt, perhaps for purposes of discussion, perhaps in order to prompt the visitors to new arguments, perhaps because he is infected with the Hollywood atmosphere. "If only everything were as simple as we'd like! What about Poe, my favorite author? I can't discover in him anywhere a trace of love for the disenfranchised, no matter how passionately I look for it. And Shakespeare! This unbearable scorn for the common man . . ."

At this point the discussion becomes heated. We shout at him that Shakespeare heaped on his kings more than just derision and that Shakespeare was a rebel against absolute monarchy and that he wanted to show that the next class of society, the nobility, were not plebs . . .

"No, no," Chaplin drowns us out, "Shakespeare was a homosexual; homosexuals, maybe against their will, are a caste, and each caste thinks aristocratically. All of Shakespeare's men are disguised women and all his women are disguised men. Julia is up above and Romeo down below; she leans over the balustrade of the balcony and lectures while he is in the garden cooing. Even the royal graybeards are women, but Lady Macbeth is a man, and Portia goes so far as to dress herself in the appropriate clothing and makes an appearance as an attorney-at-law. No man speaks to a woman the way Hamlet speaks to Ophelia; there's no eruption here, no sexual sublimation, just contempt, something obscene . . ."

And Chaplin plays Hamlet, declaims Shakespearean blank verse, the kind that crack like whiplashes above a slave girl. "No, no, this isn't any social consciousness, just genius."

(He's been given the last word here, although he hardly observes it.)

We often spoke about film. Charlie doesn't know any of the Russians. (Hollywood!) He was in a movie theater yesterday and now is terribly upset about the fact that the dance performance given as a curtain-raiser had a wavy silver background that ruined the effect.

He also tells stories about his own films. The monkeys in *Circus* scratched him badly and for six weeks he had to be in a doctor's care. Even now he has two clearly visible wounds.

Then there was the bellowing of the monkeys' owners. The monkeys, you see, belonged to four different extras, each of whom regarded his own as the main attraction. "Turn the camera downward," one of the them yells to the cameraman. "Can't you see that Johnny's on the ground?" Another: "Now, now! Mungo's turning his face this way." Charlie plays the scene: four monkeys, four tamers, himself, and the cameraman.

Nights of a Beautiful Woman was a flop. What do I, Mr. Kisch, think of *Shoulder the Arms?* I don't know the picture; I don't think it was shown in Germany.

"And it may not be shown in America now, since Hindenburg appears in it as the president of a friendly state. Moreover, he's not derided in it in the slightest, nor are the kaiser and the crown prince. I didn't go along for a second with the smear campaign; I didn't caricature anyone except for a single Prussian officer who treats his Prussian soldiers badly. And the German soldiers came and shook my hand in gratitude because I gave him a good trouncing. This didn't sit well with the militarists: an American soldier exchanging handshakes with the 'Huns'! I'm very proud of this film; it arose in the midst of the insane war psychosis and shows the utter idiocy and horror of war. It's a revolutionary film—no, not pacifistic, but revolutionary in view of the times. You have to see it, you have to see it at once."

He tosses his bamboo cane and hat aside and runs into the projection room. Well, here I am again sitting where, a few days before, at a showing of the clip of *City Lights,* I sat next to someone who forbade me any expressions of approval. Now someone is sitting next to me who constantly grabs me by the knee and raps me on the shoulder. "Pay close attention now; there's a fine scene coming up." You ass sitting on my left, don't poke me—who has to tell me to pay attention during a Chaplin film!

"You understand, I was also taken to task for palming off a moldy cheese as an American gift. And because the trench is flooded . . ." (Chaplin the soldier lies down in the water but breathes through a trumpet to keep from drowning. Early in the morning he pulls out of the water his feet, which had gone to sleep, and rubs them until he notices that they belong to his neighbors.)

"The scene here" (Chaplin is disguised as a tree behind the German lines) "we shot in the open. No double could stand in for me. We had to chase around in murderous heat until I collapsed. You see the fat fellow there? Do you know him?" Yes, I recognize him; it's Bergmann-úr. He's sitting peacefully in front of me remembering the chase after a running tree in murderous heat.

"You see? See . . ."

For heaven's sake: *yes,* I see. See everything; don't bother me!

But then there's a scene that's nicer than Gorky's story about the old whore who has a writer compose letters for her to an imaginary lover.

To Chaplin the soldier's disappointment, the army mail service brought nothing, not even a single letter. So he makes do with looking over the shoulder of a comrade who is reading a letter from home. Chaplin nods, satisfied to learn that everyone there is OK. Chaplin laughs at the remarks made by the two children. But eight days ago the brown speckled cow got sick and died, and Chaplin's tears fall on the neck of the person to whom the letter is addressed. The man turns angrily around and Chaplin just shrugs his shoulders in a Chaplinesque way. He waddles away, burdened with guilt, since he had no right to this joy and this sorrow . . .

At this point I lay my hand on my neighbor's knee.

Egon Erwin Kisch, "Arbeit mit Charlie Chaplin," "Paradies Amerika," *Paradies Amerika. Landung in Australien,* 229–42.

1. *Úr* in Hungarian, placed after the name, means "mister."

In the Afghan Jungle

Everybody laughs when you tell them you'd like to hunt tigers.

"There aren't any more. Tigers and tractors don't go together. Five years ago, it would have been a different story! But now . . . "

"That so? What about this skin here on the wall? And the tiger cubs sent to Moscow last month? And the donkey that was torn to pieces in Sarai-Kamar? And the watering-hole on the Vakhsh?"

"Nobody denies it. It happens. Four years ago a pack of wolves appeared in Sokolniki; can you then say that there are wolves in Moscow? How the Muscovites would laugh their heads off at the idea of someone wanting to go wolf-hunting! Yet in Sokolniki there was a whole pack of them, while with us it's just single animals straying in here. Maybe they crossed the river—the devil only knows how—since there are tigers over there."

"Where?"

"On the other bank of the Amu-Darya, but that's already Afghan territory. You might find tigers there in the jungle, especially at night."

"Good, that's where I'm heading!"

"But that's even more impossible than hunting tigers here."

"Why?"

"There are no bridges and no ferries over. Our sentries make sure that nobody crosses one way or the other—no spies, no smugglers, no Bassmachi,[1] no criminals."

"You don't mean to tell me that nobody ever crosses the border?"

"There used to be a lot of traffic back and forth. People would float over on their *burdyuks*. But now that's been stopped. Of course, someone makes it every now and then; the border is too long—the Amu-Darya alone flows almost a thousand kilometers between the Soviet Union and Afghanistan. When the sentry sees someone swimming across, he fires, and the Afghan is even faster on the draw."

"The Afghan? Why should he shoot? He could just as easily arrest anyone trying to come over."

"You think the sentries are posted every few yards? Besides, the guard can't tell where the current will deposit the swimmer. And as soon as he's ashore, he can disappear into the jungle without a trace. That's why the sentry shoots first and asks questions later."

"One has to take the chance, I guess . . ."

"Don't be foolish. A foreigner in Afghanistan, in the border forest, with a Russian rifle . . ."

"But there are tigers over there?"

"Yes, and even more poisonous snakes and scorpions."

At first it was impossible to scare up anyone to act as interpreter for such an undertaking, no one in fact who would even say where the *burdyuk* ferrymen could be found. When I finally discovered them on my own, they made up all kinds of excuses not to go: they had no horses (what did they need horses for, I'd bring my own), the nights were now too light . . . I offered them forty rubles. They agreed to sixty.

No one knew why I rode out alone one evening around seven to the outskirts of the village. From there we started out at dusk: five men, draped in goatskins and armed with large sticks, and I, leading my horse by the bridle. We passed some Tajiks working on the canals. At the bank of the river we came to a halt behind a clump of bushes. Three of my five companions removed their *chalats* and their pointed shoes, rolled up their trousers, and finally even removed the *tyubeteyka* from their heads. I too wanted to undress, but they said there was no need to.

The skins they had brought along were immersed in water, weighted down with stones, and kept there for five minutes. Then by means of small wooden tubes held to their mouths the men breathed the breath of life into the fleece, which began becoming a body again, began breathing and moving. Stumps of legs, tied off with string and sticks, like liverwurst, swung impatiently as they woke to life, even the scrotum growing taut.

The more breathless the blowers, the more bodily the hides became. They glistened, wet, in the moonlight. The night was hellishly light. I put my rifle on the ground, climbed up a slope, and, hidden behind a tree trunk, surveyed the scene.

The valley stretched before me all bedecked in lavender. The mathematically straight, mathematically parallel furrows of the cotton fields ran almost to my very feet. Not long ago, beasts of prey roamed at will in the wild thicket and there was no cotton. Now tractors turn around almost at the river's edge. The pastel fields seem endless; on their farthest edge the silhouette of a caravan wends its way toward the harbor.

On the slope of Hodja-tau, the Holy Mountain, the bends of the new highway that binds this corner with the outside world coiled like a yellow snake. No patrol was to be seen. Mosquitoes swarmed all around us, but, old soldier that I am, I didn't light the cigarette I had mechanically pulled out of my pocket but instead put it back.

Just then the others unhitched and unsaddled my horse, since it would have to swim with us. "My horse" belonged, of course, to my host. I should not have taken advantage of him so recklessly; if something were to happen to us, who would reimburse him for the horse? Shouldn't I leave a will behind promising to compensate him for his loss? Nonsense.

The inflated skins were plugged with corks and arranged in the water in the shape of a square. They formed a raft a meter wide. The center of it, naturally, consisted of water. Is that where I was expected to sit? Wait a moment; why had they brought all those branches? They were laid crisscross above the watery square. "There, now sit down, comrade."

Beneath me and around me everything swayed and wobbled; there is no way you can sit comfortably on crossed branches. There was something un-animal about one of the skins; it was patched up and looked more like a football.

I could already feel the current under me, yet I was still on the bank. The current was trying to drag me along with it, but five men on the river bank held the float firmly by means of two ropes they tied to the horse. One man swung himself on the unsaddled back of the horse and drove the unwilling beast into the stream; two other men jumped in at the same time.

The waves took hold of us. I had thought that we were going to head straight for the opposite bank. But one glance at the two Tajiks who remained behind made it quite clear that we were racing downstream. We were doing thirty-five kilometers an hour, or so I estimated (the *burdyuks* don't come equipped with speedometers).

The horse was harnessed to the four-branched vessel and was itself cradled by three larger swimming belts made out of goatskins. Thrusting its head anxiously above the treacherous current, the horse made for the other bank in a direct line. Its rider also drove it in that direction by blows from a stick. But because of the current, our desire to go straight across was thwarted, and as a result we were carried far downstream.

The two men who were lying portside in the water acted as a rudder, holding fast to my seat and kicking like frogs.

One of them had a curved back, which at every stroke arched higher than his head, causing his pale-blue eyes to bulge out. He reminded me of someone, but I didn't know of whom.

The banks streaked by. One of the wooden-slatted lookout towers of the sentries appeared like a line etched in the dusk, but hardly did it come into view when a long row of bushes sprang up between us and the tower. On the Afghan side there was nothing but tall reeds. In the moonlight the eternal snow of Pamir and the Hindu Kush shone blue . . . The rifle I had with me served as a balancing pole. But it didn't help. The sticks under me gave way and I was sitting in the water.

Three shots, in rapid succession, rang out. Were they aimed at us? Did they come from this side or the other? We neither saw them nor heard them hit as the raging water swept us along.

The younger of the two swimmers was yelling all the time, the rider yelled too, and I had no idea whether their cries were from fear because of the shots, whether they were trying to spur on the horse, whether they were quarreling about the direction of our trip, or whether some danger threatened. But with comforting regularity the rounded back and blue eyes of my neighbor kept on surfacing. Whom did he remind me of . . . why, of Neuerl! Of course! It suddenly came to me . . . of Neuerl! He looked just like Neuerl!

Neuerl and I had met some thirty years before. At the time I was earmarked
for a career in banking. I was recommended to a junior departmental manager
in the provinces. But if things didn't work out for me in the banking business,
I could return to my studies without anyone learning about the failure of my
effort. Besides myself, another young man entered the bank on trial. Whichever
of us proved the better was to receive the position.

The other fellow was Neuerl, and the moment we made each other's
acquaintance, he directed his pale-blue eyes toward me with undisguised
anxiety. We had to add up columns of figures and draw up account statements.
Neuerl noted down the amounts lightly with a finely sharpened pencil. He
added from left to right and from top to bottom and from right to left and
from bottom to top before he deemed his finding worthy of an entry in ink or
before placing a check mark—the sign of accuracy—on the sheets.

We sat on opposite sides of a desk, and I can still see Neuerl's head
popping up from the ledger and his curved back, like a concentric circle,
rising above his head. Then, one after the other, his chin and back sank again
into the papers, exactly the way the chin and back of the swimmer alongside
me now sank into the waves after each stroke.

The goatskin sacks were panting and snorting, the same as horse and
man. Neuerl swam beside me, his legs moving like a frog's, his eyes bluer
than the water of the Amu-Darya, which in fact isn't blue but brownish. But
the moon was blue, a sapphire brooch pinned on the bosom of the clouds.

In those days, thirty years ago, I had taken things a lot easier than my
colleague Neuerl. I relied on the dependability of the original accounts keeper,
when in fact I was supposed to check up on him. It went well. I had no doubt
that the victory would be mine, and I was happy about it, since I liked the
work.

Fräulein Freihöfer, the accounts clerk, who shared the office with us,
began taking me under her wing, perhaps because I struck her as more cheerful, hence a more desirable colleague than the shy Neuerl. He became increas-
ingly more self-conscious. On the one hand, he saw my lead; on the other, he
noticed, to his chagrin, that I had additionally acquired a promoter. He made
a clumsy effort to win Fräulein Freihöfer's favor. Whenever she was about to
put the accounts ledger back on the shelf, he rushed over to help her; when
she was unwrapping her breakfast, he grabbed the paper and threw it into the

wastebasket. But none of this made any real impression on Fräulein Frei-höfer. It was to me she gave the regular deposits, which consisted just of March payments, while she loaded up Neuerl with the accounts of speculators like Poldi Foundry and Škoda and Kosmanos and July-South. In order to calculate the deposit rates, he had to immerse himself uninterruptedly in the stock quotations, sporadically coming up for air, just like now in the moonlit river.

The contest with Neuerl seemed uneven to me, so I began easing up. If in the beginning I had accidentally omitted the (actually superfluous) notation "1 March coupon" from the March bond payments, I now did it deliberately, although the junior department manager gave me back the statements. A few times I also arrived late at the office. So after a fortnight Neuerl got the job, and for a while I cursed the lack of endurance I had shown in the banking business.

Now, thirty years later, when without authorization and shot at, I was swimming in a vessel made of patched-up goatskins from the Soviet republic of Tajikistan toward the kingdom of Nadir Khan, from a rational collective economy toward the dark forest primeval, in order to hunt tigers, Neuerl came to mind. I was struck by his similarity to the man at my side and his downward plunging blue-eyed back.

The rider and swimmers continued yelling at each other. I noticed that their shouts related to the horse or, more exactly, to one of the inflated goat's bellies that was supporting the horse. It was shriveling up, and the rider tried to close the cork more tightly. The man who had been shouting the most swam over to help him, yelling all the while.

Up to my navel in water, I held the rifle high to keep the lock from getting wet. Neuerl was doing the frog kick. We were already close to the bank. The rider struck the horse, which in any case wanted to reach land as quickly as possible, but the current mustered all its power to prevent this fat booty from escaping. It tossed us to the left, while we wanted to go straight. Where were we rushing? Were we rushing to Lake Aral?

Finally the rider managed to grab hold of a reed. But he had to let go of it again, since the current thrust us farther. Nevertheless, we had made a push forward and before long there were two of us who were able to grasp reeds.

The Amu-Darya tugged furiously at us. But it was too late. The horse had ground beneath it, and we too had ground to believe that we would be coming ashore a moment later.

Neuerl was already standing, though only on his tiptoes, but his head with the pale eyes and the rounded upper part of the body were above the surface of the water. We waded ashore.

The horse was tied to a bush, the goatskins were pulled ashore, the swimmers shook themselves, spraying water all around, I waved to Neuerl to come with me, he tossed one of the branches over his shoulder, and so we started out on the tiger hunt.

At first we had to wade through puddles and swamps, as if this were a continuation of the river on land. When we finally had solid ground under foot, I looked alternatively up and down, looking for the snakes and monkeys of the jungle. But there were none to be seen.

What I did see—the moon shone brightly—was thousands, tens of thousands, hundreds of thousands, of bird's nests. One in every fork of a branch, countless nests in a single bush. Were we at a resort for migratory birds; were we at their destination or at just a junction on their annual journey? Or were they birds from local skies who nest and hatch here? Truly, a more undisturbed region could scarcely be imagined. There were enough mosquitoes for food, and no people to bother them. Only tigers creep through the thicket at night, but that doesn't disturb the inhabitants of the bird's nests in the slightest; tigers can neither shoot nor fly. In the battle that was now about to break out between man and tiger, I could not, therefore, count on the sympathy of the birds.

I vaguely remembered having read that for a tiger hunt by night (or was it a lion hunt?) native beaters set out with torches and that you needed special bullets. Nonsense! If I land a shot between the beast's eyes, in the middle of the forehead, that is, right in the brain, what else can it do but sink dead at my feet, a bedside rug for the making? Besides, I am not going to fire just *one* shot but several, just to make sure!

Was that something gleaming in the bushes? There was nothing gleaming in the bushes, not even a glow worm. I could again relax my grip on the rifle, which I had grasped tightly. Was that something rustling in the bushes? Nothing was rustling in the bushes, not even a grasshopper.

I remained standing, Neuerl alongside me. I went farther, Neuerl alongside me. No, not he, but his Asiatic counterpart. The resemblance (unless it just happened to be imaginary) was a grotesque joke of nature.

The Tajik, who was accompanying me, a stranger, in a strange land, who for the sake of another person's whim was making his way through the jungle at night, a stick over his shoulder, into the habitat of tigers—what he must already have experienced! The overthrow of the emir; revolution; outlaws' raids; smuggling; refugees from Afghanistan; refugees to Afghanistan; the arrival of the machine age; learning to read and write; collectivization; the teachings of Marx and Lenin. The inhabitants of this Soviet region on the border of the English colony have experienced more and learned more in their lifetimes than their ancestors did in a thousand years.

And the other one, the real Neuerl? He's sitting with his finely sharpened pencil point in Leipa, Bohemia, adding up IOUs and stock shares from right to left, from top to bottom, from left to right, from bottom to top. Maybe he has since become a junior managing clerk, married Fräulein Freihöfer, and convinced himself that it was really *his* career she had advanced in the old days, since she was already in love with him.

I'm certain he has become a managing clerk. I imagine myself working under him as an unpaid trainee. Again I have omitted the notation "1 March coupon" from the March bond payments, and he has me summoned. He looks at me reproachfully, presses his pencil against the tabletop almost to the point of breaking its fine point, when crack—he ducks down, his back arched, ready to leap, like a . . .

Was there really a cracking sound just then? Something did make a cracking sound, but no matter how sharply I peered out for them, I didn't see the glowing eyes of a predatory cat shining anywhere. After all, the great Afghan tiger doesn't do you the favor of crouching down when it's ready to leap, making itself ready, in other words, to be shot at. You have to creep up to it. I didn't creep. I stepped forward stoutly, wanting to leave tracks behind, in order to find my way back to the *burdyuk*. To be sure, according to my compass I was heading due south, but if it began raining I wouldn't be able to make out the needle anymore and would have to spend the night right where we were.

Was it nostalgia for Neuerl's settledness that made me keep thinking of him? Or was it the contrary? Was I glad to be able to wander through the jungle during office hours? That's something Neuerl certainly can't do. On the other hand, how can my adventure compare to everything the other Neuerl, the one at my side, must have experienced here in much fought-over Central Asia?

Nothing snarled or snorted in the underbrush. No beast of prey was allowing itself to be knocked off. We turned to go. It was unnecessary to check the compass, unnecessary to follow our tracks; before us, in the direction of where we had landed, it was all ablaze. We hurried there.

What did we see? What did we hear? The trusty ferrymen had made themselves a bonfire and were singing at the top of their lungs—in order to frighten off the tigers. And they succeeded handsomely!

The *burdyuks* were lying in the marsh grass already inflated and bound together, and with branches again spread across diagonally. The horse was hitched in front, driven into the water, and we shoved off. However, we did not return to where we had started out. The Amu-Darya was carrying us still farther downstream. We had to row, ride, and balance ourselves for another three kilometers before we reached the Soviet shore.

I gave one of my escorts the sixty rubles; he handed them to Neuerl. He appeared to be the leader of the group. I mounted the horse. (One of the Tajiks who had not gone on the swim with us had taken it on himself to return the saddle the next day.)

"Todi-dana—good-bye!" I shouted, and they returned the farewell in chorus. Neuerl mumbled something to himself as I put my horse into a trot.

I was twice detained by sentries, to whom a rider along the Amu-Darya—a man on a horse without a saddle and carrying a rifle—seemed suspicious, even though he was able to show proper papers. My bottom was soaked through and stuck to the horse's back. The suspicious patrols did not suspect that I had undertaken an unauthorized border crossing and had been in Afghanistan on a tiger hunt.

But I was moved not by this experience so much as by the doubt as to whether what the hunchbacked Tajik had mumbled in farewell was really the words "Servus, Kisch" or something that just sounded that way . . .[2]

Egon Erwin Kisch, "Im afghanischen Dschungel," "Asien gründlich verändert," *Zaren, Popen, Bolschewiken. Asien gründlich verändert. China geheim* (Berlin and Weimar: Aufbau-Verlag, 1980), 380–89.

1. The Bassmachi were members of a movement opposed to Soviet rule in Central Asia in the early 1920s. They were mercilessly suppressed by the Red Army.

2. A popular Austrian term of greeting or farewell.

The Execution

A man died by the executioner's hand. Blood gushed from his neck in a long, broad stream; life spurted up out of a man who had seemed dead beforehand.

Unreal, his yellow face pale, he flitted this morning from the interior of the police car, his hands handcuffed, his long, lanky body in a gray Chinese coat. His hips swaying, he glided along like a ghost in a churchyard wind.

While I waited, I did not try to imagine his features and form. I know that murderers in general do not have bulls' necks, protruding chins, or receding foreheads. But this one looked all too much like a non-murderer; he looked rather like someone who had been murdered, not like one about to be advanced from life to death.

Tsang Kya-ying swung his shoulders, his legs, and even his manacled hands as they led him away to the cell of the Lower Court, to the thirty or forty people who were also due to come up for trial today and were awaiting their fate uncertainly. But he, he had no need to await his fate uncertainly; he was dead and could not escape this state of death. His two police companions had remained outside the iron door, which was sufficiently guarded without them. So he could insinuate himself like an equal among equals into the crowd of those who were not his equals. They did not notice that one of them was now only a phantom.

Suddenly the iron door opened respectfully wide. With a sense of superiority, swaggering, life entered—in the person of a policeman. Jingling keys, it moved toward Tsang Kya-ying. Only now did the others realize . . .

Don't Europeans maintain that death means either nothing to the Chinese or at least less than it does to us? "The guys laugh during their own execution," the inspector told me outside.

Well, Tsang Kya-ying, from whose body life was to spurt, had a half-opened mouth with the corners drawn up, which, together with his halting speech and continuous swaying of his entire body, created the impression that he was amused. But was he really amused? Or was it fear that moved his mouth and body? These questions are pointless now; we'll see soon enough if he makes his way cheerfully or sorrowfully from life to death.

What death means to his cellmates, we have already seen: from all corners their eyes, like the muzzles of rifles, were trained on the condemned man when life, embodied in the figure of a policeman, approached him with jingling keys. The inspector, a Scot, has served long enough in the Shanghai courts to be able to ask a Chinese prisoner in Chinese what he would like to eat before going to his death. Tsang Kya-ying asks for warm meat dumplings, cold fish, rice, and soup. And cigarettes.

In the courtroom, the Lower Court is coming to order. In itself an execution is hardly a small matter; but this court has no more to do with the execution than to ask the condemned if he wishes to make a statement or have the court deliver a message to relatives or friends.

Tsang Kya-ying is led to the defendants' dock. He has precedence over his cellmates; he is not a man accused, he is more than a man accused, more than a man condemned—he is someone who has been executed. The upper part of his body flits above the wooden dock. Tsang Kya-ying sees an acquaintance sitting on the detectives' bench and directs a torrent of words first at him and then at the judge.

Is he greeting the acquaintance? Is he berating him? Is he confessing his guilt? Is he protesting his innocence? I have no idea. The drawn-up corners of his mouth, the twisting and turning of his shoulders, express nothing; and the assessor of the international settlement, who with the help of a translator customarily transcribes every word of an accused person, witness, policeman, or detective for the records of the foreign police, this time has nothing translated. Tsang Kya-ying is of no further interest. He's finished.

Tsang Kya-ying has no final statements to make to the court and can be led off to the courtyard, where an uncovered table has been laid for him. A pack of cheap cigarettes is tossed to him; he tears it open even before his hands are freed and lights one up. Since his crime—burglary and the fatal shooting of the watchman who surprised him—he probably hasn't smoked once.

And probably hasn't had a decent meal. The wooden chopsticks with the pieces of fish and meat, and the rice, over which he poured the soup, fly to his mouth. According to a Chinese superstition, dumplings ease the way to the next world. Another cigarette. He offers the pack with the rest of the cigarettes to a policeman. You want them? You don't want them? Shrugging, Tsang Kya-ying throws them on the table; one falls out. As he stoops to pick it up, he remembers: it's pointless to pick it up. How greedily he would have grabbed for it five minutes earlier. Everything changes quickly when life is racing to its end.

The possessions that were taken from him at the time of his arrest are returned to him in a little bag: forty-four coppers, a pawn ticket, a key. Tsang Kya-ying counts his money the way the Chinese count, slinging five coppers at a time from one hand into the other. For a long time he stares, frowning, at the pawn ticket; then he tears it up carefully and places the money on the table.

"Let's go!" Tsang Kya-ying gets up with a jerk, pushes up his sleeves, and holds out his hands, crossed, to the policeman so that he can be manacled again. The thin man then climbs into the big police car. A second car follows, with a machine gun next to the driver's seat. "That's the rules," the sergeant sitting next to me in the second car explains, referring to the machine gun. "It really makes sense only when we're conveying politicals."

"Are politicals often executed?"

"Oh, my goodness,[1] almost every week! Only communists, of course. Maybe a European'll be next, this Noulens—you know about it?"

"Yes, I've heard about Noulens. The European newspapers call him Ruegg. When do you think he's going to be executed?"

"The devil knows. Should have been knocked off half a year ago. Since the war started and the papers kicked up such a row, the damned Chinks keep putting it off. Now they're even holding a public trial."

Clearly annoyed, the sergeant took a shot of whiskey. His annoyance is understandable. The international police corps makes the arrest and turns the person arrested over to the Chinese so that they can pass the death sentence. The international police corps then keeps the person condemned to death in custody, finally surrendering him again to the Chinese for execution. How can those damned Chinks dare delay the fulfillment of their responsibility!

Our cars drive through the French town, past the Canidrome, the dog track, across the Soochow Canal. They stop in front of a new building, before which, as is obligatory before state buildings, two stone lions stand guard. The sergeant goes inside to fetch a Chinese official to take charge of the official proceedings. This is, after all, a "purely Chinese execution."

A dead man thus rides to his death, but no one knows it; not the ricksha coolies who make way for our speeding column of cars; not the street peddlers hawking their wares in long-drawn-out guttural sounds; not the workers carrying their burdens on bamboo poles, half groaning, half singing a duet; not those squatting in the eating houses; not the ones standing before the money changers' cages; not those having their heads shaved and their ears tickled by the street barbers. The man in the car in front of us does not look out of the vehicle. For the one who is riding to his death, there is nothing more to see.

The sergeant has another shot of whiskey.

"Does an execution like this last long?" I ask him.

"You mean you've never seen one?" He removes the flask from his mouth, astonished at my question, since he has already taken part in hundreds of executions. "Not even a single one?"

I confess: "Not a single one yet."

"Well, it doesn't take much time. At least in general. If the offender lets himself be baptized at once, it goes fast, but if not . . ."

"What are you saying? I don't understand . . . Did you say 'baptized'?"

"Of course. A Catholic missionary comes to every execution. Some offenders at first don't want to hear a thing about being converted, but the priest doesn't give up, and then they become nervous and submit.[2] Only the politicals hold out to the end. The others all let themselves be baptized."

Impossible! And why necessarily a Catholic priest? In China all kinds of religions and sects carry on the most ferocious competition. Adventists and Christian Scientists, Quakers and the United Free Church of Scotland, Wesleyan Methodists and the Salvation Army. They all buy souls, plots of land, and military secrets; they build churches and gas stations; they promise heavenly bliss to the person who lets himself be baptized by them and casualty insurance to the person who has himself insured by them; they represent the Kingdom of Jesus Christ as well as that of Henry Ford on Chinese soil.

Even Buddhist missionaries come to this thousand-year-old religious territory of the Buddha—Japanese, for example; Japan wants them to play the role that the Christian missionaries play for the European-American state and trade interests.

With so many churches, each of which offers the one and only guaranteed way to paradise, why should those sentenced to death just follow the Catholic one?

"Tell me, sergeant, why just a Catholic missionary?"

"Don't know."

Nonsense, I think to myself, that's the whiskey talking. Has the Catholic church any interest in winning over Chinese criminals two minutes before they're executed? Nonsense.

The drive continues, past the shops of the tradesmen and craftsmen. At one intersection I turn to the right and, as if by chance, cover my face with my hand.

I don't want to be recognized. You see, there's a secondhand bookshop on the left. The bookseller doesn't know—or does he?—what kind of pamphlets his regular Chinese customers sell him secondhand. English, German, Russian. But he knows that he sells every one of these works the very same day to another Chinese regular, who, after he has read them, will dispose of them again in this same bookshop. Besides illegal revolutionary literature he also carries, like all secondhand book dealers, Chinese-English and Chinese-German dictionaries, textbooks, and grammars.

What would my friends in the bookshop say if they saw me riding next to a uniformed sergeant behind a prison van? And what would the consequences for them be if the uniformed sergeant sitting by my side should happen to notice that book-reading, book-buying Chinese were friendly with a European? Soon they'd be traveling the same route being taken by the police car ahead of us. Truth is, reading books leads to the scaffold, but not reading books is also no salvation; the dead man we are taking with us is not going to the place of execution for having read books.

We wind our way among swampy rice fields, past coffins made of stone. On the Whangpoo River the sails of the junks are billowing in the May wind.

A wide-arched gate opens. This is not the first time it opens for a dead man: it leads to the prison and the place of execution. My companion points out a patch of grass: that's where it will happen. That's where the dead man is going to die.

For the moment he is still in the police car. A table is brought out. Children are playing in sandboxes and climbing trees. As our car approaches, they beckon to other children to come over. An official photographer clumsily and fussily unpacks his tripod and sets it up. "Now each one has to be photographed before and after death," I am informed. "In the past, the Chinese simply sent a proxy to the execution, the brother or the son of the condemned, or sometimes just a coolie whom they paid to let himself be killed."

The Chinese official has taken his place at the judges' table. Police stand around, the executioner, you can be dead sure, among them. On the gravel path between the green, pleasantly fragrant patches of grass, a closed police car pulls up; in it a dead man awaits his death. Why aren't they starting?

"The missionary isn't here yet."

The sergeant, who has breakfasted on whiskey, resumes making jokes at my expense. Since I've never taken part in a Chinese execution, he wants me to believe that a missionary is on the way.

And then, by God, one really rolls up. At precisely the same moment a sacristan opens the door of the small car for the barrel-bellied priest and a policeman opens that of the big one for the spindly-thin corpse; at precisely the same moment the priest and the dead man get out. So that he should feel free when he embraces Christianity, the handcuffs are removed from Tsang Kya-ying.

The priest is a Chinese. He speaks Chinese. I don't know how he manages to make the Old and the New Testaments intelligible to a novice, to convert him so quickly from Buddha to Christ. Tsang Kya-ying is at first astonished, then unwilling, then mad; he doesn't want to hear a word of it. Unfazed, the fat living man pleads with the emaciated dead one until the latter, shrugging his shoulders, finally lets himself be baptized and a medal with the Virgin Mary on it hung around his neck.

Now he has to make the sign of the cross, but he shakes his head, and so the good father makes the sign of the cross over the neophyte. Meanwhile the sacristan has opened the box of ointment. The priest takes some, but again the dead man makes a vigorous gesture of refusal; he will not receive extreme unction. Well, so be it. On command, he kneels down and repeats rapidly (he becomes nervous) a prayer recited by the missionary.[3] He then has to stand up. But he doesn't stand up.

He doesn't stand up but instead beats his head against the ground, as if he wanted to smash it, shouting all the while.

"He's shouting that they shouldn't torture him so long," the sergeant translates for me spontaneously. "He's shouting: 'Shoot me and get it over with.'"

Right away, right away, my son, have Christian patience, everything is ready.

Look, there beneath the open sky, waiting, sit the director of executions and his officials.

The photographer, clumsily to be sure, snaps you. You are led to the place where the grass is especially neat and especially thick. The children press in as close as they can—four-year-olds and six-year-olds; surely they have often watched, but a shooting is always interesting to little kids. You are told to kneel down.

The man near you fires the revolver into the back of your head and jumps back so as not to be splattered by the blood that shoots up out of you for several minutes in a stream the thickness of a finger, while you, Tsang Kya-ying, as though suddenly filled with life, rear convulsively and then fling yourself down as if wanting to strangle the earth. You hold fast to your adversary, on whom you have thrown yourself.

You resist when they try to pull you from him, turn you around, place a stone under your head in order to photograph you for the last time. Terrible eyes, a vivid, bloody, unforgettable face you present to the lens.

That's it then. I drive home, along the banks of the Whangpoo and through the Nantao district, past the junks with their billowing sails, past the patrons of the revolutionary bookstore, past the tradesmen and craftsmen, the ricksha coolies and beggars; they all look dead. Tsang Kya-ying looked like them when he was still dead, when he moved like a will-o'-the-wisp, when he ate his last meal, when he addressed the court, and when he knelt on the place of execution and repeated a Christian prayer and was shot in the head.

Now, alive, he drives in front of me, runs past me, sits at the street corner, always the only living person; his blood shoots up, his body struggles, his eyes are wide open, his face turned red.

Egon Erwin Kisch, "Die Hinrichtung," "China geheim," *Zaren, Popen, Bolschewiken. Asien gründlich verändert. China geheim* (1980), 450–57.

1. In English in the original. Kisch is quoting the Scottish sergeant.
2. "Then they become nervous" is in English in the original.
3. The words in parentheses are in English in the original.

Chance Visit with Eunuchs

It was one of those summer strolls in the vicinity of Peking that have nothing at all to do with Peking and its vicinity. Our brain was crammed with impressions, our eyes overexposed. Here was a pagoda, fourteen stories high; the roofs floated in the ether like fourteen malachite-green parallel waves with golden crests; there a brightly painted triumphal arch vaulted over the path. We barely glanced at the pagoda and arch; we were tired of being constantly delighted.

On such strolls, this mood is apt to vent itself in a conversation about the Chinese landscape.

There is no Chinese landscape, observed one of us. The western mountains here, they're just mountains, nothing more. They could just as well be mountains in Switzerland or in the Eifel. The fields? Fields are corn-yellow everywhere, and meadows green everywhere.

His adversary in conversation—tomorrow the roles could be reversed—cites something specific: the shape of the poplar trees, the silvery gleaming strips of the rice fields. And this caravan of nodding camels—do you also find that in Switzerland or in the Eifel?

No, but in Turkey or in Africa!

You've got to admit that it's only in China you see such porcelain fences and the catafalques in the fields!

They've got nothing to do with the landscape. They're architecture. Maybe you'd also like to include in nature the Tiger Bridge and the Ming tombs?

So we talked, for the sake of talking. As we did so, we kept moving ahead, always in the same direction, up the top of a temple mound and down again on the opposite side. In the valley a wall cut across our path.

Possessed by the stubbornness of the aimless, we insisted on sticking to the direction we were going in and strode along the wall in order to reach a place where it would leave our path free again.

After a hundred paces, there was a wide opening; it was the gate of a dairy farm through which—our direction, our direction!—we had to pass. Dogs jumped all around us, yelping; they kept chasing about us, at a distance of three paces, cowardly and aggressive at the same time. They stopped, waiting, when we stopped, at a distance of three paces. An escort like this wasn't exactly pleasant. "One should always carry a stick along," we said.

Nevertheless, we soon forgot about the dogs. The people who were coming toward us resembled each other in an odd, disturbing way. With each new encounter this similarity became all the stronger, until finally it was uncanny.

They were all elderly women, evidently farm workers. Some were leading cattle on a rope, others were carrying sacks on their backs or walked past with rakes and pitchforks. They were wearing dark-blue trousers, as is the custom among working women in this country. However, contrary to all convention, their upper bodies were naked, their breasts hanging down shamelessly.

The matrons were conversing with each other, and although they weren't yelling, their voices sounded shrill, or, to be more precise, a shrill static accompanied each sound.

A sturdily built woman stood atop a wagon piled with straw; her face was etched with countless little wrinkles. Below, people were working grain in the old biblical and still-new Chinese way: the grain ground in the treadmill is thrown upward with a wooden shovel; the weight of the grains causes them to fall vertically to the threshing-floor, and the light chaff, blown away like a cloud of dust, lands on the ground a few paces to a side.

All the work was done by the old women. Their chins wobbled loosely in their jaws. Their heads were shaved clean, except for a "bun" on the crown, a tuft of hair so thin, so gray, that it revealed the advanced age of its wearer. There was no evidence of infirmity; they all went at their work hardily.

Then suddenly we were surprised and confused by a small action, which at the same moment afforded us a glimmer of understanding: one of the women, her back turned to us, relieved herself, standing—standing the way men do.

"Whom does this farm belong to?" we asked another old woman, who for a long time now was creeping around us, together with the barking dogs. She came closer: "We are officials of the imperial court, and this is our retreat."

Now we understood completely. Without knowing it, unintentionally, we had happened upon an old-age home for eunuchs.

Grain and chaff were thrown upward; little donkeys were driven around in a circle, grinding the grain; sheaves were loaded onto wagons. We stood staring at these people. Five minutes before we had looked at them as women; then they seemed to us to be men; now we knew what they were.

These and their kind had from time immemorial played an important role in Imperial China as favorites and patrons. They were statesmen, advisers, wire pullers, and intriguers; panders for the palaces and hangmen for the hovels. The eunuchs forced up the amount of tribute in unminted gold, cast taels,[1] garments embroidered with dragons, and painted silk so high that the provinces rose in revolt. Through coup d'état or murder by poison, the eunuchs brought about the end of dynasties for the sake of helping better-paying masters to the throne. The eunuchs diverted the money earmarked for the building of the navy to the building of the Peking Summer Palace, and the war against Japan in 1895 was thus lost.

Five years later efforts at reform threatened the position of the castrated sycophants. Quickly they seized control of the Boxer sect and methodically nurtured the belief of the Imperial Court that the Boxers were bulletproof and altogether invulnerable. Under this influence the empress supported the hopeless rebellion against the foreigners. But when the movement collapsed, not a single eunuch was on the long list of those whose public execution the European Great Powers were revengefully and bloodthirstily demanding. The yellow courtiers and the white diplomats knew how to come to terms with each other.

The people were unanimous in their hatred of the palace eunuchs, who resembled each other internally and externally like a couple of eggs, if such a comparison is appropriate here. They hated them more than emperors and princes, more than concubines and mandarins, and many memoranda of the "censors," the official listening posts distributed throughout the country, demanded the elimination of the court eunuchs—"the gelded candles in the shadow of the throne," as they referred to them.

In fact, after abortive attempts, many a eunuch was sent into the desert as a scapegoat, although organically he was more lacking in sin and in what it takes to be a he-goat than the other gentlemen of the court.[2] To be sure, not every one. An Te-hai, for example, bore the title of Head Eunuch, which he was not, since he produced a son—who is still living in China—with the imperial widow Tsu-Hsi. The other imperial widow, Tsu-An, who was jealous of An Te-hai, had him executed and had to atone for her order by poisoning herself. An Te-hai's successor was Li Lien-jen, who occupied the position of Head Eunuch until the year 1911, up to the fall of the empire.

There were no changes possible in the institution itself; the seraglio needed guards of proven competence and demonstrable incompetence, otherwise, in view of the principle of succession, empresses and concubines would have availed themselves of every available male for the purpose of having children. The eunuchs stood watch before the imperial women's chamber and guarded the conjugal honor of their masters. But if a guardian of the harem ever permitted a stranger to turn the key, the imperial mother who arose in consequence was, together with her offspring, in his greedy power.

Before us sheaf was being loaded onto sheaf, chaff separated from wheat, and grain ground by these once mighty ones. The old fellow asked us if we'd like to visit the temple. The way to the temple led through the middle of the institution's residential premises. The dogs, tongues hanging out, accompanied us. We passed the vestibule, which got its light only through the half-opened door, a more than sparse light. Over the tea table swayed old ladies' heads, their pigtails sticking up. Nagging, or something that sounded like it, grated on our ears.

The retreat had been very rich, our guide explained, and since he did not trust our understanding, he showed how rich the retreat had been by repeating the gesture of taking money out of his pocket. But now they had to work hard. He illustrated: they had to carry burdens, thresh grain, drive wagons.

We understood. In the imperial period the almost omnipotent head eunuchs had not been sparing of grants to the cloister into which they might at any time tumble from the heights of imperial grace. So long as a eunuch remained active in court service, regulated the traffic in the harem, and raised a loud voice heard in the council of state, he was easily able to care for his comrades-in-gender already in the retreat and at the same time, if the need arose, for his own old age.

The political procreativeness of the eunuchs went under with the dynasty. The emperor went, the generals remained. The generals share rule with the foreign colonial lords and the Shanghai bankers. Their business is looked after by a pale stock exchange profiteer and his gang of bosses, who now are what the eunuchs used to be.

The palace eunuchs of days past work their farm. Sheaf is loaded onto sheaf, chaff separated from wheat, grain ground. They work well, though they don't have to provide for wives or children. They work well, though they can't change their condition with the fruit of their labor. Say, isn't that an argument for reactionaries? After all, they're constantly inveighing against making a person conscious of his class status. That's how to make him dissatisfied. They want to keep the poor fellow in ignorance, superstition, and dirt, because that's where he feels at home. Shouldn't one go further—it'd be consistent!—and protect him by castration from those emotions, feelings, and ideas that distract him from work? But certainly only after everyone has brought into the world the requisite number of *proles,* offspring. Isn't it clear, from the above report, how hard the eunuchs work?

But enough of this political program of the future for reactionaries. There is the temple, a Buddhist temple just like others. In the shrine there is a historic halberd, so huge that one would think it would take a real man to swing it. But on the contrary, it was a eunuch who swung it; his name was Kang-Kung, and he killed many enemies in battle. That is why his memory is sacred to all eunuchs. Over his grave there arose "Hu-Kuo-Szü"—"The Temple Defending the State," together with the cloister and cemetery.

The cemetery is noteworthy for the fact that it is a cemetery. In general the Chinese has himself buried in the open, preferably in the place where he was born, where the members of his family live. However, eunuchs don't do that, since they have no family, no lineage, even when they are princes.

Yes, there is a prince buried here too, that Li Lien-jen referred to above, who for forty years ruled at the side of the imperial widow Tsu-Hsi and in her name and to the advantage of both of them pitilessly plundered the Chinese people.

We voice the rumor (in the form of a question) to our guide that Prince Li Lien-jen had been no proper eunuch. Boundless contempt was the reply. Was it because of our deplorable Chinese, or because of the fact that by our remark we had cropped the honor of a eunuch?

The fifty-cent guide's tip did not at all placate the old man; perhaps he had been a high chamberlain or court marshal. Nor did the dogs give up their distrust of us; with tongues hanging and eyes following our every move, they accompanied us until we were again beyond the wall whose domain we had happened upon unawares.

Egon Erwin Kisch, "Zufälliger Besuch bei Eunuchen," "China geheim," *Zaren, Popen, Bol-schewiken. Asien gründlich verändert. China geheim,* 470–75.

1. A monetary unit once used in China having the same value in this weight (approximately 38 grams) as standard silver.

2. A pun in the original that is difficult to do justice to in English. Kisch writes: ". . . wurde . . . mancher Eunuch als Sündenbock in die Wüste geschickt, obwohl ihm organisch mehr zu Sünden und zum Bock fehlte als den andern höfischen Herren." "Sündenbock" (scapegoat) in German is made up of the words "Sünden" ("blame," "sin") and "Bock" the word for a he-goat.

In the Dungeons of Spandau: From the First Days of the Third Reich

I. The Arrest and Apprehension of Cultural Bolshevism

In the evening the Reichstag burned, and the next morning I was arrested.

I had moved into the room on the Motzstrasse just four weeks before, on the day, to be exact, when power over Germany passed to Herr Hitler from Hindenburg, that same Hindenburg whom the Social Democrats had clamorously supported for the presidency a few months previously.

On Tuesday, 28 February, at five in morning after the Reichstag fire, the doorbell rang. I could hear my landlady ask who was there, and, when she opened the door, someone asked if I was at home, and if there was a second door to my room . . . A moment later, the landlady knocked on my door: "Herr Kisch, please open up!" No sooner did I unlock the door than a man jumps in. "Police! Hands up!" I show him that I have nothing in my hands. A second man jumps into the room as well. "Herr Kisch, we have orders to conduct you to police headquarters."

"Please sit down, gentlemen. I'll get dressed, if I may."

"Do you have a gun?"

I reply in the negative. They check out my night table, my clothes. No gun.

Can I wash up? Yes, by all means. I can even visit the toilet, but in the presence of strangers it doesn't seem the right thing. While dressing myself, the gentlemen—one was a secretary, the other an inspector—converse and ask me when I came home that day.

"It must have been about twelve-thirty at night."

"Hm. And where were you?"

"Here in Berlin West. I had nothing to do with the fire in the Parliament."

"So how do you know about the fire? You were doubtless expecting our visit?"

It seems clear to them that in my person they had seized the arsonist. They had no idea of what all of us had assumed that night—that a hundred other leftist radicals were taken into custody by a hundred other officers at precisely the same hour.

I told them that I most certainly was not the arsonist, but they replied that that didn't matter at all, since they were under orders to bring me to headquarters. Moreover, they also had to conduct a house search.

Only one of my books caught their attention. It was called *Tijdopamen*.

"What kind of a language is that?" "Dutch," I answered. "Ah, Dutch! Have you got a lot of connections with Holland?" "Nothing special, why?" "What kind of a book is that?" "It's by me. The translator gave it to me a few days ago." "What's his name?" "I can't recall. He introduced himself to me in the café."

It didn't enter their heads to check the book for the translator's name. I have no idea, incidentally, why they were so interested in it. They took a few notes of mine and some newspaper clippings with them.

"I don't have any money on me. Can I borrow some from the landlady?" "Of course." The woman lent me five marks; the sum amounted to nothing at police headquarters, since from the money confiscated from prisoners seven marks sixty goes to cover the cost of official fees. Only if you have more than seven marks sixty can you get cigarettes or some improvement in your living conditions.

"Have you any intention of escaping or of putting up any resistance?" my two guests asked me.

"None whatsoever."

"Good. We'll take that into account, otherwise we'd have to put handcuffs on you."

We head for the subway station Viktoria-Luise-Platz. A worker there was distributing printed leaflets: "The burning of the Reichstag was ordered. Provocateurs at work!"

My escorts look at each other. Should they arrest the scandal monger? The commissioner shakes his head. He only has orders to bring Kisch to headquarters. Why should he jeopardize the fulfillment of this express order through some zealous police action? We take the subway to Alexanderplatz.

And now we're on our way to I A, the political police. The hallway is swarming with people. The first I catch sight of from a distance is the attorney Dr. Apfel, the defender of Max Hoelz.[1] Good, good that he's here, I think, he can intercede immediately in my behalf. "Hello, Dr. Apfel, I've been arrested."

"Me too," he replies.

And then I see others. Carl von Ossietzky, the editor-in-chief of the *Weltbühne;* the novelists Ludwig Renn and Kurt Kläber; Hermann Duncker, the publisher of socialist classics; Felix Halle, a member of the Supreme Court; Dr. Hodann, the sex researcher; Lehmann-Russbüldt, the exposer of the bloody international arms trade and a human-rights activist; Dr. Schminke, the socialist municipal physician; the doctors Klauber and Boenheim; the member of parliament Geschke, who looked after Germany's political prisoners following the death of Menzel[2]; the member of parliament Schulz, over whose unauthorized radio address (the "radio putsch") all Germany laughed . . . and many, many others.

My guests turn me over to the political police after getting a receipt, and I was shown the corridor. The benches are occupied, the space between them blocked. All of Culture-Bolshevism is supposed to find a place to sit or stand here. Everyone knows each other, and whenever someone new is dragged in by the police, the others all greet him.

I can't help thinking of a September morning in 1914 when we were sitting on the Austrian bank of the Drina River, the remnants of a decimated division that had been hurled back across the river. Barely a squad of what the day before had still been a regiment. And whenever a wet, ragged figure that belonged to the regiment staggered across, the gang greeted him with a melancholy smile then hunched closer together to make room for him. Today's situation is strikingly similar, except that the smile of the greeting is more melancholy. At first, I didn't understand why so many people were upset and pale; later I heard how they had been mistreated by the auxiliary police at the time of their arrest, and still later I was to experience to my greater horror and disgust and see with my own eyes what the National Socialists did to helpless prisoners in their barracks . . .

The police, who barred us from the other part of the corridor, are young boys, but already decked out in armbands bearing the swastika of the auxiliary police. They seem very excited, since they have just begun their duties, but because of that they try to conceal their excitement all the more. They make derisive remarks, and when they warn someone to stay put and not wander around, they just address him as "bastard" or "hey you."

Names are called out, the first group of prisoners is formed, right turn, then down to the lockup. First stop: the deposit where watches, pens, and cash are collected and placed in envelopes. Second stop: the surrender of knives, scissors, nail files. The third stop is already in the cellar below; that's where we get rid of everything else we still have on us—wallets, notebooks, cigarette cases, matches, handkerchiefs, keys, gloves, pencils—everyone has to dump whatever he has into his hat, untie his shoelaces, and remove his coat. Then grasping hands check to make sure nothing has remained in any pockets, and gliding hands feel if anything has been sewn into any lining or concealed inside a shoe or sock.

During this procedure the new chief of police, Herr von Levetzow, drops in, followed by a police adjutant, a party adjutant, and an entire staff. He was a naval officer whom the Social Democrat Noske had promoted to admiral. Now all puffed out, he paces off his navigation bridge in police headquarters.

"This is the scruffy lot, is it?" he asks, casting a contemptuous glance at us over his shoulder.

"Yes, Chief!" the adjutant hastens to bark back.

"Where were you arrested?" he asks Hermann Duncker. But before the old scholar can reply, he is struck dumb with: "Snap to attention when I speak to you, you scum!"

And Chief Levetzow already spotted another one who seemed not to be standing erect enough: "Take the blockhead immediately to solitary and clap him in irons till his bones crack."

Two jailers rush zealously at Otto Lehmann-Russbüldt, the old leader of the League for Human Rights, and drag him off.

We stand there as pale as ghosts, but the Admiral By the Grace of von Noske has already left, and we can hear him bellowing at another group.

They then shove us into a common underground cell, where we soon discover that there are forty-seven of us there. Plank beds run along the walls. In the middle of the wall facing the courtyard stands a bucket—one for all of us, all of us for one. On the opposite side, on the wall facing the corridor, there are two built-in funnel-shaped protrusions. The pointed end is the "Judas," the peephole; an observer can cover the entire area either with one eye or with an automatic weapon.

II. Traveling in a Police Van

On 1 March, toward evening—how late it was, the approximate hour, none of us had a clue—they opened our individual cells. "Out with you!" We all had to stand in front of our doors, on the iron gangplank from which the cages hang. We were thus able to see each other again, those of us who had last said good-bye to each other when we were summoned individually out of the common lockup. Hardly a day had gone by, but how the comrades had changed! Their faces reflected the sleepless night in the stinking cell, into which the racket of new transports, names being shouted out, and alarms going off penetrated incessantly from all the corridors, while the rowdy noise-making of the emboldened Brown Shirts resounded from the street and any moment threatened a reverse storming of the Bastille, a raid on unarmed prisoners. We had been left without food, without cigarettes, without news. At three in the morning the cell door suddenly opened, and there in the light of the glaring bulb stood a policeman, who handed me the copy of a notification, my arrest warrant, for which I had to sign; order had to be preserved at all cost:

Chief of Police   Berlin, 28 February 1933
Precinct I
I^{2a}61^{03}II/43

To Herr Egon Erwin Kisch

You are under grave suspicion of having committed a punishable
offense according to Statutes 81 to 86 of the Penal Code.

On the basis of Article 22 of the decree of the President of the
Reich for the defense of the German people of 4/2/1933—State Legal
Code, p. 35—I hereby order you to be taken into custody until further
notice in the interest of public security.

By order of:
Sgd. Schneppel.
Certified by: Dommitzsch,
Official employee

Well, we already knew that we were going to be taken into custody,
otherwise we wouldn't be here. What we didn't know was on the page of a
newspaper that a comrade who was rounded up later slipped us in passing. In
three columns on the front page: "Immediate execution of those guilty of
high treason according to Statutes 81 to 86 . . . emergency degree . . ." Where
are they taking us now?

"Where are they taking us now?" we ask a guard who is checking that
all of us are present.

"You'll find out soon enough," he snorted.

They line us up two abreast; we greet each other silently. Here is Otto
Lehmann-Russbüldt, the peaceful friend of peace, who yesterday was placed
in irons on the personal command of the chief of police because he wasn't
standing straight enough when Herr von Levetzow walked by. Here is Deputy
Torgler, who turned himself into police headquarters as soon as the official
reports implicated him in the burning of the Reichstag and just as quickly
was tossed in the hole. Here is Felix Halle, member of the Supreme Court,
and the writers Ludwig Renn, Kurt Kläber, Erich Baron, and Carl von

Ossietzky. Here is the old Berlin town physician Schminke; socialist attorneys like Apfel, Barbasch, Litten; members of Parliament for whom five million Germans were still going to vote tomorrow . . . Each one of us receives his hat, but not the other things that were confiscated on our arrest.

Our procession stumbles down the iron steps. The guard of honor of National Socialist auxiliary police seems to have just the task of flanking our way to make sure that nobody escapes. But now the Brown Shirts-become-policemen want to show the stuff they're made of and regale us with kicks and derisive shouts: "Now you'll see what's you're in for, you bunch of red pigs. Now you're going to get it right on the head . . ."

Fine, we know that now too. A paddy wagon was waiting for us in the courtyard.

The compartment can barely hold ten people, just five on each side. But all twenty-one of us had to fit in, with the result that we practically had to pile on top of each other, sit and stand crammed together. Finally we were compressed into a conglomerate, then they said six more had to squeeze in. They squirmed their way into us like a drill into rock.

I can't see who's standing next to me; I don't know if I'm standing forward or backward, if the van is moving in the direction I'm standing or the opposite way, to the right or to the left. It's pitch dark; the only thing you can see is a red light through a crack. A neon sign, I think. But the red light keeps on appearing, which leads me to conclude that it's the dashboard of our van. That's up front, then.

Where are we headed? We haven't the slightest clue which road we're taking, which streets we're passing, only that squashed together, swaying to and fro, tossed back and forth, a defenseless tangle of people, the trip was lasting a long time, more than half an hour, perhaps a whole hour, and that Berlin must already be behind us.

Suddenly, a sudden jolt. The tangle of people slams against the steel wall of the van, which stands at a lopsided angle. A second, or a minute, or a quarter of an hour goes by. The driver starts the motor, but nothing happens. Once again. Again to no effect.

Outside they begin pounding, screwing, and hoisting. But we, the cargo, must in the meantime remain inside the van. Perhaps, or probably, removing the wheel or the tire, or whatever it is they're doing outside, won't accomplish anything with such a load. What then? Even then they won't permit us to get out. There aren't enough guards to keep us all together if we get out at night. So they'll turn the machine gun next to the driver's seat 180 degrees, toward the van's interior. It's all the same.

For the time being we hear them still trying to get the crate afloat. A quarter of an hour goes by, or a half an hour, or is it two hours?

The motor is turned on again . . . it starts up . . . the journey continues.

After several kilometers the van turns to the right, again at a right angle. The speed slows. Are we going through a residential district? The machine stops. There are shouts. It seems that a gate is being opened. The van moves carefully forward. Stop.

We all have to get out. The dreary overhead light of a driveway dazzles us; huge iron gates stand to the right and left. Officials in uniform, revolver in hand, surround us.

We learn that we are in Spandau.

III. Prisoner No. 1067, Cell No. 33

"Hands out straight!"

We extend our arms: a mattress, two blankets, a covering for the mattress, which certainly needs a covering—but what kind of a covering is it?—are placed in our hands. Then come a sheet, a towel, a dishrag, a white enamel bowl, a mug of the same material, a spoon, a fork, a tin washbasin. Each of us has to carry this equipment in both hands up the stairs to the individual cells. There still other inventory awaits us: a table, a chair, a toilet pail, a wash bucket, a whisk broom, a garbage scoop, a shoe brush, a water pitcher.

Spandau is an old prison. Two hundred years ago an adventurer by the name of Matthison wrote a description of his Spandau experiences. The thief Käsebier, whom Fridericus Rex used as a spy during the siege of Prague, did time in Spandau. Maybe Matthison had lain on the same mattress that I brought up; maybe Käsebier had already used my towel. The table ware, however, must date from much earlier times.

I am number 1067. This is inscribed on a card fastened to the wall. My cell is number 33. There is a little barred window up above. If you push the chair against the wall with the window and stand on the back of it, which is nothing more than a vertical board, you can then grab hold of the grating and look down into the courtyard. Farther in the distance are the residences of the prison officials, storerooms, and some public building above which flutters the flag with the swastika.

As long as the light burns in the cell, though, a person can't even think of balancing himself on the chair, grabbing hold of the grating, and nibbling a bit of freedom with a glance. Immediately a piercing voice resounds upward from the darkness below: "Away from the window!"

In many prisons the number of the cell is inscribed on the wall beneath the window so that the guard outside can tell from where someone is looking out or even calling out. That way he can report on the individual. But not in Spandau; here you're shot at once. Even now.

In the evening a kettle containing hot liquid is carried through the corridor. When the transport passes my cell, the door is opened; I then have to stand, mug in hand, on the threshold and receive my portion from a ladle. Mornings it's the same thing. Only the liquid is called tea in the evening and coffee in the morning. In the afternoon you get the brown soup you're already familiar with from police headquarters. Twice a week in the evening you get a herring or a boiled potato. The potatoes are sweetish and moist like the bread, a hard bread that is softened a little in water. I can manage only a few bites; I am weak and hungry. And still no cigarettes. The others haven't had any for a long time either.

We get to see each other in the courtyard hour; that's the treadmill. For a half an hour you walk around in a circle, three thousand steps in all, hands folded behind your back. From somewhere constant smoke in black clouds invades our lungs; but no, not a word against the free period. It is the ray of light in our imprisonment. For twenty-three and a half hours a day you sit inactive in a cage; for half an hour you see the others sharing your fate.

You can even exchange a few words with them. One of them came a few days after us and had read the newspapers. Thälmann arrested.[3] Schneller arrested! Kaspar, Torgler, and several others walk around in our circle, men for whom and for whose party almost five million votes will be cast on Sunday despite indescribable terror, despite the ban on even the slightest election propaganda, and despite the ban on all communist and procommunist newspapers and periodicals. Here walk representatives of the people chosen by the people, here they walk, hands folded behind their backs, thirty times around the courtyard, and then to spend the rest of the day sitting in their cells.

During our walk we look up at the prison wall, from which we usually peer down. We see those who can no longer muster the energy to take the walk—our sole relaxation—with us, sick, old comrades, the color of their faces turned bluish gray from beatings at the hands of the SA and from the incarceration.

The comrades who march in front of us and behind us, and the comrades up above behind the bars, are the only people we get to see. We are never summoned to the visiting room—visitation rights with relatives have now been expressly denied the political prisoners. Except for Torgler, whom they would love to be able to connect in some way to the Reichstag fire, none of us are even brought in for questioning.

In the cell you feel like a madman. You wash the dishes, put things in order, wash the dishes again, change the order of things, do a few exercises, read for the nth time the book you've already read, fold the bed linen for the tenth time, sweep the floor for the tenth time, relieve yourself for the tenth time, go from the door to the window, from the window to the door, four steps forward, four steps back.

The criminal prisoners wear institutional clothing and institutional underwear, while we are still dragging around in the same suit and underwear in which we were taken into custody. In any case, we can put our coat under our heads when we go to sleep, since we don't have any pillows.

We come into very little contact with the criminals. We see their guarded single-file march in the courtyard circle; they see us as well and by means of gestures ask us if we can toss them down some cigarettes, but that's impossible. Here and there a trusty stops in front of the door of a political colleague while cleaning the hallway, peeps through the "Judas," and asks: "You mean to say you don't like it here?" Most are here for falsifying an entry on an ID card or a work permit. These petty offenses were treated like document forgery or cheating on welfare benefits and were punished with heavy prison sentences.

The hatches of the underground solitary cells open out to the courtyard. We hear cries of: "Help! Help! People are being beaten to a pulp here!" It sets your teeth on edge, but we no longer have the nerves to be affected by this outcry of strangers; we hear too much as it is about the fate of our comrades who were taken into custody by the auxiliary police and the SA and beaten horribly.

IV. From Spand Back to the Police

On the evening before and the evening of election day the witches' sabbath of the privileged party is in full swing also in Spandau. The racket of drums, trumpets, choruses of shouts, and shots moves closer and closer to us, first driving the guard dogs in the courtyard to wild yelping, then setting off ringing and shouting inside the building. We can no more think of sleep now than we could during our police arrest.

You can't catch up on sleep during the day; even sitting on the chair in your cell, you can't snooze, even if you're dead tired, since there is a constant "telegraphing" going on. I'm talking about the criminals who converse from one cell to another, across a considerable distance, by means of a language of knocks. The six pipes of the central-heating system pass through all the cells, an ideal system of transmission. Communication passes along it all day long, with indescribable speed. At first I thought someone was entertaining himself, day and night, by banging drum rolls on the hollow metal. Since the time I understood that these are really conversations, and the noise going through my cell and through my brain makes me absolutely shudder at the thought that people are being forced to communicate with one another as if both speakers were twice handicapped, as if they were dumb and blind at the same time.

When we want to write a letter, we receive paper, pen, envelope, and ink, which are taken away after some twenty minutes. Our letters go to police headquarters in Berlin, which then decides if they will be passed on.

In the second week of our incarceration new figures suddenly put in an appearance: auxiliary police. On every cell landing a double sentry takes up position; an entire detachment has been put up in the guardroom below. Have they been ordered to remove us from here, perhaps to a concentration camp?

Gradually it comes out that they are here to augment our guard; they observe our courtyard periods from all sides, make sure we do not converse with each other, let alone slip each other something, and that we climb the steps again in strict single file. Our old prison guards feel themselves under greater supervision than we do and are therefore twice as strict with us as they had been. Additionally, in front of all iron gates and at all stone walls now stand the revolver-carrying "men in blue."

On 10 March, during the courtyard period, Otto Lehmann-Russbüldt was called into the office. When I was back in my cell, my neighbor bangs on the wall, a sign that I should come to the window. "Lehmann-Russbüldt has been freed; he sent me up his package." He is the first of us to leave. Some have already gone off to the hospital, among them Kurt Kläber, the proletarian poet. A half hour later we learn that Dr. Apfel was also let go.

And a half hour after that the guard comes to me. "You're coming down to the office with us."

I pass an area where packages for prisoners are dropped off. Many of the comrades' wives standing there rush up to me when they see me. "Is my husband still alive?" "How is X doing?" "Is Y well?" "Say hello to Z for me."

As quickly as I can, I answer; I'm not allowed to stop, it's not permitted by my uniformed escort, who in turn is observed sternly by other uniformed men standing in front of the gate.

"You're coming back to police headquarters," the official says to me. "Why?" "Are you a foreigner?" "Yes." "Well, you'll probably be expelled from Germany. Collect your things, you're going with the two gentlemen here." I look at the "two gentlemen." Typical "bulls," Berlin secret police agents.

I have to sign a number of places in thick books, probably that I received my meals daily, that the things taken away from me were returned to me, and so on. Then I am ready to be moved out.

"If you try to make a break for it, we'll drop you on the spot," one of the two gentlemen here says to me.

A police passenger vehicle waits for me and the two gentlemen here; we ride through Spandau, along Heerstrasse. I look out at the National Socialist–whitewashed Berlin: officers of the old imperial army march at the head of Nazi units, a troupe of fraternity students brandish sticks, children in brown uniforms . . . I take it all in, astonished.

"You don't know Berlin?" asks one of the two gentlemen sitting on either side of me. "I was gone a long time," I answer, "in China." "So how do things look there?" "Not too nice either." "What's that supposed to mean: 'Not too nice either'? Things are very nice now in Germany, everybody's celebrating the fact that we're finally making mincemeat out of the Jews and Marxism . . ." ". . . and all the other rabble," the other one chimes in zestily.

Have a look, see, the two gentlemen here have changed their thinking quickly enough. Eight days ago they surely hadn't heard about the National Socialism program, but now they can recite by heart the four words it consists of: Jews, Marxism, rabble, and mincemeat.

I make no reply and just continue to look out: posters for the local elections on the fronts of all houses and even on the glass advertising columns, which are usually rented out to a cigarette company for tens of thousands of marks for the whole year. National Socialist posters, all paid for from state funds, just for the purpose of announcing the election results, which have been cooked up by officials of the new deputy government and the town council in some back room. The National Socialists, who had lost two million votes in the last election, generously allotted themselves five million votes last Sunday; in some districts, such as Pomerania, more votes than the number of people actually registered to vote.

"Hopefully the municipal elections will turn out just as nice as the parliamentary elections last Sunday, so we can make mincemeat out of the Jews and Marxism . . . ," says one of the two gentlemen, with the other adding dutifully ". . . and all the rabble."

I don't answer. We roll into the courtyard of police headquarters; the place is swarming with Nazis-become-police, who already feel at home here. Again into jail; again the check of my pockets.

Then I'm shoved into a common cell full of prisoners. I'd like to ask tongue-in-cheek who the head man is I've got to report to, but the question sticks in my throat . . . These people here, workers, look dreadful, wounded, mutilated, bandaged. Where are they from? Who did such a job on them?

I hadn't yet folded my coat on the plank bed to make a place for myself when all the others surrounded me, fifty or sixty arrested workers, all talking away at me, showing me dreadful wounds and relating their terrible experiences.

They crowded in on me, pushing each other aside; the descriptions overlapped, making it impossible for me to grasp any more than details out of context; someone new kept taking the floor in order to tell me his own story and to show me his own wounds.

They had been kept together for five or six days and made to undergo the most indescribable tortures; and now a comrade arrived who hadn't been with them—they wanted to unburden themselves to him, they wanted to register their charges with him, to give him evidence of the bestiality of their tormentors.

On election day, or the day after, they were all pounced on by the SA in their own residences and beaten in the presence of their horrified families; their furnishings were smashed and their books torn to shreds. Without being permitted to dress completely—some didn't have their shoes on—they were dragged off to the Nazi barracks, initially to the Frisian barracks, later into a factory building converted into a Nazi barracks on Friedrichstrasse.

For five days and five nights the effort was made to exorcise communism from them in any way possible.

The now aroused noncommissioned officers' spirit had itself a field day. The prisoners were compelled to do exercises in the courtyard; on command they had to throw themselves down into excrement and then jump up, and whenever their energy flagged, they were beaten with sticks and whips, so that they had to keep going up and down until they collapsed into such a degree of unconsciousness that no blow of a stick or a whip could bring them around any more.

Every day they had to line up and for hours at a time, their arms raised in the fascist salute, and call out in chorus: "To our beloved Chancellor Adolf Hitler a mighty Sieg Heil, Sieg Heil, Sieg Heil!" Whoever failed to keep his arm straight enough, or to yell loud enough, was kicked and beaten.

They also had to recite the Lord's Prayer in chorus. Other procedures were under way in the barracks. The prisoners had to drink castor oil, then drop their pants, bend down over a table, and were then so showered with blows of a stick that their skin burst and red flesh bulged out. (Almost all my fellow prisoners in police headquarters had these wounds; I saw them with my own eyes.) When the laxative took effect during this beating, the company of tormentors burst out laughing.

V. "Red Front" Out of the Common Cell—That Is the Answer

An arm on my knee, my head resting in my hands, I squat on the plank bed and stare at the other inmates of the common cell who crowd around me, talking incessantly and showing the evidence of the abuse suffered in the Nazi barracks—gaping wounds and inflamed swellings.

Who were the people into whose hands they fell? Political opponents? They showed little of politics—just sadism and anal eroticism. Castor oil played the greatest role. Where did they get so much castor oil?

"Oh, they have row after row of bottles of the stuff."

The prisoners had to drink it, turn naked facing the wall, and then do knee bends until, to the delectation of those in command, the knee bends were accompanied by the action of the medication.

One of the workers was made to stand opposite his son, both were given sticks, and they were then compelled by means of blows and a revolver aimed at them to hit each other. "Harder, harder," they were ordered, and "faster, faster." Both of them are now in the same cell with me; father and son lie next to each other on the plank bed, their heads and necks frightfully beaten, the father's right eye all black and blue and bulging, his jaw swollen, possibly broken.

The prisoners were constantly told that they would be shot, that five people were shot today in the cellar; at night for fun they'd shoot into the dormitory where we all slept.

Every torture was accompanied by mockery. They were especially fond of such remarks as "You don't enjoy us, do you? That's why your wife enjoyed us all the more. In nine months your wives will be getting lively little Hitler youths."

These remarks were all the more worrisome and disturbing because none of the prisoners had even the slightest contact with his family and had no idea if, in fact, his wife had also been dragged off.

To the question where his wounds came from, the injured inmate had to answer: "I fell drunk against a stove."

Beards were cut off, hair cropped, mostly on only side of the head, or singed off and torn out in tufts; with some, the hair was shaved in the form of a swastika.

One SA major, who had had enough of the incessant beatings, finally stamped his foot and called out to his party comrades in the presence of the prisoners: "It's really enough now." But Count Helldorf, the *Osaf* [SA leader] of Berlin, who inspected the barracks in person and had the prisoners brought before him, ordered new corporal punishments. His special interest was in ferreting out Jews; he made prisoners show their genitals and then asked: "Your father's religion?"

"Protestant."

"Your mother's?"

"Catholic."

"Come on, you're a typical Jewish half-breed; your mother f——d around with Jews."

The Jews among the prisoners had it the worst; they were the most furiously beaten, and were conducted daily to their "execution"—they were lined up against the wall, a revolver was aimed at them but fired over the head in order to frighten them.

There was also a fourteen-year-old boy in the barracks who had been arrested because they wanted to find out from him the address of his mother, who was in hiding.

From others they wanted to learn the addresses of functionaries or residences where secret presses, explosives, or weapons were kept. Only one of the prisoners turned over the names and addresses of comrades; he is also in my cell, but none of us talk to him.

The light in our cell is not turned off at night, since new prisoners are being brought in all the time. There are more than seventy here now, and the newcomers have to sleep on the floor, since there aren't enough plank beds for everyone.

We also have three foreigners among us. The first is a Portuguese Esperantist who turned up at a left-radical bookshop to inquire after the address of the Berlin Esperantists' Society; police happened to be in the shop at the time and immediately took him into custody. The two other foreigners are Czechoslovaks, a waiter from Prague and a cabinetmaker from Czernowitz; both of them were beaten on the street and finally carted away by the police on the grounds that they had shouted "Hitler, croak!"

Until late at night the injured surround me and besiege me with descriptions; my nerves are stretched to the limit, I jump up and walk around. "Why don't you leave him alone," one calls out and comes over to me. "You must understand us; we've gone through hell, take me for example . . ." And now he tells me what they did to him all over again.

They really did experience in four or five days what I was bombarded with in a few hours; but they suffered it, while I just have to listen to it.

None of these inhumanly abused workers, no one—with only one exception—betrayed anything; no one speaks without hate and contempt for this type of opponent; no one, no one was driven insane by the cause for which he has to endure such horror!

At noon on 11 March I am summoned from my cell and informed that I am going to be deported across the border. Only for a moment do I go back, to fetch my coat. I take my leave of my cellmates with "Red Front";[4] more than fifty right fists are raised in farewell; more than fifty cries of "Red Front!" ring out in answer.

Red Front—from the common cell . . .

"In den Kasematten von Spandau," *Mein Leben für die Zeitung 1926–1947: Journalistische Texte, 2* (1983), 320–37.

1. Max Hoelz (Hölz; 1889–1933), a communist activist who in 1921 commanded an uprising in the Mansfeld area of central Germany (the so-called Middle German Uprising). After its suppression, Hoelz was given a life sentence. Kisch and other leftists worked tirelessly in an effort to win his release. Hoelz was amnestied in 1928.

2. Adolf Menzel (1815–1905), a well-known German painter and book illustrator.

3. Ernst Thälmann, the communist candidate in the 1925 German presidential elections.

4. The Red Front Fighters' League, a militant communist organization, was founded in Berlin in 1924; by 1928 it had more than 100,000 members. It was declared illegal in 1929 following riots in the city's working-class districts, during which thirty-one people were killed by police fire.

Ex Odio Fidei
[Out of Religious Hatred]

This much is certain: the boy Simon Abeles lies buried in the Teinkirche. If you enter the church from the street through the main door, you find in the right nave, beneath the choir, the brown grave slab of some citizen set in the ground. The sexton insists that that is the exact resting place of the copper coffin of Simon Abeles. According to old chronicles, however, it is supposed to be in the Chapel of the Holy Cross, on the epistle side of the altar, not far from the tomb of Tycho de Brahe, under the marble tablet containing twenty-four lines of Latin chiseled into it:

> Simon Abeles, a little Jew of twelve years, followed God and fled to the Collegium Clementinum of the Society of Jesus, for the sake of holy baptism, in September of the year 1693. Treacherously dragged away from this hospitality a few days later, beset in his home by flattery, threats, abuse, starvation, and frightful incarceration, he showed himself stronger than all this and died by the hand of his father and a friend of the same on 21 February 1694. The corpse, which had been buried secretly, was exhumed on the sixth day and officially examined. Until the coffin was sealed, the body did not emit a single offensive odor, was of a natural color, was not in the slightest stiff, indeed was pleasant to behold, with rose-red blood flowing from it. It was carried from the town hall of the Old Town in funereal splendor, amid a singular throng of people and the emotional participation of the folk, and here interred the last day of March 1694.

In the sacristy of the Teinkirche hangs a portrait of the Jewish boy, sweetly idealized, in a red doublet, white wig, dress sword, and with a crucifix in his hand; a cartouche bears the inscription: "Hic gloriose sepultus est Simon Abeles Catechumenus, ex odio fidei Christianae a proprio parente Hebraeo occisus" [Here lies gloriously interred Simon Abeles the catechumen, slain by his own Jewish father out of hatred for the Christian faith].

The burial of the Jewish boy in the Christian church occurred during a lawsuit that provoked a great stir. The century of the Thirty Years' War of religion was drawing to a close. The grandsons of the rebels, the defenestrants, the executed, the imprisoned, and the exiled had learned to acknowledge the new nobility, the new officialdom, the new learning, and even the new state language. But deep in their consciousness the feeling of having been defeated gnawed away at them and grew into a complex passed on from generation to generation. Did that all have to happen? Look at the Jews—persecuted for many centuries, yet they managed to preserve their religion and their customs and their language! The brethren of the Society of Jesus, who came as a religious army of occupation into a militarily defeated country, sensed only too well that they would have to prove to those of other faiths that they were the apostles of the only true religion, hence not only enemies of the Bohemian Brethren and other Protestants but also enemies of the Jews. Gustav Freytag[1] read the little piece by the Jesuit fathers Eder and Christel on the case of Simon Abeles, which was published in 1694 under the title "The Manly Steadfastness of the Twelve-Year-Old Boy . . . ," and on the basis of it characterized the entire affair in these words:

> Whoever judges this Jesuit report without prejudice will find things in it that the authors wish to conceal. And whoever regards the fanatic murderers with disgust will show the fanatic priests no sympathy. Through spies and informers, by promises, threats, and by exciting the imagination, they recruit for their god, who is quite unlike the God of the gospels, a host of proselytes for "cleansing." With the skill of experienced theater directors, they employ a pitiful murder in order to stage a real tragedy, and the dead body of a Jewish boy for the purpose of recommending their religion to Jews and Christians alike by pomp, show, and mass processions, and, if possible, by miracles. Their fanaticism, in alliance with the civic authorities and a compliant law, confronts the fanaticism of a despised, persecuted,

and passionate tribe—cunning and violence, outrage and stunted morality on one side and the other.

The judgment of the cultural historian Freytag would doubtless have been even more damaging to the Jesuits if, in addition to the private brochure of the two brothers of the order—which seemed to him suspect in itself—he had read the official report published by order of Emperor Leopold under the title "Processus Inquisitorius, which the Court of Appeals has initiated against the two Prague Jews Lazar Abeles and Löbl Kurtzhandl on behalf of the twelve-year-old Simon Abeles, the son of Lazar, who was murdered Ex odio Christianae Fidei, and which for the greater exaltation of the Christian faith as well as for the fruitful edification of one and all has been put into print together with the relevant chief-inquisitorial records and other very remarkable events then occurring. Prague, Caspar Zacharias Wussin, Book Dealers."

In this pamphlet, however much it strives to represent the proceedings in the case of Simon Abeles as just and the verdict handed down as justified, Freytag would have discovered not only a number of things the "authors wish to conceal," but he would also have had to come to the conclusion that the "fanatic murderers" might not in fact have been murderers, but on the contrary victims of a dreadful judicial murder—*ex odio fidei,* out of religious hatred.

As numerous as the accounts of this matter were, not one of them dared concern itself with the defense of the accused, who had not even been permitted any legal counsel. A hundred years later, in the case of the Huguenots of Toulouse, just as in the case of the Prague Jews, neither the intention of the son to change his religion nor the murder itself was proven, and in both cases the fathers fell victim to priest and rabble. But while Jean Calas found posthumous acquittal through Voltaire's flaming pamphlet,[2] Lazar Abeles and his friend found no one to take up their defense. Only the indictment—quite involuntarily—speaks sufficiently in favor of both men, both in what it remains silent about and in what it declares.

The "Processus Inquisitorius" begins with the sentence: "On the 25th of February in the year 1694 a Most Esteemed Royal Chancellery in Prague received a written but unsigned denunciation of a murder committed against a Jewish child in the Jewish quarter of Prague, the full contents of which follow . . ."

That this denunciation came from the Jesuits is obvious from the first glance and is confirmed in every line. It states, for example, that in September of the previous year the boy had declared his readiness to receive baptism "to the Very Reverend Father Andrea Müntzer, of the Collegium of the Society of Jesus, here in Prague at the Parish of Clements, and had repeated the same desire in the presence of several other priests, among them Fr. Guilielmi Dworski, Fr. Johannis Eder, and Fr. Johannes Capeta, ardently requesting it . . ."[3] Without exception, these facts and names could have been known only to those within the Collegium.

Indeed, Fr. Johann Eder boasts in his pamphlet that it was he himself who persuaded a clerk in the chancellery, who had received a report of this incident from a Jew by the name of Josel (Joseph, that is), to submit the denunciation: "After I received this news and the Jewish informer had been repeatedly and seriously admonished to deliver himself of a true report, on the next day he committed to paper the whole deplorable course of events in order to deliver it over to the Most Eminent Chancellery." This sentence—quite apart from the Jesuitically employed pronoun "he"—is entirely false, since "although he ('he' being the chancellery clerk, Herr Constantin Frenkin, who has been revealed to be the author of the written denunciation) has been at the same time strictly constrained to produce his first Jewish informer, by the name of Josel, he has nevertheless been unable to locate such a person." The report of the official takes care, however, not to claim any such vigorous interrogation of or admonition to the alleged informant, since he would then have had to explain why in such a thorough discussion he had not at the very outset inquired after the full name of the informant.

The very next day the exhumation and transport of the body to the town hall are undertaken, a number of arrests are made (the male nurse Hirschl Keffelet, the cemetery overseer Jenuchem Kuranda, and two maids), and inquiries initiated. Rumors circulate about the city, which soon is aflame with unrest. The chancellery, in the decree with which it transmits the investigation to the Court of Appeal, implores the latter "that anything that may *in hoc passu* [in this case] gradually emerge and become known to the public at large should forthwith also be brought to the attention of the chancellery, so that with respect to said public its rightful needs may be met in a timely manner." The entire matter now stands under the influence of public opinion, which has been whipped up by the zeal of the authorities.

In the denunciation, on whose basis the inquiry was initiated, only one thing was stated unequivocally: that the child had been poisoned, ". . . mercilessly executed by means of poison given it in wine." During the investigation—whose use of torture we can read between the lines—Hennele, the Abeles' cook, who was kept in custody in the Kleinseite (Malá Strana) town hall, finally confesses that little Simon was done in by poison. Until now she had maintained, as had the dead child's father and stepmother, that it had died of convulsions. But now she gives the answer: "I will tell the truth; the father gave him something to eat, after which he fell to the ground." And to the question as to what this might have been, she replied: "He gave him a herring."

Hence a confession by an accessory, a firm declaration of murder by poison by an eyewitness! The only problem was that in the meantime it turned out that no poison whatsoever was found in the body of the deceased. The basis from which the inquiry had arisen was thus shown to be just as false as the testimony wrenched from the cook.

Nevertheless the two medical doctors and the two surgeons who performed the autopsy did not dare ascribe the death to natural causes in view of the proceedings initiated by the officials and the outrage that had already been unleashed. In the short account of the autopsy, which in its carelessness makes a mockery of the fact that eighty years before an anatomist of the stature of Jessenius[4] had worked in Prague, the doctors report "a fresh round wound the size of a penny above the left temple due to a blow" (but not a word is said as to whether the blow was mortal, deep, or just superficial) and "a fracture of the vertebra colli." There were thus at least two blows, yet the terse account concludes with the words that "the young boy must have died of a powerful blow."

The Court of Appeals, in no way disturbed that the denounced and already "proven" murder by poison had indeed not even been perpetrated, excuses the error on the grounds that "the poison and the secret burial" (the claim that the boy had been interred at night was also proven to be false, since the burial was public) "could not so accurately and truthfully be described *in limine* [from the very beginning] by a stranger and a Jew who was, moreover, not especially well known in the Abeles' house."

"Josel's" information was therefore wrong, since he was not very well known in the house of the secret murder. But these assertions have nothing to do with the alleged assertion; the information of the informer is still valid—the murder must have been committed! The expert opinion of the medical faculty, demanded "by urgent decree," rules that the violent death of the boy must be considered and concluded. The Jewish community asks the investigating authority if the body might in some way have been injured during the exhumation; this question, though prompting solicitation of the medical faculty's opinion, remains unanswered.

Tragic-comic are the efforts now being made by the tribunal to explain the contradictions in the evidence in the case (e.g., murder by poison or murder by a blow) while at the same time attempting to discredit as mutually prearranged the fact that the testimonies of the accused and the witnesses for the defense correspond. All those taken into custody testify independently of one another that the wound to the temple was the remnant of a scab that had been scraped off, "which thus to declare even a little boy of eight, who was with them in the house, was taught and instructed ahead of time." And so Lazar Abeles, foreseeing possible exhumation of the body, instructed not only his wife and servant (who are now in custody) on what testimony to give but also a neighbor's little boy, whom he could not have imagined would be summoned!

The accused dispute the contention that little Simele [as he was known] had ever run away in order to become baptized. At this point the Jesuit fathers, from whom the first accusation had obviously come and who subsequently maintained that they had actually conducted a disputation with the child on the matter, should have been called as witnesses. But this does not happen. Besides, the alleged flight of the child presumably occurred four months earlier and thus could not have been the motive for a fatal assault. Had one intended to accept both escape and murder as proven and mutually related, the explanation would have been far more plausible that the child had attempted to run away from the ill-treatment of an abusive father and had later succumbed to the continuation of this ill-treatment. But even for this there is nothing to go on in the records of the Processus Inquisitorius.

They say that the child was placed by the Jesuits in the lodgings of a baptized Jew named Kafka, and that Lazar Abeles took him away from there. This Kafka then disappeared, and the role assigned him in absentia is quite unclear. Once, it is said, the child was abducted from him; another time, that he had been in collusion with Lazar Abeles.

Then a new witness surfaces, a baptized Jewish child, little Sara Uresin, who has in this case assumed the mission of Semael.[5] She is thirteen years old, crippled in body, and—as even the prosecution cannot conceal—a morally depraved creature whom the Jesuits would not have tenderly described as a "little maiden" but as a "brazen Jew-brat" had she been introduced by the defense. She appears as if "heaven-sent." Hear this:

> Since an Esteemed Court of Appeals, in mature consideration of all this, further desired that every effort be made to furnish several additional witnesses, particularly Jewish, through which a confrontation *in contradictorio* may be arranged (as it had often been observed in Jewish inquisitions that a confrontation in which one Jew says something straight to another Jew's face proved far more effective in making the truth known than even torture), there appeared quite unexpectedly a certain little Jewish maiden by the name of Sara Uresin, about thirteen years old, who had spent time in true Christian apprenticeship with a Christian woman and had heard of this inquisition from afar, and who of her own accord and free will . . .

And this prompt fulfillment of the court's wishes by the name of Sara Uresin (Father Eder explains her appearance through supernatural means) delivers testimony before the Royal Supreme Court, to which she is presumed to have found her way alone, regarding everything the investigating judges want to hear at that particular point in the investigation: that she had the year before served in the same house (!) just at the time Simon ran away in order to become baptized; that the boy's father had said it would be better if the boy died and had then beaten him with a wooden stick until his blood ran. The girl is confronted with Lazar Abeles. "May God punish me if I ever laid eyes on this girl before," he cries. Nevertheless, the little maiden repeats everything to his face, "quite steadfastly, courageously, and without the slightest timidity or fear."

After this inconclusive confrontation Lazar Abeles is "led back to his previous place of confinement near the clock in the tower of the town hall, with both feet and one hand well secured."

A few hours later he is found strangled.

Justice cannot help but express surprise at this deed, which is described as suicide. In the first place, the little Jewish maiden "did not know what to say to his face save for a few *preliminaria* about the Christian-Catholic zeal of the boy," and in the second place, suicide is rather complicated for a prisoner fettered and watched the way he was. He "removed the belt with which the Jews are wont to gird themselves, tied the same to a double iron grating high above, which he reached by means of a piece of wood, and placing his neck through it, hanged or rather strangled himself."

It appears, the memorandum relates, that because of the insignificant reproaches of the girl Uresin, "his callous, brutal heart and conscience had become so touched" that he killed himself.

Although an active repentance is thus asserted, this cannot protect the dead body from condemnation. The dead man is declared legally guilty and the sentence executed. His heart is torn out and he is beaten around the mouth, following which his corpse is quartered and burned at the stake.

His wife and the cook Hennele are told nothing of the death of the chief accused. Despite threats and the pretense that Lazar Abeles had confessed everything, they continue to protest his innocence. The little maiden, "privately attired in Jewish style," is confronted with the cook, who now agrees to everything the child says and finally has to add that the father killed the boy. By means of poison. There then follows the confrontation between the cook and Mrs. Lea Abeles, who the night before had suffered chest pains. She too sees that since the cook has already been made to serve against her better judgment as a witness for the prosecution, everything is lost. In order to save her husband, of whose death she has not the slightest idea, she declares that a man she knows, a certain Löbl Kurtzhandl, who is no longer in Prague, had strangled the child.

Kurtzhandl is arrested in Manetin and the inquiry against him runs its course. In the meantime, the boy Simon is buried publicly with unprecedented pomp as a Christian baptized "in proprio sanguine" [in his own blood], as decided by Archbishop Hans Friedrich von Waldstein on advice obtained from the theologians and canons. On 25 March 1694, "in ipso festo Simonis Tridentini pueri, aeque a Judaeis martyrisati" [on the feast-day of the boy Simon Tridentinus, who was also tortured to death by the Jews], a commission decides where the child is to be interred.

A week later, the funeral takes place; the body, which had been buried on 22 February in the Jewish cemetery, exhumed five days later, and kept in state in the town hall for an entire month, is officially found to be without the slightest unpleasant odor. The second test of beatitude also proves positive: ". . . as no less the mortal wounds received on the broken neck always and ever without surcease had thrown up the freshest and loveliest blood like a fountainhead, at which occasion many of those present attempted" (attempted!) "to soak their kerchiefs in this running blood, the example of which even a physician of the Evangelical religion followed."

Löbl Kurtzhandl, against whom not a shadow of doubt is to be found in the official proceedings of the case, is condemned to death on 19 April 1694. How he was treated is evident from a decree of Emperor Leopold I to the Royal Court of Appeals: "The enclosure" (a complaint) "brings to your attention among others that the Prague Jew Löbl Süsel Kurtzhandl, who was sentenced to death by you, was not permitted himself, nor were any of his friends, to receive any copy of the sentenced passed on him nor was any legal counsel made available to him *ex officio*." The emperor orders the appropriate legal procedure followed, the execution temporarily postponed, and provisions be made that "the life of the condemned man not be shortened *in carceribus* [in prison], as is reported to have occurred with his accomplice."

The Court of Appeals answers His Majesty that the condemned is merely seeking to delay matters, whereupon Leopold "in this very distressing criminal affair" grants Kurtzhandl a respite of just fourteen days and finally confirms the death sentence: "Insofar as the swift execution of the same is so much in the public interest, it is to be carried out without further delay and the filing of further appeals."

Stripped of his clothing, bound to the three-edged crowbars placed under his limbs, he stands on the scaffold so that his thighs and lower legs may be shattered by "thirty-some blows" of the eighty-pound wheel and his chest crushed with iron bars. A priest keeps on shouting to the malefactor to accept the Christian faith; after the eleventh blow Kurtzhandl is said to have answered that he was prepared to do that; he is now baptized and assumes the name "Johannes," whereupon the executioner blindfolds him and he "receives the last mortal blow on the neck, and thereby deprived of his senses, bleeding heavily from nose and mouth, after two further blows passes blissfully unto the Lord, to the proper admiration of all present, who could not laud and praise the miracle-working hand of God and His inscrutable mercy enough."

The former "impenitent murderer" Löbl Kurtzhandl is buried in the Church of St. Paul as a "penitent Catholic Christian" named Johannes.

Egon Erwin Kisch, "Ex odio fidei," "Geschichten aus sieben Ghettos," *Geschichten aus sieben Ghettos. Eintritt verboten. Nachlese* (Berlin and Weimar: Aufbau-Verlag, 1973), 39–49.

1. Gustav Freytag (1816–95), German novelist and playwright, known especially for his historical novels.

2. Jean Calas (1698–1762), a burgher of Toulouse who was innocently condemned to death. Voltaire succeeded in reversing the decision through his pamphlet "Sur la tolérance à cause de la mort de Jean Calas."

3. The three different versions of the same name—Johannis, Johannes, Johann—appear this way in the original.

4. The Czech physician Jan Jessinski (1564–1621).

5. A figure in Jewish mythology who appears as seducer and corrupter.

Kisch on crutches after jumping ship in
Melbourne.
Courtesy Museum of National Literature,
Prague.

Journey to the Antipodes

A king has been murdered. Alexander II of Serbia, who had come on a visit to France the day before yesterday, was shot on his entry into Marseilles. And not just he. The French Minister of Foreign Affairs, Barthou, who was sitting in the car next to he king, was also killed.

The assassin was cut down on the spot. A Czech passport was found in his pocket. Accomplices who had stayed in the same hotel with him had also checked in with Czech passports.

Raids on Czechs and Yugoslavs; 418 were brought into the Marseilles prefecture alone; in Paris more than 300. The departure stations of the French rail lines as well as ports are under surveillance.

Agitation is raging everywhere, especially in France and especially in Marseilles. The place where the assassination took place is besieged. People are pushed against one another in the middle of a crowd; those in the back stand on their toes in order to see what they can of the pool of blood—a king's blood, a minister's blood, an assassin's blood.

Posters of Action Française and other fascist groups shout that the foreigners are to blame, France's unwelcome guests, and cry for their blood: down with the red traitors to the fatherland, the agents of Moscow, out with all foreigners.

Posters of the antifascists answer back: The car the king was traveling in was unprotected, the same way three years earlier the president of the republic had been left unprotected. At that time the Bolsheviks were accused of murdering Doumer. The fact that the assassin happened to be a White Guardist who wanted to take revenge against France for not initiating a war against Red Russia in no way put a stop to the terror than had erupted against the left. It's going to be the same thing all over again now.

Groups of people are standing around holding discussions and arguing in front of the houses into which police had forced their way. The crowd is waiting.

A man makes his way through this raging, suspicious Marseilles; he's not feeling very comfortable at all. He is heading from the train station to the pier of the P. and O. Company. He hopes to leave France today; his passport is Czechoslovak. He is neither a monarchist nor a fascist; on the contrary. Will the ship take him on board, will it?

The ship accepts him. It's supposed to put out to sea at midnight, but that's just in the timetable. When the ropes are untied the superstitious passengers are asleep and so don't notice that they are departing on the thirteenth of the month, to be exact, on Saturday, 13 October 1934, at five in the morning.

To the man with the Czechoslovak passport, it's all the same. He's just happy to be sailing away from Europe. Now he has a long break ahead of him before entering another danger zone.

Nothing is further from our mind than the desire to lead the reader astray. Hence we shall say straightaway that the man has nothing to do with the assassination of King Alexander and Minister Barthou.

Nevertheless, we have more to do with the man than either he or we would like. We, that means we who are writing this book; the man is the hero of this book. "Hero"—that's the word we would have preferred avoiding although we are employing it, of course, not in the traditional sense but rather in the sense of "literary figure." We have no desire to present the man with whom we are going to be preoccupied as a hero. But it would be quite pleasant in this instance not to brand him to the contrary. That is because he is near to us, as a fellow countryman, like-minded, and so on. We show solidarity with him; indeed, we identify with him.

As we said, the man also finds it unpleasant that people are concerned with him. If he had to do it himself, describe the adventures yet to befall him after the fact, he would surely take just as deep a breath and just as long a windup as we have.

There's the *Strathaird,* a 22,500 ton liner. A big ship; anything bigger wouldn't be able to pass through the Suez Canal.

"What does the name *Strathaird* mean?" our man asks a cabin mate. By coincidence, he's a Scot (the coincidence isn't too great, since almost all the passengers are either Scotch or Irish or English), and he answers that Strathaird is an area in Scotland, and that there's another one called Strathnaver, after which the sister ship is named. "Gaelic is still spoken in Strathnaver and Straithaird, a variety of Celtic; not what's spoken in Ireland, but Scotch-Gaelic."

"Very interesting," our man says, though Celtic doesn't interest him in the slightest, to say nothing of the fact that there are different branches of it.

As for us, we just rub our hands. Just wait, my dear fellow, Scottish-Gaelic will yet be of interest to you! . . .

Four days ago our man was sitting in an October-cold place on the north coast of France writing about something from the eighteenth century. A telegram then arrived from Henri Barbusse: "Can you come to Paris immediately?" In Paris our man was asked if he wanted to go to Melbourne as a delegate of the world committee against war and fascism.

"When?"

"Tomorrow evening to Marseilles, the day after from Marseilles to Australia, but not by boat to Melbourne, since you'd get there too late for the congress. From Freemantle, the first Australian port you reach, take the train to Melbourne. The fare is twelve English pounds. The ship's passage, tourist class, comes to around eighty pounds round trip. The Australians sent travel money by telegram, but . . ."

"But?"

"But they cabled it to England, since it's cheaper, and London will reimburse us for what we lay out now."

"Can you lay it out?"

"We have to, since the Australians sent the money after all. Tomorrow you'll get the money from us."

"Yes, but . . ."

"But? But what? Don't you want to go? We thought you'd be excited about the prospect."

"And I am. But there's one catch: I was expelled from England."

"Does it say so in your passport?"

"It did, but I've got a new passport now."

"Splendid, so you can now go."

"Shouldn't I first ask at the British consulate if there are going to be any problems? It would be senseless to take a trip around the world and then not be able to land."

"You'll be able to land."

"If there's any doubt, wouldn't it be better to send someone unknown in my place?"

"Nonsense! They'll stop someone else as well. They're always stopping delegates to congresses against war and fascism. Hitler's diplomats make sure of that in the countries involved."

"That means I'll be stopped twice."

"Maybe. But *you'll* make it."

"May God keep your faith."

"Fine. Now you're off to Cook."

They had no idea in the travel bureau if a berth on the *Straithard* was still available. "Centenary celebrations in Australia, you know."

Of course he knew that, our man replied, naturally, *naturellement,* that's why he too wanted to go to Australia, because of the celebrations.

Cook inquired of Marseilles by telephone, and a berth in a four-bed cabin was available. The price of the round trip was seventy-eight pounds sterling. "Should we make the reservation?"

"Please."

"The fare must be paid immediately."

As it happened, our man didn't have that much money on him.

"A down payment would suffice."

As it happened, our man didn't have any money on him. Could it wait until tomorrow?

"We can't guarantee it."

Our man asks if an entry visa is necessary. No, he learns. Czechoslovaks with a return ticket do not need a visa.

All that was missing now was the travel allowance. To Marseilles 175 francs, 78 pounds sterling to the western tip of Australia, 12 pounds from there to Melbourne. And something to live on en route, since the trip alone takes five weeks. And if you weren't allowed to disembark, the trip would then last not five but ten weeks. The ship wasn't turning around immediately. It was sailing from Australia to New Zealand. As a precaution, our man consulted the timetable: the *Strathaird* was scheduled to return to Marseilles only on the fourth of January the following year.

Our man has exactly 22 French francs and 25 centimes in cash. It's clear that that hardly suffices for a trip to the Antipodes. But tomorrow he's going to get money.

Tomorrow proves to be a bad day. Murder, regicide, the murder of a minister, scream the newspapers. Murder, murder, people murmur everywhere. Out with the foreigners!

Before he leaves his hotel the next day, our man has to explain to two curious visitors why he has been living in France, why he is a Czechoslovak, and if he knows Yugoslavs or any other suspicious people. No, he doesn't know any. He may go. All hell has broken out in Paris: house searches, raids on political émigrés, imprisonments, interventions.

From the committee he learns that up to now only a part of the travel money has been raised, just enough to cover the journey from Paris to Marseilles and the ship's passage, but not the train across the Australian mainland. "But our friend Ulrich is bringing you the rest to the station this evening."

At Cook our man is told that he does indeed need a visa. "Outrageous," he cries, "didn't you know this yesterday?" He makes such a fuss that the British Consul General finally has to be called. "Hello, Cook speaking. Listen, we have a gentleman here who because of a mistake on our part has not applied for a visa for Australia. Could you please issue it to him at once; he's leaving this evening for the centenary."

The Consul General has a blacklist—our man knows it well—lying on the left side of his desk. "Are you the gentleman Cook told us about?" he says and stamps the passport:

British Passport Control
Paris
Date: 11.10.1934, No. 51 853
Visa for Australia
sgnd. C. E. Collinson
Good for any number of journeys within
twelve months from date hereof.
Temporary visitor.

Then a trip to the library of the Geographical Society and the return with a suitcase full of books. For as long as our man is away from France there won't be any literature there on Australia.

Evening. The Gare de Lyon. Friend Ulrich, who is supposed to bring the rest of the money, isn't here yet. Fortunately, someone shows up who can lend him a thousand francs, which will be enough for the Freemantle-Melbourne leg.

Friend Ulrich is still nowhere to be seen, and our man says: "He's usually so reliable. This is the first time he's leaving me in the lurch."

But friend Ulrich had already been there. He simply didn't know that at about the same time two trains were departing for Marseilles. So he waited on the wrong platform and the next day reported to the committee that the delegate had not departed. "He's usually so reliable. This is the first time he's leaving us in the lurch."

Friend Ulrich soon learns that he had made a mistake. Our man will not learn that for some time. . . .

There are 1,204 passengers on board, among them the archbishop of Bombay, the lord bishop of Madras, many nuns on their way to India, and a number of high-ranking officers. It would be irreverent to believe that perhaps they're traveling tourist class. (Certainly the nuns.) The crew of the ship numbers 400 men. The officers and seamen are English, the stewards are English, the pages—exceptionally handsome lads from sixteen to eighteen years of age—are English; their white kid gloves are tucked under their aiguillettes like epaulettes. Indescribably emaciated Indians, with the puggaree, or turbanlike wrapped bag, on the head, and with a purple sash girding the body, wash and scrub the deck barefooted, without pause. . . .

Our man sits in the writing room in order to prepare his lecture for the congress, present the problems of war and fascism in the king's English, and construct sentences out of those words that he commands. This dependence on, and limitation of, language doesn't please him at all. He would happily enlarge his English vocabulary, but now all he's hearing around him is Australian. This is what he's learning: that every noun, verb, and adjective is preceded by the word "bloody"; that a chair can be called "a fucking bastard" and bad beer can be called "a fair cow"; that a man is a "bloke"; that whereas an Englander is a regular Englishman, a regular Australian, however, is a "dinky-dye-Aussie"; that every conversation ends with "goodo."

Without any particular enrichment of his vocabulary and therefore without satisfaction as a writer he composes his lecture. The work is most likely going to be in vain anyway; the landing officials most likely are going to confiscate the manuscript and charge the author with offending a head of state. For this reason he refers to the "bloody bloke" only by the initial H. [Hitler], but then crosses that out and substitutes an X for it. But he thinks, whom can I deceive this way? Who else but H. can be meant by "bloody bloke." . . .

The *Strathaird* will not put in at any more ports before reaching Australia. The passengers heading there have to fill out disembarkation forms: columns and headings crisscross, occasional tricky questions, the purpose of the trip, if you have landing funds of forty pounds, names of acquaintances or relatives in Australia, your political views, and so on and so forth.

That our man would have forty pounds ready cash on him is out of the question; but he hopes that this would probably not be necessary for passengers with a return ticket. He has even fewer acquaintances and relatives in Australia, but he hopes that for visitors to the Melbourne centenary this would probably not be necessary.

In the Australian newspapers that he bought in Colombo, he found nothing about the antiwar congress. He doesn't even know in which auditorium the congress is scheduled to meet. What would happen if his friends didn't know that a delegate was disembarking from the *Strathaird* in Freemantle and was then proceeding on to Melbourne by train? What would happen if they came to the railroad station and didn't recognize him?

We, invisible observers, can give him the answers. You won't be landing in Freemantle, nor will you be taking the train to Melbourne. Destiny of an entirely different sort awaits you, so in the meantime enjoy your freedom of movement! But we won't give anything away. . . .

Two days, thirteen hours, fifty-seven minutes—that's about how much time remains before our man reaches Australia, and it's already four weeks since he left Europe. His lecture for the congress is written out, the Australian reference library almost exhausted and excerpted. In the first book he read, the official work *The Commonwealth of Australia* by Bernhard R. Wise, our man came across an odd law by means of which an arrival can be kept away, without his being denied entry, and can be sentenced, without his having committed any punishable offense. . . .

According to this law, every person on landing may be given a dictation test from some European language. Our man read that socialists and other progressives had opposed the law when it was first proposed on the grounds that it gave the government then in power a pretext to block the entry of its opponents into the country.

Our man nodded in approval at this point, for he shared the fear of the radicals. But on reading further he realized that the opposition to the law was illogical and ludicrous:

> Nonetheless, and in spite of this assurance and definite understanding, the opponents of the government persisted in the assertion that white immigrants would be excluded, and opponents succeeded in giving a widespread currency to this mischievous falsehood. In fact, however, the promise given by the government to Parliament has been faithfully adhered to; and from the day of the passing of the law till the present time (1908), *no white person has ever been submitted to the language test, nor has any white person ever been refused admittance to the Commonwealth.* (Bernhard R. Wise's italics.)

When he began reading the book, our man had the intention of bringing such a curious law to the attention of Europe, but then dropped the idea as unfair, since he saw in black and white that it had never been applied. So he crossed out the excerpt, but see here—in a newer work, the last that he read, he found that the dictation test had also been used against whites, though to be sure only against paupers, the insane, invalids, prostitutes, and criminals. To make certain that he would definitely fail the test, some con artist was even dictated the prescribed fifty words—in Gaelic. An amusing incident, thought our man, and he entered in his notebook: "Gaelic Test." The notes he was keeping on board closed with these two words.

The night before Freemantle, the port of the Western Australian capital of Perth, the night of 5–6 November, he didn't sleep. In the morning a launch brought the mail on board; a letter and two telegrams from Australia were for our man. . . .

The passports of disembarking passengers are being examined in the first class lounge. Our man goes there only to learn that British nationals are being dealt with first. He could thus avail himself of the opportunity to look around the world of first class, which until now he had been forbidden to enter. The day before he would doubtless have done so, but today he prefers to fix his gaze sharply on the long-awaited shore. . . .

Just then two impressively built, stern-looking men stride across the deck and make straight for our man. "Are you Mister Kisch?"

They conduct him to the customs official, who in the name of the Commonwealth, the All-Australian Federal Government, informs him: No admittance. Any attempt to trespass or otherwise set foot on land will have serious consequences. His passport remains in the possession of the authorities.

The customs official then proceeds to inspect the suitcase of our man in his own cabin. Locked out, our man protests against this; either a ban on entry into the country or a baggage inspection—a state should not permit itself both pleasures. Nonplussed, the official stutters something to the effect that he has his instructions, that he does indeed take the protest into account, but the inspection must proceed.

Backed up by two deadly determined West Australian Sherlock Holmeses, he undertakes a thorough inspection. Every handkerchief is spread open, every book leafed through, the sides of the suitcase expertly tapped, the tube of toothpaste fingered.

"No bomb inside," says our man; this observation provokes neither a smile nor an answer.

The three men earnestly continue their work. It lasts about half an hour, during which time our man ponders his fate.

He could, for example, be escorted onto the next steamship heading for Europe; that's one possibility, and just about the worst. He could be isolated on the *Strathaird*, in which case his Australian friends might not find out whether in fact he arrived or disembarked and where he could be found; that was another, equally bad, possibility. If the authorities were not in a position to keep his arrival and disembarkation ban secret, our man would be able to establish contact with his friends. That way all wouldn't be lost.

In the meantime the custom authority's internists continue to percutanate and auscultate the little suitcase. When they finally snap it shut, their boss repeats with still greater emphasis: Any attempt to set foot on Australian soil will have serious consequences.

Our man accompanies the gentlemen out of his cabin. At the end of the corridor he sees a group of people who looked as though they were waiting for the official procedure to come to an end. These were no pursuers; pursuers are usually not young fellows with such gangling movements. Moreover, pursuers rarely carry cameras perched on their stomachs. These were representatives of a profession who might help him out of the fix he was in.

"You're the blokes from the press, aren't you? Let's go up to the smoking room and mix stories."

They laugh because he calls them "blokes", which means he knows Australian, and because he speaks about "mixing stories," which means he also knows newspaper talk. And once he sits down with them upstairs, he's already a colleague. But that doesn't keep their first question from being a question of conscience: "Are you a communist?"

"Splendid," our man answers, "splendid! The first question you ask me has to do with my party affiliation. Well, I can tell you straight off that I will neither make a point of my affiliation with any party nor distance myself from any party by emphasizing my non-affiliation. I come as an antifascist and as a militant pacifist. Members of all progressive parties belong to the movement against war and fascism; also millions of communists and many outstanding scholars and writers, such as Henri Barbusse, Romain Rolland, and André Gide."

"And you want to agitate against Germany among us?"

"For Germany, yes. Against the Nazis, into whose hands it's fallen, against National Socialism, which is a danger to world peace."

"You're saying that for political reasons, aren't you? You know yourself that the Hitler regime corresponds to the nature of the Germans. If you want, we won't mention that we asked you this question."

"On the contrary. I'm here to oppose the contention that the Germans are warlike, to report that everyone with whom I was in prison refused to be pressured into accepting fascism despite the atrocious tortures they were subjected to, to tell of the resistance and illegal activity in Germany carried on in the face of indescribable dangers. Only heroes can resist a bloody tyranny with such self-denial, the way the illegals in Germany do."

They make notes.

"Well now. Let's organize things so as to avoid any competition among you. You, I'll tell about the danger of war beyond the Suez Canal; the fellow over here, about Nazi terror; the other fellow, about the activities of our movement; and you, my dear colleague from the illustrated papers, will get anecdotes from my life as a reporter. That way each of you has his own scoop, OK?"

"OK."

Afterwards our man composes a telegram to the government in the capital of Canberra in which he expresses his distressing surprise over his unfriendly reception and asks that the obvious misunderstanding be set to rest. The blokes from the press write it all down.

The passengers on the *Strathaird* have gone ashore to spend the day in Perth. The two well-built detectives have remained on board, keeping a distance of three steps between themselves and our man.

Full of envy, our man gazes at the wide road running eastward from Freemantle. At the end of this road, where his gaze cannot reach, lies Perth, a large city. The passengers from the *Strathaird* can now stroll its streets among Australian palaces and Australian life, have lunch in Australian restaurants, buy Australian goods, until around three in the afternoon newspapers are thrust in their faces with the front-page picture of a man with whom they have been together for the last few weeks without having the slightest idea of the danger he represented.

The Berliners are better off. They have already learned before lunch of the detention of our man, together with all the details. They are reading about the incident the same hour that it is taking place in Western Australia, though it should be observed that on the 120th degree longitude east the same hour arrives nine hours earlier than in Central Europe. On the Wedding and in Neuköln, on the Potsdamer Platz and in front of the Memorial Church, the newsboys are crying: "Can't enter Australia! The raging reporter furious! Night edition!" We (the observers) separate our astral body from the Australian and buy a copy from a newsboy precisely when he's dramatically bellowing the word "furious" into the Berlin air.

> London, 7 November. According to a Reuter's report from Canberra (Australia), the "emigrant" Egon Erwin Kisch, who as a delegate of the world committee of the antiwar movement was to speak against war in Australia, has been denied permission to enter the country by the immigration authorities. The reason for this was the allegation that from the time he left Germany Kisch has been openly conducting communist propaganda. Kisch then sent an angry telegram to the Ministry of the Interior in Canberra in which he protests in the strongest possible terms against such treatment of a "writer of international renown."

The biggest type available to the Scherl Printing Shop, the headline underlined in costly red ink, the text extra bold and spaced, were insufficient to fill out the first page. Thus a Mister Editor so and so, who is suspected of prior relations with the front-page hero who is so put out over Australia, was called in for the purpose of adding a sharply worded gloss to it.

Just as swiftly as the Reuter's Telegraph Agency raced to Europe with the report, so it races back to Australia in order to relate what people were saying over there:

"The rebuff he got in Australia is welcome evidence of the extent to which the world is beginning to understand the character of the emigrants from Germany . . ."

This and similar extremely self-satisfying statements by the [German] Ministry of Propaganda are literally on the desks of editors in Sydney and Melbourne in the evening, and they can only be delivered under the title "General Agreement in Berlin." The English press, Reuter's tells the Australians, limits itself to the repetition of the report. Only the Manchester

Guardian finds the disembarkation ban "petty and detrimental to the prestige of the Commonwealth."

After passing Cape Leeuwin, the southwest point of the censorious continent, the *Strathaird,* with our man aboard, makes its way along the southern coast of Australia through a storm-tossed bay.

Radiogram from Melbourne: Is government statement true you are forbidden to set foot on English soil question mark reply immediately stop committee.

What can you reply to such a question by friends after getting so upset over the disembarkation ban? Our man replies that the statement that England isn't allowing him to land is simply ridiculous. The year before he gave lectures in London at Essex Hall and Kingsway Hall chaired by Lord Marley, Sir Bertrand Russell, and Lady Despard, the sister of Field-Marshal French. Only when he was on his way to the London countertrial of the Leipzig Reichstag fire trial, was he, like many foreign witnesses, detained at the English coast through the intervention of the German embassy. But it was clearly just this one incident that was involved at the time.

This radiogram reply cost eighteen shillings and was paid for out of the money that was earmarked for the transcontinental train trip.

Fifteen hours elapsed before the telegram was in the hands of the addressees. The ministry deliberated over it before it was delivered. The sender of course has no knowledge of this. He is also in the dark as to the fact that another overseas delegate is on his way to Melbourne to the antiwar congress, a delegate from New Zealand. Our man had never heard his name mentioned, but he and the other fellow are traveling toward one another, our man eastward and Gerald Griffin westward.

Moreover, as he glides past the mainland, our man doesn't yet know about the discord beginning to brew there. For the masses, the centenary celebration is no joyous holiday. Carefully screened banquets and balls have been arranged for the guests of honor, the distribution of medals has been considered, expensive ceremonial structures have been erected—is this really the time for such things?

Of all the official events, only the 19,000-kilometer international air race from London to Melbourne has attracted any attention. But its course glaringly illuminates the preceding backstage game.

The imperialistic meaning of this prelude is documented by Joyce Manton, an associate professor at the Melbourne University, in her booklet "The Centenary Celebration as a Preparation for War." An Italian airplane and the American airplane *Bellanca* were not permitted to enter the race; the master pilot Kingsford Smith and his American machine were stopped at takeoff, although he was financed by the Australian chocolate king, Macpherson Robertson; other planes were handicapped or misled into a roundabout route. Thus two Englishmen won, Scott and Black, just the way the military air authorities had wanted it to turn out from the beginning by any and all means.

The honorary committee of the anniversary is under military command, and most of the official guests are military people. The squadron of seaplanes from Iraq has not arrived for reasons of sport nor the chorus of Scottish grenadiers for musical ones. All of this is an obvious pitch for rearmament and militarization aimed ultimately at the Australian working man and woman. . . .

[An uproar erupts when Kisch's detention aboard the *Strathaird* becomes known ashore, and protest rallies are quickly organized. His case eventually goes before the Supreme Court of Victoria in Melbourne.]

A reception committee for the world delegate [Kisch] had been established in Melbourne, but it was changed to a defense committee after the landing prohibition. Local groups arose all over the country. Trade unions denounce the measures taken by the government, writers speak out against the arbitrary action taken against their European colleague—Katharine Susannah Prichard, Vance Palmer, Jean Devanny, J. M. Harcourt, Tom Fitzgerald, E. J. Brady, Bartlett Adamson, Bernard Cronin, Georgia Rivers, and Max Meldrun, Australia's greatest painter; the university professors Walter Murdoch, Beasley, Greenwood, and MacMahon Ball call the banning of the guest an insult to the Australian people; F. Alexander, the chairman of the Australian section of the League of Nations, uses even stronger language; and a bishop, E. H. Burgman, sends the committee a message of sympathy.

Cool and scornful, Mister Menzies, the attorney-general and minister, lets the storm break at his feet. To be sure it was not he who had issued the ban, he answers his first interrogators in Parliament—that had already been decided by the previous government—but he would carry it through. "The disembarkation of this individual has been prohibited by the Ministry of the Interior, and there the matter rests," he declares, and adds that the delegate "will not set foot on the soil of the Australian Commonwealth." . . .

At the same time as these events were transpiring, the case was unfolding before the Supreme Court—kidnapping or legal deportation, that is the question. In rapidly succeeding editions, the evening papers report on what is happening there and elsewhere on the mainland, news about the congress, about the trial, about the scenes on the pier, and about the arrests for distributing pamphlets, pasting up notices, disobeying police orders, and insulting the authorities. . . .

The decision as to whether or not our man may set foot on the soil of the Australian Commonwealth rests in the hands of the Supreme Court of Victoria for now. The case got under way early in the morning. Mrs. Aarons declared that the captain of the *Strathaird,* Mr. A. E. Carter, is illegally detaining her Berlin friend on board, although he is in possession of a valid entry visa issued by the British consulate general in Paris. Mrs. Rosenove, who is acting on behalf of our man, who for his part is acting on behalf of the king of Great Britain, demands an "order nisi," the rescinding of the illegal detention on board. Against this, the accused captain objects on the grounds that it is his responsibility to carry out the orders of the government of the Commonwealth aboard his ship. As it turns out, he cannot for the moment produce the orders of the government of the Commonwealth decreeing the detention of the plaintiff. Adjournment of the trial until tomorrow. . . .

The next day, a representative of the federal government appears before the court and reads out a statement of Minister of the Interior Paterson:

> On 18 October 1934, in pursuance of Section 3, Paragraph GH of the Immigration Act, the minister responsible for the said act declared on the basis of information received from another part of the British Empire through official channels that Egon Erwin Kisch is an undesirable visitor to, or resident of, the Commonwealth.

Our man's representative brands the assertions of this document as false. On 18 October the minister had no idea that the delegate was coming. The order to the port authorities in Freemantle read: "Kisch, who according to

Melbourne newspaper reports will be arriving for a lecture tour, is to be prevented from disembarking." But the first newspaper reports about the forthcoming arrival appeared only two weeks after 18 October. The ban came about in response to the wishes of the German National Socialists in Australia, and the statement of the minister, that information had arrived through official channels from another part of the Empire, bears the stamp of falsehood. Where is this information? What does it really say?

The questions are not answered. At one o'clock in the afternoon the judge arises and announces that, contrary to the usual practice of rendering a verdict only after establishing the grounds for the verdict, he would on this occasion pronounce judgment first so that the *Strathaird* would not have to remain in port any longer than necessary. And the verdict declares: The action is rejected; the detention of the plaintiff on board is legal, and he must assume the burden of all court costs.

The news is transmitted on board by telephone and the siren is sounded, announcing that the time has come for all visitors to leave the ship. Our man bids farewell and promises to appear on deck to wave bye-bye. He advises a departing young reporter with whom he had discussed politics to remain on the pier a few minutes after the ship pulls out. "I'm afraid I can't; I'll get to the office too late as it is." "Risk five minutes."

A few days later our man receives an effusive letter of thanks from the young reporter, who had after all waited. "If I hadn't followed your advice, I would have been tossed out on my ear, for I would've missed everything that happened."

What did happen?

The *Strathaird* pulled out. There was already a meter of water between the ship's hull and the side of the pier when the crowd of people were horrified to see a man swing onto the railing five and a half meters high above them. Good God, is he going to jump off?

One will understand if we ourselves do not say what happened but leave that instead to those who are less involved and more competent, if unasked. The Berlin *Angriff,* for example, declares: "Jewish insolence of the Raging Reporter.—Just punishment: Kisch breaks his legs." The *Angriff* doubtless exaggerates; the Jewish insolence was hardly so great and was content with his breaking just one leg, albeit in two places.

Those closer the scene come closer to the facts. Let us simply insert here the front page of an Australian newspaper:

On learning that the court had dismissed the petition for his release, Egon Erwin Kisch, the banned Czechoslovak writer and lecturer, jumped from the eighteen-foot-high afterdeck of the *Strathaird* just as she was about to depart for Sydney. Falling on a steel rail of the pier, he injured his leg and, after taking a step forward, collapsed. Friends tried to help him, but constables, hurrying from all sides, seized him and under the command of two detectives carried him back to the ship over his protests. "If you have arrested me on shore," he shouted at the top of his lungs as they were carrying him, "you have no right to put me back on a ship!" This protest was ignored and Kisch was taken to the ship, which had meanwhile reversed engines, turned back to the pier, and lowered a gangway. That part of the public that was standing close to the afterdeck was seized with great excitement, which was expressed in various ways and which didn't die down after the departure of the *Strathaird*. At this hour the police are clearing the pier. The leap was the result of the announcement delivered on board that Chief Justice Irvine had dismissed the action. Although he had previously assured friends and visitors alike that he did not expect to be released in Melbourne, Kisch was very upset over the court's decision. His visitors went ashore and there awaited his parting word. When he appeared at the railing, some of them shouted: "Why don't you come ashore?" He pointed to a man who was staying more or less at his side and appeared to be keeping an eye on him. Then Kisch moved off, at which most of his friends left the pier as the ship began getting under way. Scarcely three minutes later he appeared on the afterdeck, swung onto the railing, and jumped down. He landed on the pier, got up, took a step forward, and then collapsed, his face contorted in pain. At the same moment Constable I. B. Weller reached him and asked him in a friendly way if he had hurt himself. He replied that he had broken his right leg. On orders from the detectives, and despite his loud protest, he was carried back to the ship, which had again berthed. We are informed by police headquarters that the commander of the *Strathaird*, Capt. Carter, is responsible for Kisch's custody and that the moment the ship returned he demanded that the fugitive be put back on board. Before the *Strathaird* pulled out once more, demonstrators glued pieces of paper to the bow containing the words: "Kisch, deported by Hitler, 1933 and by Lyons, 1934. Kisch must land!" Two women were arrested as they were sticking the papers on. . . .

[Injured from his fall and detained on board the *Strathaird,* Kisch is forced to sail to Sydney. He is finally taken ashore for the dictation test required by the Immigration Act. When he fails the examination in Gaelic, he is taken to jail and put in solitary confinement. He is eventually transferred to a hospital and the next day taken to court to be tried for his ignorance of Gaelic. He is released on bail a week later but is returned to the Sydney Hospital. Despite the advice of his doctors, he insists on leaving the hospital in order to attend public meetings and rallies where he was expected to speak.]

An evening gathering in Australia Hall was arranged for Tuesday, three days after the Domain Meeting. Our man arrived, friends lifted him out of the car and onto the back of some Samson, who carried him up the stairs. Police right and left, alongside and to the rear. They kept pace but did not intervene, neither on the stairs nor in the entrance hall.

Only at the moment when our man entered the auditorium, which was filled to capacity, and he was greeted on all sides, did a tremendously tall detective push his way past the line of police and said to our man, louder and rougher than necessary: "Follow me at once into the cloakroom." Participants in the assembly pressed threateningly against the police cordon, there was loud shouting, and the mood was tense. The Samson, who was still carrying our man on his back, was prepared to make his way right up to the podium, but police barred his way. "Hold on," our man called out, "let's first hear what uncle has to tell us."

"I'm not your uncle," shouted the detective, "and thank God you're not my nephew."

"Now, now," said our man, attempting to calm the situation, "you're certainly not my son." Laughter all around. The detective dug his hand into our man's shoulder. But he didn't arrest him. It might have occurred to him that no one's official dignity was being insulted. If you say to someone "Perhaps you're my son," that's the worst kind of insult in Australia, since it has to do with one's mother. But our man had expressly assured the contrary: the detective was certainly not his son.

Samson and his burden moved off in the direction of the cloakroom. When they got there, the detective handed our man a summons for the hearing on Friday. Nothing else. This might just as well have been done in the auditorium or before the entrance to the building, apart from the fact that our man would have appeared at court even without the written summons. But the police didn't care about this; what they did care about was inciting a clash. In the course of the gathering, which could now get under way again, the summons was put up for auction to the highest bidder.

The next day friends informed our man of his approaching meeting with the cabinet of ministers at the fellowship's reception for the poet laureate . . .

"Hold on! I don't understand a word. Do you have a poet laureate in Australia? What is the fellowship? Why is it giving him a reception? What does that have to do with the cabinet of ministers? Or with me?"

No, Australia does not have a poet laureate, but the person who in present-day England is invested with this medieval court title had been ordered to Australia in order to take part in the centenary celebration together with the king's son. This poet laureate is John Masefield.

"John Masefield? This is also the name of a quite different poet. In Upton Sinclair's anthology of social literature there is a revolutionary poem by someone named Masefield."

"That's the same person, but he doesn't write poetry like that any more. Perhaps you'll remind him of his early verses when you meet him."

"How, in heaven's name, am I supposed to meet him?"

This is the story. The Fellowship of Australian Writers, the Australian literary union, is arranging a banquet in honor of its esteemed colleague. The national government and that of New South Wales have promised their participation.

But leftist members of the fellowship, who on the strength of their numbers were permitted by the bylaws to invite a guest, decided to invite a foreign colleague to the banquet. And, to be sure, the one who in the judgment of the government is an illegal and unwelcome presence in their country. . . .

Inspector Wilson of the Customs Office is heard as a witness as to whether and how the intelligence test was conducted. He testifies that the accused shouted so loudly that people outside the guardroom could hear: "It is unfair to test me in Gaelic. It's not me you're exposing, but Australia. The whole world will laugh at this."

Movement among the public. Policemen rush at them with rubber truncheons, barking: "Silence in the courtroom!" A man shouts, gesticulating: "A prophet! He wanted to warn you about making Australia a laughingstock." He is dragged out of the courtroom. "A prophet!" he could still be heard shouting from outside.

Witness Wilson: "The accused declared that there was no ink in the pen I gave him, and . . ."

Movement again among the public. The policemen bark: "Silence in the courtroom!"

Witness: ". . . and he tore up the paper and threw it away." (That the accused threw it at a detective, the witness magnanimously remains silent.) "He also said that he had once been in Strathnaver and spoke some Gaelic, but Constable MacKay didn't know it."

Constable MacKay is summoned as the next witness and testifies that until his sixteenth year he grew up in the village of Tongue, in Sutherland, a Gaelic-speaking district of Scotland, but that he had been educated in English.

Piddington [Kisch's attorney] asks the witness MacKay for a few words in Gaelic, but the witness replies that he didn't remember any. He doesn't even know, or mistranslates, such easy words as "no," "street," and "house." (Piddington brought along with him an English-Gaelic dictionary.)

"It's been twenty years since I've spoken Gaelic," MacKay apologizes.

Piddington asks him to read just one word from the dictionary. (Gaelic has its own alphabet.) The witness: "This seems to be Irish Gaelic; I can only read Scottish Gaelic."

Piddington: "The Scottish population is 4,843,000; barely 2.8 percent of them speak Gaelic. Therefore, it can hardly be considered a living European language in the legal sense."

A linguistic quarrel develops. Evidence and counterevidence clash; requests for evidence and counterrequests crisscross; an adjournment of the trial is demanded.

Prosecutor: "I have no objection, on condition that the defendant remains in custody until the trial resumes in order to avoid a repetition of such scandalous scenes as the clenched fist raised in the Domain, the demonstration in Macquarie Street, or the public auction of the summons."

The judge declares that the release of the defendant until the announcement of the verdict has already been ordered and cannot be revoked. The court adjourns.

The prosecutor introduces an expert at the next hearing: John McCrimmin, a retired police inspector, who was born on the Isle of Skye, one of the Hebrides Islands belonging to Scotland. He is to testify that Constable MacKay speaks correct Scottish-Gaelic. In order to prove the competence of the expert, the prosecutor puts before him the text of the dictation test.

John McCrimmin reads and translates it without faltering: "He remembers that his father had a book, called the 'Red Book,' which contained a lot of information about the Highland clans and also parts of Ossian's poems."

(The Sydney author Julian Smith[1] discovered that this excerpt derives from an old work, *The Language and Literature of the Scottish Highlands,* by Prof. John Stuart Blackie. The book cites the exact measures with which King George II, in 1747, not only sought to suppress the Gaelic-Celtic language but even branded the wearing of traditional Scottish garb a serious crime. Had the Terra Australis been a free British dominion at the time, it would have rejected every Gaelic-speaking immigrant, just as today it rejects the one who is not Gaelic-speaking.)

Because the expert McCrimmin reads and translates the test passage fluently, his decision should be accepted now without contradiction: Constable MacKay is able to read the Scottish-Gaelic words in such a way that everyone who knows this language can easily transcribe them.

Unfortunately, Mister Piddington intervenes with a question to the judge: "Would Your Worship also permit me to ask Mister McCrimmin to translate something?" His Worship permits it, Piddington holds out the book to the expert Celt but covers the last word of the place he wants him to translate.

Expert (translating): "Likewise could we benefit if we let her give herself freely to vice for her own pleasure."

Piddington: "Would you be so kind as to dictate your translation to the court clerk?"

Expert (dictating): "Likewise could we benefit if we let her give herself freely to vice for her own pleasure . . ." With an apologetic smile: "This isn't a very moral line."

Piddington: "It is in the original. It happens to be the line from the Lord's Prayer: Lead us not into temptation, but deliver us from evil. The word I covered with my finger is 'Amen'."

The police advance on the spectators. "Silence in the courtroom!" But all the menacingly swung rubber truncheons cannot stifle the laughter. The judge blows his nose long and loud.

Expert: "There are three different kinds of spelling in Gaelic, so it's easy to give it another interpretation."

Piddington: "I do not believe that a spelling can appreciably alter the Lord's Prayer. But now I doubt, Mister McCrimmin, that you translated the text of the dictation test quite so fluently when you read it for the first time."

Expert (decisively): "Yes I did."

Piddington: "And when was that?"

Expert (aware that he let the cat out of the bag): "Do I have to answer the question?"

Piddington: "But you have already admitted that you knew the text ahead of time; therefore you can tell us when it was that you saw it."

Expert: "Yesterday."

Piddington: "May I ask where?"

Expert remains silent.

Piddington: "In the office of the prosecutor?"

Expert: "Yes, but I immediately . . ."

Despite the brandishing of rubber truncheons and the barking of "Silence in the courtroom!" the rest of his statement suffers an awful shipwreck in the storm of hilarity. . . .

Prosecutor: "Don't talk nonsense, my learned friend. Your important guest will be jailed, as he deserves, and in a week or so no one will even remember his name."

He, too, seems to be a prophet, at least as regards the imprisonment. The judge, you see, has no inclination whatsoever to spend any more time on the two towers of Babylon and their language confusion. He also has no inclination to prolong the trial's proceedings by days, the evenings of which, as before, the defendant would use to hold lectures and make speeches all over the place.

What Justice Gibson is doubtless thinking of is the removal of his predecessor, Judge May. So he rises and pronounces the verdict: Gaelic is a European language; Scottish-Gaelic is a dialect of this language and is itself a European language in accordance with the immigration act; the constable who subjected the defendant to the dictation test was competent in this language; and the defendant did not pass the examination. Therefore the defendant is guilty of having entered Australia illegally and is hereby sentenced to six months' hard labor and the payment of all court costs. . . .

Once again our man is subjected to a body search. The police inspector stands beside him, a haughty look on his face, and slaps his silver riding crop against his leather leggings.

The familiar triad of door, lock, and bunch of keys subsides. Our man lies in a big cell and tries to imagine how the next half year is going to turn out. Six months' hard labor, perhaps in the Australian bush among kangaroos and poisonous snakes. It can also last longer than six months; defaulted court costs are paid off everywhere by more prison time—the only currency good anywhere.

Two hours later our man's cell is used by others. A batch of twelve prisoners has arrived from Parramatta, he is told by the policemen, who carry him into a smaller cell in a friendly and careful way. This one stinks even more than the big one; it stinks the most of all the cells he has become familiar with here. Without light, without reading material, without pencil and paper, he lies on the plank bed. For supper he gets coffee (or is it tea?), which at least isn't as bad as it was in Spandau, and three pieces of toast. . . .

Gerald Griffin is also sentenced to six months' hard labor. Clad in prison garb, he is confined to the Parramatta jail. Griffin was born in Ireland, so he is a Celt, even a Gael. His crime is that he doesn't know Dutch.

The two sentences stir up people's feelings. Among workers especially the action of the authorities is viewed as a challenge. The protest movement grows and manifests itself more radically than would have been imaginable just a few years earlier. . . .

[Kisch's appeals are carried as far as the Australian Supreme Court, held in Parramatta, the old capital of New South Wales. No sentence is passed on him. But at the same time the High Court in Sydney reviews the matter and decides in Kisch's favor.]

Its five-man panel deliberates for a week the question of whether an immigrant can legally be tested in Scottish-Gaelic and decides, four to one, in the negative.

Scottish-Gaelic may well be a language in the philosophical sense, and doubtless a European one; in contrast, however, to Irish-Gaelic, the official language of the Free State of Ireland, it is not a language in the political-legal sense, therefore not in the sense of the immigration law. The rapidly declining way of speaking of some remote parishes in no way corresponds to this sense. Therefore the verdict of the police court is rescinded, and any further persecution based on ignorance of the Scottish-Gaelic language is expressly prohibited by the High Court.

Our man is thus a free man in Australia for the first time, not just one at large. He requests his passport and his return ticket, which were taken away from him in Freemantle, but he doesn't get them. . . .

[Kisch then travels by train from Sydney to Melbourne, where he attends rallies, makes speeches, and goes sightseeing. But he soon discovers that the case against him, especially his failure to pass a dictation test in Scottish-Gaelic, is being waged by the Sydney *Morning Herald*.]

After the overturning of the police verdict by the High Court, a campaign is undertaken to influence public opinion against the delegates. The Sydney *Morning Herald* daily publishes column-long anonymous letters to the editor in which Scottish-Gaelic is touted as indeed a world language. Scots! Highlanders!—the cry resounds from the mouths of the masks—does not your blood boil when a foreigner reviles the language of your homeland and Australia's highest court agrees with him?

Every New Year's Day Sydney's Scottish colony gathers on the grounds of the Agricultural Fair for a festive compatriots' reunion. On this occasion they also come—the Macphersons, Macdouglases, Macintoshes, Macgregors, Macdonalds, and Macdarishes, wearing kilts and bonnets and playing bagpipes, but instead of dancing and merrymaking, they hear denunciations of the man who does not know the ancient tongue of their ancestors and yet was acquitted. In his sermon a priest goes so far as to express himself in these unpriestly words: "If an Australian court of law were to declare in the Scottish Highlands that Scottish-Gaelic ought not to be regarded as a living language, these gentlemen themselves would no longer be regarded as living, for they would be struck dead." . . .

[Kisch brings a suit against the Sydney *Morning Herald.* At the same time the Australian government brings a new suit against Kisch. After his previous acquittal, the Australian authorities asked the British government to send an uncoded cable stating its attitude toward Kisch's exclusion. The following reply was received: "The situation is that in September 1933, Egon Erwin Kisch was prevented from landing in the United Kingdom because of his notorious subversive activities. Nor would he be now admitted into the United Kingdom." Armed with this information, the Australians bring a new case against Kisch whereby they attempt to prove that he is a prohibited alien. However, in order to spare everyone concerned further embarrassment, including the Sydney *Morning Herald,* the Australian authorities will not go to trial if Kisch agrees to leave the country on the next departing boat, in which case his passport and return ticket will be immediately returned. But Kisch resists deportation on a German ship and is consequently sentenced to three months' hard labor and a further 106 days for the costs of the trial and the appeal. Released on bail, Kisch attends a gala evening organized by the Writers' Fellowship in honor of both the Australian novelist Katherine Susannah Prichard and himself. He then goes on a speaking tour of Queensland, where he is received enthusiastically. He later returns to Melbourne to take part in an antifascist torchlight procession.]

For 27 February, the anniversary of the night the Nazis torched the German Reichstag, the Melbourne antifascists have organized a torchlight procession, a demonstration against the terror in Germany. The two delegates [Kisch and Gerald Griffin] are to lead the procession.

Right after the first announcement of the event the German consular officials protested this "unparalleled provocation" and demanded, on threat of German economic boycott, that the event be banned.

Easier said than done! Bans have already caused enough damage as it is in this matter; should those ministers who managed to get rid of their colleagues because of bans themselves be slapped now by similar actions? Would the workers of Melbourne tolerate a ban instigated by the Nazis? There is only one solution: the European delegate [Kisch] must "voluntarily" leave the country before 27 February, silently quit the scene, crawl away, without anyone being any the wiser that his departure had been arranged by the government.

The crown attorneys telephone Miss Jollie-Smith [Kisch's solicitor] and propose: Your client obliges himself to depart on the next ship leaving for Europe via New Zealand and not putting in at any Australian port. Your client further obliges himself, until the time of his departure, not to take part in any demonstrations, not to speak in public, and not to give any interviews to the press. The government will for its part assume responsibility for the costs of all criminal proceedings and the defendant's legal counsel; moreover, his passport will bear no indication of the Australian landing prohibition. But if even one of these conditions is rejected, he will be required to serve the sentence of hard labor, will be liable for the payment of all costs, and his sentence and deportation will be duly noted in his passport.

Not just one of these conditions is rejected, but all of them. The representative of our man informs the crown attorneys of this, and they reply: "Your client can do what he wants; we will not concern ourselves about him any more. We will pay his costs and will send him his passport so that he can leave. Hopefully that will happen very soon."

The costs are damned high; including those of the captain of the *Strathaird,* who was convicted in due course, they come to £1,524, which is just about as much as the great [Nellie] Melba paid a generation ago to keep her Czech rival, Emmy Destinn, from entering Australia. Do you recall, dear reader, that when we first mentioned this prima donna tragedy we cited a quotation according to which all great deeds of history occur, as it were, twice, the first time as tragedy, the second time as farce?

Gerald Griffin and our man travel to Melbourne, straight to the torch-light procession. The head of the procession is in front of the Trade Union Building, while the various organizations and professions form columns in the side streets. The two delegates are called on to deliver an address before the microphone of the Trade Union Building transmitter. Our man would very much like to see the faces of the gentlemen from the German consulate while he compares Hitler and Thälmann, Göring and Dimitroff, Goebbels and Ossietzky.

For the first time in the history of Oceania, aborigines are taking part in a demonstration together with whites. On the most primitive instrument imaginable—a leaf of the rubber tree that they press to their lips—they play revolutionary songs; their Marseillaise sounds like a jungle storm.

Twelve hundred torches have been passed out, ten times as many people make up the procession. Thirty thousand people, cheering loudly, disapproving silently, or just curious, line the route. Between the procession and the onlookers march the police and constabulary of the state of Victoria, at their head the detectives of the Political Squad.

At the corner of the Bourke Street hill and Swanston Street, the head of the procession comes to a stop because of the crowds. In the sky above, a procession of torches also seems to pause, five very brightly burning torches standing high next to each another, and far beneath them, beneath the Southern Cross, the earthly torches rock like the lights of a fleet at sea.

Their sails spread wide and high, and when the light hits them, words can be made out: "Free . . . ," and again "Free . . . ," or "Thälmann," or "Ossietzky." Shouts resound in chorus, and then the sailors of this fleet raise their voices in song.

Night of 27 February. Where are they now, the friends, colleagues, comrades who, two years ago this day, were thrown into the cells of the Berlin police headquarters, then crammed into police cars, "to be shot," they were told, a grim journey to supposed death? But death did not come to them then, it came later, in a more long-drawn, more agonizing way. How many were hanged on window grilles, shot while trying to escape, drowned in sacks, beheaded, beaten to death, delivered to relatives in soldered tin coffins! And how many are still languishing in dungeons, every day, every night, expecting the same end!

"Free . . . ! Free . . . !"

With torches and banners the columns are moving; you can see them as far as the bend in the street, almost a mile long. New ones tramp after them from Russell Street; the stream is endless—it forges its way not only through the streets of Melbourne, it flows through Europe, America, Asia, Africa. . . .

[With all the demonstrations behind him, Kisch boards the liner *Orford* in Melbourne for his departure from Australia. His last day in the Commonwealth is 11 March 1935, when the *Orford* puts in at Freemantle, the port of Perth, and he is able to spend his remaining hours with Australian friends before the long journey back to Europe.]

The liner *Orford* lies in Melbourne harbor, ready to depart, and from the pier onto which our man jumped four months ago, he now limps his way up the gangplank. As he does so, he is almost knocked down by curious people who, without paying him any attention, are running around all over the ship. . . .

Monday, 11 March 1935, is our man's last day in Australia. The veil of morning cloaks the hour at which the ship docks at Freemantle, the port of Perth. His Perth friends took the last train at night in order to see him off. . . .

Peppermint trees and red gum trees, giant ferns and giant cacti, line Forest Drive. Below it, to the right, winds the Swan River, at one point so sharply that the shore lies like an island in the liquid noose; the conical tower of an old mill nods from the seeming isle up the street.

Fourteen kilometers more and Perth appears. A meeting is set for midday; it is still early morning and our man has time to roam around Perth. A monument to two policemen rises up before the police station; they were shot to death in Coolgardie by gold thieves (since it's about gold, shouldn't one say "robbers"?). "The criminals were hanged," the inscription says tersely, a warning to all. . . .

Our man spends the hours before the departure of the *Orford* with some friends in the Darling Ranges, where Katharine Susannah Prichard lives, in the middle of the bush. Only one shrub of bougainvillea stands in blood-red blossom, otherwise it's all bare, as if a forest fire had swept through here. But if rain falls tomorrow or the day after, the grass will shoot up to a man's height in just a few hours and the twigs of the trees and bushes will be in full bloom.

The fauna is unaffected by the aridity; in the garden, which is unbordered, you can hear the dingoes yelping, an opossum eyes us from a branch and leaps from it. Two koala bears play clumsily with each other on a tree without giving us a glance or jumping aside, and a kangaroo trustingly approaches little Ric, the writer's son, and lets himself be fondled.

In the arbor made of planks—looking more like a log cabin—everyone drinks tea and his friends tell our man to persuade their European colleagues not to send letters and other material destined for Australia only to Sydney. "Everything passes us here, and the mail takes days to go from Perth to Sydney, and days to go back to Perth from Sydney. We're much closer to Europe, you know, than Sydney and Melbourne, much closer."

Western Australia counts itself part of the Commonwealth only reluctantly, its longing is for Europe. His Australian friends would like to go with him straight to Europe, where there isn't such banal daily life with howling dingoes, hopping kangaroos, shrill-blooming bougainvillea, and with bears and opossums on the branches of the jungle, which withers and dies one moment and the next springs to life again. . . .

Farewell, last farewell! The *Orford* is breaks loose from the pier and slowly glides past a German ship, the *Justin*. "Hip, hip, hurrah!" shout the crew lined up on the deck of the *Justin* at a sign from their commanding officer. And after this *captatio benevolentiae*, there follows a demonstration against the red flags and songs on the pier. "Heil Hitler, Heil Hitler, Heil Hitler!" the lineup shouts in booming chorus and with outstretched arms.

But this is too much for the passengers on the *Orford,* and even those who don't at all like our man ask him: "Give us a slogan against Nazism." "Raise your fist and shout 'Red Front.'" "How's that? Road Front?" "Yes."

They then raise their fists, and the "Red Front, Red Front!" is so resounding that even the four bent legs of the *Justin's* flag, which a moment before had flung themselves around in the air so enterprisingly, seem to stiffen.[2] A command is barked: "Atten-tion! The Horst-Wessel-song!"[3] It is sung at the top of the voice, and with equal strength the counterpoint falls into every softer passage, explodes into every line of verse:

> Die Strasse frei,
> > Rot Front!
> die Reihen fest geschlossen,
> > Rot Front!
> Der Tag für Freiheit
> > Rot Front!
> und für Brot bricht an.
> > Rot Front!

(The streets are free, / Red Front! / The ranks closed tight, / Red Front! / The day for freedom / and for bread is dawning, / Red Front!)

Aren't the singers on the *Justin* stifling a laugh? The commander's face is distorted with rage. Between chorus and counterchorus the command is suddenly heard: "Fall out!"

The two ships have glided past each other, the shore is again visible, and friends waving farewell. Way over on the left waves the flag of the Paris Commune. That is the last thing our man, and we, can still make out on the Australian shore, that is the finale.

Egon Erwin Kisch, "Weg zu den Antipoden," *Landung in Australien* (Berlin and Weimar: Aufbau-Verlag, 1973). My translation is excerpted from pages 311–440.

1. Kisch provides his own footnote on Julian Smith in the original text: "On the Pacific Front: The adventures of Egon Erwin Kisch in Australia." By Julian Smith; Sydney 1936. Australian Book Services Ltd., Manchester Unity Building (230 pp.; 14 photos).
2. The reference is to the swastika in the Nazi flag.
3. The German anthem under the Nazis.

Kisch with members of the International Brigades during the Spanish Civil War, 1937.
Courtesy Museum of National Literature, Prague.

Soldiers on the Seashore

The usual picture of a hospital is of a long, barracks-like, unadorned, dreary kind of building, something suitable as a temporary refuge for poor people who are not only poor but also sick, hence twice burdened.

But once we mention that a Spanish coastal town has become a hospital for the International Brigades, we have to ask our readers to discard the above popular image of hospitals. For this hospital consists of many lovely villas in palm gardens. One of the lovely villas serves as the hospital administration; another one has become the main surgical section; two or three others are used for lesser surgery, while still others house the internal medicine, dental, X-ray, and pharmacological sections. More of the lovely villas have been designated as a warehouse, a kitchen, a workshop, a laundry room, a cultural club, and a home for children.

What would the owners of these villas, who used to spend two months a year here, say about their splendid homes being kept open all year round and each villa, which had been designed to the taste of a single family, now serving as a residence for upward of fifty people? How ghastly, a flophouse!

And Doña Conchita—if she learned of such a degradation of her summer abode and accidentally ran into a former villa neighbor in Seville—would add indignantly to her report about the transformation of the villas: "If you only knew, Doña Rafaela, what has become of the glass dining room of the Hotel Riviera!" "Well, tell me, Doña Conchita, what has become of it; I'm prepared for the worst." "A soup kitchen, Doña Rafaela, a mess hall for soldiers!" "My God!" (Doña Rafaela falls in a dead faint).

On one side of the beach promenade stand the lovely villas, while on the other side is the beautiful beach of the beautiful sea. Less pretty is the street itself. It is no asphalt "Promenade des Anglais," as in Nice; no parqueted "Avenue des Planches," as in Trouville. The main street of the seaside resort is bumpy and shabby. The owners of the villas preferred to bounce around in their cars than spend even a centimo on anything that didn't belong exclusively to their own private paradise—each one's villa being his paradise. The bad road running alongside the good villas is one of the symbols of Old Spain. Another symbol is the sewerage system. Such an egoistic sewerage system exists nowhere else on earth.

But now that we are living in New Spain the path of convalescents is being improved, so that the comrades arriving in ambulances aren't done in by the last stretch of the route from the trenches to the hospital.

"And, Doña Carmencita, if you could only see the types hanging around now on our promenade!"

No, for sure it isn't the fashionable public of a fashionable seaside resort. They are soldiers. Oh, Doña Carmencita, if they were only soldiers like our dashing General Franco, for example, or like our entertaining General Quiepo de Llano, or like their sturdy Moors. But they aren't at all professional soldiers, not even draftees pressed into service for God, king, and our bank accounts. They are, I am afraid, the men of those damned International Brigades. And wounded ones at that.

And the outfits they venture out in on our beach! To be sure, they wear pajamas, but not the silk pajamas with cords and tassels, but just coarse woolen hospital gowns, and over them coveralls made of blue-and-white-striped linen instead of a colorful bathrobe. There was a time here when people admired bathing costumes together with what they covered, the women the figures of the men and the men the figures of the women. But now, God help us. One is missing an arm, another a leg, a third has a bandage around his head instead of a bathing cap, a fourth is half-packed in plaster, the fifth and sixth are on crutches, the seventh and eighth have an arm in an "avion," that is, a three-cornered, woven, and padded wire splint.

Yes, my dear Doña Carmencita, that's the way they look, the figures knocking about our beautiful beach, swimming in our beautiful waves, breathing our beautiful sea air. They've been thrown together from every imaginable land, Doña Carmencita, and they speak Belgian and Negro and Austrian and Balkan and heaven knows what else. Thanks a lot for these kinds of international beach guests.

Whatever the man might have thought who forty-eight years ago undertook to establish a local newspaper in the nearby provincial capital, however bold his imagination, in no way could he have dreamed of the readership his paper found forty-eight years later.

Have a look over there. Three wounded soldiers, all from the same city, are sitting on the lower embankment. One of them is Chinese and at home used to read only his paper written in Chinese and printed in Chinese; the other is a Jew from San Francisco who read either Yiddish or Russian newspapers; the third is an Armenian who his whole life never read anything printed in any alphabet but the Armenian. Together they are trying to decipher the army communiqué that is printed in Spanish in the *Heraldo de Levante,* which had been founded forty-eight years ago. There's also something about yesterday's bombardment of the resort. Everyone here knows more details about the incident that the official communiqué, yet the little newspaper vendor sells out all his copies of the *Heraldo de Levante* to Englishmen and Poles, Cubans and Germans, Frenchmen, Balts, Hungarians, Yugoslavs, Italians, Scandinavians, Romanians, Turks, and the polar-fox hunter from Alaska who is always so hot here yet insists on dragging around in the summer heat in a thick sheepskin coat and a sheepskin cap.

As I said, even though we know nothing about the founder of our *Heraldo de Levante,* we do know that this kind of a polyglot readership could never have entered his mind. We also know that he founded his paper forty-eight years ago, since "48th Year" appears on the title page.

"And these people, dear Doña Luisita, are today living in our lovely villas, which bear our lovely names—Villa Conchita, Villa Carmencita, Villa Rosita, Villa Lola, Villa Luisita, Villa Eulalia, Villa Rafaela . . .

"Our villas are no longer bearing our names, Doña Luisita! The Reds, these faithless heathens to whom nothing, absolutely nothing, on earth is sacred, have removed our names and now call our villas after people no decent person ever heard of: Garibaldi, Masaryk, Maxim Gorky, Louise Michel, Dombrowski, John Reed, Henri Barbusse, Rosa Luxemburg, Lina Odena, Diakovic, Paul Vaillant-Couturier, Hans Beimler, Ralph Fox, Edgar André, Pavlov, Sozzi, Henri Vuillemin, Jacquemotte and Durutti, Ernst Thälmann, Matyas Rákosi and Anna Pauker, Dimitroff, Azaña, Marcel Cachin, Miaja, La Passionaria, André Marty, Jacques Duclos, Maurice Thorez and Alvarez del Vayo."

After the end of the swimming season, just a watchman and his family used to live in the resort. Now there are 1,600 to 1,700 people here the whole year. Hundreds of them are constantly leaving, but the population never goes down. The killing machines of war are constantly manufacturing new supplies.

The battles rage high up, in the mountains. In the first railroad station behind the front lines the wounded are loaded in the ambulance train, which, if it is transporting soldiers of the International Brigades, pulls into one of their hospitals.

About the ambulance trains it can be said that in terms of the workmanship of their furnishings, their nickel railings, their operating tables, their instrument and medicine cabinets, their bath facilities, and the like, they often surpass leading sanitoria. Isn't that luxury, inappropriate luxury, asks many a shaking head; is all of that necessary for such a short trip? The questioner receives the answer that it is indeed not necessary for the sick being transported, but that it is urgently necessary for the workers who manufactured it and made a present of it and who wanted to make only the nicest and best and costliest for their wounded comrades.

By means of this mobile paradise the wounded soldier glides away from the realm of hellish fire, of super-hellish fire that is ignited and nourished by hand grenades, mortar shells, incendiary bombs, artillery rounds, machine guns, and rifles.

Upon arrival at the train station, the sick are loaded into ambulances. Then the trip to triage, to assignment. In the gray days before the war a huge garage had been built on the highway. Since one couldn't drive comfortably on the beach promenade (see above) and there was no interest in making it drivable (see above), the owners of the villas left their cars in the garage and went the few steps to and from their villas on foot. There was ample room in the garage and, moreover, room for the cars of those guests who came to the Hotel Riviera from the entire Spanish Levant to dine in a circle of equals.

The new, present-day inhabitants of the transformed seaside resort have no private autos, and so the garage was turned into a theater with a stage, flies, cloakroom, wings, and whatever else goes with a proper theater. "Teatro Henri Barbusse" was the name given this theater with its changeable auditorium And the auditorium is changed more often than the repertoire. The latter consists mostly of evening variety shows. A Bessarabian surgeon demonstrates that he is not only a Bessarabian and a surgeon, but also a baritone, and rather a good one at that. A nurse and a teacher from the children's home perform with castanets; both Andalusians, they sing and dance the three-quarter time of a malagueña. An American patient, first cellist of the Metropolitan Opera in New York, plays a composition by Saint-Saëns. Two Bavarians stage a shadow show from their homeland and then a second one in which they poke fun at a military bureaucrat. A Negro driver tap-dances, and in the middle of the dance Adolphe enters singing a song reminiscent of Chaplin. But this Adolphe by no means appears as a comic, nor as a dance partner to the Negro. He makes an announcement: a transport of new wounded has arrived.

The stage, orchestra, and auditorium immediately empty out. A change of scene and set takes place, as fast as can be done in the technically most up-to-date big-city theater. Instead of chairs and benches, the hall is at once filled with beds, with sixty beds with snow-white sheets. Instead of the cold buffet, kettles of tea or coffee and soup stand on the counter. Even cigarettes, an otherwise rare commodity, are suddenly extracted by the cartons from a hiding place nobody fortunately knows. As many as there are wounded—and there can be as many as 250 of them—that's how many packs of cigarettes are distributed.

At the entrance, where the box office stood before the theatrical performance, or at least might have stood, there are now tables laid out with papers and stamps.

The ambulances, into which the patients had been hoisted from the train just five minutes before, roll in from the station. Borne by the strong arms of the Brancardiers, they are carried in on stretchers, past the barrier, where papers are checked. Nimble attendants help them out of their clothes, into new underclothing, and into the beds.

The doctors spring into action then. They remove bandages, put on new ones, make their diagnoses, and based on these and the count of the available beds in the individual villas they assign each of the wounded his future quarters in the town. Everyone is given a good feed, the squadron of nurses ministering throughout the hall, which gradually empties of people and finally also of germs, since in the course of the night everything has to be disinfected.

By morning, the wounded soldier who arrived at night is a regular patient—that is, someone who looks forward to the day when he can return to the front and when the Teatro Henri Barbusse, which was his receiving station, becomes his place of departure.

All here have the same wish to . . .

No, the sentence doesn't permit of an easy ending. Something that contradicts all theory concerning the instinct for self-preservation and can arouse the suspicion that we are indulging in hero worship and idealization can't be expressed so easily. One cannot conclude the sentence as a simple assertion if one has lived through World War I, with its mass desertions, feigning of illness, self-mutilation, and other varieties of shirking duty. Before one declares that it was different with the International Brigades, and why, the genesis of these organization has to first be recalled.

Entire columns, centurions, companies, battalions, brigades from every single foreign country, many non-Spanish formations are arrayed on Spanish soil. These formations did not come as formations, not as troop transports, not in the manner of brigades, or battalions, or companies, not dragged into the war as a group. Nearly every person appeared alone, as an individual, on his own decision, out of personal conviction.

Such a voluntary army of such national diversity and such ideological unity had previously been unknown to military history, and never before had there been volunteers whose journey into voluntary service was burdened with such a mass of difficulties, strains, and sacrifices. Where would they get the money for the trip? . . . wives and children left behind . . . one border . . . then another . . . passport check . . . more interrogation . . . more imprisonment . . . the distance ahead . . . hunger . . . ambling along on foot, feet aching . . . a persistent, strange dog accompanying you . . . as a stowaway on a train or in the hold of a ship . . . will you get there on time? Will you get there on time?

At long last the Pyrenees were crossed, you could breathe Spain in the air, you were among comrades. At long last you got a weapon, after you had been for years a defenseless victim in the clutches of scornful henchmen. At long last the time for a settling of accounts with fascism was at hand.

And . . .

And now you're lying in a field hospital. Is this why you dragged around the world? Should this shooting at and getting shot at amount to my entire share in the war against fascism? Should it be all over for me then?

No, the battle isn't over yet. Nor is the sentence begun above. It goes: All here have the same wish to return to the front as soon as possible. Whereas there are deserters in armies elsewhere, here there are their opposites, for whom we're tempted to use the term "inserters." They "flee" from bases and hospitals in the quiet back areas into the trenches. Just as in other wars they punish soldiers guilty of criminal offenses by sending them to the front, in this unusual army soldiers are punished by being sent out of the country. And—and isn't this still more unusual?—many of these punitively repatriated soldiers try to return to combat.

Ask any brigade doctor what the most striking aspect of his war practice is and he'll answer: "Pretense. The guys pretend to be healthy. Reverse Schweiks![1] They lie about their wounds no longer hurting and their bowels functioning as smoothly as those of a prince consort's. They lie about their temperature chart, and if they could pull it off, they'd also retouch their X rays."

At two in the afternoon an ambulance drives along the beach, takes on passengers from the villas, and transports them to and from the X-ray lab.

Battlefields are mass graves of shells. On the Sierra de San Just or on the flat shores of the Ebro, at Teruel and at Saragossa, myriads of bullets buzz past each other in all different directions; most of them bore into the ground or remain lying in furrows, but many, far too many, sink into human bodies. Finding these projectiles and the damage they cause the organism is the task of the X ray. The point of entry of the foreign body and the point of exit, if there is one, don't always show the way to the damaged organs. Here a piece of rib bone has splintered off and, deviating from the line of fire, has penetrated a lung, causing more damage there than the shot itself. Over there, on the other hand, a bullet ricocheted against a bone and crouches, as if it hadn't penetrated the body, near the hole through which it entered.

With accidents in civilian life, the manner of the accident and the structure of the bone to some extent permit the nature of the wound and the location of the foreign body to be limited. In the medical wards of the war you almost never find the typical fractures that the surgical clinics and first-aid stations of peace-blessed cities treat day in and day out. Shots know no rules and have no habits. Except for one, and it isn't a good one: they connect the inner wound with the outside world. Every fracture is consequently an open fracture, and infection can creep in along the channel of the shot, even when the dressing is thick and tight. The dark lantern of the radiologist searches the body, and more than once, for anything hostile. Is there any tissue damage? Where is the blood flowing from the wound? How high is the exudate in the hemo-thorax; is the level going down? Is the projectile traveling?

"Come back in four days, comrade."

Every day at two in the afternoon the big van drives to and from the X-ray lab.

Minor surgery is no minor matter, although it barely undertakes amputations— except for a finger or a toe—and although it manages without anesthetics apart from the very short-term one. The operations are septic operations—or, in lay terms, they treat puss-filled wounds. But shell wounds, even if superficial, can be dangerous, depending on the number of them. I remember one comrade, a sculptor from Vienna, who had received eighty-two shrapnel fragments, but you couldn't see them or him; he was one huge abscess. But a good-natured abscess, by the way; he spoke so optimistically of his recovery that he brought tears to the eyes of the two young women doctors, who didn't share his optimism. Then he suffered another bout of pneumonia . . .

Someone is walking along the beach in front of our window. "Hi, Franz, I'm just now writing about how you looked when you arrived here."

Major surgery functions aseptically, with anesthetics and saws, in abdominal cavities and brains, sewing and plastering, fitting bones, muscles, and tendons together. The *Manual of Military Surgery* is a thick, encyclopedic book with twenty-three main chapters and more than a hundred secondary ones. Yet the doctors of the International Brigades could add another chapter to it, one possibly titled "Effects of War Injuries on Organs Mistreated in Concentration Camps." Certain conditions of the kidneys or the intestines facilitate the diagnosis as to which German concentration camp the patient had been in.

Sometimes a medical orderly can be seen coming out of the Villa "Pavlov" with some object wrapped in linen. It is an amputated leg or arm.

"What is the hardest thing in surgery?" we ask. "Amputation, isn't it?" "No," answers the head of major surgery, "it's harder not to amputate than to amputate."

The medical supplies available in the pharmacy are for the most part gifts from foreign organizations, factory workers, and also from physicians who pass on to the Spanish soldiers the samples that come to them. Such an International of medical supplies is not easy to conduct as long as the donors rather than the donations are filled with the international spirit. Despairing, the comrade pharmacist tears her fox-red hair. For what the Germans call strophantin is quabaine to the French. The imaginative names of the preparations that the American doctor urgently requests are completely new to her. She doesn't even have time to pull her red hair, since she has to ask again what the active ingredient is of the thing requested in order to be able to offer her customers something similar. It often happens that the doctor is unable to make out the directions or dosage on the wrapping of the strange preparation; they may, for example, be printed in Russian letters.

Not just the medicaments themselves, but even weights and measures are a nightmare. The English make out prescriptions in grains and ounces. How, then, is the red-haired pharmacist supposed to mix ointments and liquids on the basis of such prescriptions when she was trained at the Faculté de Pharmacologie in Paris to mix according to grams? How should she know her way around the beakers, syringes, and test tubes that have been sent from England and are calibrated according to a medieval Anglo-Saxon measure?

There are far too few thermometers, and these few are divided, so to speak, into sects and factions. One kind measures in Celsius, another in Fahrenheit; a third, the indigenous Spanish, consists of such thin little tubes that you can hardly make out the mercury, let alone being able to read at which degree of latitude it actually stops.

"What damned kind of gauze have you sent me?"[2] someone calls out for whom any gauze that is not antiseptic or impregnated with cyanide or boric acid is a "damned kind of gauze."

"Was für ein verfluchtes Zeug von Mull haben Sie mir da hergeschickt?"[3] resounds a few minutes later. Hello, who's speaking? A German physician for whom only aseptic gauze counts and the cyanide and boric acid gauze is "ein verfluchtes Zeug von Mull."

In such circumstances all you can do, oh, you bandage material of all kinds, is to join together in a single unit. Preparations of all companies, agree on common names. Medicinal containers, unite in the international standard for an international standard and come to Spain. You are needed. . . .

The main place of residence of today's guests, if they are not bedridden, is the "Maxim Gorky" leisure center. Earlier, it had been a particularly lovely villa and has now become lovelier. To be sure, not everything in this ideal club is ideal. Of the library someone said, for example, that it holds more languages than books. In fact, there are fifteen hundred books in twelve languages; but that is too little for the more than enough time and appetite for reading at the disposal of the ill. With the copies of newspapers—some of which are on display in the leisure center, while others are delivered to the seriously ill—the need is covered just as little, and those who are responsible for the distribution sing their song of complaint in messages posted on the walls.

Courses and meetings are held on the club's premises and are separated by language. Once a week each of the larger language groups has the main auditorium at its disposal for a meeting, to which members of other nationalities are welcome if they are somewhat fluent in the particular language.

The general bulletin of the hospital, which is written and illustrated by hand, appears in a format of four square meters and ten columns. It appears on the grating of the Villa "Azaña," and in each column a different language group reports on the life of its frontline units and events in its homeland.

The self-criticism in the wall newspapers of the individual villas is multilingual, and beside this each language group has its own wall newspaper in the leisure center. Sometimes the titles are witty—"The Eavesdropper at the Wall," "Put against the Wall," "The Spanish Wall (newspaper)," and so on—and sometimes the contents. Journalistic brilliance goes to—who else—the Hungarians. They invented the motorized wall newspaper, whose notices and caricatures move electrically on crankshafts and are shown in the correct light by different-colored little bulbs.

The competition between the different language groups is also vented in other ways. For the benefit of refugee children from Asturias, donation chits were sold for ten centimos apiece. Each language group pasted the front page of one of its national dailies with these chits. Everyone who bought ten chits got to stick them on. The day before yesterday the Germans took the lead, yesterday the Spaniards, today the Americans. The record of the Americans seems secure, since they already have 1,230 chits on their *Daily Worker.* All of a sudden, a Chinese newspaper is stuck to the wall with 1,250 chits; a single Chinaman sacrificed his entire savings so that his nation of 400,000,000 should stand in the place due it, first.

There is a lecture almost every evening; lecturers are in anything but short supply. One of them was with Franco. He crossed the lines over to the republicans, and can now talk about the other side, the unimaginable, remote other side of opposing trenches. Another one is from the sobering, remorseful, despairing Saar region. A third is a specialist in union affairs, a fourth in Spanish history and culture. Often several people speak on the same subject: the comrade who was an army lieutenant in Germany publicly discusses the Ukrainian question with the war commissar from the Polish Palafox Battalion and with an émigré from Kiev who through his service in the Spanish People's Army hopes to atone for his previous desertion from the Soviet Union. Doctors deal with popular-scientific topics.

Whoever comes to Spain from abroad, whether he be a politician, a scholar, or an artist, makes a stop here to visit countrymen. And hardly anyone who has something to say gets away without having had his say. Translators of all languages are astonished at the fine flow of words, and when the speaker believes that he has finished his talk, he still has to answer questions and earn his safe-conduct pass to continue his journey by the sweat of his brow.

Musicians provide little occasion for discussions, but they still don't get off any easier. On his way through, the black singer Paul Robeson, to take one example, had to give concerts, each capable of filling an entire evening's performance, in all the villas housing the severely wounded in the space of a single morning.

Classes for all non-Spanish groups are jointly held in the Spanish language; all language groups, including the Spanish, participate jointly in concerts, chess tournaments, and sports. Music is, in a sense, the unofficial service language of the International Brigades. If you can sing, no matter in which language, make yourself at home; if you own a mandolin or harmonica, can play or sing along, you fit in wherever you come from. But even if you don't know any songs, you won't miss a concert any Thursday.

The programs consist in the main of classical pieces. Among Spanish composers the only ones known in the rest of Europe are those who captured the attention of the world as virtuosos, such as the amazing violinist Sarasate or the cellist Casals. (Incidentally, the hope that Pablo Casals would concertize in the hospital was not fulfilled. If he were to accept every invitation, he'd have to travel the length and breadth of the country.) Just like Pablo Casals, Spain's greatest musician, Spain's greatest painter, Pablo Picasso, and Spain's sole Nobel Prize–winner for literature, Jacinto Benavente, are enthusiastic advocates of the republican cause and haters of the fascist general's clique. Shouldn't this fact alone suffice to eradicate everywhere the lies about the "vandalism of Red Spain"? Shouldn't this fact alone manage to explain to those who always advance the supremacy of art which side the cause of culture and humanity stands on?

It is entirely questionable if the international and Spanish soldiers ever before heard the Spanish concert pieces that they now hear on Thursday evenings. They sit with heads thrust forward and mouths open, as if they wanted to capture the melodies like the stream from a tapered wine bottle raised high. Their applause is frenzied. But don't think that the non-Spanish compositions have any lesser effect on the audience of the Spanish wounded, nurses, and villagers. There are often enough motifs that have been inspired by Spain's folk life or at least by the composer's conception of it and that are now returning to the people by whom they were originally inspired. . . .

While the concerts need the largest auditorium in order to accommodate the crowd of listeners, truth to tell, the football public needs even more space. The football team of the International Brigades competes every Sunday against guests from cities throughout the province. It is widely renowned, although it's a different team that takes the field almost every week. After all, whoever can shoot goals can also shoot fascists and heads for the front as a forward or fullback. . . .

There is a cuisine for Spanish stomachs, which can stand gallons of olive oil, whereas a dab of butter makes them vomit immediately. They're not used to it; Spain has never been a cattlebreeding land. Also noteworthy is the fact that the Spanish fly (not the male potency kind, but the real Spanish fly) has the same aversion to butter as the Spaniard himself. They swarm all over in thick squads. It feasts on everything: on people, their uniforms, their boots, and especially their excrement. It nibbles on wood, on stone walls, on sheets; it covers everything like a black surface. The one thing it leaves alone and doesn't swarm all over, the one thing it distances itself from in disgust, is butter.

The non-Spanish soldiers, however, can't stand olive oil or any dishes prepared with it, and any cooking for them is done with butter—or, better said, margarine or some other fat of unknown origin, if it's at all available. What the innards of the Spaniards also like and those of the Internationals not at all is garbanzos, a fortunately untranslatable growth that occupies a middle ground between chickpeas and broad beans and produces flatulence.

During the conquest of Mexico, Fernando Cortés and his conquistadores are said to have sighed longingly for their native garbanzos and decided on retreat because they missed this ambrosia in the land of the heathens. This occurs in Heinrich Heine's ballad "Vitzliputzli," but in "Atta Troll" Heine warns foreign digestive organs against this food, a hundred years before the International Brigades felt the machine gun–like clatter of the garbanzos on and in their own bodies:

There I also ate garbanzos,
Big and hard as shotgun pellets.
Even Germans can't digest them,
Though they're all brought up on dumplings.

Nothing to be done, the stomach has to endure these shotgun pellets, since it seldom has any other ammunition available to it. Obtaining provisions and feeding troops in a country torn apart by a war of intervention is a more than serious problem. As a small contribution to its solution, the Interbrigades maintain a modest chicken farm and rabbit hutch. Roosters and bucks do what they can, eggs are laid and rabbits are born; nevertheless all increasing of the small animal population is, if one may say so, only a drop in the bucket where fifteen hundred soldiers' stomachs are involved.

A warehouse exists for additional foodstuffs, such as eggs, fat, cans of meat and milk, cocoa, and marmalade. There's plenty of room left in the warehouse; whole shelves are standing empty. Extra provisions the world over, come on!

Even for someone confined to his bed, life in the villa town flows differently from how it does for those laid up in some quiet out-of-the-way area. Countrymen, even if they didn't know him before, visit him and provide him with reading material; smaller language groups conduct their courses of instruction or compatriot get-togethers at his bedside, so you can easily find yourself in a hospital room where Finns on one side and Macedonians on the other side are gathered around a bed singing their national songs by turns. The Spaniards among them, who take considerable pride in belonging to the International Brigades, join in the singing, even in Finnish and Macedonian.

Sometimes the person being visited provides the entertainment by singing solos or playing the mandolin, like Franz Luda, for example, a true Viennese who's not going under; his bed was the concert podium, the hospital room of the Villa "Marcel Cachin" was the crowded concert hall, the program consisted of Viennese Lieder, and the performer bubbled cheerfully, his two amputated legs notwithstanding.

Whoever can move, if only on crutches, betakes himself to the beach, as far as the surf. You can still swim in the sea in the first half of December. It's also nice to sit with different comrades on the seawall cracking hazelnuts, peeling oranges, and talking about wounds and bandage changes and other aspects of the healing process.

Don't believe for a moment that the wounded soldier has no possession he can boast about. He carries it on him day and night, carefully wrapped in gauze, and this possession is a bullet that had previously stuck in his throat or in a bone or in the chest. It can also be a cigarette lighter; it happened to be in a breast pocket and stopped the fascist shot whizzing directly at the heart.

The food is cursed in all dialects of all the languages spoken here. The mule that was served for lunch—something that can be counted on day in and day out—must have been the granddaddy of all Spanish mules. From comrades employed in food service you find out what special delights are to be expected today: whether vermouth or beer (alas, it's not real beer) is being served in the canteen, whether maybe sausage sandwich, cake, or grape juice can be purchased. Or even cigarettes?

No, cigarettes are never available; you have to make do with whatever you get your hands on, and unfortunately those are almost always the ghastly colored, ghastly tasting Spanish cigarettes known as "antitanks" in soldiers' lingo. Sometimes Galoises come as presents from France, Vlasta from Czechoslovakia, Guard's Parade from England, and Lucky Strike from America, but all together don't fill the smokers' mouths for long. Aren't there any other brands in France, England, and so on, other countries that manufacture tobacco? Cigarettes of all brands, soldiers want to smoke you!

From the balcony of the Dombrowski villa, entrance to which is forbidden to non-typhus patients, half-healed typhus patients hold court; below, on the beach promenade, the audience gathers. If a nurse comes along, the Danes and the Poles, sick and healthy alike, call out to her, as if from one mouth, "guapa" ("hey, good-looking"). They learned that this homage is obligatory even before they began taking the Spanish language course, and the nurses, even those who were still nuns less than a year ago, have already learned to reply with a "guapo" of their own. Only the inevitable rhymester stands off to a side and mutters into his unshaved chin: "So what if Carmen's a tease, if my embraces she hastily flees?"

One of the nurses is Trini, who is especially popular among German speakers if only because of her name. But Trini is no Bavarian or Austrian

Trini, but a Catalonian Trini, no abbreviated Katharine, but an abbreviated Trinidad. A delicate little thing with the complexion of a child, her hair combed simply over her ears, modest and brightly smiling. A connoisseur of women would determine at the first glance that the life of this girl flowed calmly and without mishaps. She performs her chores in the Villa "Paul Vaillant-Couturier," bringing the food and the medication, rolling up swabs, making bandages, and coming with a bottle or bedpan at the faintest call.

Before she became a nurse she fulfilled her military service another way. On 20 June 1936, when the building of the Capitanea in Barcelona was stormed—it was here that the would-be dictator of Catalonia, General Godet, had entrenched himself—Trini was there at the time and got a pistol shot in the shoulder. At Tardiente, with the militias, she was among the first to learn how to throw a hand grenade, and she threw well. But a piece of shrapnel tore her right ear off. In the battle of Huesca in the fall of 1936, Trini was struck in the hip by a rifle shot. She had to quit the front, and in fact forever, since the Ministry of War forbade women to serve in regular units.

"Guapa," a soldier calls out to her as she goes by. "Guapo," answers Trini with her girlish smile.

In front of the orphanage, children are playing with the soldiers during their school breaks. The kids had lost their parents in the war; father had been shot to death by Franco's Mamelukes, mother torn to shreds by Franco's bombs. The international uncles have taken the place of parents. That's the way it has been and is in every war—the soldier loves the foreign children; they remind him of the home he misses. The International loves the children even more, since he misses home even more than other soldiers; he has been cut off from his homeland even more abruptly, no military postal service leads from the theater of war to his home, and since his family lives in Germany, Italy, Austria, Yugoslavia, Poland, or Hungary, no mail at all reaches there from Republican Spain.

He plays with Spanish children on the Spanish beach, and the little ones are delighted that the sand castles they can build with the soldiers' help exist nowhere else, sand castles built according to all the rules of fortress construction. And there are the funny dances the black uncle swathed in white bandages teaches them. And the big camaradas always have presents in their pockets: a box of crayons or hand-carved marionettes or some sweets. . . .

Nightlife on the beach in the seaside resort now begins earlier than it used to. After the sun sets, it's pitch dark; no light must shine on street or sea. You can't see your hand in front of your eyes, you keep stumbling over garbage pails standing in front of the villas, and you bump into someone coming toward you. The swearing that accompanies such collisions or the snatches of conversation of the unseen passersby establish their nationality.

The evening wind combs the brunette locks of the sea into phosphorescent curls. A small star hangs in the sky, hangs so low it scrapes the horizon. You'd swear it was the light of a mast. When the waves surge up, it's not the waves that move in the eyes of the viewer but the little star, which goes out and then flares up again. You'd swear it was a ship sending signals.

A shooting star flashes across the sky on the right. It can be a flare pistol or a falling incendiary bomb, perhaps a new type that burns during its flight. Sheet lightning, a storm with thunder and lightning—are they not a ship's guns? Is there a battle at sea going on, or a troop landing, or the usual bombardment of a harmless coastal city?

In June you could a see a freighter at sea being bombed by a squadron of planes. The ship was the *Legazpi;* it was carrying an "autochir," a mobile operating room, and tons of medical supplies. Just short of its destination the ship was struck by an incendiary bomb; shortly thereafter, wood and ether and demijohns full of pure alcohol and boxes of surgical cotton and balls of gauze stood in bright flames. The crew dove into the sea.

Convalescents set out in boats to save whatever there was to save. The head of the hospital, although he had a weak heart and was suffering from jaundice, stayed outside the whole night and the following day until only the hull of the ship was turning in the water. Then he went home and went to bed with a high fever. He died a few days later. He was an emigrant from Germany named Günther Bodetzk.

Dark is the night of the spa, dark the sea in whose depths ships with foodstuffs and medicines are torpedoed under the strictest observation of the Non-Intervention Committee, which in fact does not intervene against the non-intervening interventionists.

With the wailing of sirens comes the new day; it comes from the Balearics, from the Italian naval base at Mallorca, as an obtuse angle of slowly approaching bombers. They fly high above the sea, then low over the villas of the field hospital so that the antiaircraft guns can't fire at them without hitting the houses. The Capronis stay so low that it seems their wings would sweep the roofs from the houses. They drop bombs on the highway and on the railway, circle the orange groves and fire their machine guns at the people running to take cover in them.

Children jump here and there, yelling; feverish patients run out of the villas; a group of nurses scatters in all directions, casting the too visible target of white linen smocks from their bodies; because a plane roars above his head a wounded man throws himself down so violently that his cast and the meticulously healed bone crack; another tears the stitches of his wounds running and they begin bleeding again, while from the air the machine gun clatters and bullets whine.

One of the birds of prey is so near above us that we can feel the flapping of its wings. Lying flat against the ground, we follow it with our gaze, a bomb frees itself from its underbelly, in the morning sky it shines, flashes, and falls— the cornucopia of the fascist Fortuna, loaded with gifts of powder, shrapnel, and explosives, loaded with death, fire, and destruction for the purpose of striking orphans and nurses, of crippling seriously wounded men even more or killing them.

Who gave the order for the bombs to come whistling down? Generals. They deceived the state, to which they swore an oath of loyalty and which paid their salaries; they stole the army that had been entrusted to them; and directed and supported by foreign powers, by world fascism, they spread horror and slaughter across their own land and its people.

So it happens that the bomb attacks a hospital, and nothing and nobody stops them. In a split second, it will have accomplished its business of murder. In a split second . . . We lie there, we do the same as the leaders of the democratic states, we stick our heads in the sand.

We have no weapons against the squadron of planes, we have no means with which to stop the bombs that whistle down. But those statesmen have the means and the weapons.

Fire and smoke leap up high like a scream.

May the human humans hear it, this scream against barbarism: Progressive mankind, become an International Brigade for freedom and justice.

Egon Erwin Kisch, "Soldaten am Meeresstrand," "Nachlese," *Geschichten aus sieben Ghettos. Eintritt verboten. Nachlese* (Berlin and Weimar: Aufbau-Verlag, 1973), 311–35.

    1. A reference to the eponymous hero of Jaroslav Hašek's famous World War I novel, *The Good Soldier Schweik*. Schweik is a simple recruit who uses his wiles to avoid combat as much as possible.

    2. In English in the original.

    3. "What damned kind of gauze have you sent me?"

Kisch visiting Mayan ruins, Yucatán, 1944. Courtesy Museum of National Literature, Prague.

An Indian Village under the Star of David

The night was pitch dark and on the cool side when I got up this morning at seven sharp in order to be in Venta Prieta.

I had already heard something about this village and its Jewish inhabitants in Mexico City, but I had no idea where it was and had also forgotten its name. Then the day before yesterday I happened to be riding toward Pachuca, the silver city, when some eighty-three kilometers from the capital I came across a sign that read "Venta Prieta." Wasn't this the name? I got out and uncertainly asked about the Jews. The person I asked replied, pointing: "The *caballista* over there is one of them."

The caballist? As far as the eye could see there was no one around who could be taken for an authority on the Cabbala, an interpreter of numbers and signs. Only a peasant who was dismounting quite unmystically from a horse. Then it dawned on me: horse in Spanish is *caballo;* hence a *caballista* would be a rider. I went up to him, asked what I wanted to know, and he answered: There is a service every Saturday at seven in the morning.

Seven is hardly a pleasant hour. But what was there to do? So I jumped from the warm feathers of Pachuca in the gray of dawn in order to greet the cool Sabbath. I must confess I was ready for something grotesque, and was in a bit of an ironic frame of mind. An old song was running through my head that had been popular in the days of harmless dialect humor. All decked out in Indian feathers and Apache war paint, but with the side curls of an orthodox

Jew from East Europe and in the prayer shawl worn in the synagogue, the Viennese comic Eisenbach leaped onto the stage and belted out:

> Mein Vater war ein klaaner
> Jüdischer Indianer,
> Meine Mutter, tief in Texas drin,
> War eine koschere Gänslerin . . .

(My father was a lit-tle / Jewish Indian; / My mother, deep in the heart of Texas, / Raised kosher geese . . .)

I got to Venta Prieta too early. Some Indians or Mestizos, in no way distinguishable from other Indians or Mestizos, were standing around in the November fog in linen pants, shirts, and sandals. One of them, stocky and wrapped in a red wool *sarape,* was Señor Enrique Téllez, the head of the Jewish community. He was the person I was supposed to check with for authentic information. Señor Téllez also happens to be the richest man in the village, which in itself is no indication of real wealth.

Venta Prieta consists of a hundred and fifty people and relatively few houses.

Two-thirds of the inhabitants are Otomí Indians, although no longer purebred. They work in the mines of Real del Monte, cultivate the corn fields in back of the village, or raise *havadas,* guinea fowl, which, like their owners, are products of crossbreeding.

Houses, slapped together from adobe, street mud, and horse dung, stand on only one side of the country road. The only building made of stone is the school. A boundless plain stretches on the other side of the road: an army base and an airfield for a branch line to Guajutla in the district of Tampico. A row of barracks gleams in the distance. "The other third of the town," Señor Enrique Téllez tells me, "is made up of us Jews, thirty-seven adults. We are just a big family, or actually two families, related by marriage, the Téllezes and the Gonzálezes."

"Have you been here a long time?"

"For almost two generations. We used to live in Zamora, in the state of Michoacán. But forty years ago a pogrom against the Jews broke out and my maternal grandfather was seized. His name was Roman Gison. They demanded that he be baptized and that he renounce his old beliefs. When he refused, they sewed him into a cowhide and set fire all around it. The cowhide shrank and in this way crushed my grandfather. All the Jews then fled from Zamora. My father found this ranch here, which belonged to a distant hacienda. The earth is completely dry, nothing but clumps of soil. But my father bought it nonetheless, since there weren't any houses here; he had no desire any more to live in a city or even in a village." Don Enrique points behind himself: "There is where I was born."

"There" is a house, no more dilapidated or neglected than the others, but bigger. Creatures of all kinds—guinea fowl, children, a horse, and a lot of dogs—move in a lively flow in and out of the courtyard. During my conversation with Don Enrique and his group, a black cow sticks its head out of the gate, lows from time to time, as if to warn others of my presence, and doesn't venture out of the yard, as if harboring in its udder deep mistrust toward me.

I look at my watch. Don Enrique says: "The service will be beginning soon; we're not very punctual. The women first have to prepare breakfast for their husbands going to work."

"They work on Saturday?"

"There's no other way."

"Then how can they take part in the service?"

"That's why we hold prayers three times; we come in three shifts."

"Do you conduct the service yourself, Señor Téllez?"

"No, I'm afraid I don't know a lot about it. Our rabbi is an Abyssinian."

"An Abyssinian? How does an Abyssinian land in Mexico?"

"He works as a baker in Pachuca. A young man with a keen interest in religion and knows the Bible. He can even read Hebrew. He'll be here in a moment."

Don Enrique enumerates the religious rites observed by the community. They fast on Yom Kippur—on "Ayuno major"; he translates so that I can understand. At Easter they eat matzos—"galletas de la semana santa," he translates, which I would translate into German as "Waffeln der heiligen Woche" [Holy Week wafers].

"We also celebrate the new year and fast on the anniversary of the destruction of the Temple. We eat no pork. Fowl and cattle we slaughter kosher."

I ask if circumcision is practiced. "Yes, but we don't have a circumciser here. We take the newborn boys to the capital to Señor Klipper." Imagine, that's the onomatopoetic name of the circumciser of Mexico.

Next to the black cow, which still keeps observing me mistrustfully from the entrance to the gate, stands a blond Norwegian-looking boy, about four years old, and looks my way just as mistrustfully.

"Come here," Don Enrique calls to the boy. But instead of obeying, he runs away. "That's my nephew," says Uncle Heinrich, "I wanted him to tell you his name."

"What is his name then?"

"Reubeni. All our children's names come from the Old Testament: Elias, Abraham, David, Saul for the boys, and Rachel, Rebecca, or Sarah for the girls. Do you know that the widow of Francisco Madero is also named Sarah?"

I had already heard in Mexico that the martyrs of national liberation, the brothers Francisco J. and Gustavo Madero, were illegal Jews; so too is Madero's widow, living in New York, who was born Pérez, a typical Sephardic-Jewish name. The Madero brothers are not the only prominent men said to be of Jewish origin. Many of the victims of the Inquisition were singled out as *judaizante* in Spanish, "of Jewish inclination." Even the father of the nation, the priest Miguel Hidalgo, is listed as *judaizante* in the records of the Inquisition.

"Our children," continues the head of the community, "go to the public school. Have you seen the school? Nice, isn't it? A few years ago the 'Cristeros' (a clerical-fascistic movement) demanded that a church be established in Venta Prieta. The inhabitants of the village—they're mostly miners and unionized, and no anti-Semites—asked the government that since the village already had a church, could they instead have a school? They made no mention of the fact that the church happened to be a synagogue. We got the school; it was founded under President Ortiz Rubio. One of our children, Saúl González, attends the military school over there. One of our people also works at the airfield; he first began helping out as a mechanic and then passed his pilot's examination."

Don Enrique's knowledge of the history of the Jews of Mexico is limited to the fact that he knows the name Carbajal, the Portuguese whom Phillip II sent to New Spain for the purpose of pacifying the rebellious coastal regions on the Gulf. Luis Carbajal the Elder took a hundred Maranos families with him, and it is from these people that the Mexican Jews derive their origin. Their greatest reverence, however, is reserved for his nephew, "Carbajal el Mozo," who together with his mother and siblings was tortured in the dungeons of the Inquisition; but he never renounced his Mosaic faith. On 5 December 1596 he and his entire family stood atop the funeral pyres, forty-five Jews. This figure does not include the dead whose remains had been scraped out of the cemetery, or the refugees, who could be burned only in effigy. A German also stood on the scaffolding; as a Lutheran who refused to become converted, he was thrown into the prison of the Inquisition where he was converted to Judaism by Carbajal. Luis Carbajal el Mozo and his family went into the flames as unpenitent Jews.

Don Enrique has more to tell of his own generation. "In Michoacán we had a rabbi who was not beardless like the Indians, but wore a huge silver beard. The peasants called him the 'bishop of the Jews.' He sometimes traveled to other Jewish communities to deliver sermons. In our district there is no other Jewish community besides us. The nearest one is two hours by train from here, in San Augustín de Zapoctis, a village in the state of Mexico. Ah, here comes our rabbi. Hola, Etiope!"

The Ethiopian came over to us, carrying a package carefully tied with string. Since I know it, I shall at once state that he is a typical Falasha from Abyssinia. In the Jewish Christianity of the Falashas, the Jewish element tends to prevail; abroad, most of the Falashas become Jews. In Harlem, in New York, I saw their huge synagogue, and now I am meeting here a rabbi from their tribe.

His name is Guillermo Peña. He is barely thirty years old, was born in Mexico, and understands only a few words of Kuara, the language of the Falashas. Guillermo Peña lives with his father in Pachuca, where be bakes as much bread as he can deliver, which means not much. Therefore, he has time to learn Hebrew on his own and to read the Bible. Every Saturday morning he comes to Venta Prieta, without remuneration, conducts the service, and gives religious instruction. This rabbi is a shy, retiring person who is uncomfortable talking about himself to me and happy when I follow his repeated request to enter the *jardincito* [little garden].

The *jardincito* is a small garden surrounded by a red brick wall; the synagogue is located here. It can hold at the most forty people. A spirit lamp dangles from the ceiling of the synagogue. A shabby piano in one corner, a blackboard in the other with Hebrew script chalked on it, and as a second pedagogical tool a battered globe for illustrating biblical geography. Three vases made of mirror fragments and containing paper flowers are meant to decorate the piano.

On the embroidered cover of the altar stand a candle (instead of a seven-branched candelabra), a glass (instead of a golden goblet), and instead of a handwritten Torah scroll of vellum lies a folio: the Old and New Testament in the Spanish language, published by the Bible Society. In truth, this book doesn't fit here in the slightest. The Jewish community neither acknowledges the New Testament, nor did the Bible Society publish the book for the purpose of helping the Jews persist in their faith.

Whitewashed walls. One has a Star of David painted on it; two lions with flowing manes and naked bodies support it. For want of real candelabra, two are painted on the other wall, but—lest anything be left out—their pedestals and candles are decorated with every conceivable kind of emblem. On the front wall the "Hear, O Israel" stands out in Hebrew and Spanish: "Oye, Israel, el eterno es nuestro dios, el eterno uno es" [Hear, O Israel, God is eternal, God is one].

Don Guillermo anxiously followed my inspection of the frescoes, and when I ask him who the painter is, he replies, hesitantly, "me," then adding: "I am a baker, Señor."

"The pictures are very pretty, especially the Hebrew letters," I nodded affably and observe his dark-brown African face blush. "I am a baker, Señor," he whispers again. Don Guillermo may not be much of a painter, but he's not just a baker either. He is first and foremost a priest, as one can see when he lovingly unties his bundle and spreads out its contents: song books and prayer books, equipped with many bookmarks. Then a white shawl emerges from a small bag, which the rabbi immediately dons, and a cap that perches on the back of his head.

The assembled congregation consists of thirteen people of the Mosaic confession, thus three more than the prescribed minimum. Yet the thirteen do not make up a proper assemblage for prayer, since women and children do not count. But can Jehovah be so strict about this in Mexico, where for hundreds of years His people have been holding their ground against terrible threats and subtle temptations?

From hut to hut the summons was whispered "Let us pray," with the information when and where. Only in the jungle could they find a place to hold services. On the way there they could be met by arrows or seized by servants of the Inquisition, be thrown into a crater, or be torn to pieces by wild animals. If one failed to make it, perhaps the tenth, did that mean that the nine remaining should disperse without fulfilling their spiritual obligations? "Oh well, let us pray," they said and did. And while Jehovah at the time looked the other way, a minyan is a minyan in Mexico, even if fewer than ten men are assembled.[2]

Today there are four men here. In addition, four women or girls. They are the ones who embroidered the altar cloth with flowers and sayings from the Bible and are now interrupting the monotonously murmured words of prayer with their singing. The children sing along, among them the Norwegian-Jewish-Indian Reubeni Téllez, who ran away from me, and the nine-year-old Saúl González, who attends the military school, a future Mexican general.

The service was simple, but in essence a Sabbath service like anywhere else. At the end the congregation stood before the altar for the prayer for the dead. Children are not permitted to recite the prayer until they have been accepted into the religious community through confirmation. But two boys, probably orphans, stepped forward together with the adults—another of the exceptions God has permitted the village of Venta Prieta in Mexico.

I too stepped forward, brought my feet together, and repeated what the rabbi recited; each worshipper adds just the names of his own deceased.

My father and mother were born in Prague, lived there, and are buried there. It never could have occurred to them that one day one of their sons would be reciting the prayer for the dead for them amid a group of Indians, in the shadows of the silver-laden mountains of Pachuca. My parents, who lived their entire lives in the Bear House of Prague's Old Town, never dreamt that their sons would sometime be driven out of the Bear House, one of them to Mexico, another to India, and the two who were unable to escape the Hitler terror, to unknown places of unimaginable horror. My thoughts roamed farther—to relatives, friends, acquaintances, and enemies, sacrifices of Hitler, all entitled to be remembered in the prayer for the dead.

A procession of millions: men and women who their whole lives strove to nourish their families and to make useful members of human society of their children; employees and laborers who earned their daily bread by the sweat of their brows; doctors who were ready day and night to help the suffering; people who were dedicated to spreading the truth and improving the situation of their fellowmen; scholars who lived from learning; artists who wanted to bring beauty to life; children who dreamed of a wonderful future . . . all kinds of people, full of zest for life or sentimental, good and bad, strong and weak.

The procession of them is immense, constant. Passing cold faces, they stagger on to their goal. There it stands, a smoking building. Everyone knows what this building means, what the smoke rising from the chimney consists of. It is a death factory; producing corpses. What are the thoughts of this army of people consecrated to murder? No more hope, no more hope for themselves, for their children, for their remembrance, not even hope for vengeance, for punishment for mass murder. They have to push toward the gate, they have to undress themselves, they have to proceed into the chamber, where a terrible gas suffocates them, burns them, disintegrates them. Smoke rises from the chimney.

Immense is the column; it drags on, as if mankind had never existed, as if the idea of mankind had never existed, never the aspiration to bring into the world more bread, more right, more truth, more health, more wisdom, more beauty, more love, and more happiness.

I am the last to leave the altar to which I came a few hours before in such a good mood.

Egon Erwin Kisch, "Indiodorf unter dem Davidstern," "Entdeckungen in Mexiko," *Marktplatz der Sensation. Entdeckungen in Mexico* (Berlin and Weimar: Aufbau-Verlag, 1993), 6th ed., 528–36.

1. In the Jewish faith, a congregation cannot hold services unless at least ten men, constituting a *minyan,* are present.

A Deed of Collective Optimism

"A German performance in Mexico, eight hundred spectators in the auditorium, twenty-six performers and singers onstage, to say nothing of the stage painters, costume designers, and technical personnel . . . It was not only a display of the intellectually interested and not just a brilliant new performance by the Heine Club, which created a center for the spirit that had been forbidden in Germany. Above all it was a deed of collective optimism by all those who refused to permit Hitler to rob them of their pleasure in culture. Even if the undertaking had met with no success, it would still have been a success. But as a performance it was also an outward success . . ."

That's what I wrote about a theater evening at the Heine Club. The same can be said for the overall achievement of the Heine Club: a deed of collective optimism, a success.

In case there is a small grain of truth in the observation attributed to Goebbels that the German émigrés had unleashed the hatred of the world against the Third Reich, the Heine Club should take credit for having been an atom of this grain. On a distant and small section of the front, it fulfilled its duty, despite all the hardships and considerable misunderstanding and malice in the camp of the émigrés themselves.

Egon Erwin Kisch, "Eine Tat des kollektiven Optimismus," *Mein Leben für die Zeitung 1926–1947: Journalistische Texte 2* (Berlin and Weimar: Aufbau-Verlag, 1983), 523.

Index